D0744815

MORE THAN TALK

Communication Studies and the Christian Faith

THIRD EDITION

Bill Strom
Trinity Western University

KENDALL/HUNT PUBLISHING COMPANY
4050 Westmark Drive   Dubuque, Iowa   52002

Scripture taken from the HOLY BIBLE, NEW INTERNATIONAL
VERSION®, Copyright © 1973, 1978, 1984 by International Bible Society.
Used by permission of Zondervan Publishing House. All rights reserved.
The "NIV" and "New International Version" trademarks are registered in
the United States Patent and Trademark Office by International Bible
Society. Use of either trademark requires the permission of the
International Bible Society.

Photo Credits:
p. 9, 367 – Keith Brofsky/Getty Images
p. 17, 107 – PhotoLind
p. 60, 62, 65 – Chris Borland/PhotoLink
p. 141 – Buccina Studios/Getty Images
p. 26 – Zach Bulick
p. 158 – SW Productions/Getty Images
p. 177 – Monica Lau/Getty Images
p. 181 – Skip Nall/Getty Images
p. 372 – Alan Pappe/Getty Images

Copyright © 1998, 2003 by Bill Strom
Copyright © 2009 by Kendall/Hunt Publishing Company

ISBN 978-0-7575-5874-0

Printed in the United States of America
10 9 8 7 6 5 4 3 2 1

To Shelaine,
as always, and forever.

CONTENTS

ACKNOWLEDGMENTS

I FIRST ENVISIONED *More Than Talk* as a resource for students at Trinity Western University where it continues to serve a significant role. Thanks to instructors in our department and in continuing education who have provided helpful feedback regarding its utility.

For the third edition I enlisted colleagues for the task of proofreading individual chapters, although any concerns that remain are entirely my own. I want to thank Marilyn Edwards, Linda Matties, Carole Davis, Fred DeVries, Ken Pudlas, Dave Heidebrecht, Melinda Dewsbury, and Ron Braid for their help down the final stretch. Your eyes often caught what my tired ones missed! Ron also deserves special acknowledgment for conforming the endnotes to Chicago Manual of Style standards, a task he offered to do.

Also deserving of appreciation is Zach Bulick, the layout editor for this third edition. His willingness to work with the previous design yet bring new ideas indicates his servant heart and flexible spirit. The cover design is his original work.

Approximately thirty schools in the United States and Canada adopted *More Than Talk* its first ten years, and feedback from instructors has shaped this latest edition. Thanks to all who completed surveys, or passed on comments at National Communication Association or Religious Communication Association conferences.

I am indebted again to regional and developmental editors at Kendall/Hunt Publishing Company. Their belief in the book, and eagerness to contribute to its revision, fueled the vision for a third edition.

To my sons Taylor, Clark, and Eric, I want to say thank you for showing interest in *More Than Talk*. I am so pleased that you love to read, and pray that God will bless you as you continue to commit your studies to him.

Finally, I am grateful for my wife, Shelaine, who supports my writing projects, whatever they might be. Your humor and wisdom continue to marvel me. I am blessed a hundred-fold by you.

Above all, I give glory to God by whom the mysteries of communication were given us, and to my Savior, Jesus Christ, through whom all things hold together, and to his Spirit who encourages me with truth and hope. May this book be a sweet-smelling sacrifice to the Lord God Almighty.

PREFACE

FACEBOOK HAD YET to start up when the last edition of *More Than Talk* came out. During the run of this third edition, readers probably cannot imagine a day without logging into a Facebook or MySpace profile.

In the early years of computer-mediated communication (CMC), critics thought it spelled doom for genuine community by labeling it superficial, inauthentic, and bent toward deception. Others thought the blurring of private and public boundaries would lead to fragmented and disconnected personal identities. Critics offered scary examples of individuals presenting multiple online profiles in order to get what they wanted from unsuspecting targets. In addition, church spokespersons felt online communication would erode church attendance and lessen personal accountability.

We have become more savvy Internet users of late, and research on social networking indicates that we don't engage strangers online or stay behind closed doors at the price of face-to-face community, or at least not much. In fact, Christians are avid online social networkers who connect regularly with friends and family.

The difference between Facebook and First Baptist is that online communication tends more toward individualism and control than face-to-face interaction.[1] Online individualism shows up in CMC's bias toward thoughts of *my* email, *my* profile, and *my* friends on *my* computer. Online control shows through in choices to "ignore" a would-be "friend" on FB, to enter and leave chat groups at will, and to organize *my* pictures, *my* videos, and *my* songs, in order to customize *my* digital world to meet personal needs.

But the social networking research also speaks of a covenantal theme, one that indicates our love for and dependence on others, especially within our faith community. As Heidi Campbell writes, "[Researchers] found that being an Internet user was positively associ-

---

1 Heidi Campbell, "Challenges Created by Online Religious Networks," *Journal of Media and Religion 3* (2004): 82-99.

ated with being a member of a community or religious organization, with users being slightly more likely than nonusers to belong to more religious organizations. Overall, their findings demonstrated that involvement in religious organizations seems unaffected by Internet usage across the years, neither encouraging nor distracting from participation in religious groups."[2] Christians seem to engage many means, including electronic ones, to enjoy support from and identification with Christ's body in covenantal community.

This edition of *More Than Talk* expands on the biblical idea—and ideal—of covenant and covenantal communication. The careful reader will see a shift in language from simile (communication is like a covenant) to adjective-noun form (this book is about covenantal communication).

This edition builds on the second with updated examples, current research, and new ideas. The opening two chapters address communication generally and then covenantal communication specifically. The case study from Burkitt Financial brings an organizational communication perspective not found in earlier editions.

In addition, the language chapter introduces storytelling as a biblical guideline, and the self-perception chapter suggests that personal virtue, more than high esteem, should be our goal for self-development. The interpersonal chapter continues to feature the sad story of Robert and Vicky, but with a new discussion on how a humble heart shapes our thinking and communication toward reconciliation with others.

The family communication chapter continues with the theme that covenantal commitments thrive or die close to home, and that verbal abuse is a fact for some. New is the idea that God wants families to be sanctified, or holy, as we encourage each other toward Christlikeness.

The two media chapters have received the most editorial attention as the cultural landscape has continued to change with the upswing in social networking, and with the sober fact that mediated sex and violence show up in television almost doubly as often as a decade ago. The quadrant model of Christian responses to media still shapes these two chapters. I have also added the argument that we can judge media with our values while engaging a critical and godly eye for the good.

---

2 Heidi Campbell, "Challenges…" 90

Instructors and students continue to show sufficient appreciation for the last three chapters on the social sciences, humanities, and skills. My goal is to describe how scientists and critics do their scholarly work, so that readers may prepare for future studies.

The third edition of *More Than Talk* continues to invest space for illustrations, pull-quotes, cartoons, and tables. My hope is that they enhance your understanding of communication.

It is a mystery that ink on paper might change one's thoughts and heart. My prayer is that these words will go beyond talk, so that by God's grace, we might enjoy his peace and wisdom.

Whatever you do, do it all for the glory of God.
1 Corinthians 10:31b

Speaking the truth in love, we will in all things grow up into him ...

Ephesians 4:15a

What Is Communication?

Two Views

IT'S HARD TO solve problems through communication when the problem is communication. Burkitt Financial, a small services firm, suffered from toxic interaction. Its seven employees fostered a culture of disrespect, particularly toward the owner, Sally Burkitt. Sally struggled to articulate a unified vision to which her employees might buy in, and this led to multiple voices attempting to shape the purpose and direction of the company. Sally also lacked a concept of team as she worked one-on-one with her staff. This individualistic style discouraged group identity and resulted in employees pairing off around mutual grievances they held against Sally. Rather than share lunch hours together in the staff room, employee duos slipped away from the office to nearby restaurants where they would unload. Their leaving the office early and returning late signaled their low morale and disinterest in community.

Employees also nurtured a culture of disrespect through angry outbursts and blatant insubordination. One employee, frustrated with Sally's top-down management style, burst into her office shouting with expletives that Sally reminded her of her ex-husband. Sally just took it. In another scenario Sally requested that a woman change her office location. The employee agreed, but never did. Other forms of disrespect included back-biting, gossiping, grumbling, complaining, accusing, sarcasm, hurtful joking, and triangulation (she told me that you told her that I said X). Along with playing these toxic language games, Sally's group offered up unhealthy portions of icy silence, averted eye contact, and shoulder turning. Junior high kids were often more mature.

Compounding disrespect were workload territoriality and resistance to change. Each of Sally's employees managed a unique client portfolio with little cross-servicing. Therefore when Jane was sick or Don on vacation, no other employee could effectively serve Jane and Don's clients. Even when asked, employees felt little obligation to pick up another's load. This fencing of responsibility nurtured strong allegiances between employees and their clients but eroded employee commitment to Burkitt Financial. One employee abused this relationship by leaving Burkitt and taking her most lucrative clients with her.

Despite Sally Burkitt's shortcomings, she knew she needed help, so she hired a communication consultant. The consultant diagnosed the culture of disrespect toward Sally, as well as Sally's tendency to not support her staff. In a manner of weeks, all but one employee either quit Burkitt, or was let go by Sally. It was time to start over.

What Is Communication?

We begin with this case study to underscore the role communication plays in creating a healthy workplace. And yet the problems at this firm represent much more than issues with organizational communication. They represent issues of intrapersonal communication—how Sally views herself and talks to herself (the topic of Chapter 5). The problems more obviously concern interpersonal communication—how Sally and her employees treat each other with icy stares and harsh language (Chapter 6). They also concern small group interaction (Chapter 8) and intercultural communication (Chapter 10) as the seven-person staff developed group dynamics within a multi-background mix. So our first observations about communication is that it is ubiquitous and eclectic—it is everywhere and diverse. For this reason I sometimes dub our field the "adjective" discipline. A look at some divisions in the National Communication Association indicates that most begin with an adjective designating the context or application of communication. For example:

- African American Communication and Culture
- Communication Ethics

- Family Communication
- Intercultural Communication
- Mass Communication
- Peace and Conflict Communication
- Performance Studies
- Religious Communication
- Small Group Communication
- Visual Communication[1]

Such complexity may cause one to wonder what holds the field together. Straightforward definitions are a start, but even there we have a hard time agreeing. Two of our scholars canvassed our research thirty years ago, and even then discovered over 120 definitions![2] However, this lack of agreement on a particular definition does not mean we fail to agree on anything. We do agree on two broad approaches to how communication happens and how we should study it. How we picture communication will direct our journey in exploring it.

The Objectivist Picture

The objectivist school of communication pictures communication like FedEx—a complex but efficient system for moving messages from here to there, from me to you, with intentional impact.[3] This approach views communication as the conveying of information (my idea, your feelings, or our story) from person to person, by way of various means or channels (our conversation, your Facebook profile, a new DVD). And like a FedEx package, information might get lost or damaged along the way due to unfamiliar words, poorly chosen pictures, or simply someone's misinterpretation. In everyday communication, this school of thought favors efficiency ("We sure got a lot accomplished at today's meeting"), speed ("I can't believe anyone still has dial-up"), and communicator performance ("You sure gave a great speech"). Communication, in this vision, might be defined as the process by which two or more people convey messages via diverse channels with some effect and the likelihood of interference.

Harold Lasswell, a media researcher in the late 1940s, epitomized this objectivist view when he outlined a linear model of five questions to assess a communicative event. His model of "*Who, Says What, In What Channel, To Whom, With What Effect?*" considers each link in the communication chain.[4] We might consider what researchers have discovered about each link as they apply to Sally and her colleagues.

Who? Who is the sender? What is their motive? Their personality? Their cultural background? Their gender? Their level of credibility? In our example, the answer is Sally Burkitt, a fifty-something Canadian who owns a business in western British Columbia. Objectivist research has discovered that Sally's employees will likely view her more credible if she 1) speaks the truth, knowledgeably, 2) proves she is trustworthy and reliable, and 3) shows care and concern for them.[5] If she fails at these features, her credibility will continue to suffer.

Said what? Can one describe the content of the message? Is it informative or persuasive? An intimate self-disclosure or a threat? Newsy facts or editorial opinion? Objectivist studies in marital communication indicate that couples usually divorce when they treat each other in ways similar to the Burkitt employees. In particular, couples who criticize, show contempt, become defensive, and/or stonewall (get silent) kill hope for their relationship.[6]

By what channel? How is the message conveyed, and how does this channel shape the message? Messages we hear have less impact than those we hear and see.[7] Sally's employees sent powerful messages of dissatisfaction when they attacked her face-to-face—messages that would be less potent if conveyed through email.

To whom? Who is the receiver or responder? What is their gender? Level of listening? Cultural position? Current beliefs and values? Sally's employees took her blunt manner in different ways. A Chinese female exercised face-saving behavior by never complaining about Sally, a pattern common among people who value group identity more than individual identity.[8]

With what effect? Do receivers change their minds or attitudes? Are they persuaded to act on a new belief? Are they numbed or sensitized to the world's realities? The conflict Burkitt employees experienced very likely spilled over into their family life, resulting in strained relationships and ripple-effect stress.[9]

While Lasswell was writing about the way media function in society, you can see that they apply to interpersonal communication as well. Following Lasswell's work, other linear model enthusiasts added more features, including the ideas that senders *encode* messages by using a *symbol system* (that is, language or nonverbal behavior), and receivers *decode* this information into personalized meaning. In addition, the idea of interference was broadened to be understood as any *physical noise* in the environment, *semantic noise* from word-confusion, and *technical noise* from static in the channel (such as a person's strong accent, or a strange-looking font). Conceived this way, senders are like FedEx customers who mail messages to passive receivers who accept and open them in patterned, law-like ways. Only later did transfer theorists add the idea of responder *feedback* and communication *context* to recognize that receivers respond mindfully, and that symbols take on situational meaning. Figure 1.1 depicts a common understanding of the objectivist transfer model.

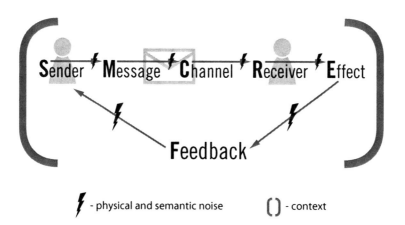

Figure 1.1: Who (S = Sender), Says What (M = Message), by what Channel (C), to Whom (R = Receiver), with what Effect (E), with the opportunity for Feedback (Fb) and the potential for physical, semantic, and technical Noise (⚡), all in a social and geographic context {C}.

Communication scholars have built on the objectivist transfer idea to develop many other models. For example, the elaboration likelihood model has shown that the more people elaborate (that is mull over or carefully consider) the ideas and evidence in a good persuasive message, the more likely they will be persuaded by that message, whereas sleepy or distracted people who pay superficial attention to less critical things (such as the speaker's tie or handsome smile) may be persuaded, but only for the short term. Or consider the face-negotiation model, which has shown that people who see their personal identity as connected with others (as opposed to independent) are more likely to avoid embarrassment with other people by avoiding conflict. Or, finally, in the cultivation theory, researchers have discovered that the more television people watch, the more they tend to see the world as a dangerous place. (Or, the more people believe the world is dangerous, the more they tend to watch the tube).[10] In these models, researchers have run experiments or gathered answers on questionnaires with people in order to observe, measure, and picture communication objectively.

We call these researchers social scientists because they use the scientific method to study people (social beings). Their way of thinking thrives in marketing and public relations where CEOs and politicians seek efficient and effective means to change our attitudes, shape our buying habits, and influence our vote. We will examine how scientists study communication in Chapter 13, and consider their assumptions about reality and methods for describing it.

The Interpretivist Picture

Whereas objectivists cast communication in terms of information transfer and effect, interpretivist school advocates assume meaning-making is more creative and cooperative, like friends playing charades.[11] Charades requires two active partners working together, thinking like each other, and using symbols that the other might recognize. To play by the rules they constrain their gestures to ritualized motions (two fingers on one's arm mean two syllables in the word). They pay attention to the feedback their partner provides, and make adjustments accordingly. Sometimes charade players' efforts are rewarded with guessing the word; other times they only succeed in generating new meanings or wrong meanings.

Along similar lines, interpretivist scholars see communication as active, dynamic, creative, and flawed. They are less likely to think that a film or speech causes a single meaning in passive receivers, but rather that active partners engage personal thoughts to create subjective meaning. This applies not just to playing charades or having a heart-to-heart chat, but also to how we interpret popular media and culture. For example, a movie such as *Juno* may be understood from diverse points of view, and critics may ultimately disagree on the message it sends to young girls. In the film, 16-year-old Juno MacGuff (played by Ellen Page), gets pregnant by her friend Paulie Bleeker (Michael Cera) and decides to give up her baby for adoption. Conservatives might affirm Juno's decision to not abort the child, but lament her modeling premarital sex. In contrast, pro-choice advocates may feel the movie oversimplifies the difficult decision pregnant teenagers encounter, and point out that the feel-good ending is rare in real life.[12] Both are probably right.

So interpretivists believe in *polysemy*, or "many meanings"—the idea that a word, speech, or film might be understood variously. If this is true, one would think we would experience communicative chaos, but

> Interpretivists are not surprised that people interpret *Juno* differently, but they also attempt to construct theories for how people might interpret *Juno* well.

generally we do not. The reason is because through interaction over time we tend to build up similar meanings associated with words and actions with people from our background or culture. The tighter knit our worlds, the greater the likelihood our ease in constructing shared meaning. When entire communities share similar assumptions, values, and rituals, its members will regularly create shared meaning with high fidelity. As interpretivist scholars reflect on these common ways of making meaning, they write theories that articulate the particular assumptions, values, and rituals that guide communication. Thus, interpretivists scholars rely on reason, observation, and concepts to articulate what they think is going on between people or in the media. They do not rely on science.

Interpretivist scholars have created dozens of theories to make sense of everything from grammar and vocabulary (e.g., how do we explain the difference between "she dropped her pen" and "she dropped her eyes"?) to epic films (e.g., what criteria might we use to determine if *The Matrix* trilogy represents allegory, tragedy, prophecy, or a blend?) Interpretivists are uneasy if we go through life as film-goers, book readers, and speech listeners with little between our ears to help us understand, judge, and explain what we engage. Their theories also explain organizational communication.

Consider for example how you might analyze Burkitt Financial's communication malaise with Michael Pacanowky's cultural approach to organizations.[13] While most people describe businesses in terms of job descriptions, lines of authority, and product management, Pacanowsky suggests organizations are best regarded as cultures where people spin "webs of significance" through communication. This theorist believes that an organization doesn't *have* a culture, but *is* a culture, and employees create culture through the stories they tell and the metaphors they invoke. If we conjecture what metaphor Burkitt employees might use, the idea of a "dysfunctional family" comes to mind with Sally and clan looking a lot like a controlling mother with ticked-off teenagers. While Sally wants her employees to respect her, she has yet to earn respect or trust from these "children." In terms of stories, Pacanowsky suggest three types: corporate stories are told by senior management to inspire rank-and-file), personal stories are individual tales that situate people in the cultural web, and collegial stories are off-the-record comments from employees to newcomers that inform them "how things really work around here." Sally's personal story of being berated by the swearing employee defined her as a victim who felt justifiably defensive. This narrative helped the consultant discern that Sally needed to be proactive and positive with her new employees.

James Carey, a respected interpretive theorist, defined communication as "a process whereby reality is created, shared, modified, and preserved."[14] What he means is that how you make sense of Burkitt Financial, "dropped her eyes" and *The Matrix* depends largely on how you engage, interpret, remember, and respond to each one. Quentin Schultze, once a student of James Carey, echoes his mentor's views in his own definition:

> [T]he study of communication is the art of subjectively interpreting the meaning and significance of people's shared cultural activities. Communication is a partici-

patory ritual in and through which we create, maintain, and change culture. Rituals include the daily routine of reading the newspaper and eating meals together, and the weekly patterns of gathering for worship, viewing television, attending courses, taking exams [and] dating.... We do not merely exchange messages; we cocreate and share cultural rituals that define reality.[15]

So while objectivists attempt to answer who, says what, by what channels, to whom, with what effect, the interpretivists are more likely to look at communication through a principled question such as "what concept best helps us to interpret (appreciate and evaluate) a cultural performer's ritualistic symbolic expression?" Or, for example, how might this interpretivist theory help us make sense of a director's film or speaker's speech?

The Whole Picture

FedEx efficiency and charades-playing fun are contrasting yet complementary images of communication. My intent in analyzing the Burkitt case study was to underscore the usefulness of both models to understand complex interaction. The objectivist approach is supported by social scientists who discover regular patterns in human communication. The interpretivist school is enacted by artists and critics who argue for conceptual lenses to make sense of human communication. Both will play a role in the rest of this book.

My personal orientation to communication studies has been influenced by my education as a social scientist at the University of Iowa, and my faith commitment as a follower of Jesus Christ. I am convinced that God is LORD of all, including my scholarship, and so I look for biblical lenses to understand communication. The next chapter describes a communication model you will not find in standard textbooks as it seeks to wed the interpretivist idea of covenant with scientific research. If all truth is God's truth, as some Christian philosophers assert, then such an approach might give a more complete picture than either-or images.[16]

 **WORTH THE TALK**

1. The two pictures of communication in this chapter are the FedEx (objectivist) model and the charades (interpretivist) model. The first might define communication as "the process by which two or more people convey messages via diverse channels with some effect and the likelihood of interference." The second might define communication as "a process whereby reality is created, shared, modified, and preserved." Which do you agree with more? Why?

2. What objective meanings do you think the movie *Juno* communicated to all viewers? What diverse subjective interpretations do you think viewers of *Juno* created on their own?

 **CONSIDER THE WALK**

1. Tell or write a story of when you and a friend miscommunicated, and explain where you think things went wrong by using the objectivist model of who, said what, by what channel, to whom, with what effect. Try to see the breakdown as possibly occurring at multiple places along the way.

2. Create your own interpretive theory as to what principles should guide movie watching. That is, what concepts or ideas should form the lens for understanding and interpreting a film? You may have done something like this before when studying literature.

3. Compare and contrast the claims of the objectivist approach with those of the interpretivist school and argue for one being a more valid way of viewing communication. Do research on both models, use real-life examples, and try to come up with three to five good reasons for favoring one model over the other.

ONLINE CHALK

Communication models abound, but the two general schools we presented capture two distinct poles of a diverse continuum. If you Google the following terms, you will find good sources on both approaches.

- Models of communication
- Linear model of communication
- Objectivist model of communication
- Interpretive views of communication

ENDNOTES

1 The National Communication Association is the premier academic organization in the United States for the study of communication. See their website at http://www.natcom.org.

2 Frank E. X. Dance and Carl E. Larson, *The Functions of Communication* (New York: Holt, Rinehart and Winston, 1972).

3 For an introductory overview of objectivist theorizing see chapter 3 in Em Griffin's *A First Look at Communication Theory*, 6th ed. (Boston: McGraw-Hill, 2006).

4 Harold D. Lasswell, "The Structure and Function of Communication in Society," in *The Communication of Ideas*, ed. L. Bryson (New York: Harper, 1948).

5 James C. McCroskey and J. J. Teven, "Goodwill: A Re-examination of the Construct and Its Measurement," *Communication Monographs* 66 (1999): 90-103.

6 For a description of this study and others like it, see John Gottman and Nan Silver, *Why Marriages Succeed or Fail—and How You Can Make Yours Last* (New York: Simon & Schuster, 1995).

7 S. Chaiken and A. H. Eagly, "Communication Modality as a Determinant of Message Persuasiveness and Message Comprehensibility," *Journal of Personality and Social Psychology* 34 (1976): 605-614.

8 John Oetzel and Stella Ting-Toomey, *The Sage Handbook of Conflict Communication: Integrating Theory, Research and Practice* (Thousand Oaks, CA: Sage, 2006).

9 C. A. Higgins, L. E. Duxbury, and R. H. Irving, "Work-Family Conflict and the Dual-Career Family," *Organizational Behavior & Human Decision Processes* 51 (1992): 51-76.

10 See Griffin, *A First Look*, for descriptions of these three models.

11 For an introductory overview of interpretivist theorizing see chapter 3 of

Griffin's *A First Look.*

12 See David Cray's article "On Film and in Real Life, Two Pregnant 16-year-olds Spark Moral Debate," *Associated Press,* http://www.mytelus.com/ncp_news/articlePrint.en.do?pn=arts&articleID=2841806 (accessed December 21, 2007).

13 See Michael Pacanowsky and Nick O'Donnell-Trujillo, "Organizational Communication as Cultural Performance," *Communication Monographs* 50 (1983): 127-147.

14 James W. Carey, *Communication as Culture: Essays on Media and Society,* (Boston: Unwin Hyman, 1998), 33.

15 Quentin J. Schultze, *Communicating for Life: Christian Stewardship in Community and Media* (Grand Rapids: Baker Academic, 2000), 54-55.

16 One philosopher who has advocated this view is Arthur Holmes. See his *All Truth is God's Truth* (Grand Rapids: Eerdmans, 1977).

You …keep your covenant of love with
your servants who continue wholeheartedly
in your way.

I Kings 8:23

Covenantal Communication
Changing Together through Committed Agreement

CHAPTER 1 ENDED with the idea that objectivist and interpretivist scholars complement each other to paint a fuller picture of communication than either may do alone. It is also true that a single model may blend both approaches. For example, Aristotle's idea that speakers persuade by making appeals to emotions, logic, and their own character has attracted much attention from scientists seeking to support his claim.

I suggest that the biblical model of covenant, and the idea of covenantal communication, hold similar promise. The covenant concept dates to Old Testament times among the Jews, Hittites, and Assyrians, yet its principles appear to hold today with measured regularity. This chapter explains covenants and covenantal communication and how both may help us understand and interpret life around us. To do so, I would like to tell you what happened with Burkitt Financial.

Burkitt Goes Covenantal

After the communication consultant discerned that Burkitt Financial was suffering from a culture of disrespect and hurtful individualism, she encouraged Sally to think team communication and to put redemptive policies in place. Sally agreed, and soon after Sally gathered her new employees along with the consultant to lay down a vision for organizational structure, communication flow, professionalism, authority, and, most of all, handling conflict. Through brainstorming, sharing, and debating, the newly hired Burkitt Financial group developed seven guiding principles. They even labeled them their "covenant."

Our Company Covenant

Together we desire to create a workplace environment where our behavior, attitudes, and actions are guided by the following:

1) A commitment to communication that reflects the values of honesty, friendliness, respect, harmony, and fun.

2) The establishment of a professional environment characterized by respect for our employer, our coworkers, and our clients. We will show respect by maintaining organized and clean work places, dressing semi-formally, and playing non-offensive music at low volume.

3) A willingness to change, continue to learn, be cross-trained, ask questions, help one another, and be flexible.

4) A posture toward our clients that values service, friendliness, appropriate addressing of clients (i.e., "Mr. Reimer"), and adopting the philosophy that "the customer is always right."

5) A desire to operate our business in an ethical, moral, and legal manner.

6) When conflict arises, we are committed to communicating openly and honestly, letting the other person know what our needs are—no mind reading required—and working together to understand one another and find workable, achievable resolutions.

7) When this goal is not achieved, we commit to extending grace and forgiveness and continuing to work toward the greater goal.

This set of guidelines resembles covenants from ancient times. What is a covenant? A covenant is an agreement between two or more people that guides how they will treat each other. In expanded form, a covenant is an enduring relationship created between two or more people who agree to standards of behavior for their mutual benefit, and if broken, results in significant consequences. Equally important is that covenants develop through a particular process we will call covenantal communication. Sally could not simply declare "Here's our covenant." She and her employees were required to work together, with good intentions and mutual commitment, to put ideas to paper. This process of relating covenantally is as important as any covenant people might forge.

Covenantal principles represent a biblical and Christian lens for understanding communication around us. It is my conviction that a covenantal approach to our field brings together the best of objectivist and interpretivist thinking. It is interpretive in that it consists of six ideas for what constitutes covenantal communication—ideas you might use to make sense of your own communication, or a slice of popular media. It is also interpretivist in that we might use its ideas as ideals to reform communication in our social worlds—a motive that interpretivists value.[1] Covenantal communication is also objectivist, because its ideas appear to be supported by scientific research. That is, you can observe these principles through empirical inquiry. However, unlike full-fledged objective theories, the covenantal model is not intended to predict communication behavior so much as to explain it. Let's start afresh with the concept of covenant.

Covenantal Communication

The first reference to covenant in the Bible is in Genesis 6 when God promised Noah he would spare him from impending doom if Noah built an ark. Noah accepted God's offer, built the ark, and guaranteed survival for his family. Gary Chapman observes that in biblical covenants, such as God's with Noah, Jonathan's with David, and Ruth's with Naomi, one person initiates an agreement for the *other* person's benefit, not their own. In Noah's story, God did not need the ark; he wanted Noah to survive. Chapman goes on to show that covenantal relationships are created by making unconditional promises to one another, for example, when God promised to prosper Abraham no matter what. People make unconditional promises to show their steadfast love to another, and intend to back them up forever. These promises, when accepted by the other, form an agreement that binds the two in mutual accountability.[2] The covenantal marriage, for example, requires two people unconditionally dedicated to each other in an enduring, accountable bond.

Professor Moses Pava captures similar yet new dimensions when he defines covenant as "a voluntary agreement among independent but equal agents to create a 'shared community.' The primary purpose of the agreement is to self-consciously provide a stable social location for the interpretation of life's meanings in order to help foster human growth, development, and the satisfaction of legitimate human needs."[3] Pava's definition highlights that covenants yield stability for people to interpret and manage what life throws at them.

Today contemporary scholars use covenant to understand culture and communication. For example, Pava is a business professor who suggests that covenantal ideals should shape how business leaders do shop in the corporate world. Eric Mount Jr., a religion professor, believes covenant principles explain how American culture developed through most of the last century as Americans valued "obligation, commitment, promise, responsibility, fidelity and vocation" to hold each other accountable in neighborly love.[4] Jack and Judith Balswick, relationship experts, recognize covenant as the biblical image for marriage, and contrast it with traditional male-centered models and self-centered contract models.[5] Or consider theologian Russel Botman's claim that covenantal principles are required of politicians and clergy in South Africa as they negotiate equality and reconciliation between black and white people following so many years of apartheid.[6]

So we should not be surprised that covenant principles crop up in small businesses such as Burkitt Financial. When they do, it is usually in two ways. One way is in the *quality* of communication that takes place. When communication is motivated by unconditional love, long-term commitment, and a desire to hold others accountable to agreed-upon standards for each others' benefit, we might say we have observed covenantal communication. Such interaction provides participants a "stable social location" from which to find purpose and meaningful talk. The other way covenantal principles show up is in communication *outcomes*, or bona fide covenants, whether spoken or written. The employees at Burkitt Financial penned a written covenant that guides future behavior, and between them they created unwritten trust and respect to see it out. Whether written and explicit, or unwritten yet relationally created, covenants represent the end result of covenantal communication.

Let's now consider more fully the characteristics of covenantal communication. As we do you will see that I am both descriptive and prescriptive. A descriptive account, like the objectivist approach, attempts to explain communication. A prescriptive account, like the interprevist approach, argues how communication might be. When combined, our analysis will show that most communication reflects some covenant principles, and that much communication practice might be shaped to these ideals.

Principle 1: Covenantal communication recognizes us as persons-in-community more than as individual selves. Our culture commonly preaches the opposite as it glamorizes individual expression, personal rights, and untethered freedom. However, in Christian perspective, we are created by God to be in community with others. For good or for ill, we not only live in relation to others, but we owe a great deal of who we are to them, and to God, as they speak into our lives.

We were designed to connect with others: connecting is life.

In *The Covenanted Self*, theologian Walter Brueggemann summarizes how this insight burst on the scene in 1918 in the works of Jewish philosopher Martin Buber and other writers. Brueggemann writes that Buber's dialogical principle, also known as the I-Thou principle,

> made clear that the human self is not an independent, autonomous agent but is always and necessarily preceded by a Thou, one radically other than us, who evokes, summons, authorizes, and 'faiths' us into existence as persons. This 'other' is endlessly inscrutable mystery and endlessly problematic for us, for we can neither escape from that other, nor are we able to seduce, capture or possess that other who always stands free from and over and against us.[7] [And again, this dialogical principle] is the insistence

that the self is always a self in relation and therefore reality is at core a relational interaction, that is, no autonomous, fixed, self-sufficient self.[8]

The observation that our self identity is more a "we" than a "me" is underscored by psychologist Paul Vitz when he suggests that our nature mirrors a triune God. He writes, "Because we are made in the image of a trinitarian God, we are made to be *interpersonal.*"[9] Rabbi Jonathan Sacks makes the point that God doesn't create individuals, he creates persons, and persons belong to a people. Our people—our relatives and cultural group—precede our birth and live past our death, and all along "people" us unto into personhood, or as Brueggemann suggests, "faith" us into existence. In Jewish thought, persons-development is fueled by *chesed*, or compassion, or more accurately "covenantal love." No baby enters the world alone, but as a child-in-community.

John Oetzel and Stella Ting-Toomey, two communication researchers, have shown that embracing a we-identity rather than a me-identity influences how we manage conflict. They found that no matter if people were Asian or American, the ones who saw their self-identities as interdependent (i.e., as connected to, responsible to, and identifying with a social group) were more likely to use an avoidance strategy for dealing with conflict than were people with independent (me-based) self-identities who tended to use dominating (in your face) strategies.[10] While long-term avoidance can be unhealthy, its immediate benefits likely outweigh power-over moves. Other research indicates that people with big personal egos and a sense of entitlement are less willing to forgive others, or ask for forgiveness, in conflict situations. They are more likely to wonder if engaging in forgiveness is necessary, worthwhile, or even due.[11] Picturing your self-identity as connected to others, and exercising forgiveness in conflict situations, signals covenantal values.

Principle 2: Covenantal communication is motivated by our steadfast love for the benefit of the other. This principle addresses the *why* behind our communication. Why do salespeople show up at our door? Why do film producers invest millions into our next DVD rental? Why do teachers teach us or preachers preach? As one of our scholars noted, human beings do not merely go through motions; humans act with intentions. Our intentions compel us.[12] But compel us to what end? To sell? To win over? To entertain?

In Noah's story, God was compelled to preserve Noah's family and animal life on earth. In Jonathan's case, Jonathan wanted to protect David from the murderous envies of King Saul. In Ruth's covenant, she promised life-long companionship to her mother-in-law Naomi who had lost her husband and two sons. These examples help illustrate that in covenantal perspective, the purpose of our communication is intended to benefit the other. When we invest in others at our own expense, we call this altruism. When we do so with affection toward the other, we may call it steadfast love.

God's steadfast love toward us is a defining feature of his nature and the covenantal relationship he seeks with us. David referred to God's unfailing love in good times and bad. In I Chronicles he records a psalm of praise with "Give thanks to the Lord, for he is good; his love endures forever" (I Chronicles 16:34), and after his affair with Bathsheba he cried out "Have mercy on me, O God, according to your unfailing love; according to your great compassion blot out my trans-gressions" (Psalm 51:1).

David's praise and lament hinges on God's steady, expectant love— a love that blesses us while inviting our obedience. God's guaranteed love does not free us to sin, but lures us to love in return. As Charles Kraft observes, in scripture "we see a God who refuses to stay on the other side of an enormous communication gap. He seeks relation-ship with us that will elicit from us a commitment to himself and his cause."[13]

Talk of unfailing love plays well in the scriptures or in a romantic novel, but does it play well among everyday people? Vincent Jeffries, a social scientist, argued affirmatively when he suggested that human personality can be explained in the terms of altruistic love and virtue, and by doing so we can understand why relationships flourish or fail.[14] (His idea is radically different from the usual habit of describing per-sonality in psychological terms such as "extroversion" and "introversion" or animal types such as beavers, otters, lions, and golden retrievers!) Jeffries believed that altruism (helping others with no expectation in return) was best expressed through St. Aquinas' five virtues of tem-perance (self-control), fortitude (patience and long-suffering), justice (correct action), charity (love), and prudence (wisdom). His review of the marital conflict research showed, for example, that wise couples knew how to distinguish between big and insignificant issues in their marriage, focused on the problem (not each other), and engaged diverse ways to solve their problems. His research showed that, everything else being equal, the five virtues explained why couples treated each other equitably, managed their anger, and chose not to withdraw after conflict. In similar research, I found that the more husbands and wives thought the other virtuous, the more satisfied they were with their marriages.[15] Is virtuous love possible in less intimate relationships? I think so. The Burkitt employees leaked their commitment to steadfast love when they noted how they wanted to respond to unresolved conflict: "When [a workable solution] is not achieved, we commit to extending grace and forgiveness and continuing to work toward the greater goal."

Principle 3: Covenantal communication requires responsible symbolic expression. That is, a covenantal approach assumes that words count, and actions tell, and therefore you cannot say whatever you please without consequence. This cloak of responsibility weighs significantly in two domains: how we name our world, and how we enact social relationships. Both require responsible language and action.

> The mystery of symbols is that they not only point to our world, but also enact relationship with others.

When God asked Adam to name the animals, he affirmed the power of words to point to, label, and order his creation. We continue Adam's task as scientists discover and name new species, or as social critics observe and label human behavior. For example, the term "sexual harassment" was added to our dictionaries only in the 1970s as scholars and activists observed and described this abuse of power.

Words also represent one's identity—the who and whose we are. When God changed Abram's name to Abraham and changed Simon's name to Peter, he did so to signal their new role in his plan to bless the world ("Abraham" means "father of many nations") and build his church on a solid foundation ("Peter" means "rock"). So when the Burkitt employees envisioned a workplace that was clean and organized where they dressed semi-formally and played low-volume music, their words pointed to, labeled, and ordered a tangible vision for change. Their discussion was more than talk—it began to shape their reality. Scholars call this the referential function of symbols.[16]

But words do more than point to our world; they can also create new social realities. When God made his promise to Abraham, he created a new world order. God promised to bless Abraham's family and guaranteed them the Promised Land (see Exodus 32:13). Similarly, God promised Noah to never destroy all of life again by flood, and said the rainbow would be a reminder to him of this "everlasting covenant" (see Genesis 9: 12-16). Promises are powerful speech acts in that they cement social bonds, picture an ideal world, and show steadfast love for the other. Promise-making and promise-keeping characterize covenantal communication.

Professor Hak Joon Lee relies on covenantal logic to create a guide for ethical communication, and suggests that moral decisions require all stakeholders to have a fair say through open and honest dialogue.[17] I think Burkitt Financial held to Lee's rule when Sally, employees, and the consultant sat down to agree on their covenant. And what is this covenant but a wonderful promise for better communication? The Burkitt group promised to show respect, be honest, and act friendly. They committed to share openly, conflict graciously, and forgive liberally. By coming together and agreeing on this vision, the members created a corporate promise through their language, and will hopefully prove their intentions true with their actions.

Unfortunately, our words also hold potential to unravel covenantal trust, as evident in distressed couples on the verge of divorce. John Gottman, psychologist and respected leader in marital communication, has identified criticism, contempt, defensiveness, and stonewalling as the "Four Horsemen of the Apocalypse" which destroy marriages.[18] While a simple complaint targets someone's behavior, such as, "That music is too loud," a criticism diminishes the identity of the other person, as in, "You *always* play your music too loudly!" and contempt goes further by trying to hurt others psychologically, as in "I *hate* you for playing such loud music!" Such attacks may lead a partner to respond defensively by denying responsibility or making excuses, which does nothing to solve the issue. If defensiveness continues, partners may give up, shut down, and withdraw—stonewall the other—all the while rehearsing and nursing wounds with mental strokes such as "I can't believe she plays that music to hurt me!" Gottman's research affirms that words count, and cannot be taken lightly in their role to build or erode covenantal relationships.

Principle 4: Covenantal communication results in redemptive pacts as to how we will live together. That is, our communication results in written or unwritten agreements about what is best for both parties and their collective good. These agreements, whether personal or organizational, represent full-scale promises to live according to a shared vision. For example, couples make vows on their wedding day to protect and honor for life. Committee members pass agendas with topics R, S, T, but not W, X, Y in order to focus their business. Some of us agree to sign statements of faith and community responsibilities to join our college or university. Journalists and the Federal Communications Commission agree on what is ethical coverage of news events. We even show agreement when we obey traffic signs, pay our taxes, and water our lawns on city-approved days.

In each case these redemptive pacts create a "shared community" and a "stable social location" to interpret life and "foster human growth."[19] But what do they look like in everyday friendships like your own? To find out I asked students in my relational communication course to jot down agreements they have made with close friends and family. Students wrote down between two and fifteen pacts, but on average about seven or eight. I then asked them to categorize their list by type, and to give a label for each category. We then made a master list of the categories and tried to find overlap. While this process was not too scientific, it did reveal an interesting pattern. Students in my course entered into:

1. Agreements about *practical living*, for example who washes dishes, cleans the room, and pays the bills.

2. Agreements about *communication and relational health*, such as being open, addressing conflict, setting physical boundaries, and supporting one another

3. Agreements about *money*, as in who pays rent, who pays tuition, how much one should save, and whether one had to pay back another.

4. Agreements about *involvement with extended family and other friends*, such as visiting each others' parents, going out, recreating, and handling difficult people.

5. Agreements about *spiritual commitments*, such as praying together, attending church together, and ministering to others.

6. Agreements about the *future*, for example, rooming together, going on road trips, getting married, having kids, and attending grad school.

My students had to think long and hard to generate some of these examples, because, in their own words, "we just assume so much; we don't necessarily talk about it." Their comment signals a feature of closely knit covenantal relationships—when we act in good faith for the other's benefit, we may not feel it is necessary to express our needs or negotiate a deal to meet them. Friends just know.

This observation sets up another important point: redemptive pacts within covenantal relationships bear little resemblance to business agreements made under legal contracts. It's not as if my students wrote down hard-and-fast rules that their partners required of them, but small and large agreements that generally guided their relationship. However, in some relationships (business and otherwise), people operate with a strong contract orientation. Gary Chapman describes the five features of contracts:

1. Contracts are most often made for a limited period of time.

2. Contracts most often deal with specific actions

3. Contracts are based on an "If…, Then…." mentality.

4. Contracts are motivated by the desire to get something we want.

5. Contracts are sometimes unspoken or implicit.[20]

It's not surprising that people who enter relationships with a contract mentality generally suffer. Their tendency toward immediate pleasure and "this-for-that" affection keeps them from loving lavishly at their own cost. Not surprising, they tend to keep track of when others hurt them, and forgive only after the other person apologizes. Such people spin *unredemptive pacts* with friends in the name of keeping things fair and even. But relationally they wilt.[21]

When God calls us into a covenant relationship with himself, he is all the while modeling how we ought to relate with others. The

terms of God's redemptive pact are summed up succinctly by Jesus in Matthew 22:37: "Love the Lord your God with all your heart, and with all your soul and with all your mind" ... and (vs. 39) "Love your neighbor as yourself." Theologians take the last half—loving our neighbor— and suggest we do so through two other great commandments. One is God's *great commission* to go and proclaim his salvation and make disciples of people everywhere (Matthew 28:16–20). The other is the *great mandate* to take dominion over the entire created order and steward it as a gardener would a garden (Genesis 1:28–31). The first concerns the well-being of people's souls and their eternal destiny; the latter concerns extending God's kingdom and righteousness on earth by acknowledging Christ's lordship over all. The call to be witnesses of his gospel requires us to know the story of salvation and the hope that is within us. The call to be gardeners requires us to denounce evil, seek justice, respect others, exploit no one, and serve everyone.[22] When we covenant with God, we look forward to his agenda. We indeed become co-laborers with him in the redemption of the world (1 Corinthians 3:9).

Principle 5: Covenantal communication changes us together. Put another way, when you and I agree on a redemptive pact, communication will play a central role in transforming us to its vision. It is one thing to agree, yet another to make it happen.

The history of the word "communicate" underscores how this process changes us. The Indo-European roots of "communicate" are *ko* and *mei*. *Ko* means "together" (as in cooperate or coauthor), and *mei* means "change." Together they capture the crux of covenantal communication: to change together. This understanding makes clear why models of "information transfer" and even "co-creation of meaning" noted in Chapter 1 often fall short. Communication is more than mere information transfer, or meaning creation. When we communicate, we also nurture and nudge each other toward some ultimate vision of life. In covenantal communities, communication reflects God's justice and agape love so people can grow in him. Or as Moses Pava said, it meets legitimate human needs. Without a vision to love God or see his justice, life can become meaningless and debilitate into the pursuit of things or merely our own happiness.

Organizational CEOs understand the principle of change through communication, and act on it strategically. Often they use a company mission statement to embody and engrain the organization's ethos. Jack Hawley writes of the leader's communicative challenge:

> "The leader's first task is to define reality, to make sense of the organization . . . what it means, why it is in business, what its great purpose is, and what kind of place you want it to be...."[23]

As we know, Sally Burkitt led her employees in defining their organization's reality. Their covenant directly addressed the kind of place they wanted Burkitt Financial to be. Their value on professionalism cut out jeans and loud music. Their value on cross-training promoted flexibility and sharing each others' loads. Their concern for respect meant that complaining and condemning had to go.

While Sally and group might aspire to these ideals, you can bet they will fall short from time to time. And then what? Does showing steadfast love mean turning a blind eye to each other's shortcomings? The answer is no. Living in covenant requires holding each other accountable to the shared vision, even if it means expressing difficult truth.. It also means praising where kudos are due as colleagues meet and surpass expectations in creative ways.

Communications scholar Mark Gring argues that when we hold to or steer from our covenantal community's moral vision, we should expect "sanctions"—blessings and curses that guide our course.[24] Blessed sanctions might be material, as in pay raises and company trips to Palm Springs, or symbolic, as in receiving an award or a supervisor's words of approval. Similarly, cursed sanctions may be a difficult year-end review and a supervisor's request that we receive more training. I am sure that Sally Burkitt and her employees will not bless or curse on whim, but with sound reasons in light of their new vision, a vision everyone drew up together and bought into.

Our communication reflects a similar economy of blessings and curses as people change through relationship. We will pick up this line of thinking in Chapter 5 when we consider the power of self-talk to change how we see ourselves. It plays out again in Chapter 6 when we consider how deep interpersonal relating allows for mutual influence in friendship communication. In Chapter 7 we will consider the dark and bright side of family communication where parents and children shape each other. Finally, the theme of changing together also applies in Chapter 8 as we look at how small groups build community to complete their tasks.

> Couples married over twenty-five years often cite loyalty and commitment as reasons for their success.

Principle 6: Covenantal communication exercises long-term commitment for maximum benefit. This principle was implied when we said covenantal interaction is motivated by steadfast love. "Steadfast" means "everlasting," and to remain loyal in relationship requires commitment.

Making long-term commitments runs against the grain of our cultural values. We are people on the go. We value mobility, not active local enmeshment. Students in my classes indicate that they have moved to a new house or apartment about eight times by the time they are twenty years old. That means a new place every thirty months. Moreover, the statistics on divorce indicate we jump from house to house for more than the view. The divorce rates of 50 percent for married couples and 60 percent for remarried couples in the United

States are the highest in the world. Seems many would rather switch partners than hang in there. However couples who have been married for over twenty-five years often cite "lifetime commitment," "loyalty," "commitment to sexual fidelity," and "commitment to spouse and marriage" as reasons for their success.[25]   Furthermore, research indicates that we are quite aware of our reasons for committing to someone else, rather than believe it is a mystical, unavoidable union.[26]

The case for commitment as the Holy Grail of thriving, satisfactory relationships is really nothing short of amazing. When married couples measure high on commitment, they also tend to adjust their lives for their partners, and willingly sac-rifice their own needs for their partner's benefit.[27] Committed people are more sexually responsive than uncommitted ones (a fact that entertainment media twist to the opposite), and have less need to scan their social environment for other partners.[28] Communicationally, commit-ted partners show more lively emotional expression, support each other's feelings, and open up about their lives more than do the uncommitted.[29] We should not be surprised, therefore, to learn that com-mitted couples feel less trapped in their

marriages, have fewer affairs, have longer marriages, and rate their rela-tionships more satisfactory than uncommitted people.[30] This golden litany proves that long-term commitment yields maximum mutual benefit for married couples.

It is my sense that commitment works because it indicates that someone will accept responsibility for what he or she says. It means one will stick around even when taken to task. The National Communication Association underscores this principle in their credo for communication ethics. Alongside other statements to speak truth-fully, value diversity, promote human potential, and condemn violence, they also stand by the ethic that "We accept responsibility for the short- and long-term consequences of our own communication and expect the same of others."[31]   When we abide by this rule, we avoid the eject button in relationships at the first sign of conflict, and try to work things out. When we agree to this ethic, we admit our fault and ask for forgiveness when we hurt other people. Similarly, when others have hurt us we exercise the courage to approach them and address the issue. Media moguls who respect this principle accept responsibility for viewers' responses to damaging programming rather than defending themselves behind a "free speech" argument. Missionaries who understand this rule attempt reconciliation with nationals when past evangelism strategies have destroyed valuable heritage. Commitment serves as holding power through stormy seas until we harbor in reconciliation.

Ultimately, commitment resonates with God's promise to never leave us nor forsake us. As Joseph Allen writes, "This characteristic of God's covenant love is readily suggested by the very meaning of covenant, a relationship in which the parties have an enduring responsibility to one another . . . not momentary concern, but enduring loyalty."[32]

Given these six principles, we might offer a full definition of covenantal communication to summarize.

Covenantal communication is the process
by which people-in-community, who are motivated by
unconditional love, use symbols responsibly to agree upon
redemptive pacts in order to change together through committed
loyalty over generations

"Covenant" and "covenantal communication" provide a biblical lens for understanding and evaluating human communication.

WORTH THE TALK

1. This chapter describes a covenantal model of communication. Is this model more like the objectivist transfer model or the subjective interpretivist model discussed in Chapter 1? Explain your reasoning.

2. A covenantal model seems most true of close relational communication and small-group communication. How might it apply to the world of media and culture?

3. Which of the six covenantal principles do you think sheds the most light on your communication? Explain why.

CONSIDER THE WALK

1. Covenantal communication may occur between friends, among members in a small group, and between media producers and media consumers. Take one of these contexts and explain how the six principles of covenantal communication apply.

2. "Covenant" is one biblical theme that helps us understand communication. Research other themes that do the same. Some suggestions include: redemption, revelation, shalom, incarnation, and communion.

3. Look at your own communication with a friend, parent, or professional acquaintance (e.g., professor, pastor) for its covenantal qualities. Use the six principles to describe how your communication is, and to evaluate how you would like your communication to be.

ONLINE CHALK

Covenantal communication embraces an array of concepts and skills. These search terms put you in touch with sites that reflect that diversity.

- Covenantal communication
- Covenantal relationships
- Contract versus covenant
- Change through communication

ENDNOTES

1 For a discussion of interpretivist theorizing see chapter 3 in Em Griffin's *A First Look at Communication Theory*, 6th ed. (Boston: McGraw-Hill, 2006).

2 Gary Chapman, *Covenant Marriage: Building Communication & Intimacy* (Nashville: Broadman and Holman, 2003), 11-25.

3 Moses L. Pava, "The Many Paths to Covenantal Leadership: Traditional Resources for Contemporary Business," *Journal of Business Ethics*, 29 (2001): 86.

4 Eric Mount Jr., *Covenant, Community, and the Common Good: An Interpretation of Christian Ethics* (Cleveland: Pilgrim Press, 1999), 8-9.

5 Jack O. Balswick and Judith K. Balswick, *A Model for Marriage: Covenant, Grace, Empowerment and Intimacy* (Downers Grove, IL: InterVarsity Press, 2006), 38-48.

6 H. Russel Botman, "Covenantal Anthropology: Integrating Three Contemporary Discourses of Human Dignity," in *God and Human Dignity*, ed. R. Kendall Soulen and Linda Woodhead (Grand Rapids: Eerdmans, 2006), 72-88.

7 Walter Brueggemann, *The Covenanted Self: Explorations in Law and Covenant* (Minneapolis: Augsburg Fortress, 1999), 1.

8 Ibid., 19.

9 Paul Vitz, "A Christian Theory of Personality: Covenant Theory," in *Man and Mind: A Christian Theory of Personality*, ed. T. J. Burke (Hillsdale, MI: Hillsdale College Press, 1987).

10 See John Oetzel and Stella Ting-Toomey, "Face Concerns in Interpersonal Conflict: A Cross-Cultural Empirical Test of the Face-Negotiation Theory," *Communication Research* 36 (2003): 599-624.

11 See Julie Juola Exline and others, "Too Proud to Let Go: Narcissistic Entitlement as a Barrier to Forgiveness," *Journal of Personality & Social Psychology* 87 (2004): 894-913.

12 Rhetorical scholar Kenneth Burke argued that understanding a person's motives is key to understanding their communication. His dramatic pentad suggests that we

may assess someone's talk by considering 1) the scene (where), 2) the agent (who), 3) the agent's means (how), 4) his or her act (what), and 5) their purpose (why), the last of which concerns motives.

13 Charles Kraft, *Communication Theory for Christian Witness* (Nashville: Abingdon, 1983), 34.

14 Vincent Jeffries, "Love: The Five Virtues of St. Thomas Aquinas," *Sociology and Social Research* 71 (1987): 174-182, and Vincent Jeffries, "Virtue and Marital Conflict: A Theoretical Formulation and Research Agenda," *Sociological Perspectives* 43 (2000): 231-247.

15 Bill Strom, "Communicator Virtue and its Relationship to Marriage Quality," *Journal of Family Communication* 3 (2003): 21-39.

16 For a full treatment of the referential and performative function of language, see John Austin, *How to Do Things with Words* (Cambridge, MA: Harvard University Press, 1962) and John R. Searle, *Speech Acts: An Essay in the Philosophy of Language* (New York: Cambridge University Press, 1969).

17 Hak Joon Lee, *Covenant and Communication: A Christian Moral Conversation with Jürgen Habermas* (Lanham, MD: University Press of America, 2006), 125-156.

18 John Gottman and Nan Silver, *Why Marriages Fail or Succeed, and How You Can Make Yours Last* (New York: Simon & Schuster, 1995).

19 Moses L. Pava, "The Many Paths to Covenantal Leadership: Traditional Resources for Contemporary Business," *Journal of Business Ethics* 29 (2001): 86.

20 Gary Chapman, *Covenant Marriage*, 8-10.

21 For an engaging comparison of covenantal and contractual relationships see Margaret F. Brinig and Steven L. Nock, "What Does Covenant Mean for Relationships?" in *Covenant Marriage in Comparative Perspective,* ed. John Witte, Jr. and Eliza Ellison (Grand Rapids: Eerdmans, 2005), 265-293.

22 For a fuller understanding of God's call for us to be his witnesses, both in terms of evangelism and establishing righteousness on earth, see the Lausanne Covenant of the Lausanne Committee for World Evangelism at http://www.gospel.com/ and search for "covenant." See also Klaus Bockmuehl's helpful commentary in the social ethics article of the Lausanne Covenant in, *Evangelicals and Social Ethics: A Commentary on Article 5 of the Lausanne Covenant,* trans. David T. Priestley (Downers Grove, IL: InterVarsity Press, 1979).

23 Jack Hawley, *Reawakening the Spirit in Work* (San Francisco: Berrett-Koehler, 1993).

24 Mark A. Gring, "Communication as Covenantal" (paper presented at the National Communication Association Annual Convention, Chicago, November, 1999).

25 For a thorough and very readable study of commitment in marriage across several nations, see S. Sharlin, F. Kaslow, and H. Hammerschmidt, *Through Thick and Thin: A Multinational Picture of Long-Term Marriages* (Binghamton, NY: Hawthorne Clinical Practice, 2000). See also R. Lauer, J. Lauer, and S. Kerr, "The Long-Term Marriage: Perceptions of Stability and Satisfaction." *International Journal of Aging and Human Development* 31 (1990): 189-195.

26 See Catherine A. Surra, Michelle L. Batchelder, and Debra K. Hughes, "Accounts and the Demystification of Courtship," in *Explaining Family Interactions,* ed. Mary Anne Fitzpatrick and Anita L. Vangelisti (Thousand Oaks, CA: Sage, 1995),

132. The authors argue that it is a myth to believe that people are naïve about commitment and about why they get committed, based on communication research.

27 For reference to accommodating behavior see J. Weiselquist, C. Rusbult, C. Foster, and C. Agnew, "Commitment, Pro-Relationship Behavior, and Trust in Close Relationships," *Journal of Personality and Social Psychology* 77 (1999): 942-966. For reference to sacrificing behavior see S. Miller, "Inattentive and Contended: Relationship Commitment and Attention to Alternatives," *Journal of Personality and Social Psychology* 73 (1997): 758-766.

28 For reference to sexual responsiveness, see S. Sprecher et al., "Domains of Expressive Interaction in Intimate Relationships: Associations with Satisfaction Commitment," *Family Relations* 44 (1995): 203-210. Regarding not seeking alternative partners, see above S. Miller, "Inattentive and Contended."

29 For reference to lively emotional expression and supportive communication see S. Sprecher et al., "Domains of Expressive Interaction," and for opening up (also called intimate self-disclosure), see S. Sprecher and S. Hendrick, "Self-Disclosure in Intimate Relationships: Associations with Individual and Relationship Characteristics Over Time," *Journal of Social & Clinical Psychology* 23 (2004): 857-877.

30 For reference to feeling less trapped, engaging in fewer affairs, and being more satisfied in marriage, see S. Stanley, H. Markman and S. Whitton, "Communication, Conflict, and Commitment: Insights on the Foundations of Relationship Success from a National Survey," *Family Process* 41 (2002): 659-675. For reference to longer-lasting marriages see C. Rusbult and J. Martz, "Remaining in an Abusive Relationship: An Investment Model Analysis of Nonvoluntary Dependence," *Personality and Social Psychology Bulletin* 21 (1995): 558-571.

31 For a complete look at the National Communication Association's ethical credo visit: http://www.natcom.org.

32 Joseph L. Allen, *Love & Conflict: A Covenantal Model of Christian Ethics* (Nashville: Abingdon, 1984), 72.

In the beginning was the Word,
and the Word was with God
and the Word was God.

John 1:1

High-Fidelity Speech
Putting Faith in the Spoken Word

THE PLAIN ENGLISH Campaign is a not-for-profit organization established in 1979 and dedicated to improving English in public use. This group plays watchdog for phrasing that is vague, over-written, or simply unintelligible. Its services include granting a Crystal Mark designation for documents that meet the Plain English grade, and a weekly Gobbledygook designation for ugly copy we should avoid. At year's end the group determines a Golden Bull Award for the worst of the worst Goobledygook candidates. One winner from 2007 included:

> *From Virgin Trains in a letter to customers about problems booking online:* Moving forwards, we as Virgin Trains are looking to take ownership of the flow in question to apply our pricing structure, thus resulting in this journey search appearing in the new category-matrix format. The pricing of this particular flow is an issue going back to 1996 and it is not something that we can change until 2008 at the earliest. I hope this makes the situation clear

And a weekly Gobbledygook recipient was:

> *From a notice on the Amazon.com.uk website:* We are currently experiencing an issue which is impacting the appearance of availability for some seller offerings.

The *Virgin Trains* writer appears to be explaining why online pricing information is hard to find, and he or she dodges responsibility by labeling it a long-term problem. The *Amazon's* language seems equally culpable in that it avoids saying the company's computer problems are keeping them from posting customers' books for sale. In covenantal perspective, the writers might aim to use language more responsibly to create shared meaning as well as to own what is theirs. You and I are probably equally guilty of such evasive talk. I have used the phrase "righteous indignation" to avoid saying I *hate* someone, and used the line, "Let's discuss their needs" to avoid being called a *gossip*.

While evasive language is not trivial, I think it is but one symptom of a larger issue. That issue is that many North Americans lack faith in the ability of words to communicate truth in the first place. Or, put conversely, many believe you can use words to create any truth you like. Without the basic starting point that truth is knowable, surface words have little foundation. Words become a commodity to be twisted and inflated, packaged and sold for some personal or corporate gain. It is no wonder we distrust the words of companies such as *Virgin* and *Amazon*, as well as those of our leaders.

This distrust began as early as the seventeenth century when philosophers and scientists divided human experience between the material (such as atoms, earth and technology) and the immaterial (such as faith, reason, and language). They considered the material *real* and the immaterial, well, not *really* real. You can see the implication of this duality. If words are not real, then they may do a lousy job of referring to or creating anything real. Practically speaking, one can say almost anything and get away with it, because, as the saying goes, "it's only words."[1]

Despite the popularity of this view, it runs contrary to other philosophical and theological positions. It must also pain God who seems committed to the idea that, in language, he has given us a tool for not only claiming truth and pointing to reality, but also creating important truths and realities. As we noted in Chapter 2, responsible symbolic expression helps us create key meanings as we come together to shape agreements, pursue the good, and change our reality. It is important, however, to point out that there's a difference between physical, social, and mental reality. But first, we need to appreciate how language operates as one enormous redemptive pact.

Language in Covenantal Perspective

From the sounds we utter, to how we debate an opponent in speech class, language and its use are a set of social agreements—a meeting of minds within a people group as to the sounds, words, and conventions that will signal their faintest emotions and grandest dreams.

First of all, acquiring language is a social process as much an innate one. We have the natural ability to learn language, but we still need a language community around us to develop it. Feral children—those raised by animals or with minimal human interaction during the first years of life—do not speak. Even when re-introduced to human life, feral children struggle to learn language fluently, if at all, affirming that full personhood blossoms as others "faith" us into existence.[2]

For people raised in usual settings, the language acquired represents a diverse set of social agreements. Consider that the twenty-six letters in our alphabet are not naturally occurring, nor the only symbols we might have chosen, but were agreed upon over time until standardized. From these twenty-six letters we derive about fifty-two sounds (called phonemes), including, for example, the letter "A" which we agree to pronounce as "short" (as in f*a*t), "long" (as in f*a*te), and "aw" (as in f*a*r) among others. Other cultural groups agree on similar as well as different sounds. For example, in Indian Marathi, one version of the "r" is pronounced while the tongue is touching the uvula at the back of the throat.

We also agree on meaning units called morphemes, which are usually words, but also prefixes and suffixes, which we pick up through interaction or learn by rote in school. The Oxford English Dictionary represents our lexicon, or collection of words deemed usable as "English." When used regularly, a word acquires "conventional meaning," or its usual association in everyday life.

We combine letters by way of long-established spelling rules (e.g., "i" before "e" except after "c"), which allows for "receipt" but not "recieve," and then order words by way of syntax rules (e.g., subject-verb-object generates "Gina loves cake" but not "Loves Cake Gina"). When we engage in a simple conversation, we hold to "cooperative rules" such as saying enough (not hogging nor yielding the floor too much), saying what's true, sticking with the topic, and being direct and clear.[3]

Sanctions of blessing and cursing respectively await those who hold to or ignore these linguistic agreements—as our command of language will influence the grades we earn, the careers we pursue, and the people we call friends.

Given that we learn language in community, agree on its elements and rules, and enjoy benefits of its mastery, one might consider a covenantal definition of language. In covenantal perspective, language is an agreed-upon linguistic pact that empowers people to order and make meaning of their world, and if never learned, or intentionally disregarded, yields dire personal and social consequences. Let's now consider how language empowers us in relation to our physical, social, and mental worlds.

Words and the Physical World

A pastor once asked his congregation, "Why did Adam name the elephant an elephant?" His answer? "Because it looked so much like one!" There is a temptation to think that objects cry out a label, as if large pachyderms command, "Call me *elephant*." If all of creation did this, we would speak one language—"universese." But in fact God's creation does not emit a natural language, which explains in part why there are over 6,000 languages, and why few use the same word for even common objects. For example, English-speakers refer to shaggy canines with "dog," while the French use "chien" and Germans utter "hund."

A more accurate model of how words relate to the physical world is depicted in Figure 3.1.[4] The dotted line between *symbols* (words) and *referents* (what they refer to) indicates that this relationship is arbitrary, meaning words do not resemble or sound like the things to which they refer. The word "dog" does not look like one any more than does "chien." Even still, ever since Adam had the job to name the animals, people have had the responsibility of labeling the cosmos. Humans name the physical world.

Just because these labels are arbitrary, however, does not mean claims we make about the world are fickle. For example, the words "dog," "sleeping," and "mat" may not imitate the things to which they refer, but my claim that "The dog is sleeping on the mat" is by no means arbitrary. That claim can be judged true or false depending on where Buddy is and what he's doing. The same is true if you make an abstract claim such as "God is sovereign." Just because a French speaker may say "Dieu est souverain" does not render this claim meaningless, irrational, or hidden from investigation.[5]

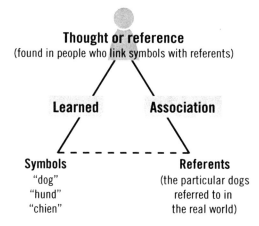

Figure 3.1. The Meaning Triangle (from *The Meaning of Meaning*, C. K. Ogden and I. A. Richards. Reprinted by permission of Routledge and Kegan Paul.)

The dotted line in Figure 3.1 also represents a language pact in that we agree to associate "dog" with actual hairy canines. We also agree that some words (such as "restroom") are preferred over others (such as "toilet") in certain social contexts, because we can emotionally manage the image of a small tiled room, but not its porcelain potty. We also agree that the history of a word's meaning is a good basis for developing new words. You will recall that from *ko* and *mei* we agreed to derive words such as communication, community, communion, and commune, each denoting change together through sharing in common. The practice of communication studies that examines word histories is called etymology.

Words and Our Social World

The solid lines in Figure 3.1 that connect "symbols" and "referents" via the person icon represent how others teach us to speak. Unlike wolf children, we had the advantage to learn word-referent linkages (remember those Richard Scarry books?) and develop a relationship with our caregiver. This bonding process begins with the slightest imitative exchange between parent and infant, as when a father returns a "coo" to his newborn daughter, and later celebrates her first words with praise.

These exchanges are like tiny social contracts, and communication scholars call them *speech acts*.[6] Speech acts are behaviors we make with language that we cannot make with our bodies. Promises, greetings, blessings, and praise are prime examples. I may throw a ball with my arm, but I lob an insult at you with hurtful words. You may sculpt a sandcastle with your hands, but you build up my spirit with helpful words. Our relationship develops through the speech acts we engage with one another.

While speech acts are largely interpersonal, they also function in the media to develop relational bonds. Take this printed book for example. Although it refers to dogs and train companies (that is, physical objects), it is also establishing a relationship between you and me. And, even though you cannot give me feedback as quickly as you could in conversation, words in a book still nurture relationship. Or consider how soap opera enthusiasts develop para-social relationships with their favorite characters, talking to them on the television, and worrying about their situations.[7] You may catch yourself promising your favorite soap star that you will be right back after the commercial break. In worse case scenarios, para-social relating can lead some fans to stalk favorite celebrities in real life.

Our language is so meat-and-potatoes that we are apt to forget that everything from our greetings, phone calls, coffee chats, and emails depend on words to create trust, show affection, and shed light among us. Therefore, we must remember that words can break trust ("Oops, I forgot I promised"), show hate ("She's nothing but a #%&*!!"), and deceive ("Officer, I was going only 57 m.p.h."). In extreme cases, words contribute to mental disorders such as schizophrenia and add pain in abusive relationships.[8] We will look more at the destructive social potential of language in the chapters on interpersonal and family communication.

Words and Our Mental World

Another drawback of Figure 3.1 is that it does not recognize the amoeba-like nature of meaning in our heads. Even if we all agreed on the *denotative* (that is, dictionary) definition of "train" as "a means of transportation consisting of assembled cars which runs on a track" we would likely differ in the connotative (that is, emotional) meanings we attach to it. Osgood and his associates examined affective meaning (another term for connotative meaning) and discovered that we tend to favor three emotional dimensions when attaching meaning to terms: evaluation, potency, and activity.[9] You will get the point of their study if you check your associations with "trains," on the scale below, and compare it with a friend's.

TRAINS

Good ___ ___ ___ ___ ___ ___ ___ Bad (evaluation)
Weak ___ ___ ___ ___ ___ ___ ___ Strong (potency)
Fast ___ ___ ___ ___ ___ ___ ___ Slow (activity)

Sports car enthusiasts who value speed and personal freedom would likely rate trains closer to bad, weak, and slow, whereas a retiree who has time to visit both coasts might rate the trains nearer to good, strong, and fast. Like the ever-fluxing perimeter of an amoeba, the emotional meaning attached to "trains" changes from person to person, or within the same person over time.

Figure 3.1 also hides the fact that words may blind us to alternative ways of thinking. This is the hypothesis of Edward Sapir and Benjamin Whorf.[10] Rather than say our thoughts precede our language, they propose that our language precedes and molds our thinking. The strong version of their theory claims that the language we speak determines our higher level thought processes. They call this linguistic determinism. Their soft version suggests that the language we speak helps or hinders our ability to perceive the world. They call this linguistic relativism. It is not that our brains and senses cannot perceive the world in different terms; it is that our language discourages us from doing so. In our car-crazed culture we find it easy to picture and discuss cars because of words such as *sedan, Ford, compact, Toyota, sports coupe, convertible, four-wheel drive, prairie cruiser, commuter car, Chevrolet,* and *two-door.* However, we may struggle to picture or discuss trains until we master other labels such as *trainset, motive power, consist, rolling stock, carriages,* and *third rail.*

This shows how difficult it is to visualize a concept without a word to represent it. For this reason my wife and I expanded our children's vocabulary so they could knit together a tightly woven word-net with which to "catch" their experience. We are pleased they grew up voracious readers and enjoyed language arts in school. We also kept some ugly words from entering their vocabulary in hopes that their response to life's challenges would be lexically biased toward grace, not garbage.

Great System, But Still Flawed

The rich potential for language to point to the physical world, create relational bonds, and nurture right thinking should compel us to study its intricacies. God made his entire creation good, including our gift of speech. But since Adam's sin and the consequential fall of the human race, all of creation, including language, carries the burden of the fall in some form or other. Language, for all its potential, still has pitfalls. We might regard some flaws as inherent to a language's grammar and vocabulary, while other shortcomings are due to our misuse of it. What are some of those pitfalls?

Abstract Language. One problem is that words differ in their degree of concreteness, some being tangible and others opaque. Linguist S. I. Hayakawa pictured this problem with his abstraction ladder.[11] Imagine a ladder grounded in bedrock that reaches skyward. The bedrock represents tangible words, and the clouds represent abstract words. In between are rungs (other words) that separate tangible words that you can almost taste, touch and feel from abstract ones that refer mainly to other words.

Take, for example, "Buddy," our Maltipoo pet. "Buddy" refers to one particular dog with his unique yelp, shape, and demeanor. Up one rung is the word "dog" that refers to all canines (the Buddies, Rexes, and Scuppers of the world), and up another rung is the word "pet" that refers to all animals owned for human pleasure (such as cats, fish and gerbils). Each new word refers to a more abstract referent, as in "animal" and "organism." Buddy *is* a dog, pet, animal, and organism, but I would never say, "I'm going to walk the organism."

While abstract language has its place, it can also cause confusion. We promise, "I'll be home early," and mean midnight, but our partner reads it as 10:00 P.M. We say, "I want to be more committed to God," and mean, "attend worship regularly," but our friends think "she's going to become a nun." A simple verbal check often avoids the misunderstanding. "What do you mean by *early*?" "What do you mean by *more committed*?"

Euphemism. "Through euphemism we substitute mild, vague, or less emotionally charged terms for more blunt ones."[12] When I refer to my hate for someone as "righteous indignation," I am using euphe-

**"I didn't promise you a company car.
I promised you a set a wheels."**

mism. I may be kind, but I'm not honest. Some Christians suggest that Ephesians 4:15 is a good standard for guarding against euphemism. If we "speak the truth in love" we will choose words that are kind and accurate. In good conscience I can call a friend "rotund" even though he is overweight, because "rotund" extends mercy while still admitting he is fat.

Some cultural groups favor euphemism because such words act like social salve and keep the peace. Asian groups who have been influenced by the teaching of Confucius may use euphemism to avoid embarrassment in an awkward social setting, or to show kindness when they really feel anger.

While euphemism might be conveniently used to keep relations harmonious, our conscience may revolt when euphemism covers up mistakes and horrors that could be avoided. For example, when American pilots accidentally killed four Canadian soldiers who were performing anti-aircraft maneuvers in Afghanistan, the event was labeled a case of "friendly fire," not "our horrendous mistake." Similar labels attached to military initiatives hide their bloody destruction. In 1991 President George W. Bush's war on Sadam Hussein was cast as a natural and uncontrollable event by naming it "Operation Desert Storm." Hitler recast his horrors as "the final solution;" the rest of us have since called it "holocaust."

Equivocal Language. A word is said to be equivocal when it has two or more legitimate interpretations. The more abstract a word, the more equivocal its potential. Equivocation can lead to humorous clash between meanings. Consider the headlines that read "Red Tape Holds Up New Bridge," "Man Struck by Lightning Faces Battery Charge," and "Farmer Bill Dies in House." More strategic use of equivocation was Nike's successful "Just Do It" slogan. Nike advertisers were content to let the audience decide what "it" is.

Equivocal terms come in all too handy if you want to deceive someone.[13] You can answer the question, "How was your day?" with "It was terrific," and whoever asked will probably think you studied hard or got a desired grade on an assignment. Only you know that you skipped class and enjoyed a day in the park.

Equivocal language has redemptive quality in legal and business communication. A job description may read, "The employee will continue in the current role until altered by future mutual agreement." The word "future" might refer to one month, one year, or one decade from now, but it gives both parties desirable leeway.

In relationships, equivocal communication is ambiguous phrasing that may dodge the topic but be more socially appropriate.[14] For example, when your friend emerges from the changing room wearing an unbecoming outfit, and asks, "How do I look in this dress?" you might lie ("It's gorgeous! Buy it!), speak point blank ("It's ugly. Don't get it."), or equivocate: "It's definitely your style." Saying so is hopefully true, and it also affirms your friend, even if you personally dislike the dress.

Dichotomies. Dichotomies, or polar words, are terms that color a person or object entirely one way or another. Polar terms stem from the verb *is* as in "John is lazy. He does not like to get up in the morning." But John might be energetic between noon and two A.M. All of John is not lazy, but "John is lazy" makes him appear so. Suppose Gina, the student government president at your school, is a whiz at math, an average public speaker, and a terrible cook. If we call her "successful," we are bound to lose some of the truth about her. Few of us are essentially one way or another, but our language tends paint us so. Two ways to avoid false dichotomies is to ask the degree question ("to what degree is John lazy?") and the specificity question ("What specific behavior appears to indicate Gina is successful?" Both help us avoid sweeping generalities.

Abstract language, euphemisms, equivocal phrases, and dichotomies represent a handful of challenges with language. Interestingly though, these problems rarely render our talk completely meaningless. Through feedback, body language, and context we understand what others say with uncanny accuracy. These successes and joys convince many people that language is more than mere talk; it is a gift from God that we use for his pleasure and our own. God seems to have faith in language to accomplish his ends, whether divine or human.

God as Word-User

The Bible testifies that God puts high value on communication, and particularly on words. In the Genesis account he speaks the cosmos into being with his first declaration "Let there be light" (Genesis 1:3), and in Revelation he guides John to warn anyone who "takes words away from this book of prophecy" (Revelation 22:19). He is the God who defines himself as "I am," relies on words to instruct us in his moral way, and will one day defeat Satan by the words of his mouth. God's words lack no ontological force.

The Bible tells us that God created everything *ex nihilo* (from nothing). Indeed, he spoke it into existence. Sometimes we forget this fact or we fail to appreciate its relationship to our study of language. The word "said" is a non-exotic verb, but its use in Genesis 1 takes on monumental meaning.

> And God *said*, "Let there be light."
>
> And God *said*, "Let there be an expanse between the waters . . .
>
> And God *said*, "Let the water under the sky be gathered to one place . . .

and on it goes in verses 11, 14, 20, 24, and 26. Moreover, after God spoke his creation into existence, he declared it "very good." The scriptures also record that this "speaking forth" the world into existence was done through Christ, the *logos*, or word. The Gospel of John, Chapter 1 begins

> In the beginning was the Word, and the Word was with God, and the Word was God. He was with God in the beginning.

Through him all things were made; without him nothing was made that has been made.

In one sense God was saying that Jesus is his Word—his message incarnate for us. In another sense God was saying that through Christ he exploded the cosmos into existence. As the psalmist writes, "By the *word* of the Lord the heavens were made, and all their host by the breath of his mouth" (Psalm 36:6). Jesus was co-creator of the universe, and remains the sustaining logos behind its intricacy and design. This mystery is difficult to fathom.[15]

God also communicates his covenant relationships with us through words. To Moses and Aaron he promised, "I will help both of you speak and will teach you what to do. He [Aaron] will speak to the people for you [Moses] and it will be as if he were your mouth and as if you were God to him" (Exodus 4: 15b–16). In this case, God promised to be Moses' source of wisdom and guidance. When Jesus raised his cup with his disciples at the last supper, he said, "Drink from it, all of you. This is my blood of the covenant, which is poured out for many for the forgiveness of sins" (Matthew 26: 27b–28). Here God, through Jesus, indicates that the wine is his sign of salvation.

Finally, one would expect that God-in-the-flesh would exercise speech that attracted attention, and Jesus' language did so. Of Jesus' words the temple guards said, "No one ever spoke the way this man does" (John 7:46). Huston Smith writes of Jesus' language: "If simplicity, concentration, and the sense of what is vital are marks of great religious literature, these qualities alone would make Jesus' words immortal. But this is just the beginning. They carry an extravagance of which wise men . . . are incapable. The language is part of the man himself, stemming from the urgency and passions of his driving conviction."[16]

People as Word-Users

Given God's faith in language, it is fitting that he gave us the gift of language, and that it is a sign of being made in his image. Even the Gentile rhetoricians who lived before Christ believed speech separated us from the animal kingdom. A Greek orator, Isocrates (350 B.C.), noted that some animals are stronger and swifter than us, but language sets us apart.

. . . [B]ecause there has been implanted in us the power to persuade each other and to make clear to each other whatever we desire, not only have we escaped the life of the wild beasts, but we have come together and founded cities and made laws and invented arts; and, generally speaking, there is no institution devised by man which the power of speech has not helped to establish.[17]

King Solomon played a similar song for the gift of speech when he wrote "A word aptly spoken is like apples of gold in settings of silver" (Proverbs 25:11) and "From the fruit of his lips a man enjoys good things" (Proverbs 13:2).

Out of context, it would appear that Isocrates and King Solomon believed that speech and language are inherently good. But neither was so naive. For Isocrates, eloquence was the outward sign of being a university-educated individual—one who knew philosophy, mathematics, history, and other subjects. Solomon had a different idea. To him, one's words revealed the condition of one's heart, whether it be folly or wisdom, evil or good. He wrote: "The tongue of the wise commends knowledge, but the mouth of the fool gushes folly" (Proverbs 15: 2) and "The lips of the wise spread knowledge; not so the hearts of fools" (Proverbs 15:7). This theme is repeated throughout the proverbs.

Jesus' teachings about the tongue follow the same way of thinking, as indicated when he addressed the issue of blaspheming the Holy Spirit (what some Christians consider the one unpardonable sin). His strong words indict the Pharisees: "Make a tree good and its fruit will be good, or make a tree bad and its fruit will be bad, for a tree is recognizable by its fruit. You brood of vipers, how can you who are evil say anything good? For out of the overflow of the heart the mouth speaks" (Matthew 12:33–34).

The principle here is that the tongue is not good or evil, but the heart is; the tongue simply "spills" the contents of our heart. This theology aligns with the science of Vincent Jeffries, cited in Chapter 2, that the altruistic personality plays out in redemptive conflict management, while a selfish heart struggles to do so.[18]

We are fortunate, however, that this heart-tongue connection is not automatic. If it were, we would mouth off like inconsiderate idiots, spewing every minor thought and fleeting emotion. We would be a lot like the Jim Carrey character in *Liar Liar* who spoke his mind but had no social grace. For good or for bad, we can override our heart condition with a choice of the will. The Apostle James affirms this view when he observes that the same tongue can praise God or curse people, and implicates that the choice is up to us.

> With the tongue we praise our Lord and Father, and with it we curse men, who have been made in God's likeness. My brothers, this should not be. Can both fresh water and salt water flow from the same spring? Can a fig tree bear olives, or a grapevine bear figs? Neither can a salt spring produce fresh water. (James 3:9–12)

George Campbell, an eighteenth century Presbyterian pastor and speech scholar, suggested that human nature consists of the intellect, the emotions, the imagination, and the will.[19] I think his views help us piece together how we use words. In some cases our emotions rule and we blurt what we feel—redemptive or not. Other times we first carefully think through what we should say, and then speak. Still other times our language reflects our imagination and creative side (as in poetry and theatre). But governing each case, mostly, is our will and moral sense of what is right. As Proverbs 10:32a reads, "The lips of the righteous know what is fitting." Whether we follow through on what we know to be right is a matter of choice.

Because God has made us responsible creatures, it is worth asking how we might speak responsibly. Put another way, how might our speech please God?

Biblical Guidelines for Language

1. Speak Intelligibly. To speak intelligibly means to be easily understood. In his letter to the Corinthians, Paul encouraged the believers to prefer intelligible words over unintelligible ones. The issue he was wrestling with was *glossolalia* or speaking in tongues in the worship service. Though he spoke in tongues himself, he writes "But in the church I would rather speak five intelligible words to instruct others than ten thousand words in a tongue" (1 Corinthians 14:19).

Paul seemed to know what communication theorists claim: symbols do not contain meaning, rather people do. You can stare at "mi atta war camalla jato' all you like, but it is as *glossolalia* until you spend time with a Marathi-speaker to understand it means "I am going to work now." If we want our speech to be intelligible, we need to link it to people's experience. Don Smith makes this point when he asserts, "communication is involvement."[20] Missionaries who spend three or four years with new people groups before attempting any kind of translation work reflect the wisdom of this principle.

The more time we spend with our own group, the more likely we will develop jargon, or specialized terms. However too much jargon gets in the way when relating to outsiders. Theological terms such as "redemption," "justification," "Eucharist," "predestination," "apostolic procession," and "NIV" may bear rich meaning to Christians, but little to the unchurched. Biblical concepts such as "peace," "love," "justice," and "hope" are likely to be more intelligible, and serve as good bridges to begin dialog with others about spiritual matters. Codeswitching is the habit of changing our vocabulary or style of talk for different audiences so each can understand us and identify with us. We would be wise to switch from "Christianese" to a more fitting vocabulary if we want our message to be intelligible.

2. Speak Culturally. To speak culturally means we engage the home-grown language of our receivers, in vocabulary and grammar, such that upon hearing us speak they might say "you are one of us, for that is how we would say it."

Mike Walrod is the director of the Canadian Institute of Linguistics, and gives a presentation to show how translators write down language sounds unknown to them. The presentation requires a volunteer from the audience. On one occasion the volunteer was a chap from Africa who had been at our school for over a year. Dr. Walrod asked him to use his native language to describe his experience at Trinity Western University. As the student spoke, Mike converted the sounds into the International Phonetic Alphabet on the blackboard, and then repeated them aloud to the student. He then created a new sentence and spoke it to the student. The young man's response was first shock and then tears! He had not heard his language in over twelve months, and the sounds tumbling fresh on his ears triggered a mix of emotions.

Kenneth Burke suggests that the goal of communication generally and of persuasion specifically is not to change attitudes but to engender *identification*.[21] If you can say of my words "Yep, that's me; that's my experience too," then I have succeeded in identifying with you. We have connected. That is what Mike Walrod did. His effort to speak a relatively little-known language communicated respect and kindness to a culturally stressed student. His effort conveyed an appreciation for the student's primary symbol system for thinking and connecting to the world.

The guideline to speak culturally also applies in our communication with diverse ethnic groups in the United States and Canada. P. K. McCary took this to heart after she saw how the archaic English of the King James Version Bible simply did not wash with young black kids in her church. Her vision was to retell the greatest story using inner city black slang. The result was *Black Bible Chronicles* (African American Family Press), a paraphrase of the Pentateuch (Genesis through Deuteronomy) and *Rappin' With Jesus: The Good News According to the Four Brothers* (Matthew, Mark, Luke and John).[22] For example, after Adam sins, God confronts him by asking, "What's up, brother? Who hipped you to the fact you don't have on any clothes?" Or consider her rendition of Jesus' teaching that the meek will inherit the earth in the Sermon on the Mount:

> "You know, there's a little something for everybody," Jesus told 'em. "Brothers who are down in the way they feel, they ain't got nothing to worry 'bout 'cuz the Kingdom of Heaven belongs to them. Even those who feel like they've lost, can be on the one again 'cuz there will be arms 'round 'em to make 'em feel better. And you know those brothers who seem weak and on the bottom of the tadpole, the world is theirs. No kidding."

While some may criticize the book, calling it irreverent or an endorsement of nonstandard English, the fact is that God's message may now be more understandable to readers on the streets. Keep in mind though that what is "hip" today may be "lame" in five years. Language evolves as people add, subtract, and revise it to meet their needs. Astute communicators pay attention to these changes for the benefit of their audience.

Missiologist Charles Kraft would endorse books such as *Rappin' with Jesus* as long as he was assured that McCary's translation was true to both black culture and the biblical text. He terms this fidelity "appropriate Christianity," and defines it as "a Christianity that is appropriate to the *Scriptures*, on the one hand, and appropriate to the *people* in a given cultural context, on the other."[23] If a translation misses what Jesus or John or Martha intended to mean (to the best that can be discerned), its cultural expression misses the mark.

3. Speak with Stories. Several years ago an acquaintance of mine was criticizing his pastor for telling too many stories, and doing too little exegesis. To preach exegetically means to "extract out" from scripture what it means by taking it apart phrase by phrase using definitions and context. When I asked my acquaintance if Jesus' main preaching style was exegetical or narrative (storytelling), he admitted it was narrative, but then quickly added, "But lucky for him, he was *speaking* scripture, and now our job is to explain what he said." I smiled but did not fully agree, "Jesus could have spent most of his time in the synagogue preaching exegetically from the Old Testament, but from what I can tell, he more often told fresh stories."

You probably figured out why I began this section with a story! Stories draw us in, develop a plot, and make a memorable point. I bet most of you can finish these stories told by Jesus and indicate their moral teaching:

Who is your neighbor? Consider a man who was beaten and robbed on his way to Jericho....

For the word of God is like a seed planted along the way. Some of it fell on the path, some on the rock, others among weeds....

Then the son took his inheritance and traveled to a far away land where he lived a life of merriment until....

Jesus' tale of the Jew on the Jericho road reminds us to love Samaritans, whoever that may be in your neighborhood. His farming story reminds us that our role is to sow the gospel, and then let it go, for others must make up their minds about God's good news. And Jesus' story of the prodigal son turns at the end when we realize that the brother who stayed at home was just as lost in his embitterment as was his wayward brother who spent his fortune on wine and women. Stories stick.

Richard Swanson wishes we would speak God's stories more. Stories, he argues, project worlds that envelope us, engage us, and give us a platform to view the whole parade and play a role for ourselves. Stories create expectations that someone will "do what's right," and with that moral urge provide a "durable way" of seeing the world.

According to Swanson, "In story we can experiment and explore where we would never otherwise go."[24]

Since the last edition of this book, I have become a regular teacher in my church's children's ministry. Once a month I teach in "the big room" to fifty to sixty kids. While I have had some success with puppetry and ventriloquism, I believe the most engaging times have been telling compelling stories. Once I dressed as the rich young ruler complete with suitcase bulging with carnal possessions. I told the children of my expectant visit with Jesus and then, in monologue form, I spoke with the Master. When asked to sell all and follow him, I sadly packed up my possessions and left. Show and tell made the point.

4. *Speak actions.* We speak actions when we strategically use speech acts to nurture healthy relationships with friends and family. Jesus seemed to appreciate this performative function of language as he showed compassion and correction. Consider how Jesus

> *Blessed* children.

> *Warned* evildoers.

> *Comforted* the sick.

> *Expressed* love.

> *Forgave* people their sins.

> *Commanded* the dead to rise.

Two most important speech acts we perform as believers are confession and forgiveness. Confessing our sins to a friend or priest changes us for the better. It kicks in a loop of accountability because we know that the confidant may ask us how that area of our life is going. Our burden is made lighter when we confess because someone else now shares it, and supports us. Receiving forgiveness from someone we have wronged doubles the blessing. Not only do we purge our guilt, but we restore the relationship.

If a friend were to describe the speech acts you perform with your lips, what would they sound like? Would they consist of verbs such as *complained, whined, snapped, moaned, grunted, scolded, demanded, jabbed, swore,* and the like? Or, would it be a litany of righteous language such as *instructed, encouraged, promised, joked, corrected,* and *blessed?*

The value of positive talk is underscored in a long-term research project conducted by John Gottman.[25] He wanted to chart features of communication that cause divorce. To do so he audio-taped several hundred couples' conversations during the first year of marriage, coded them for positivity and negativity, and then kept track of which couples divorced and which ones' marriages thrived. He found that satisfied couples were those whose interaction maintained a five-to-one ratio of positive-to-negative moments. However, unsatisfied couples measured at five-to-two or five-to-three ratios. Some of these "moments" were nonverbal shows of positive or negative emotions, but a good number of them were couples' talk. Those who weighed in with significantly more praise and encouragement were more likely to thrive compared to the whiners and blamers.

5. Speak Worthily.   Finally, the scriptures encourage us to engage in valuable talk, not pernicious, silly, or godless talk (see 2 Timothy 2:16 and Ephesians 5:4). This is not easy in a culture that turns virtue on its head and glorifies evil. Once while visiting a skate and snowboard shop, my eye caught the tread of a "sinful sole" shoe. The manufacturers had listed, in raised relief, the seven deadly sins: greed, lust, anger, pride, gluttony, sloth and envy.

Shocking others with this type of values inversion is easy, but being a person truly worth listening to is difficult. How many of us have slipped away from a sermon or switched channels because neither offered a worthwhile message? How many have sweated over a speech because we wondered if we were worthy to give it?

Several years ago one of our TWU Communications graduates was asked by his former principal to speak at the graduation ceremony of his high school alma mater. Derek, only 23 at the time, felt unworthy of the honor and was nervous of the occasion. Nevertheless, he agreed. Would his speech reflect the worth of such an honor? He took up the challenge and logged twenty to thirty hours to construct a twenty to thirty minute speech. He meant business, and his investment paid off.

In the book of Jeremiah, God lays out his criteria for the prophet to be his ambassador. Among other things God says "If you repent, I will restore you that you may serve me; if you utter worthy, not worthless, words, you will be my spokesman" (Jeremiah 15:19). God first called him to repentance, and then to worthy speech. Only then did God make Jeremiah his ambassador.

You can bet that Derek did not fill his time with crack-me-up one-liners, sexual innuendoes, and lists of his accomplishments. Rather, he began his speech by encapsulating what graduation meant to his audience and then quoting Winston Churchill. He followed the guideline in Ephesians 4:29 to "not let any unwholesome talk come out of your mouths, but only what is helpful for building others up according to their needs, that it may benefit those who listen" and Colossians 4:6 to "let your conversation be always full of grace, seasoned with salt, so that you may know how to answer everyone."

Personally, my struggle involves an area I've termed gray talk. It is not pernicious or venomous, neither is it seasoned with salt nor grace. A lot of it qualifies as godless chatter, foolish talk, and even coarse joking (see 2 Timothy 2:16 and Ephesians 5:4). I struggle with that gray area between obvious trash talk and what is truly edifying.

Worthy words communicate truth, correct wrong thinking, reveal a thankful heart, encourage the downtrodden, plead the case of the less fortunate, and show love. The words of Christians should also be delightful, winsome, informed, and gentle. This type of talk exemplifies disciples who love God with their heart, mind, soul—and even their language.

Summary

People have a suspicion about language today, a suspicion that language is "mere talk" with no real force and with a weak link to reality. This chapter seeks to dispute that way of thinking.

Language is God's gift to us, distinguishing us from animals. Language delivers the bulk of our communication with others—whether to describe God's creation, form human bonds, or pattern how we think. Language is by no means a perfect system, as noted in discussions about abstract terms, euphemisms, equivocal terms, and dichotomies.

God's value for language is shown in his speaking the universe into existence and Christ's sustaining the universe as the personal *logos*. God also relies on language to reveal himself to us and knit covenantal bonds. Our language indicates our heart's condition as well as our choices. Because we can mask the condition of our heart by what we choose to say, I described five responsible ways we might choose to speak: intelligibly, culturally, with stories, in speech acts, and worthily.

WORTH THE TALK

1. What do you think of someone who remarks "He's only saying that"? What view of language does this depict? What might one's response be to someone with such a view?

2. Which of the five biblical guidelines for language speaks most to your use or misuse of words? If word choice points out a weakness, what might you do to improve in this area?

CONSIDER THE WALK

1. Make a list of "Christianese" terms or phrases that are well known by believers. Beside each term write down how other religious groups might interpret them. For example, the term "born again" might mean "reincarnation" to a Hindu. Then write down a definition that you think a person from the other religious group might understand.

2. Do an analysis of a magazine or television advertisement for its use and abuse of language. Use the five criteria provided in this chapter to ask whether the ad uses language intelligibly, culturally, worthily, with stories, or in a speech acts manner. Try to determine the linguistic strategies the advertisers have used to persuade people to buy their products.

ONLINE CHALK

Principles from this chapter represent a variety of topics on language. The following search terms and phrases put you in touch with many of them.

- Plain English Campaign
- Language and social reality
- Language pitfalls
- Logos as word
- Speaking culturally, speak culturally
- Concrete language
- Storytelling as communication

ENDNOTES

1 Communication scholar, Greg Shepard, writes "in the seventeenth century, the world was firmly divided into linguistic and nonlinguistic spheres, and the strategy of claiming materiality for something by contrasting it with 'mere' words, talk, or rhetoric was fixed in literature, philosophy, science, and social theory until, by the close of the century, communication was rendered immaterial, an idea void of ontological force." See G. J. Shepherd, "Building a Discipline of Communication," *Journal of Communication* 43 (1993): 83-91.

2 A helpful website regarding feral children may be found at: http://www.feral-children.com/en/index.php.

3 See H. P. Grice, "Logic and Conversation," in *Syntax and Semantics*, ed. P. Cole and J. Morgan (New York: Academic, 1975), 3:41-58.

4 See C. K. Ogden and I. A. Richards, *The Meaning of Meaning* (New York: Harcourt, Brace & World, 1946), 1-23.

5 For an advanced look at this idea, see John R. Searle, *The Construction of Social Reality* (New York: Free Press, 1995).

6 For a full treatment of how we use words to perform actions see John Austin, *How To Do Things With Words* (Cambridge, MA: Harvard University Press, 1962), and John R. Searle, *Speech Acts: An Essay in the Philosophy of Language* (New York: Cambridge University Press, 1969).

7 The seminal article on para-social relationships is Donald Horton and R. Richard Wohl, "Mass Communication and Para-Social Interaction: Observations on Intimacy at a Distance," *Psychiatry* 19 (1956): 215-229.

8 See P. Watzlawick, J. H. Beavin, and D. D. Jackson, *Pragmatics of Human Communication: A Study of Interaction Patterns, Pathologies, and Paradoxes* (New York:

Norton, 1967), and P. Evans, *The Verbally Abusive Relationship: How to Recognize it and How to Respond* (Holbrook, MA: Adams Media, 1996).

9 Charles Osgood, George Suci, and Percy Tannenbaum, *The Measurement of Meaning*. (Urbana, IL: University of Illinois, 1957).

10 Edward Sapir, *Culture, Language, and Personality* (Berkeley: University of California, 1970), and Benjamin L. Whorf, *Language, Thought, and Reality* (Cambridge, MA: MIT Press, 1964).

11 S. I. Hayakawa, *Language in Thought and Action*, 4th ed. (Orlando: Harcourt Brace Jovanovich, 1978).

12 Stewart L. Tubbs and Sylvia Moss, *Human Communication*, 7th ed. (New York: McGraw-Hill, 1994), 84.

13 Buller and Burgoon's "Interpersonal Deception Theory" identify falsification, concealment, and equivocation as three deceptive strategies. Falsification is a bald-face lie, concealment is a half-truth, and equivocation is a vague true statement. See David B. Buller and Judee K. Burgoon, "Interpersonal Deception Theory," *Communication Theory* 6 (1996): 203-242.

14 See Janet Beavin Bavelas et al., *Equivocal Communication* (Newbury Park, CA: Sage, 1990).

15 The centrality of Christ as the *logos* of the world and the basis for intelligible use of language is not shared by eastern religions. Huston Smith writes of the Hindu religion and notes that in its view "man is forever trying to lay hold of Reality with words, only in the end to find mystery rebuking his speech and his syllables swallowed by silence" (*The Religions of Man* (New York: Harper & Row, 1965), 71.) Similarly, Buddha's followers gave him the name Sakymuni or "silent sage." This name denotes the idea that, in Buddha, there existed a mystery and depth beyond what could be said or thought with words. Finally, those who are Taoist (pronounced Dowist) strive for the goal of "creative quietude" as they live in the force which has no name but which they simply call the Tao (the Way).

16 Ibid., 305

17 Isocrates, *Antidosis*, trans. George Norlin (Cambridge: Harvard University Press, 1929; repr., 1956), 2:327.

18 Vincent Jeffries, "Love: The Five Virtues of St. Thomas Aquinas," *Sociology and Social Research* 71 (1987): 174-182, and Vincent Jeffries, "Virtue and Marital Conflict: A Theoretical Formulation and Research Agenda," *Sociological Perspectives* 43 (2000): 231-247.

19 See James L. Golden, Goodwin F. Berquist and William E. Coleman, *The Rhetoric of Western Thought*, 5th ed. (Dubuque, IA: Kendall/Hunt, 1993), 129-138.

20 Donald K. Smith, *Make Haste Slowly: Developing Effective Cross-Cultural Communication* (Portland: Institute for International Christian Communication, 1984), 43.

21 Kenneth Burke, *A Rhetoric of Motives* (Berkeley: University of California, 1950).

22 See P. K. McCary, *Black Bible Chronicles: From Genesis to the Promised Land* (New York: African American Family Press, 1993), and P. K. McCary, *Rappin' With Jesus: The Good News According to the Four Brothers* (New York: African American Family Press, 1994).

23 Charles H. Kraft, ed., *Appropriate Christianity* (Pasadena: William Carey Library, 2005), 5.

24 This paragraph was written with ideas from Richard W. Swanson, *Provoking the Gospel: Methods to Embody Biblical Storytelling Through Drama* (Cleveland: Pilgrim Press, 2004), 10-15, with the final quotation found on page 14.

25 J. T. Gottman, "Why Marriages Fail," in *Making Connections: Readings in Relational Communication*, ed. K. Galvin and P. Cooper (Los Angeles: Roxbury Publishing, 1996), 219-227.

Do not merely listen to the word, and so deceive yourselves. Do what it says.

James 1:22

Nonverbal Communication
Exercising Congruency and Grace

MY SPIRIT STILL twinges when I recall the incident. Shelaine and I were attempting to exit a parking lot onto a busy divided thoroughfare. I kept looking to my left for a break in traffic, and then came my chance. Without looking back to my right, I gave the van some gas. FLASH! BRAKE! What was that?

A twenty-something male on a mountain bike skidded abruptly to a stop to my left. He had just ridden in front of us on the sidewalk from our right, and I had almost hit him. He was furious. I was shocked.

"What the ---- do you think you're doing?" he shouted, straddle-walking his bike back to my open window. "Don't you know how to drive!" he raged, his eyebrows slanting downward like a Japanese warlord. "You almost killed me!" His nose was eighteen inches from mine, his eyes seared my own. I expected that he would punch me any moment. "Look both ways, you idiot!" His shirtless chest and neck-length black hair made him an intense image as he squeezed the bike's handle-grips and bumped the wheel against my door. Yep, I thought, I am going to lose at least two teeth. What to do?

"I'm sorry," I intoned softly. "You're right," I managed with some humility. "I'll be more careful next time," I offered slowly, my hands still on the steering wheel and the rest of my body frozen with fear.

The biker huffed one more look of disgust and pulled back, and in another second was gone.

Any passerby did not need to hear a single word of our exchange to figure that trouble brewed deeply. Raised voices, squared-off posturing, rapid speech, and gnarly faces usually mean an easy read for anger—emotional cancer for covenantal relating. But seldom are nonverbal behaviors linked to such intense emotion, and rarely are they interpreted so easily. How did the biker make sense of subtle cues such as my short hair and wire-rimmed glasses? How should I have understood his helmet-less head or scratched-up CCM bicycle?

> Our nonverbal communication is less controllable than our tongue.

Pick up a book on nonverbal communication and you will get two distinct but not incompatible claims. One is that nonverbal behaviors are less controllable than our tongues. This fact makes it sound as if we are like the *Far Side* cartoon character whose leg thumps wildly on the floor as a dog scratches his stomach. This view is pretty depressing, but it is true of auto-responses such as sweaty palms, when we are nervous, and dilated pupils, when we like someone. We cannot control some cues.

The other claim is that despite our lesser ability to control them, we can improve sending and interpreting nonverbal signals through awareness and practice. Some authors even provide tips for skill development.[1] Of course this implies that there is a standard for competent nonverbal communicating and hints that we are responsible for improving our baseline ability. So there is hope—hope that with God's strength we may choose to act redemptively toward others whether with micro actions such as winks and body angle or with macro statements such as lives of service and earthly sacrifice. On the receiving end, the hope is that we exercise caution and alertness as we decipher other people's mosaic of nonverbal signals.

"Nonverbal" means "not of words" and it is strange that we define this field by what it is not. Nonverbal communication "includes all the nonlinguistic things a person does to which others ascribe meaning" whether we intend so or not.[2]

Nonverbal behavior falls into numerous categories. Some have to do with our appearance, such as body type and attractiveness, artifacts, such as clothing, jewelry, glasses, and body movement, such as gestures and posture. Nonverbal cues include our facial expressions, eye behavior, personal space and territory (also called *proxemics*), touch or tactile communication, voice (also called *paralinguistics* or *vocalics*), smell (or *olfaction*), use of time (or *chronemics*), and physical environment, such as room décor and building layout. To begin making sense of these diverse cues, let us consider how they differ from our use of words.

The Lay of Nonverbal Land Compared to the World of Words

First, verbal messages tend to be single-channeled and received one at a time, whereas nonverbal messages are multi-channeled and received in mosaic simultaneously. The words the biker-guy hurled at me crashed one by one on my ears like cars of a train spilling from a bridge. However, his appearance, voice, spacing, and van-bumping touch arrived as a package to my ears, eyes, and skin. These cues—or clues if you wish—are like tiled bits of an intricately crafted mosaic. Researchers encourage us to read cues in clusters in order to make full sense of them.[3] We need to consider the whole mural others paint for us.

Second, nonverbal messages differ from verbal ones in the degree that we can turn them on and off. Because we are either

Like tiles on a mosaic, a person's nonverbal cues
come at us all at once.

speaking or not, we call verbal messages *discrete*. In contrast, we are not as able to turn off nonverbal cues like a spigot does to water—they are *continuous*. I could not stop using some kind of eye behavior with the cyclist as well as some kind of posture and some tone of voice. Since others may interpret these continuous cues at any time, we acknowledge what is a communication truism: We cannot *not* communicate.[4] All behaviors carry communicative potential, whether or not we intend them so.

Third, verbal messages tend to be deliberate, whereas nonverbal messages are often unconscious. I assumed this when I encouraged you in Chapter 3 to speak intelligibly and worthily. The same goes for how we act responsibly around others, with the understanding that simultaneously managing our left hand, right foot, palms, and voice is challenging. I bet a ghostly white face and dilated pupils accompanied my calm voice and resting hands. Biker-man probably knew I was scared silly.

Fourth, verbal messages tend to be clear while nonverbal messages tend to be ambiguous. I knew the meaning of every word the cyclist shouted in my face (you, idiot, watch, drive, killed . . .), but I still do not know how to read his riding on the sidewalk at 15 miles per hour. Or what of his riding helmet-less? Since the city of Surrey has a helmet bylaw, my ungracious read was that he was an insolent rebel or a forgetful oaf. But maybe he was rushing to help someone in an emergency. Maybe he could not afford a helmet. Some research indicates that we tend to be more confident about our cue-reading than we ought to be. Both women and men tend to report higher levels of confidence in their decoding accuracy than their actual performance merits.[5] The rule of thumb appears to be that we use caution and grace when reading ambiguous cues.

Fifth, verbal codes convey raw data well, whereas nonverbal systems are best at signaling relational messages. We play on this bias to show love to pre-language infants by the way we hold, cuddle, and coo them. We return to this bias when we want to show strong emotion toward adult friends. One researcher estimates that as much as 93 percent of the *social* meaning (that is, emotional meaning) we derive from others stems from facial expressions and tone of voice, and only seven percent from what people say.[6] We might fuss over these specific percentages, but I think you will agree that nonverbal signals tell us much about how others feel, and the nature of your relationship with them.

Finally, people tend to put stock in nonverbal messages when they clash with what someone says. Suppose the cyclist shouted, "You drive better than Michael Andretti—I wish everyone drove like you." Would I believe him? Probably not. Given his outraged look and tone of voice, I would know that he was being sarcastic.

The weighing of nonverbals more heavily than words reflects a value God seems to put on this code as well, as least as an indication of our heart. As Eugene Peterson renders Paul's words, "Merely hearing God's law is a waste of your time if you don't do what he commands. Doing, not hearing, is what makes the difference with God." And later, "You can get by with almost anything if you front it with eloquent talk about God and his law."[7] Almost anything. Consider the messages we send when we claim to love fellow sinners but give them looks

> Our nonverbal communication often serves as an indication of our heart.

that could kill or shoulders that freeze them out. I think our greatest challenge is to show the balance between justice and love—the first so often delivered through what we say, the latter through how we say it.

Worthy Goals: Congruence and Grace

How then should we act? And to what standard should we aspire? The answers may come to light with an illustration. In *The Jesus I Never Knew*, Philip Yancey writes:

> I know of one AIDS patient who traveled eleven hundred miles to be with his family in Michigan for Thanksgiving dinner. He had not seen them in seven years. The parents welcomed him warily, and when dinner was served everyone got a heaping portion of turkey and all the trimmings on the best Wedgewood china plates—except their son the AIDS patient, who was served on Chinette, with plastic utensils.[8]

The parents might defend their behavior by claiming that they were only being authentic with their sentiments. Who can argue that being genuine is good? Carl Rogers suggests that when we are real with our emotions, when we know them, feel them, and show them genuinely to others around us, we exercise *congruence*.[9] Being congruent with our nonverbal communication lets us be ourselves. Keeping emotions bottled up is unhealthy, for ourselves, and those closest to us.

However, being congruent with our emotions in this case failed to encourage their son. If anything, it pronounced judgment. Thus, while we should aim to show on the outside what we are experiencing on the inside, we still need grace and wisdom to communicate what will edify.

Consider the difference the Michigan mom and dad could have made if they served their son the Thanksgiving meal their Wedgewood china, and included his place setting with the others in the dishwasher. Their behavior would have signaled acceptance, or grace. One definition of grace is that it is all the good in human life and relationships; treating their son thus would have simply been good. Another definition of grace is that it is the slack we cut others—the unmerited favor we grant them as we make sense of their confusing or seemingly nasty behavior—just like the grace God grants to us. This kind of grace is especially important when interpreting ambiguous or hurtful nonverbal behavior. Consider how these parents could have engendered hope had they treated their son graciously, even royally. Consider the covenantal bond they could have established had they extended grace. The next step is to recognize the range of cues at our disposal and their primary messages so we may engage them for responsible covenantal relating.

Voice

During my college years I met a woman with Elizabethan features. Karen's light skin, shoulder length dark hair, and 5'8" frame would cast her well on an A&E production of *Hamlet*. When she spoke though, something did not seem right. Rather than hear a full, mellow voice one heard a tinny, high-strung, nasal twang. One had to fight the stereotype, but it was easy to believe that Karen was immature, insecure, indecisive or weak.[10] From what I knew about Karen this stereotype did not fit, but strangers would not know better.

Vocalics include the pitch, volume, rate and quality of voice as well as disfluencies such as "um" and "ya' know." Our bias is to favor people who speak with lower pitches, average to above average volume, moderate to quick rate, and rich quality. Extremes usually turn us off. Too high pitch equates with youthful inexperience; too low with mental dullness. Too quick a rate speaks of nervousness or slick sales tactics; too slow a rate may indicate incompetence. Too breathy a voice can be interpreted as spinelessness; too full as pompous.[11]

Our voice is as unique as our fingerprint, and, along with our face, a key source by which others infer our credibility and how likable we are. Maybe you tend toward a voice like Karen's or more raspy or throaty. If we want others to take us seriously, it is worth asking, "How do I sound?" Audio capturing our conversations or using voice-lesson exercises might improve our vocal habits, as well as sensitize us to people less blessed like Karen.

Eye Behavior

If the eye is the window to the soul, I know very little about Sid's soul. I bumped into Sid on the sands of Cannon Beach, Oregon one summer and liked him immediately. Within minutes we learned that we shared the faith, loved vacationing in the sun, and struggled as parents of young children. Only one thing bugged me—Sid wore his shades during the entire conversation. Try as I did, I never met Sid "eye to eye."

In western cultures we use our eyes to communicate liking, attention, respect, and control.[12] And we do so through two modalities: location (where we look) and duration (how long we look there). If I had learned that Sid was actually checking out the beach during our conversation, I might figure him to be rude or distracted. The normal North American rule is to give people ample eye contact with the occasional glance away to provide psychological space. Whether sending or receiving, people who stare 99 percent of the time, are usually considered oddballs.

Pictures of Christ usually depict him with warm, welcoming brown eyes, but I doubt that love gushed from them every waking moment. Remember when Peter rebuked Jesus for predicting his death by saying "This shall never happen to you!"? How do you suppose Jesus looked at Peter when he responded, "Get behind me, Satan! You are a stumbling block to me; you do not have in mind the things of God, but the things of men" (see Matthew 16:21–28). Or how did Jesus eye the moneychangers as he flipped their temple tables in righteous anger? If we hold to a flannel graph view of Jesus, we limit his human ability to use his eyes to speak with authority as well as love.

Facial Expression

One reason I took a liking to Sid was because even without eye contact his smile told me he was a congenial guy. We rely on the face more than any other source to read people's feelings. There is even evidence that people interpret basic emotional states similarly from culture to culture in the smiles, grimaces, and furrowed brows we muster. "Japanese, Americans, English, Spanish, French, German, Swiss, Greek, and South Pacific Islanders recognized happiness, surprise, fear, anger, sadness, disgust, contempt, interest, bewilderment and determination in the photographed faces of people from other cultures."[13] Be careful though. Just because someone is smiling is not a guarantee they are happy. In cultures where saving face is especially important, people become adept at obeying display rules. *Display rules* dictate when someone should override their true feeling with a false mask. For example, whereas employees in the United States and Canada might be allowed to show mild shock at a bosses' mistake, Japanese subordinates are encouraged to play a poker face or polite smile.

We know that women are better than men at expressing their emotions with their faces and at interpreting other people's faces as well.[14] One reason is because women have a biological edge in that the corpus callosum that connects their right and left brain hemispheres is more developed than men's. This enables women to recognize facial expressions with their motor-dominant right hemisphere *and* attach a word label to an expression with their language-dominate left hemisphere.[15] Men recognize emotions well, but have a harder time calling one "contempt" and the other "disgust."

A second reason is accommodation—the tendency women have of paying attention to channels considered polite and controllable by others, but ignoring impolite and less controllable channels. The control hierarchy is face (first), body, then voice (last). On a first date, for example, where nerves run high, the gal might attune to her date's face more than his tapping foot because this eases tension and is kind.[16] We can all learn from this practice of favoring the more controllable channels when we want to respect others.

Judith Hall's primary explanation for why women read faces better than men is sociological: Women's role in society prescribes it.[17] Women have been socialized as "relational experts," whether at home or at work, and this expectation sensitizes them to facial cues. For example, traditional society expects a stay-home mom to know why baby Emma is crying, and to meet her need. Similarly, we expect women health professionals to exercise more sensitive bedside manner because they can read their patients' faces. When my counselor friend Kurt heard this explanation, he suspected he might be as adept as most women because his role requires reading clients' faces daily. I take Kurt's point as hope for all guys—practice makes perfect.

Gestures

In the movie *Shine*, David's sisters lean out a window to watch their pianist brother and their father return from a music talent competition. "Did he win?" one sister asks. The second one studied the gait of her father and brother. "No . . ." her voice trailed off, "he lost." And she was right. What gave it away was not David's playful hopscotch on imaginary chalked lines, but the father's stiffened walk and businesslike pace. His body read bitterness.

Gestures are body movements made from the neck down. Deciphering what gestures mean may be a cinch at times and bedeviling at others. Lest we claim that we can read others like books, it is better to admit that, like a good novel, some behaviors are open to multiple interpretations. Asking friends to verbalize their ideas is probably the best check for understanding their gestures.

Is this woman using an illustrator to make a point, or an emblem to replace a word?

Emblems are behaviors with precise verbal equivalents. The raised finger in a restaurant means "service, please." The shrug of the shoulders when asked a question means "I don't know." The hook and wiggle of the finger in front of us indicates "Come here." A cue attains emblem status when we can interpret it correctly about 95 percent of the time.[18] Emblems flourish within close-knit circles. For example, gang members use complex hand signals to indicate group solidarity and membership. To outsiders these emblems are like visual jargon—they are virtually un-decodable.

Illustrators accompany our words and make sense in conversational context. They illustrate what we are saying. Suppose I made my hands in the shape of an over-sized football. Without accompanying this gesture with words means little to North Americans. But when I say "A rugby ball is about 30 percent larger than a football and shaped the same way," the illustration makes sense. Good public speakers are especially adept at picturing ideas and objects with their hands, arms and, bodies.

Affect displays are bodily expressions of emotion. Some are automatic, like our hopping about on one foot after stubbing a toe, our sweaty palms when nervous, or dilated pupils when interested in someone. Other affect displays are more intentional and symbolic. In worship, the Kenyan believer dances, and mystic monk sits in silence. Another believer raises her hands, while others feels compelled to kneel. My own resolve is that discussions about worship style create more division than multiplication of God's kingdom in part because affect displays are more about preference and tradition than biblical edict. A covenantal approach suggests that church members agree on a uniform worship style where most are at ease with the degree of emotional expression, so that the form of worship does not become a distraction to praising God.

Regulators are gestures that guide the flow of conversation. A head nod "yes" and an open palm invite others to chime in; a head nod "no" and a palm turned down announce you want to keep the floor. Picking up on regulators and reading them well takes mindful skill. They make the most sense when viewed with the rest of the mosaic—including what is being said.

Adaptors are gestures left over from past associations that give release to present tension. As I write, I pause occasionally and find myself chewing on a nail. It is a bad habit I picked up in my youth when under stress, and it still provides strange comfort today. You might bounce a leg or twirl a pen or curl your long locks when under duress. We do not intend to use adaptors around others, but due to their deep roots, they creep in anyway. Fortunately, we use fewer adaptors as we get to know people well, by which time they care less about our nervous fidgeting anyway.

Artifacts and Appearance

Artifacts are adornments we make to our bodies, such as clothing, hairstyle, jewelry, and the like. *Appearance* refers to the look we present to others based on our physical attributes. While we can control what we wear and how we style our hair, we have less control over our body type and facial contours. But people still read both.

Sometimes good looks and stylish clothes can get us in trouble. Who can forget the papparrazi's pursuit of Princess Diana so her photograph might grace their tabloid rag? Their dogged insistence, and the poor choice of a drunken Ritz Hotel driver, led to the death of a very public woman. When asked why she was so popular with the masses, one British commentator put it bluntly: because she was so beautiful, so photogenic.

It is harsh irony that Princess Di's physical beauty would contribute to her death at an early age. Most attractive people only benefit from the long list of advantages we extend to them. So significant and influential are these advantages that some authors call them a prejudice.[19] In numerous studies, participants who observe photographs of attractive people perceive them as more sexually warm and responsive, sensitive, strong, and sociable than less attractive people.[20] Di probably benefited from similar thinking.

Physical attractiveness is generally interpreted positively, but it also has its detriments.

This bias also applies to personality stereotypes associated with body type. We tend to perceive skinny people as more suspicious, tense, nervous, pessimistic, and quiet but plump people as more lazy, warm-hearted, sympathetic, good-natured, and dependent. Muscular people get the edge as we assume them to be stronger and more adventurous, mature, self-assertive and sexually warm than the other two types.[21]

The beauty bias extends to how we treat and talk with attractive and unattractive people. Consider Table 4.1. It reports how we are more likely to self-disclose to, reward, help, pay attention to, give in to, and date attractive people more than unattractive people. While

1. We are more willing to self-disclose to a physically attractive person.

2. We are more willing to reward physically attractive people monetarily.

3. We are more willing to extend help to physically attractive people.

4. We are more likely to be persuaded by a physically attractive person.

5. If we are an elementary school teacher, we are more likely to interact with good-looking students more often and more positively than unattractive students.

6. We are more likely to date and marry someone we consider physically attractive.

Table 4.1 How Beauty Effects Communication Behavior[22]

there's nothing wrong with being beautiful, it seems that our response to beautiful people is putting value on the wrong thing.

Remember when Samuel was searching for King Saul's replacement? He thought he had a winner with tall, good-looking Eliab. But God said no—"Do not consider his appearance or his height…The LORD does not look at the things man looks at. Man looks at the outward appearance, but the LORD looks at the heart" (1 Samuel 16:7). Being tall was nothing against Eliab, but God looked past this to his heart. Eliab lacked the heart of a king for God's people. Later Samuel selected David, a man who was good-looking *and* a man after God's own heart.

Moreover, consider Peter's challenge to women of faith to seek inner beauty. He writes: "Your beauty should not come from outward adornment, such as braided hair and the wearing of gold jewelry and fine clothes. Instead, it should be that of your inner self, the unfading beauty of a gentle and quiet spirit, which is of great worth in God's sight" (1 Peter 3:3–4). Peter was not saying one should not dress stylishly, but that one's character should be based on inner qualities. By extension it seems reasonable that we should get to know people through dialogue rather than judge them from their looks.

The tabloid editors who published Princess Diana's picture month after month acted on a cultural assumption that beauty is good. Even the scriptures acknowledge the worth of that which is noble, right, pure, admirable, and *lovely* (see Philippians 8:4–9). But beauty, like life, is here only for a season.

Space and Territory

Sid and I stood just out of arm's reach as we chatted on the beach. Doing so communicated attention and respect. *Proxemics* is the study of how we use mobile space around us and *territoriality* is our penchant for calling a patch of immobile space our own and defending it. If either is intruded upon, we usually feel antsy. We do not like others butting in too close.

Space indicates status and intimacy in relationships. We keep our distance from authority figures, especially in formal, public settings. We get close to peers and friends, especially in private settings. We can use space to show covenantal commitment, as when we buddy up to a friend. We can also send cool messages by keeping our distance.

It seems Jesus enjoyed breaking the space rules that dictated first-century Palestine in order to show his inclusive love toward social outcasts. As F. F. Bruce writes, "He accepted sinners, and they were glad to accept him. He was glad to share their meals . . . He gave the impression, indeed, that he really enjoyed the company of such people—that he preferred it, in fact, to the company of those who had a good opinion of themselves."[23]

The rules Jesus broke resemble the expectations many cultural groups have as expressed by Edward Hall. *Intimate distance* (0 to 1.5 feet apart) is generally reserved for best friends and lovers, not weeping prostitutes with vials of perfume. *Personal distance* (1.5 to 4 feet) is accessible to friends and disciples, not low-life tax collectors. *Social distance* (4 to 12 feet) is where we work daily with colleagues and strangers, but usually not outcast beggars and lepers. Jesus used *public distance* (12 feet and beyond) to give himself breathing space in the boat at Galilee, yet other times welcomed children to sit with him. While we know that Jesus needed personal space to rejuvenate his spirit with the Father, his ministry with people indicated a life committed to getting close to affirm, include, and touch.

Touch

Four months after Shelaine and I married we traveled to my sister's home in San Francisco for Christmas. One evening after supper my sister Jane began washing dishes at her little kitchen sink. As she did, I gave her a little shoulder rub, which she appreciated thoroughly.

Later that evening Shelaine asked, "What was *that* all about?

"What was *what* all about?" I answered.

"That shoulder rub for Jane."

"Well . . . she was working hard; I thought she could use some encouragement."

"But I thought you only gave *me* shoulder rubs," Shelaine replied.

I could sense that my wife felt hurt. She thought, with good reason, that back rubs were just between us.

This scenario illustrates how our use of touch is a whole new ball game from space. (Had I just stood close to Jane, I think it would not have been an issue.) Touch is governed by unspoken rules massaged into place by our culture, and generally agreed upon as a local pact by our immediate family. You may have seen the bumper sticker that reads, "You toucha my car, I breaka your face!" Or perhaps your parents have said, "No you cannot wrestle with your sister. It's not appropriate." Who may touch whom, where, when, and for what reasons vary widely, but here are some rules of thumb.[24]

Touch is usually status linked. Bosses, doctors, teachers, and ministers are more likely to touch employees, patients, students, and parishioners than the other way around. We tend to accept this touch as a role prerogative, for through touch leaders may literally guide our direction or our work. Appropriate touch has many benefits to the recipient, as the next point shows.

Appropriate touch increases health and good will. We know that body massage stimulates vitality in premature babies and boosts the immune function in cancer and HIV patients. Appropriate touch by a counselor encourages clients' self-disclosure, self-acceptance, and a positive client-counselor relationship. A simple touch on the hand by a cashier improves customers' impressions of a store.[25] Jesus often touched those he wanted to heal or encourage.

Touch can be easily misunderstood in relationships. More specifically, men have a harder time distinguishing between friendly touch and sexual touch. Authors of "Friendly? Flirting? Wrong?" write, "males generally construe the world in more sexual terms than do females, and ... as a group, men were much more likely than females to judge 'friendly' behavior as 'seductive' or 'promiscuous' behavior."[26] Men need to keep from jumping to conclusions about women's touch and learn to appreciate friendly touch as intended. Women may keep in mind how men tend to interpret touch, and be judicious in its use.

Smell

Get close enough to others and their odor tells us something or reminds us of something else. A friend of mine in college gave off the same odor as my grandfather. As he and I talked, my mind would flit between Illinois and Iowa, from Scott Brue to images of Grandpa Ammer's soft face and over-stuffed chair. You too may have experienced flashbacks with the help of an olfaction trigger.

A billion-dollar personal hygiene industry indicates that we are not comfortable with our natural smell of our breath and body, although this is not universal. Arabic people consider it a sign of friendship and trust to talk close enough to smell each other's breath. People in India are slow to apply deodorant, probably for lack of availability or because heat and humidity win out anyway.

© 1996 Randy Glasbergen.

"I want my husband to pay more attention to me. Got any perfume that smells like a computer?"

Scientists have now found ways to use aromatherapy to stimulate various emotional states, and corporations are putting these findings to work. A Japanese company, Shimizu, engineered a device that releases aromas into a building's air-circulating system. With a mix of peppermint, lemon, eucalyptus, rosemary and pine they can induce alertness. Lavender and clove calm the nerves. Citrus, pine and eucalyptus refresh.[27]

Greek Orthodox believers take seriously the contribution of smell to enhance their worship experience. Priests burn incense in ornately decorated canisters to symbolize God's Spirit. Both odor and spirit are invisible yet surround and influence the worshippers.

Use of Time

Chronemics is the study of how we measure and manipulate time to fit our human needs. We derive this term from the Greek word *chronos*, which means time. Many cultures, like India, hold a *polychronic* view of time—they place people and events ahead of schedules and clocks. In India you leave for town when everyone is ready, not when the clock says so. In Nairobi, Kenya you preach until you are finished with the message, not until four minutes past noon. Interruptions and delays are the norm, not the exception. As you can tell, the "poly" in polychronic means "many," and people with this orientation are comfortable with many activities occurring simultaneously until each comes to a natural end.

Early in my visit to India, the director of the orphanage told me I could join others who were traveling to nearby Amravati the next morning. I asked when we would leave, and he said ten o' clock. In predictable North American form, I was ready at 9:55 with lunch bag in hand. But there was no car. And no people. I waited for fifteen minutes and then half an hour. Then others began to arrive, one by one. We left the orphanage at 11:15 A.M.

In contrast, North American culture holds a *monochronic* view of time. We see time like a single strand of segmented film, and we expect people to conform to its frames for the sake of efficiency. People with this orientation think of time as a commodity, and show it in expressions such as "made time," "banked time," or "worked double time." North Americans pride themselves in punctuality, and marvel at computer technology that can measure the nanosecond (one billionth of a second).

Obsession with timely efficiency can affect our communication with others. Jeremy Rifkin, author of *Time Wars*, suggests the shift from polychronic time to monochronic time in western culture has made us impatient. He cites studies showing how computer whizzes suffer especially.

> . . . [P]sychologists have observed that computer compulsives are much more intolerant of behavior that is at all ambiguous, digressive, or tangential. In their interaction with spouses, family, and acquaintances, they are often terse, preferring simple yes-no responses. They are impatient with open-ended conversations and are uncomfortable with individuals who are reflective or meditative. Computer compulsives demand brevity and view social discourse in instrumental terms, interacting with others as a means of collecting and exchanging useful information. Above all, they put a high premium on efficient communication.[28]

An email memo I received from one of the computer technicians at my school bears this out. The subject line read: "Computer system down from 1-2 today," and the body of the message read "See subject"!

A lineal, monochronic view of time does seem to mirror the Christian view that God is working purposefully through history. Taken to its extreme, however, we can easily spiritualize punctuality and exhausting schedules beyond reason. A pastor in Florida felt incredible pressure to perform. To convince his deacons they asked too much of him, he asked them to write down the number of hours they thought he should spend with various duties per week and then tallied up the hours by category.[29] The results were:

sermon preparation, 18 hours
administration, 18 hours
visitation to people's homes, 15 hours
prayer, 14 hours
worship, 10 hours
outreach, 10 hours
counseling, 10 hours
community activities, 5 hours
denominational tasks, 5 hours

church meetings, 5 hours
miscellaneous, 4 hours

The total came to 114 hours; there are 168 hours in a week, among which about fifty are for sleep.

Environment

A while ago a friend of ours took us to a new condo development in town. The furnished visitors' suite demonstrated some classic environmental research. For starters, the visual effect was most pleasing: warm taupe walls with white trim matched the drapes and woodwork in the vaulted living room and breezy kitchen. The realtor had placed a well-worn book face down on a padded chair, and added two pairs of fuzzy slippers with robes in the walk-in closet. Instrumental music soothed softly from a distant bedroom. These props were not accidental, of course, but strategic efforts to pique our interest.

In a classic study on ways our environment affects our mood, researchers placed subjects in an ugly room, an average-looking room, or a beautiful one, and had them evaluate photographic negatives of faces. People in the ugly room rated the faces more homely than those in the beautiful room. They also said that the ugly room created a sense of monotony, fatigue, headache, discontent, sleepiness, irritability, and hostility. On the contrary, subjects in the decorated room "reported feelings of pleasure, importance, comfort, enjoyment, energy, and the desire to continue the activity."[30]

How beautiful your school is will likely effect the grades you earn. In another study, students who received lectures in a pleasantly decorated room scored significantly higher on exams and rated the teacher's performance more competent than did students in a sterile classroom.[31] You can quote this kind of research when your department needs a new facility.

What is the lesson for believers? It is at least to recognize that how we keep our homes and build our churches may not only reflect our values, but nurture them as well. Or as Winston Churchill once put it: "We shape our buildings, thereafter they shape us."

Summary

Nonverbal communication is the process by which we create meaning from nonlinguistic cues. Nonverbal behavior differs from language in important ways, most notably that they are continuous, less controllable, more ambiguous, and packaged in clusters that hit us all at once. We convey our feelings for others, and for our relationships, through nonverbal cues.

Due to the relational nature of nonverbal communication, I suggested that we try to be congruent—to express our emotions fully and freely. Faking emotions can take its toll in the long run. Our congruency, however, should be filtered through grace, so we act in ways that will edify others. Grace also gives others the benefit of the doubt when their nonverbals are ambiguous or hurtful.

People often infer our credibility and how likable we are from our voice alone, so it is worth asking, "How do I sound?" Similarly, the placement and duration of our eye contact can communicate liking, attention, respect, and control. Where do you look? For how long?

Gestures range from quirky twitches to intentional embraces. We would do well to master the language of the body. Our fashion and looks can bring us blessings and trials, but investing in character qualities, rather than cosmetics, will return a valuable premium. Covenantal relating goes beyond facades, and guards against the beauty bias.

Space often communicates degrees of liking and power as well as the tone of the relationship. Jesus broke space rules to demonstrate his steadfast love to attract people to God's kingdom. Touch is often status linked, but when used fittingly, can affirm others in spirit and physical health. Mistaking friendly touch for sexual touch is a tendency men should guard against.

Smell can draw up deep connections to our past and aid worship in the right context. How we use time will reflect our value on people or on schedules. A balance between these styles is no doubt achievable. Finally, how we keep our rooms, homes, and churches will ultimately influence our moods and even our performance. Cleanliness and aesthetics nurture a positive spirit.

 **WORTH THE TALK**

1. What other criteria besides congruence and grace may guide our use of nonverbals?

2. When are you least liking to give eye contact with someone else? Can you determine why? What might you do to improve your eye contact with others?

3. When you give an oral presentation, how might you use your facial expressions, gestures, and voice to your advantage?

4. What do you think of people who dress well daily? What of people who dress casually? Do you think these judgments are true or fair?

5. Think of instances where Jesus touched others. Can you surmise a general truth or pattern from his actions?

6. What do you think about using aromas to artificially induce certain moods in office buildings? In churches?

7. What does your arrival time to class communicate to your professor? What does your professor's arrival time communicate to you?

8. Bedrooms often depict a person's style. What does your room say about you? How does your room influence you or your roommate?

CONSIDER THE WALK

1. Visit a lounge on campus, find a comfy chair, and watch people. Use the nonverbal ideas in this chapter to describe some lounge-goers in terms of how much they like each other, and their general emotional states as you watch them. Interact with the research in this chapter to support your analysis.

2. Try the following nonverbal experiments and observe how people respond to you. Report back to your class if possible.
   - Sit in the front row of class and give unyielding eye contact to the professor.
   - Enter an elevator but don't turn around to face the door; face the people.
   - Put on some cologne you wouldn't normally wear. Extra strong.
   - The next time you shake hands with a new acquaintance, don't let go for five seconds.
   - Wear the most uncharacteristic blouse or shirt for a day.

ONLINE CHALK

Here are nine search phrases that hit rich pay dirt in Google. As usual, discern better sites from mediocre ones.
   - Body language communication
   - Appropriate eye contact
   - Facial communication
   - Clothing communicates
   - Appearance communicates
   - Proxemic communication
   - Interpersonal touch
   - Human olfaction
   - Chronemics

 **ENDNOTES**

1 For example, Dale Leathers offers lists of guidelines for every sort of nonverbal behavior in *Successful Nonverbal Communication: Principles and Applications* (New York: Macmillan, 1986).

2 Em Griffin, *Making Friends (and Making Them Count)* (Downers Grove, IL: InterVarsity Press, 1987), 114-115 (italics added). See Griffin's entire chapter 6 in "Nonverbal Communication" for a discussion of nonverbal communication in relationships particularly.

3 Roy M. Berko, Andrew D. Wolvin and Darlyn R. Wolvin, *Communicating: A Social and Career Focus*, 6th ed. (Boston: Houghton Mifflin, 1995), 154.

4 Paul Watzlawick, Janet H. Beavin and Don D. Jackson, *Pragmatics of Human Communication* (New York: W. W. Norton, 1967), 49.

5 Reported on in Judith A Hall, *Nonverbal Sex Differences: Accuracy of Communication and Expressive Style* (Baltimore: Johns Hopkins, 1984), 24.

6 Albert Mehrabian, *Silent Messages: Implicit Communication of Emotions and Attitudes*, 2nd ed. (Belmont, CA: Wadsworth, 1981), 77.

7 See Eugene Peterson, *The Message: The New Testament in Contemporary English*, (Colorado Springs: NavPress, 1993), 306 and 307. These passages are renditions of Romans 2:13 and 23.

8 Philip Yancey, *The Jesus I Never Knew* (Grand Rapids: Zondervan, 1995), 172.

9 See Carl Rogers, "The Interpersonal Relationship: The Core of Guidance," in *Bridges, Not Walls: A Book About Interpersonal Communication*, ed. John Stewart, 4th ed. (New York: Random House, 1986), 352-358

10 See J. D. Burgoon, D. B. Buller and W. G. Woodall, *Nonverbal Communication: The Unspoken Dialogue* (New York: Harper & Row, 1989), 70.

11 These findings reported in Gay Lumsden and Donald Lumsden, *Communicating with Credibility and Confidence* (Belmont, CA: Wadsworth Publishing, 1996), 148-150.

12 Ronald Adler and Neil Towne, *Looking Out/Looking In*, 8th ed. (Forth Worth: Harcourt Brace, 1996), 249-250, and ibid., 153.

13 Ibid., 154.

14 Judith A. Hall, *Nonverbal Sex Differences*, 19 and 53.

15 Ibid., chapter 3, *Explaining Judgment Accuracy*.

16 Ibid.

17 Ibid.

18 Paul Ekman, "Movements with Precise Meanings," *Journal of Communication* 26 (1976): 14-26.

19 Roy M. Berko and others, *Communicating*, 178.

20 E. Dion, E. Berscheid and E. Walster, "What is Beautiful is Good," *Journal of Personality and Social Psychology* 24 (1972): 285-290, as quoted in Dale Leathers,

Successful Nonverbal Communication: Principles and Applications (New York: Macmillan, 1986), 104.

21 See, for example W. Wells and B. Siegel, "Stereotyped Somatotypes," *Psychological Reports* 8 (1961): 77-88, and David Lester, "Ectomorphy and Personality," *Psychological Reports* 51 (1982): 1182.

22 These findings are reported in L. A. Malandro, L. Barker and D. A. Barker, Nonverbal Communication, 2nd ed. (New York: Random House, 1986), and in Dale Leathers, Successful Nonverbal Communication.

23 F. F. Bruce, *Jesus: Lord and Savior* (Downers Grove, IL: InterVarsity Press, 1986), 46.

24 See Dale Leathers, *Successful Nonverbal Communication*, 119.

25 See Adler and Towne, *Looking Out/Looking In*, 255-257.

26 Quoted in L. B. Koeppel, Y. Montagne-Miller, D. O'Hair and M. Cody, "Friendly, Flirting, Wrong?" in *Interpersonal Communication: Evolving Interpersonal Relationships*, ed. Pamela J. Kalbfleisch (Hillsdale, NJ: Lawrence Erlbaum, 1993), 13 (see chapter 2, 13-32).

27 See T. Hall, *The New York Times*, November 27, 1991, C1 and C6, as reported in Lumsden and Lumsden, *Communicating with Credibility*, 168.

28 Jeremy Rifkin, *Time Wars: The Primary Conflict in Human History* (New York: Henry Holt, 1987), 17. Rifkin's citation of Brod comes from Craig Brod, *Technostress* (Reading, MA: Addison-Wesley, 1984), 94.

29 Reported in *The Mennonite Brethren Herald*, November 24, 1995, 26.

30 L. Malandro and others, *Nonverbal Communication,* 156, describe the Maslow and Mintz study which may be found in A. M. Maslow and N. L. Mintz, "Effects of Esthetic Surroundings: I. Initial Effects of Three Esthetic Conditions Upon Perceiving "Energy" and "Well Being" in Faces," *Journal of Psychology* 41 (1956): 247-254. See also N. L. Mintz, "Effects of Esthetic Surroundings: II. Prolonged and Repeated Experience in a "Beautiful" and "Ugly" Room," *Journal of Psychology* 41 (1956): 459-466.

31 D. D. Wollin and M. Montagne, "College Classroom Environment: Effects of Sterility Versus Amiability on Student and Teacher Performance," *Environment and Behavior* 13 (1981): 707-716.

For we are God's workmanship, created in Christ Jesus to do good works, which God prepared in advance for us to do.

Ephesians 2:10

The Anchored Self:
Image Bearers in Symbolic Communities

ALLYSSA'S APPEARANCE PICTURED an attractive, communicative college sophomore. She was slim and pretty and could flash an endearing smile. But down deep loomed an unattractive view of her self that froze her relationally and communicationally. On buoyant days she was confident, talkative, and interpersonally savvy. On low days she was confused, withdrawn, and interpersonally inept.

Allyssa belonged to a discipleship group of four women that was led by my future wife, Shelaine. All four felt comfortable to discuss their understanding of God and his word, and each was committed to growing in him. As they came to know each other better, it was evident that Allyssa's roller-coaster emotions were due, in part, to some nontraditional ideas about her standing before God. She felt that God considered her in right standing only if she had confessed all her known sins. If a recent sin went unconfessed, Allyssa believed she would drop from grace and go to hell if she died that moment. This explained her emotional—and communicational—ups and down. Some days she was confidently sure of her salvation; other days she felt she was on the brink of damnation. Allyssa bounced from feeling justified to feeling condemned, and back, day after day. She was a spiritual and psychological wreck.

As Allyssa's spiritual mentor, my wife shared with her a more biblical view of God's grace, namely, that when we repent, God welcomes us into the secure fold of his salvation. Sins we commit thereafter grieve the Lord, but they do not jeopardize our standing before him as recipients of his grace. Like the traveler in the parable, we do not need to wash our entire body after a walk on the dusty trail. We need only wash our feet.

Upon understanding God's grace more fully, Allyssa's demeanor changed slowly yet dramatically. She showed confidence in her self and her witness for God. A year later she led her own discipleship group, and now lives in China with her husband and children as a missionary. She keeps in contact with us across the miles, and remembers warmly the small community of friends who nurtured her to personal wholeness.

Self in Community

In Chapter 2 we acknowledged our need to connect with others in order to come together and change for the better. Allyssa's story captures this principle well. In this chapter we consider how our symbolic communities and God's word nurtures our sense of self through communication. Our thesis is this: All people share an anchored human identity, as made in God's image, and the symbolic communities to which we belong nurture that self culturally and morally. Therefore, while we may talk about our "self-concept" as a separate, knowable identity, we acknowledge that our selves develop in community with others.[1] Moreover, as Rabbi Jonathan Sacks observes, it is better to drop the idea of individual "selves" and think more, instead, in terms of a *people*.[2] Among a *people* we develop our *personhood* because a community is committed to shaping our identity and moral development. Put another way, each person is a self-in-community, and this symbiotic dynamic helps us understand Allyssa's communication and thousands like her.

> It is better to think in terms of a *people*, not individual selves.

Therefore, we might define *self-concept* as the relatively stable set of impressions we have about ourselves as a spiritual, social, personal, and physical being in relationship with others and with God. This definition differs from most textbook definitions because it assumes that we see ourselves as spiritual too. Even the atheist and agnostic, who believe that God does not exist, or are unsure if he exists, may define themselves as "non-spiritual." It is difficult to define ourselves without the continuum of spirituality.

Our self concept affects how we talk to ourselves (what we call *intra*personal communication) and our talk with others. How do you see your self? You can get a handle on your self-impressions by doing an exercise with me. Doing so will help you gain self-awareness that goes way beyond just reading about it. Here is how to do it. Take a blank sheet of paper and number it 1-20 on the left-hand side. Now answer the question "Who am I?" Begin each line with "I am . . ." and write down words and short phrases that describe you. Write what comes to mind, and do not worry about what others might think. Only you will see this list. Take five to seven minutes to do this now.[3]

· ·

If you are like me, you found it increasingly difficult to think of descriptors near the end of the list. This is because some images and feelings are less defining, more buried. My easy first five answers were father, husband, professor, Christian, and disciplined. I call these my workhorse images because I am enacting them daily at home and school. My last five responses were positive, energetic, conservative, funny at times, and joker. As a group they look more like Jerry Seinfeld than Bill Strom, but in some respects I see myself like Seinfeld.

The types of descriptors you chose probably fell into two categories: nouns and adjectives.[4] Nouns represent the roles, groups, and positions that define you in relation to others. For example, I am a "father" in relation to Taylor, Clark, and Eric, "husband" in relation to Shelaine, and "professor" in relation to my university community. By comparison, adjectives represent personality traits that describe your character. They are how you see yourself despite your relation to others. That said, these self-descriptors likely have root in relationship with others as well, for one is only "conservative" in comparison to "liberals," or a "joker" compared to more serious people.

The descriptors you chose also hint at three other dimensions of our self-concept: self-image, self-esteem, and importance level.[5] *Self-images* are the pictures I have of myself whether clear or fuzzy, accurate or inaccurate. *Self-esteem* is my generalized sense of personal worth—whether I like or dislike my self-images. *Importance level* is the weight I attach to any one image and related esteem. For example, I have a clear picture of myself as a rotten golfer, and my scores will prove it. I do not particularly like being a poor golfer, but because I have low value on golf generally, my global sense of self-worth remains buoyant. Keep in mind that we usually treat self-images as separate frames (such as "student" + "daughter" + "runner"), but we are more likely to speak of our esteem in general terms. The frames may change, but the mood or music of our esteem plays on. We are more likely to say "Jen has low esteem" than "Jen dislikes the part of her that golfs poorly."

Formation of the Self Concept

Christopher Columbus believed that if God made us in his image, then people raised outside the influence of the known world would automatically speak God's language—Hebrew. Columbus therefore brought a Hebrew scholar with him on his trip to the New World as an interpreter. As we know, he was wrong. God may have stamped on us his *imago Dei* imprimatur, but he left our cultural and personal identities largely in the hands of covenant communities. We may even have some genetic tendencies, as in body type and temperament, but community interaction completes the picture.

Others communicate to us who we are. Every semester at my school students are required to evaluate their courses and professors, and each semester instructors grin and bear it as they read student comments. What students say can influence a dean's decision to promote a professor, and more than one instructor has quit the profession based on poor evaluations. "I must not be a good instructor," they lament, "the evaluations tell me so."

Paying attention to what others say about us is called *reflected appraisal*, and it is the key idea in works such as George Herbert Mead's *Mind, Self, and Society*.[6] He defined the self as the picture others mirror back to us. As I interact with you, you tell me who I am in direct and indirect ways. Eventually I begin to believe that what you say about me is true. This is why Mead dubbed it "the looking-glass self," because I come to know myself through the mirror of you.

The mirrors we face each day include other people and the media. High school girls and college women in particular suffer stress in the shadows of gorgeous, slim super models who set impossible standards of beauty and sexual appeal. Although media scholars have been unable to prove a direct link between the media's "thin is in" message and eating disorders in young women,[7] others suggest that this media message combined with achievement messages at home may in fact contribute to anorexia nervosa (self-imposed starvation) and bulimia (binge eating with self-induced vomiting).[8] This means that girls whose parents expect the world of them are more susceptible to media images than girls with laid-back parents. Controlling their eating habits, even for self-starvation, gives such girls a sense of personal control.

Despite the ugly messages our parents might hurl our way, it seems most of us admire our mom and dad and their investment in our lives. In fact, parents and friends win over media personalities as our personal heroes. Harvard sociologist Arthur Levine found that young adults considered their heroes to be parents, close friends, and relatives three-to-one over musicians, entertainers, and clergy.[9] In a similar study by the Children Defense Fund, "the youths [ages 13-15 years old] said they consider their parents and other adult family members to be the most powerful influence on them—more important than friends, television, and other media."[10]

As believers the question worth considering is whether our heroes reflect God's view of us. I realize that no one has a direct hook-up to God's mind on every matter, but we can at least test what others say about us by seeing how it squares with scripture. Perhaps it was some

"I've always told little Teddy he was a mixed up kid."

well-intentioned but theologically off-base person who told Allyssa that she needed to confess sin daily to be assured of her salvation.

We compare ourselves to others. My brother Brad was my yardstick for personal development while growing up. Only fifteen months older than me, he seemed to be five years ahead in athletic prowess, leadership skills, and dating. Even though he genuinely encouraged me in these areas, I still felt about two feet short of his maturity. Fortunately for me, Brad was less able than I was in cracking jokes and carrying a tune. He made a great basketball point guard, but a clumsy wrestler. My parents could see the differences and were wise enough to encourage my interest in ventriloquism, choir, band, and wrestling. Later my brother's interests in business were cantilevered by my desire to teach, and today we are diverse in identity but enjoy each other's mutual respect.

Social comparison is this habit of comparing ourselves to others around us—whether brothers or bullies—and judging ourselves accordingly. In our better moments we probably compare ourselves to godly, humble people whom we emulate and wish to imitate. Doing so may lead to short-term low esteem ("Gee, I sure don't serve others as well as she does") but long-term maturity ("Thank you, God, for this new opportunity to serve. It makes me feel worthwhile.") In our worse moments it is easy to compare ourselves to down-and-outers in order to feel superior. The question seems to be whether or not those with whom we compare ourselves ultimately build us up in the likeness of Christ.

We infer our identity from how we behave and communicate. Another way our self-concept develops is through watching ourselves. Perhaps after a heated debate with a friend [about some issue] you have thought, "I must really feel deeply about this issue. My avid debating proves so." You may have had a weak sense of your attitude about the issue before your debate, but your behavior affirmed and heightened it. Daryl Bem would say you engaged in *self-attribution,* because you attributed (linked) your behavior to a presumed, driving identity.[11]

This idea reverses conventional wisdom. Most of us think that attitudes and identities precede behaviors. For example, I like to bike, so I do. Bem suggests the opposite: After observing that I bike a lot, I infer that I like to bike. One summer I attended a conference where the speaker used Bem's logic to challenge us. He claimed that you only believe that which motivates you to action. He asked us to make a list of where we invested our energies and then asked, "What do these things tell you about you?" He encouraged us to make self-attributions for the sake of self-awareness. You might try a similar exercise.

We organize all these impressions into a sensible whole. Three of the ten words in the middle of my list of personal descriptors include "proud," "competitive," and "old athlete." On first blush these seem at odds with my concept as believer, husband, and conservative. Does our self-concept make sense, or is it a mixed bag of conflicting images and esteems? Morris Rosenberg suggests the former. Our self-concept is "an *organization* of parts, pieces, and components...that...are hier-archically organized and interrelated in complex ways."[12] Remember how your first five descriptors came easiest? They probably govern how the others fall into line. As a father I do not think of myself as competing with my children, but as a father I teach my children that healthy competition can be fun and rewarding. I see myself as a dad (first) who enjoys competing. An Olympic athlete may see herself as a competitor (first) who enjoys mothering.

As believers we are encouraged to have the mind of Christ, which in turn informs other images. For just as Jesus saw himself as son/savior/compassionate/carpenter/rabbi/friend seeking to do the will of God the father, so we can see ourselves as students/friends/strug-gling/proud/athletes under the Lordship of Christ. Having the mind of Christ informs my image as athlete, friend, and the like. With this said though, let us not forget that the struggle we all experience is similar to Paul's. Despite his new identity in Christ he still struggled with sin. "I do not understand what I do. For what I want to do I do not do, but what I hate I do" (Romans 7:15). Our identity in Christ does not change our humanness. We may be justified in God's eyes, but we are still justified sinners.[13]

To summarize, our self-concept is molded by what others say to us, by our comparing ourselves to others, by observing our own commu-nication habits or behavior, and by organizing these perceptions. Left at that, these truths look like a postmodern view of identity formation. Postmodernists believe that people are largely (if not entirely) the product of their social environment—mere cogs in a social machine.[14] This type of thinking has birthed *victimology* and *anti-speciesism.* Victimology suggests we are not responsible for evil acts we commit because our environment nurtured our response. Anti-speciesism is the idea that we ought not assume that humans are any more superior than animals.[15] Both positions assume a community-determines-all approach to identity formation. Julia Wood, a communication scholar, argues against these positions by distinguishing between determinism and influence.[16] Society may strongly influence our self development, but it does not determine it. We still exercise self-agency—the ability to self-reflect, pursue alternative identities, and live with our choices.

I suggest that believers need to take self-agency a step further to acknowledge God's larger design for personal identity. The scriptures tell us that God knew us before we were born, has chosen us to be his people, and paid salvation's price while we were still separated from him. God empowered us with self-agency, but with a guiding purpose to know and enjoy him forever. Our identity is not subject to every symbolic wave that crashes against the helm of our person. Rather, our identities are anchored by God's design as we discern messages within our symbolic communities. We are foremost his workmanship (Ephesians 2: 10) whom he draws to himself through others, scripture, prayer, and our conscience.

The Scriptures form and inform our identity.[17] The word of God is not merely ink on onion-skin paper. Like a two-edged sword, it cuts to our conscience with the reminder that every person, from serial killer to missionary child, is made in God's image and deserving of respect. What does it mean to be made in the image of God? Traditional interpretations of this image refer to our original perfection (in the Garden of Eden), our ability to use knowledge, our moral awareness and our immortality.[18] Others have added that we are rational, historical, valuing, social, and symbol-users. Furthermore, God's word is able to judge our thoughts and intentions (Hebrews 4:12) and teach, reprove, correct, and train us (2 Timothy 3:16, 17). God's word also renews our minds so we can discern God's will (Romans 12:2).

Prayer Reminds Us of What and Whose We Are.   Prayer is a speech act that puts our identity in perspective. Even the physical act of kneeling and bowing one's head reminds us of our creature status before God.

In Matthew 6, Jesus teaches his disciples how (not what) to pray, and helps us understand whose we are. Calling God holy reminds us that we are his creation, placed on earth to worship and enjoy him forever. Asking that his kingdom come and will be done reminds us of our part as instruments of his redemption on earth. Requesting daily bread and the forgiveness of sins points to our need for physical and spiritual food. Asking for freedom from temptation and Satan reminds us that without God we are the devil's quarry.

Our Conscience Molds Our Identity. Finally, God uses our conscience to mold us morally. Our local newspaper published a story about a man accused of wife abuse. When the police laid the charges, the man was confused. All his life he had observed his father and uncles treat their wives with verbal attacks and slaps to the face; he thought all men acted similarly. His small voice of conscience had become callused by ugly models in his family community.

In several of his letters the apostle Paul speaks of the conscience which God has given us to defend and accuse our thought life and behavior (see Romans 2:14, 15, 1 Corinthians 8:9–13, and 1 Timothy 4:2). Unfortunately, sin often tilts our conscience off center. For the abuser it fell to the side of leniency. Abuse seemed okay to him. For others it may lean toward legalism. Consider how some believers interpret Christ's call to be in the world but not of it to mean that they do not speak with unbelievers. Others extend this rule and do not speak with believers who speak with unbelievers! I suggest that their consciences are too sensitive.

> God uses our conscience to mold our moral self.

· ·

A turning point in my own identity formation came on a day when I mentioned to my father that I was contemplating a teaching career. He responded with a broad smile and an energetic comment: "Yes Bill, I think teaching fits you." Neither of us looked up chapter and verse for God's plan for me, but both of us knew that God would be honored in a life of instructing others. And so goes the interplay of finding and forming who we are: by paying attention to God's voice, our own observations, and the reflected appraisals of others.

Self-Esteem's Influence on Communication

Knowing who we are has great benefits. Feeling worthwhile has even more. One author suggests that when we have a clear identity we feel unique in a good way.[19] I get a measure of satisfaction knowing that I may be the only teacher/ventriloquist/old athlete/conservative/joker on this earth.

Another asset of a clear identity is that we know what to expect of ourselves.[20] Should we say yes to the principal who asks us to speak at the high school graduation? Should we agree to lead a small discussion group? A clear sense of self can direct our decision and give us peace at heart. We can also predict fairly well how the speech or small group discussion will go if we know ourselves.

Appropriate esteeming of our identity also has its benefits. In fact, a variety of research projects suggest an impressive yet sobering list of behaviors that show up routinely with low or high esteem. Figure 5.1 summarizes some of these findings.

A fear I have in presenting this research is that you fall prey to the belief that self-esteem is a scapegoat for life's problems—communication problems included. If you experienced ugly or horrible things as a child, and today your esteem suffers because of it, you might think you have the right to be mad at the world. The issue is whether you will view your level of esteem as an "invaluable key or an irresponsible excuse."[21] It is a key when we use these findings to help us understand who we are and why we act as we do. It is an irresponsible excuse when we believe our esteem is directly wired to our behavior with no allowance for choice. Given this word of caution, let's look at each tendency in turn.

Our self-evaluation leaks out in what we say about ourselves. Remember Jesus' words? "Out of the overflow of the heart the mouth speaks" (Matthew 12: 34). While Jesus was referring to our moral self, I believe his words ring true of our esteem self as well.

Growing up in the shadow of a competent brother made me wonder when I would finally catch up. My self-doubts leaked out in statements such as "No, I can't do that—at least not as well as Brad." When others picked up on my self-doubt, they played into it whether consciously or unconsciously. When church friends considered who should be on the church youth executive, they nominated Brad, not Bill. When my brother's friends chose teams for tag football, they picked "Strom" (Brad), not "Little Strom" (me). The youth group

PERSONS WITH HIGH SELF-ESTEEM	PERSONS WITH LOW SELF-ESTEEM
Are likely to think well of themselves and voice this opinion.	Are likely to think poorly of themselves and express this view.
Are likely to make statements that show an expectation of acceptance of others.	Are likely to make statements that show an expectation of rejection by others.
Are better able to defend their ideas publicly.	Are less able to defend their ideas publicly.
Are less easily persuaded from their original beliefs.	Are more easily persuaded from their original beliefs.
Perform well when being watched (e.g. giving speeches, playing sports); not afraid of others' reactions.	Perform poorly when watched; sensitive to possible negative reaction.
Talk more freely in groups.	Talk less frequently in groups.
Find it easy to initiate conversations with strangers.	Find it difficult to initiate conversations with strangers.

Figure 5.1 Esteem and Communication[22]

members and football players were probably only applying an "older is better" rule for leadership and athletic skill, but their choices made me think poorly of myself, and it showed in my communication. Perhaps the best thing I did back then was to attend a different university than Brad and establish my own identity based on my own accomplishments. Speaking more optimistically about myself came more easily after that.

Liking ourselves usually leads to expressing that we expect to be liked by others; not liking ourselves forecasts rejection from others. We have all made nervous phone calls to people we would like to get to know better. "Hi, Leanne, this is Ted. *You won't remember me*, but I'm in your French 101 class. *I suppose you're too busy*, but I was wondering if you'd like to see the movie at the bijou tonight. I know you do a lot with

Erica, so I won't be surprised if you want to go with her instead. So, what do you say?" Ted hardly has a chance. His every line begs Leanne to decline. Using more neutral language is more likely to lead her to "yes." It is probably truer too. Compare the difference: "Hi, Leanne? This is Ted from your French 101 class—the guy who said he visited Paris last summer. I don't know how busy you are, but I was wondering if you'd like to see the movie at the bijou tonight. My friend Mike could join us too if you are already planning to go with Erica." I realize that this is a hypothetical example, but I hope the spirit of the idea is worth making. We can work at expressing anticipated approval.

People with poor self-esteem are less able to defend their ideas than people with high esteem. Preparing and delivering a public debate gives people with low esteem the willies. Somewhere in their youth they learned to hush up and not ask questions. Somewhere they were instructed to do what they were told without discussing options or asking for reasons, and now they have a tough time thinking critically and defending their ideas. Although 10 to 15 percent of the population may be born shy, it seems that most folks with low esteem have been conditioned to shut up, not speak up.[23] These individuals experience a double whammy. Not only do they doubt their perceptions and ideas, they also have less experience, and fewer strategies, to voice them.

People with low esteem are more easily swayed to new opinions. Perhaps you have seen the *Far Side* cartoon that shows a shadowy door-to-door salesman presenting a book titled *Double Your IQ or No Money Back* to a would-be customer. The goofy-looking homeowner scratches his head and remarks, "Well, I dunno. . . . OK, sounds good to me." This type of yielding to persuasion helps people with low esteem gain acceptance from others. It also makes life easier for them if someone else is calling the shots.

Lest we think that God's ideal is that we become high-esteeming shot-callers, consider the type of believers that made up the first-century church. As one author observes, "Paul notes that the early church wasn't peopled with many winners. Few of Christ's followers were wise as the world judges wisdom; not many were powerful, and only a smattering were of noble birth. Most were weak, low and despised (1 Corinthians 1:26–29)."[24] The reason why God chooses to work through down-and-outers is to convince us of his love and righteousness and to help us guard against our own proud efforts to please him.

Giving in to God, even due to a suffering self-esteem, appears to be more favored than playing solo on our own accomplishments.

People who think well of themselves tend to perform better publicly than those who think poorly of themselves. Students on your school's debate team might come to mind again. And musicians. And the best athletes. These individuals seem to glory in the spotlight where they earn acclaim and envy. For example, in the film *Hoosiers*, the star guard, Jimmy, challenges the coach's plan to pass the ball to a less capable player in a clutch situation. Jimmy retorts, "No coach. Give me the ball. I won't miss." The coach agrees, and seconds later, *swoosh*, Jimmy nets the championship game winner. People like Jimmy usually think well of themselves.

What is encouraging is that we all get better with practice. I can list scores of students who enter my public speaking course with little confidence but who leave with a surer sense of self and their ability. Esteem does not drive everything. How we choose to prepare will influence our delivery, and the feedback we receive when we give a sound speech builds our sense of worth. Speaking clubs such as Toastmasters and assertiveness training seminars are based on this optimistic premise.

People with less esteem tend to keep quiet during group discussion; those with more esteem voice their views. Put together, these tendencies mean that high esteemers carry the conversation while low esteemers suffer from missed opportunity to speak. International students experience this pattern as they lug through the doldrums of culture stress and English language learning. They may not be of low esteem upon arriving in North America, but the fear of appearing stupid with English turns many into quiet members of small group. They want desperately to be accepted, but fear embarrassing themselves and locals. Only after gaining confidence in their English do many begin contributing. Leaders of small groups would be gracious gatekeepers to ask reticent students their opinions and ideas. Sometimes the littlest encouragement can empower the meek-minded.

One's level of esteem affects his or her willingness to interact with strangers. Speaking with strangers induces more stress than chatting with a friend, but folks with a low self-image find novel interactions particularly stressful. What is at stake is their bank account called "face." Low esteem people work very hard to gather strokes and rewards to fill that account so they may present a positive public image. Interactions with strangers potentially debit that account. They wonder if they will say something stupid, or if the stranger will reject them.

At the start of my cross-cultural communication course we play a get-to-know-you game where everyone introduces him- or herself, and where certain players have to remember almost everyone's name. As students attempt to put their best foot forward, you can bet that they experience emotional anxiety and mental uncertainty in this situation with new acquaintances.[25] Low esteem people must suffer doubly here as well! The good news is that research indicates that initial interaction with strangers, even if foisted upon us, leads to increased liking and liberty to interact even more.[26]

As noted earlier, some readers may take their bruised ego as reason to be sour apples around others. I hope that is not the case. Rather, my desire is that you understand how certain communication behaviors tend to accompany a wounded esteem, and then I hope to encourage you to choose against the grain. That theme runs throughout this book—that we have choice in how we respond to others and how we talk to ourselves.

How Do We Talk with Ourselves?[27]

This is an important question. For Allyssa the answer was to berate herself for every little mistake and convince herself that she, like Paul, was chief among sinners. Theologians call this worm theology and a good number of Christians subscribe to it. They point out that Adam and Eve's *pride of self* (not their hate or lust or envy) brought sin into the world, and that pride continues to be a root of much sin. Therefore, they reason, any kind of self-pride is wrong. They also note that when people come to grips with God's holiness and grace they should respond like Jacob who resolved, "I am but dust and ashes" (Genesis 40:4).

At the other end of the continuum are believers who contend that Christians are perhaps the only group of people who have reason for a clear self-image and high self-esteem. They reason that through Christ we have taken off the old self and put on the new self—a self that is Christ-centered, but still our own identity (Ephesians 4:24). Also through Christ we are freed from the incapacitating effects of guilt—we are new creatures in him. Believers who subscribe to this good news view suggest that thinking and speaking positively about ourselves signals hallmark Christianity.

Somewhere in between are believers who suggest that both are true. They agree that we are all sinners. Consider 1 John 1:8 that reads, "If we claim to be without sin, we deceive ourselves and the truth is not in us" (1 John 1:8). But they also point out that God called us *very good* when he created us (see Genesis 1: 31), made us right before him through Christ's death, and empowered us by his Spirit to do good works—all sources for human strength. The key seems to be balance. I love the way Paul says it in Romans 12: 3, "I say to every one of you: Do not think of yourself more highly than you ought, but rather think of yourself with sober judgment, in accordance with the measure of faith God has given you." A sober analysis helps us appreciate our skills and gifts without getting pigheaded.

This makes good theology, but how does it translate into self-talk? While these suggestions are not meant to be a sure-fire, money-back guarantee for increasing your sense of self-worth, they are intended to help you guard against unfounded negative self-talk.

Guard against the fallacy of perfection.[28] If you give in to this myth, it will be too easy to berate yourself for not giving a "perfect" speech or not saying the "perfect" thing to a friend. We should strive for our best, but not tongue-lash ourselves for falling short. We are all human, and that means we are limited in our knowledge and still working out our salvation.

Don't think you have to please everyone.[29] An old wag once said, "You can please some of the people all of the time, and please all of the people some of the time, but you can't please everyone all of the time." There is wisdom here. While we strive to speak appropriately, we cannot anticipate every response others may make toward us. Honest mistakes happen, and when they do we need to cut ourselves some slack.

Avoid over-generalizing your faults.[30] Have you ever caught yourself saying "I *always* do that!" or "I *never* say the right thing!"? Are these statements true? Probably not. What happens is that we remember our flubs more than our successes because mistakes draw more attention. If you consider all the evidence though, you can probably say with proper humility "I messed up this time, but that's not characteristic of me." We should be aware of flawed communication patterns, but guard against giving them center stage.

Play to your strengths. After Paul instructed believers to view themselves soberly, he goes on to explain how God's people differ in giftedness. Some are gifted to serve; *let them serve*, he says. Others are wired

"I'VE GOTTA BE ME ... BUT I CAN'T HELP THINKING
SOMEONE ELSE WOULD BE MORE QUALIFIED!"

to encourage; *let them encourage*, he writes. He seems to be saying that we should glory in who we are, rather than pine over what we are not (see Romans 12:6–9). I can thank God for his gifts to me—that I am an old athlete/teacher/joke teller—and not compare myself to others who are gifted differently. I'm free to be me.

Make virtue your goal. Much discussion about self-esteem falls faintly away when we remember that God seeks our holiness more than our happiness. This may sound like a call to sackcloth and ashes, but hear me out. Recently a group of scholars, who call themselves the "positive psychologists," have asked why their field tends to focus on what is wrong with people rather than what is right. To stem this tide they study sources of human strength—virtue—to observe its role in personal well-being and human interaction.

Consider humility, or the ability to accurately understand, and accept, one's strengths and weaknesses. June Tangney found that humble people tend not to be self-focused, but capable of appreciating other people and valuing their advice.[31] Others have found that humble people are more willing to forgive, and accept forgiveness, while proud people withhold forgiveness, and doubt forgiveness is even right or beneficial.[32]

Twenty years earlier philosopher David Clark caught the essence of these scientific findings when he wrote, "True humility is neither thinking too much of oneself or too little of oneself; it is not thinking of oneself at all."[33] This is the spirit of Paul's writing when he says, "Do nothing out of selfish ambition or vain conceit, but in humility consider others better than yourselves. Each of you should look not only to your own interests, but also to the interests of others" (Philippians 2:3–4). Humble self-talk says, "How can I help? How can I encourage? How can I show hospitality? How can I love?" Just when we are feeling the dumpiest about ourselves is when looking to others returns a truckload of blessing.

Modern researchers have also discovered the golden benefits of self-control, which they define as exerting your self over your self to override short-term vice in favor of long-term social benefit.[34] While we might struggle to use self-control when we're tired or hungry, we also carry with us a degree of dispositional self-control that plays out across many communication situations. People who exercise self-control show it best in stopping tit-for-tat fighting, taking a "time out" to cool off, and curbing impulses that could lead one to do stupid things.[35] Not surprisingly, people who measure highly on self-control scales also tend to score highly on self-esteem scales, and vice versa.[36] There's something personally gratifying about keeping your cool when you could have flipped.

Recognize that your self is expressed diversely among your symbolic communities.

A covenantal approach recognizes the interdependent manner in which symbolic communities shape us, and we shape them. This means we interact differently across various groups, but this is okay. You express your student identity among classmates when you debate ideas, study with friends, and give class presentations. You express your sibling identity when you banter with brothers or sisters. You might express an adventurous self as you lead youngsters at camp or climb a local mountain. While you may be tempted to wonder which identity your *true* self is, it is better to regard each as an expression of your complex personhood which is interwoven with others.

The next two chapters are built on the idea of self-in-community, a covenantal tenet. Chapter 6 addresses our creation of deep, personal bonds through interpersonal communication, and Chapter 7 looks at family communication as relational systems. Both underscore that our talk conveys meaning, enacts relationships, and changes us as we come together.

Summary

Who we become is not a willy-nilly affair. God has impressed upon us his divine image and with that status comes the responsibility that we build up others into his likeness. This is not to ignore the fact that we define and discover ourselves through other means as well. Other people impress on us who they think we are (or should be), sometimes with soiled images and roles. We can also get wrapped up in comparing ourselves with others for good or for bad, depending on who that standard is and how we respond to measuring up. We also figure out who we are by observing how we speak and act toward others. We make sense of all these selves by organizing them and making some more dominant than others. It is also helpful to recognize that our self-images (the pictures we have of ourselves) are not the same as our self-esteem (the degree of self-worth we attach to those images). How important an image or feeling is will often govern our global esteem.

Left at this it would seem that the formation of our self is an entirely human affair. However believers assume that God's program anchors our image in his larger design and that we clue in to that truth from scripture, prayer, and our conscience. Realizing that we are God's workmanship helps us weather the cultural and social storms that attempt to define us otherwise.

Our level of self-esteem can have a significant effect on our self-talk and communication with others. We observed how people with low esteem are likely to verbally express this view, often expect rejection from others, struggle to defend their ideas in public, often give in to persuasive ploys, do not perform as well when being watched, speak less frequently in groups, and find it tough to initiate conversations with strangers. While these are not moral deficiencies, most people desire to improve in these areas for the sake of personal development and communicative competence. It's also worth pursuing godliness through humility and self-control as these virtues guide our communication down healthy paths. The bottom line is that we need to practice healthy self-talk and try to look outwardly to others rather than always at ourselves. Humility frees us to meet other people's needs, and self-control manages our response through difficult times.

 **WORTH THE TALK**

1. Who has shaped your self-concept? What people and media influenced you when you were young? What sources influence you today?

2. Why do you think self-esteem has become a prevalent concern in today's society? Some attribute it to the rise of humanistic psychology in universities and counseling practices.[37] Others say it is due to technology (such as telephones, computers, and television) which depersonalize our environment. What do you think?

3. What do you think of David Clark's comment that "True humility is neither thinking too much of oneself, nor too little of oneself; it is not thinking of oneself at all"? Do you agree that our goal should not be to strive for high esteem but rather to be preoccupied with serving others?

4. What degree of self-control do you think you exercise in your communication? Where do you get this sense—is it from recalling how you have communicated, or from what others have told you?

5. Do you ever feel two-faced for acting very differently in distinct environments? What is healthy about expressing ourselves diversely? Unhealthy?

 **CONSIDER THE WALK**

1. Do a full self-concept analysis to compliment the one explained in this chapter. What twenty words or phrases best define your definition of self? After you have done this, analyze the terms by type using some framework: the nouns/adjectives ideas discussed in this chapter, the images/esteem/importance level discussed as well, or the terms in this chapter's definition of "self-concept," namely, spiritual, social, personal, and physical.

> *Spiritual*: terms that indicate your religious beliefs and type of relationship with God.

> *Social:* terms that describe any relationship you have with other people as in roles ("student"), friendship ("girlfriend), etc.

> *Personal*: terms that describe personality traits, likes and dislikes, etc. (e.g., "fun-loving," "studious," "athletic")

> *Physical:* terms that describe your height, weight, color, looks, etc.

Now evaluate each term. Do you like this picture of yourself? Are there other pictures you have of your self that you like or dislike which are not in the list of twenty? Now consider the top five people, experiences, or group that had the most impact on your self-concept. Finally, comment on how your self-talk reflects the principles at the end of this chapter.

2. Do a self-concept and communication analysis. Re-read the list of findings in Figure 5.1. Which ones seem to be true of your behavior? Discuss whether esteem seems to be causing this behavior or is a result of this behavior. Also discuss how you think you might choose to communicate or behave in ways that are not consistent with these general patterns.

ONLINE CHALK

Searching the web for self-talk will generate a lot of sites committed to helping you gain a better self image or esteem. While "talking yourself to health" has its benefits, the view in this chapter is that our identity is anchored in God's image and plan for our lives, and we need to discern the clamoring voices of media and pop psychology as we fine-tune our identities and self-talk.

- How to talk to yourself
- Negative self-talk
- Positive self-talk
- Imago Dei (Latin phrase for "image of God")
- Self in community
- Intrapersonal communication

ENDNOTES

1 The position is similar to that of scholars who call themselves communitarians. "Communitarians assume that individuals in society are neither fully free nor fully constrained. They are "situated agents." Individuals have great potential for self-determination, moral autonomy, or free-riding, but are nevertheless conceived as highly socialized and deeply influenced by the values, beliefs, practices, and opportunities handed to them by their communities."This quotation comes from David Karp, "Communitarianism and the Just Community," *Contemporary Justice Review* 3 (2000): 153-174.

2 Sacks, Rabbi Jonathan, "Social Contract or Social Covenant," *Policy Review* July/August (1996): 54-58.

3 I got the idea of including this exercise from Em Griffin in his book *Making Friends (And Making Them Count)* (Downers Grove, IL: InterVarsity Press, 1987), 28. Many standard textbooks suggest a similar exercise.

4 Ibid., 28.

5 The self-image and self-esteem distinction is a common one made in communication textbooks. For example, see Rudolph Verderber's *Communicate!*, 8th ed. (Belmont, CA: Wadsworth, 1996), 34-39. The idea of importance level is my contribution.

6 George Herbert Mead, *Mind, Self, and Society* (Chicago: University of Chicago, 1934).

7 See Jane D. Brown and Kim Walsh-Childers, "Effects of Media on Personal and Public Health," in Jennings Bryant and Dolf Zillmann, *Media Effects: Advances*

in Theory and Research (Hillsdale, NJ: Lawrence Erlbaum, 1994), 389-415, especially 397.

8 See P. E. Garfinkel and D. M. Garner, *Anorexia Nervosa: A Multidimensional Perspective* (New York: Burner/Mazel, 1982), 10.

9 A. Levine, in an article published in *Change* September/October (1993): 14.

10 *The State of America's Children Yearbook 1994*, (Washington, D.C.: Children's Defense Fund, 1994), 56 as quoted by Steffen T. Kraehmer, *Heroes: Shaping Lives Through Family and Culture* (Minneapolis: Fairview Press, 1995), 16.

11 See D. Bem, "Self-Perception Theory," in *Advances in Experimental Social Psychology,* ed. Leonard Berkowitz (New York: Academic Press, 1977), 10:173-220.

12 Morris Rosenberg, *Conceiving the Self* (New York: Basic Books, 1979), 73.

13 This was a central tenet of the Protestant Reformation and the teaching of Martin Luther, namely, that we are simultaneously justified and sinful, this side of heaven. See Michael Horton, *Putting Amazing Back into Grace: Who Does What in Salvation?* (Grand Rapids: Baker Books, 1994), 165-204.

14 For a critique of the postmodern view of self from a Christian perspective see Dennis McCallum, ed., *The Death of Truth* (Minneapolis: Bethany House, 1996).

15 For another critique of the postmodern view of self, including anti-speciesism, see Gene Edward Veith, Jr., *Postmodern Times: A Christian Guide to Contemporary Thought and Culture* (Wheaton, IL: Crossway Books, 1994).

16 Julia T. Wood, *Relational Communication: Continuity and Change in Personal Relationships* (Belmont, CA: Wadsworth, 1995), 120.

17 This and the following two observations are made by Grant Howard in *The Trauma of Transparency* (Portland: Multnomah, 1979).

18 This list comes from Bruce Milne's *Know the Truth* (Downers Grove, IL: InterVarsity Press, 1983), 96.

19 Griffin, *Making Friends*, 31.

20 Griffin, *Making Friends*, 32.

21 Harold Faw, "Self-Esteem: Invaluable Key or Irresponsible Excuse?" (unpublished paper, Trinity Western University, Langley, British Columbia, summer, 1994).

22 Item 1 is reported on in Verderber's Communicate!, 38 where he cites J. D. Campbell, "Self-Esteem and Clarity of the Self Concept," Journal of Personality and Social Psychology 59 (1990): 538. Items 2, 3, and 5 are reported in D. E. Hamachek, Encounters With Others: Interpersonal Relationships and You (New York: Holt, Rinehart and Winston, 1982), 3-5. Items 4 and 6 are reported on in Griffin's Making Friends, 41 and 43 where he cites D. Hayes and L. Meltzer, "Interpersonal Judgments Based on Talkativeness," Sociometry, 35 (1972): 538-561, and G. Lesser and R. Ableson, "Correlates of Persuasibility in Children," Personality and Persuasibility, ed. C. Hovland and I. Janis (New Haven: Yale University, 1959), 187-206. Item 7 is reported on in M. Rosenberg, Conceiving the Self.

23 See "Extreme Shyness Linked to Biology, Researchers Say," *Cleveland Plain Dealer,* June 28, 1987, A-15, reporting the work of psychologists Jerome Kagan, Robert Pomin, David Rowe, and Stephen Suomi, as cited in Roy Berko, Andrew Wolvin, and Darlyn Wolvin, *Communicating,* 6th ed. (Boston: Houghton Mifflin, 1995), 65.

24 Griffin, *Making Friends*, 43.

25 William Gudykunst builds an intercultural communication theory around these two concepts. See his "Toward a Theory of Effective Interpersonal and Intergroup Communication: An Anxiety/Uncertainty Management (AUM) Perspective" in *Intercultural Communication Competence*, ed. R. L. Wiseman and J. Koester (Newbury Park, CA: Sage, 1993), 33-71.

26 M. J. Sunnafrank and G. R. Miller, "The Role of Initial Conversation in Determining Attraction to Similar and Dissimilar Strangers," *Human Communication Research* 8 (1981): 16-25.

27 This comparison of three approaches to the self is based on Wayne Joosse's booklet *The Christians' Self-Image: Issues and Implications: Occasional papers from Calvin College* (second printing, 1990).

28 See Ronald Adler and Neil Towne, *Looking Out/Looking In*, 8th ed. (Fort Worth: Harcourt Brace, 1996), 152.

29 Ibid., 154.

30 Ibid., 156.

31 J. Tangney, "Humility: Theoretical Perspectives, Empirical Findings and Directions for Future Research," *Journal of Social & Clinical Psychology* 19 (2000): 70-82. See also Tangney's "Humility" in *Handbook of Positive Psychology*, ed. C. R. Snyder and S. J. Lopez (London: Oxford University Press, 2002), 411-419.

32 J. J. Exline and others, "Too Proud to Let Go: Narcissistic Entitlement as a Barrier to Forgiveness," *Journal of Personality & Social Psychology* 87 (2004): 894-913.

33 David Clark, "Philosophical Reflections on Self-Worth and Self-Love," *Journal of Psychology and Theology* 13 (1985): 3-11.

34 Roy F. Baumeister and Julia J. Exline, "Virtue, Personality and Social Relations: Self-Control as the Moral Muscle," *Journal of Personality* 67 (1999): 1165-1194.

35 For insight on stopping fight escalation see J. Gottman, "The Roles of Conflict Management, Escalation, and Avoidance in Marital Interaction: A Longitudinal View of Five Types of Couples," *Journal of Consulting and Clinical Psychology* 61 (1993): 6-15. Regarding impulse control see I. L. Kelly and J. Conley, "Personality and Compatibility: A Prospective Analysis of Marital Stability and Marital Satisfaction," *Journal of Personality and Social Psychology* 52 (1987): 27-40. Regarding adults taking a "time out" in conflict situations see A. Lange, C. van der Wall, and P. Emmelkamp, "Time-out and Writing in Distressed Couples: An Experimental Trial into the Effects of a Short Treatment," *Journal of Family Therapy* 22 (2000): 294-407.

36 J. P. Tangney, R. F. Baumeister, and A. L. Boone, "High Self-Control Predicts Good Adjustment, Less Pathology, Better Grades, and Interpersonal Success," *Journal of Personality* 72 (2004): 271-325.

37 For an excellent book-length discussion of how "self-ism" has dominated psychological theory and practice see Paul Vitz, *Psychology as Religion: The Cult of Self-Worship*, 2nd ed. (Grand Rapids: Eerdmans, 1994).

By speaking the truth in a spirit of love, we must grow up in every way to Christ, who is the head.

Ephesians 4:15

Redeeming Our Dialogue
Looking at Interpersonal Communication

IN DESCRIBING HIS belief that hurting people heal best within communities of care, psychologist Larry Crabb wrote:

> We were designed to connect with others. Connecting is life. Loneliness is the ultimate horror. In connecting with God, we gain life. In connecting with others, we nourish and experience life as we freely share it. Rugged individualism, proud independence, and chosen isolation violate the nature of our existence as much as trying to breathe underwater.[1]

His observation underscores covenantal principle number one—that we live as persons-in-community who thrive when in redemptive relationships with others.

Unfortunately, the hard facts also show that the social bonds that bring life can also beleaguer us, as in the case of Robert and Vicky. I was surprised to hear from my wife that Robert had admitted to having an affair. This was the first case of infidelity close to home for my wife and me. We had known Robert and Vicky for nearly ten years. They were raised in Christian homes, made personal commitments to God early in their lives, went to Bible college, faithfully attended church, served on committees and taught Bible studies.

But after thirty-three years of marriage, Robert felt controlled by his wife and reported to have no feelings for her. After Vicky discovered the affair, the two saw a counselor, but it became clear that Robert did not intend to break off his adulterous relationship. His tears were not over his infidelity, but over having to choose between wife and mistress. What went wrong?

Without doubt, Robert and Vicky suffered from numerous strains in their relationship—debate about money, fatigue from a double-income lifestyle, the challenge of three children, and negotiation for affection. However one strain that seemed most telling was their basic way of interacting. When problems arose, Vicky was likely to discuss them avidly, suggest solutions, and act to solve them. Robert usually went along with her solutions but rarely voiced his own. Unknown to Vicky, Robert bottled up deep resentment toward her regarding her assertiveness. During one counseling session, Robert explained how Vicky had barged in on a business deal he was cutting with a salesperson that resulted in him losing the deal. Thirty-one years later she was now hearing about it for the first time.

> A covenantal perspective affirms the view that we don't communicate *in* a relationship, but that our communication *is* the relationship.

Marriage relationships exist because two people come together, vow allegiance to each other, and develop a bond through an array of communicative acts. No wonder we refer to it as the marriage covenant. But marital communication is but one example of relational communication, or, more broadly, interpersonal communication. All three represent potential places for serious covenantal interaction as we commit to friends, family, and workplace colleagues to change together.

A covenantal perspective affirms that we use responsible symbolic expressions to create, enact, and mold relational bonds to fulfill a need for connection. Therefore communication plays a central role in creating relationships. The tough part is visualizing how communication and relationships merge. For starters, let us begin with three pictures of interpersonal communication that extend the two models presented in chapter one. They should help us grasp the mystery of between-person communion whether among couples, friends, or workplace comrades.

What is Interpersonal Communication?

In *Making Friends (& Making Them Count)*, Em Griffin depicts in visual metaphor three common models of human communication.[2] Some people picture communication like bowling, others like Ping-Pong, and still others like charades.

What happens when we bowl imitates what some scholars call the *linear model* of communication.[3]   In Chapter 1 I referred to it as the objectivist school's *transfer* model.   In this view communication is dependent on the bowler/sender's efforts to select the right ball/message and cruise it down an alley/channel so that it strikes/affects passive pins/receivers with predictability.   The wrong ball/message results in gutter ball or split/misunderstanding, but the right ball/message scores a strike/understanding. "Understanding" is cast as knocking preferred meaning into pins/receivers who do not, or cannot, respond uniquely with feedback. Perhaps some of the lectures that Vicky sent Robert were intended to bowl him over, and she could not register his resentful silence as feedback.   In this respect, the sender-message-channel-receiver-effect model may depict how some people relate.   Down deep though, we hope for more redemptive communication and a more complete model.

A linear model of communication pictures the process as the mechanical transfer of information.

Unlike bowling, Ping-Pong requires two people to play—a better model already. Ping-Pong seems to typify what scholars call the *interactive model* of human communication.[4]   In Ping-Pong someone serves/sends and someone returns/responds, and then they reverse roles. A skilled server can put the ball/message where she wants and a seasoned opponent/responder knows how to handle what is coming.

The more each player knows the other's history, the more readily he or she can predict and respond to the immediate shot. The upside of this model is that it begins with two people, acknowledges our use of feedback, and recognizes our history with our partner. The downside includes the assumption that our human environment is predictable, and that there is only one message (ball) in play at a time. It also assumes that communication is chiefly a power game rather than a cooperative dialogue. Even still, this model seems to typify our every-day interaction with store clerks and casual acquaintances with whom we remain superficial.

Enter the idea that communication is like charades, or what some scholars call the *transactional* model of communication.[5] As Griffin puts it, "A charade is neither an action, like a strike in bowling, nor an interaction, like a point in Ping-Pong. It's a transaction."[6] The charades metaphor most resembles an interpretive approach to communication because it assumes that active, mindful communicators jointly construct meaning, enact a relationship, and are hampered by noise.

Consider how charade partners work together to share the same meaning or image. They read each other for every clue to solve the puzzle. The person acting thinks hard about her partner's experience and their shared experience. She might use symbols or sounds unique to their relationship in order to strike a responsive chord. All the while she uses every channel imaginable, from facial expressions to gestures. Together the partners figure out enough words of the clue until the penny drops: "Oh I know what you mean, 'Two heads are better than one.'" If they happen to share the same connotative meaning of the "Two heads. . ." adage, their common experience overlaps even more. Through nonverbal cues they not only conjure up the same quotation, but link in spirit and connect emotionally. They change together.

The charades metaphor is played out in definitions of interpersonal communication. In *Interpersonal Communication: Pragmatics of Human Relationships*, Aubrey Fisher and Katherine Adams write, "Interpersonal communication is the process of creating social relationships between at least two people by acting in concert with one another."[7] Along the same lines, in *Bridges, Not Walls*, John Stewart writes "For me interpersonal communication is the type or quality or kind of contact that occurs when each person involved talks and listens in ways that highlights the individual's and the other person's human-ness."[8] Note his emphasis on quality, not structure. A structural definition would depict interpersonal communication as the face-to-face exchange of messages between two or three people. But it is more than a Ping-Pong exchange—or it should be. Let's look more deeply at these definitions to understand why. We will start with John Stewart's.

Interpersonal Communication Highlights Each Others' Humanness

If you feel quirky when leaving a message on a telephone answering machine, then you can relate to Stewart's first distinctive of interpersonal communication. An answering machine is an object, not a person. It might "talk," but it is not human. Stewart defines "human" by contrasting it with "object," based on the work of Martin Buber, the philosopher noted in Chapter 2.[9] What distinguishes humans from objects? Stewart interprets Buber as standing for four qualities.

HUMANS ARE	OBJECTS ARE
1. Unique	1. Standardized
2. Unmeasureable	2. Measureable
3. Choice-makers	3. Not choice makers
4. Addressable	4. Non-addressable

People are unique, not standardized. We talked about our uniqueness in the self-concept chapter. That I am a father/professor/believer/old athlete/joke teller means I am probably one-of-a-kind. Objects are not so blessed; they are standardized with component parts. When we talk to people without consideration for their unique make-up, we treat them as objects.

If Vicky and Robert developed routine impersonal talk, we might say they failed to listen deeply to each others' dreams and fears. Scripts such as

"Hey, what's up?"

"Oh, nothing much—how about you?"

"Fine I guess"

"Well, see you later."

make for classic *phatic* communication—talk that functions as social lubricant, but remains superficial and standardized.

People are unmeasurable, not measurable. Social scientists have made valiant attempts to measure people, but in the final tally their question-naires and experiments fall short, at least in the eyes of Stewart and Buber. Stewart writes "'Pulse 110, respiration 72, Likert rating 5.39, palmar conductivity .036 ohms' might be accurate, but it doesn't quite capture all what's going on in me when I greet somebody I love."[10] Some people call the unmeasurable part of being human the psyche or personality. Christians call it the soul or spirit. Whatever the label, this feature of being human makes us unpredictable in a good way. No one can define and measure all the variables in my spirit accurately enough to predict how I will choose to act.

People are choice-makers. We have already noted that to be made in God's image is to have a will to choose (see Chapter 5). When Vicky messed up Robert's business deal, Robert had many options for response. He could have noted his concern assertively and lovingly, or hinted indirectly, or sulked, or blown up, or remained silent. He chose the latter. Objects, in contrast, have no choice.

Our interaction with others becomes more object-like when our talk squelches their freedom to choose. The salesperson on the phone might ask, "May I come by on Tuesday or Thursday to show you those knives?" This question appears to give two options, but it omits a third. It's a loaded question that assumes you want the salesperson to drop by, which you may not wish in the least. The question constrains your choice.

People are addressable. By saying humans are addressable and objects are not, we mean that one can speak *with* a person, but only *at* an object. This is what Stewart and Buber say distinguishes humans from animals. By speaking *with* someone, we engage in commu-nication of similar kind and mutuality; we engage their personhood, and they engage ours. Animals, and especially pets, seem to take on this "almost human" addressable quality. But no matter how tender a response from my dog Buddy, his actions are not human, nor mutual. Animals remain objects.

Just because people are addressable though does not mean we engage this quality with every word. Sometimes people chatter as if on automatic pilot and speak *at* us, not *with* us. You might experience this with a friend who dominates a conversation with her agenda, spilling details that bore you silly. By ignoring your addressability, she loses you.

Redemptive Interpersonal Communication

Stewart, Fisher and Adams would all agree that when we stop communicating we stop relating. Again, Stewart writes, "For me interpersonal communication is the type or quality or kind of *contact...*"[11] He could have said *connection* or *relationship*. Fisher and Adams write, "A relationship is not a 'thing.' When you are not interacting, the ... relationship ... [is] not occurring."[12]

> Interpersonal communication requires inter-person connection which weds soul with soul.

This is the rock-bottom truth that the transactional model (charades metaphor) offers us, and a covenantal perspective affirms. Interpersonal communication is not about the mechanical conveying of words; it is about creating, enacting, and becoming in relationship as we heighten each other's humanness. A covenantal approach, however, extends that view with a spiritual purpose. Yes, our *interaction* should address the whole person, but with a redemptive *goal* in mind, namely, to become more like Christ. Paul's letter to the believers at Ephesus distinguishes between a redemptive process and a redemptive end. He wrote, "... speaking the truth in love [the process], we will in all things grow up into him [the goal] who is the Head, that is, Christ" (Ephesians 4:15). To me this speaks of redeeming the process and person, the relationship and relaters. I want to recognize your sinfulness as I speak with you, but I do not want to enhance your vice. I want our communication to redeem both of us to every corner of our being.

So what does redemptive relating look like? How do we avoid the pitfalls encountered by Robert and Vicky? I think the answer extends to four areas, namely, how we 1) perceive others, 2) speak with others, 3) deal with conflict, and 4) listen.

Gracious Perceiving of Others

In Chapter 5 I suggested that you do the twenty statements exercise for self-perception. What if your best friend wrote down twenty statements that describe you? Would his list match yours? Probably not. What you wrote is what scholars call your *private self* (how you see your self in all its intimate intricacy), but what your friend wrote is your *public self* (how you come across to others).[13] As already noted, we express our self-concept differently in various symbolic communities, and, like actors on a stage, tend to portray diverse images from context to context. Moreover, we tend to process these images in less-than-rational ways. It may be of no surprise therefore to learn that "Researchers have found no correlation between confidence in our perceptions of others and the accuracy of those perceptions."[14] Robert and Vicky may have thought they knew each other as they dated, but if either was putting on a front, those impressions were but sand castles.

Research indicates that we can improve our accuracy in perceiving others by being more realistic about ourselves, by not seeing things in black and white, and by becoming better at inferring traits from behaviors.[15] This means if we are unsure about our own self-concept, we best not make outlandish claims about our friends. Chances are, we will be off target. Also, if we have grown up in a strict, authoritarian home, we are prone to think that we can peg our friends into sharply cut wholes—she's a jerk, he's cool. But as we noted in the last chapter, people are more complex than that.

Christ's call to take the log out of our own eye before we complain about the sawdust speck in someone else's (see Matthew 7:3) is more a caution not to judge than a rule for how to perceive others, but there is a principle that still holds. It is this: Acknowledging that we are complex, and not perfect, will help us exercise empathy and extend grace when trying to understand others. If we are receiver-centered and enter their frame of reference, we may understand them. Unfortunately, we often fail at empathizing with others, and therefore misunderstand them. Research testifies to perceptual biases that create interpersonal noise. Be aware of these.

Our first impressions of others go deep and die slowly.[16]   This is called the *primacy effect*, because we tend to weigh early information about others more heavily than later information. A short-term memory exercise I do with my students hints at why this might be true.   I ask my students to listen to a list of ten words.   After the tenth one I say "go." Their task is to write down as many words as they can recall in the right order.   Without fail, the most remembered word is the first one (usually 95 percent get it right), then the second word (about 90 percent) and then the tenth word (about 85 percent score a ringer). Between words two through ten there's a big dip, like a grin from left to right.   The smile is actually a smirk, because least recalled word is the seventh one. What happens, it seems, is that people rehearse or dwell on the first words more than the middle ones, so these ideas stick.   The upswing in recall at the end may explain the *recency effect*, or the tendency for us to form impressions of people based on fresh behavior while ignoring stale behavior. Both findings remind us that we are not likely to consider everything we know about someone when perceiving them in the immediate context.   No wonder we are not accurate with our general impressions much of the time.

Our first impressions guide future perceptions.   For example, once we think a person is "funny" or "sloppy" or "liberal," we look for things they do to confirm that impression, even if it means ignoring contra-dictory information.   Once again, a classroom exercise comes to mind

© 1997 Randy Glasbergen.
www.glasbergen.com

"You're more beautiful today than you were the day I met you. You had a really big pimple that day."

119

that illustrates this. On the screen I show students two words in two orders:

Side A of the class sees the word "kind" first, and "dishonest" second.

Side B of the class sees the word "dishonest" first, and "kind" second.

After exposure to each word, I ask them to form an impression of an imaginary person who has this trait. After they have seen both words and formed a melded impression, I ask them whether their image is more like Robin Hood (a good guy who does dishonest things to help the poor) or a con artist (a bad person who does kind things for dishonest gain). Each year the results indicate that the word seen first weighs more heavily in their impressions. Most of the students who saw "kind" first and "dishonest" second say their impression resembles Robin Hood; most students who saw the terms in reverse order see their person like a con artist. This gives us good reason to be careful about how we present ourselves when doing job interviews and going on first dates. It is also a reminder that, as perceivers, we should hold off on cementing first impressions of others until we see the entire load.

We are prone to pay attention to the intense, novel, and beautiful.[17] Every semester professors look out onto a sea of faces in large lecture classes knowing that they will befriend only a handful of those students. Which ones is somewhat predictable, everything else being equal: the guy wearing the purple sweater and sporting the two-tone buzz cut, and the gal with the teal Mariners cap who answers two questions the first week of school. Both students stand out against the backdrop of their less active classmates.

In conversation the same trend occurs. If your friend has a new hairdo or fidgets with her sleeve or tells you she just got accepted into medical school, you are more likely to zero in on these intense and attractive matters and forget the friend you knew yesterday. In the chapter on nonverbal communication we highlighted the benefits we extend to attractive people in particular. This is a good place to remember that we should guard against doing so at the expense of our more drab friends.

We allow negative information about others to outweigh the good.[18]   If you have ever sat on a pastoral search committee at your church, you have a good sense of this tendency.   A couple years ago I found myself sifting through eighteen resumes pregnant with information about the candidates.   But it took only a month for our committee to narrow the field to eight, and another month to whittle it down to three. How did we do it?   For good or for bad, we let negative information take its course.   When two applicants had similar strengths, but one had a stark weakness, we axed him.   Or, when a candidate had five positive traits and one negative trait, compared to someone who had three positive traits, we favored the all-positive applicant.   Were we accurate in our perceptions?   Only God knows. This reminds us that we should consider negative information about others in the most gracious light rather than jump to conclusions.   Perhaps people who report weaknesses on resumes are more honest than those who do not.

> In human relating, it is not easy to determine what we choose to do versus what others cause us to do.

We see ourselves as responding to our environment, but see others as choosing to act as they do.[19]   For example, regarding my eating lunch, I might think, "I ate lunch because I saw it was 12:30," but of your brown bagging it I might think, "You ate lunch because you chose to; you were hungry."   This is called the *actor-observer difference* in attribution-making, because as social actors we tend to see our own behavior as a response to our social environment, but, as observers of others, we see them as choosing their behavior.

Consider Vicky and Robert again.   Vicky probably explained her acting upon Robert's business deal as a response to him—"I got involved because Robert needed me."   But you can bet that Robert, who observed her behavior, attributed it to Vicky's aggressive personality.   "She butted in because she's controlling!"   Both could be right, because in human affairs it is not easy to determine what we *chose to do* or what we *were caused to do*.   As gracious perceivers, we need to balance the two and acknowledge that other people feel just as constrained by their environment as we do.

We take credit for our good behavior and blame our environment for our bad behavior, but do just the opposite for people we dislike.[20] If there were any proof that we are essentially selfish, back-side saving creatures, this is it! Consider these typical examples:

I consoled my arch rival after we won the game *because I'm a loving person.*

She consoled me after my dad died *because everyone expected her to.*

I failed to comfort her after her car accident *because I had such a hectic week.* *She* failed to comfort me after my backpack was stolen *because she doesn't care.*

The urge to blame others in conflict situations is particularly strong. What did Adam say when God asked, "Have you eaten from the tree that I commanded you not to eat from?" He said, "The woman you put here with me—she gave me some fruit from the tree, and I ate it." And what did Eve say when God asked, "What is this you have done?" She answered, "The serpent deceived me, and I ate" (see Genesis 3:1–14). They both responded with blame, blame, blame. Better that we own up to our responsibility.

Gracious Language with Others

If I had to grade Robert and Vicky's language the past ten yeas, I would give them a "C." Their public language was not bitter or calloused or attacking or explosive, but neither was it affirming, empathetic, trusting and loving. It was blah talk—lots of factual talk about other people and current events, but little inter-human sharing, as described earlier in this chapter.

The biblical record gives evidence that from our mouths come life and death for those around us. Even a short study demonstrates how "mere words" form powerful speech acts to nurture or destroy relationships.

The Power of Gracious Language
Words can bring healing   (Proverbs 12:18)
Kind words bring life   (Proverbs 15: 4)
The right words bring joy   (Proverbs 15:23)

Careful words keep one out of trouble   (Proverbs 21:23)
Apt words are beautiful   (Proverbs 25:11)
Words can bring help, encourage and comfort   (1 Corinthians 14: 3)
Helpful words build up and provide what is needed (Ephesians 4:29)
Speaking the truth in a loving manner encourages Christ-likeness   (Ephesians 4: 15)

The Power of Ungracious Language
Thoughtless words wound   (Proverbs 12:18)
Cruel words crush the spirit   (Proverbs 15:4)
Gossip separates close friends   (Proverbs 16:28)
Answering before one listens is unwise (Proverbs 18: 13)
Insulting and obscene talk are to be ridden of   (Colossians 3: 8)
Lying is bad   (1 Peter 3:10)
Slander is to be avoided   (James 4:11)

Maybe these verses underscore the obvious, but so often we treat words like computer bytes—weightless and dimensionless, therefore harmless.   Perhaps we have accepted the lie that sticks and stones may break bones, but words will never hurt us.   Recall from chapter two that John Gottman's research indicated that couples who divorce were almost certain to pepper their interaction with criticism, defensive-ness, contempt, and stonewalling.   This negative talk occurred once for every five positive statements, or a 1-to-5 ratio.   Couples who did not divorce tended toward a 1-to-6 negative-to-positive ratio, or even better.[21]

Insults and criticism at least recognize that the other person exists. But ignoring a friend entirely or denying her perceptions might be even more damaging.   Consider the times when we have

. . . chosen not to return a text message

. . . avoided saying "hi" to someone

. . . said "don't be silly—you don't really feel that way."

. . . changed a topic abruptly with no regard for what a friend just said

Not texting and not greeting others implies that they do not exist, or, at least, that they are not important. Labeling their feelings as silly or wrong suggests that they are oblivious to their own emotions! Abrupt topic switching implies that our agenda is more important than theirs. All are cases of *disconfirming messages*—messages that do not recognize nor affirm others, nor invite deep covenantal relating. *Confirming messages*, in contrast, are words and behaviors that 1) acknowledge our friend and our relationship, 2) show a relevant response to what she said, 3) affirm our friend's experience, and 4) indicate a willingness to become involved with her.[22] Confirming messages indicate that we are more concerned about the other person than ourselves, and that we are open to covenantal communion. Confirming messages affirm the redemptive role interpersonal communication performs as it creates and transforms relationship. Our talk transforms us.

Gracious Fighting with Others

Gracious language yields gracious conflict management. I am convinced that if Robert and Vicky had listened better, their marriage might have survived. Or, if Robert had spoken his mind instead of shoving resentments down deep, they would have had more to go on. Or if Vicky had not bulldozed Robert under a mountain of monologue, he would not have felt resentment in the first place.

While each of these statements is true, they tend to glorify improved communication as the saving grace in relationships. For years I believed this, but now I am less sure. Recently I have adopted a more biblical view that handling conflict doesn't begin with improved skills, but a renewed soul. Consider what Paul wrote to the believers at Colossus:

> "Clothe yourselves [rather] with compassion, kindness, humility, gentleness and patience. Bear with each other and forgive whatever grievances you may have against one another. Forgive as the Lord forgave you. And over all these virtues put on love, which binds them all together in perfect unity" (Colossians 3:12–14).

Paul mentions only one skill—forgiving grievances—as he makes the larger point that we should clothe ourselves in Christian virtue.

Similarly, in *Beyond the Myth of Marital Happiness: How Embracing the Virtues of Loyalty, Generosity, Justice, and Courage Can Strengthen*

Your Relationship, Blaine Fowers argues that great communication stems from a good heart, and that focusing on skill development, while helpful, misses the mark. From his own experience in handling conflict with his wife Susan, he writes, "We would work and work and work until we had either ironed it out completely or completely exhausted ourselves. We would often be up half the night—communicating."[23] He goes on to note their covenantal resolve: "We do use communication skills to help, on occasion; but what keeps us going is our joint commitment to ideals and goals that guide us in knowing how we want to live together."[24]

This vision of relating inspired me to carry out my own study. In it I asked seventy couples to indicate their impressions of their spouses as virtuous or not. In particular, I asked them to assess the degree they thought their spouse was self-controlled, wise, faithful, industrious, and humble. They also rated the quality of their marriage on a global measure of relational and communicative health. Perhaps not surprising, the more husbands and wives saw each other as virtuous, the more they thought their marriage was of high quality.[25]

These are simple observations, but ones worth making. Compassionate people rarely treat others as objects. Kind friends rarely use words that wound. Humble individuals rarely judge others. Gentle folks rarely cuss a blue streak. Faithful people usually follow through on promises. Being a godly person may be half the battle in managing our wars with each other. That said, we must still consider the redemptive strategies that spill from a good heart to manage conflict. Consider these biblically informed pointers.[26]

Keep Your Cool and Consider Taking a Time Out. Quick tempers can get us into a lot of trouble. The proverbs remind us that quick-tempered people act foolishly (14:7) and stir up strife (14:18). Righteous people, instead, think before they answer (15:28), and step away from quarreling in the heat of the moment (17:14). As long as that stepping away does not lead to avoidance of the issue, the idea of a cool-off period for reflection makes a lot of sense.

When you are apart, consider doing more than stewing. Two family therapists recommend that you take this time to write a letter to your friend or spouse noting your feelings, how you may have responded differently, and what you want from him or her. Married couples who use this technique seem to improve their problem-solving skills, and increase marital satisfaction.[27] Even if you don't write a letter, time apart will cool emotions and help you think through the issues so you can discuss them calmly together.

Keep Short Accounts. Robert's 31-year grudge is a sober reminder to not let the sun go down on our anger (Ephesians 4:26). If we nip it in the bud, an issue will never have time to blossom. Some couples and friends make the redemptive pact to not let a day end without addressing an issue. We can all benefit from that strategy. It may mean making a phone call late at night, or getting together for coffee at a 24-hour joint, but when each party's account has been credited with timely discussion, there is little fear of a major blow-up later.

Act Wisely, Not Foolishly. Acting wisely means discerning the best thing to say in the heat of conflict which will benefit you and your friend. In covenantal perspective, this requires steadfast love while acknowledging that you still live by important guidelines. Research indicates that wise people focus on the problem, not their partner, and appear to use more strategies for solving problems than the less wise.[28] They don't get stuck in the rut of blaming each other, or believing there's only one solution to a problem. Wise people distinguish between insignificant issues that don't matter, and the big-rock ones that do.[29] Discerning the difference saves mental and emotional energy for problems that really count. Wisdom requires brains, heart, and that elusive thing we call judgment. Brains alone will not cut it, for heady analysis may just puff up (1 Corinthians 8:1). Wise communication meets everyone's needs.

Make Understanding and Reconciliation Your Aim. If you are at all competitive, you will have the urge to win an argument rather than understand your partner and reconcile. Men in particular have this urge to conquer rather than connect.[30] As long as men are in control, they feel they are managing conflict just dandy. This posture may succeed in fixing the problem, but sacrifice mutuality. Mutuality means both parties voicing their concerns and being understood. Solomon put it bluntly, "A fool does not delight in understanding, but only in revealing his own mind" (Proverbs 18:2). Understanding begins with listening, which we pick up in the next section.

Once we understand each other—empathize with what hurts, who hurts, or why it hurts—we can better work toward reconciliation. Reconciliation means settling our dispute, reestablishing communion, and coming to an agreement. Reconciliation between you and me mirrors God's new covenant with the world. Consider Paul's letter to the Corinthian church:

> Therefore, if anyone is in Christ, he is a new creation; the old has gone, the new has come! All this is from God, who reconciled us to himself through Christ and gave us the ministry of reconciliation: that God was reconciling the world to himself in Christ, not counting men's sins against them. And he has committed to us the message of reconciliation. (2 Corinthians 5:17–19)

David Augsburger might say becoming reconciled requires carefronting—caring for others in love, yet confronting them with the issues that bug you or disturb you.[31] To confront without care may lead to domination, or the abuse of power. To care without confrontation may turn us into weak-kneed pacifists who cave to our partner's needs, or avoiders who withdraw to keep the peace. Neither reconciles the relationship. Reconciliation requires equal parties negotiating their needs in a spirit of love so legitimate human needs can be met. Reconciliation requires courage.

Reconciliation may also require extending and receiving forgiveness. Recall from Chapter 5 that egotists find this difficult. Humble people less so. To forgive someone means to grant a pardon for the hurt they caused, and to release resentment or anger against them. Forgiveness, like Jesus' death, pays the debt of the other person's sin. A woman who forgave her alcoholic and mentally ill father for sexually abusing her wrote:

Forgiveness is agreeing to live with the consequences of another person's sin. ... You're going to live with those consequences whether you want to or not; your only choice is whether you will do so in the bitterness of unforgiveness or the freedom of forgiveness. ... All true forgiveness is substitutionary, because no one really forgives without bearing the penalty of the other person's sin.[32]

Gracious Listening with Each Other

Working toward reconciliation requires an open-ears attitude. Like the charades metaphor implies, listening entails openness and alertness to what friends say and how they say it. Did you know that remembering something a friend mentioned in a conversation—even a pleasant one—is more difficult than remembering a point made by a public lecturer?[33] The reason is that during a lecture our roles are well defined, as speaker and listeners, but in transactional encounters we are speaker *and* listener. We are often thinking about what we want to say next, and this garbles incoming messages.

The ideal is to be an *active* listener. *Active interpersonal listening* engages our head and heart to hear, attune, understand, and respond to others' ideas and feelings. It is mindful, effortful, and receiver-focused. Active listening takes humility, because it assumes we turn our full attention to someone else in order to follow their train of thought and emotional spirit. Because active listening takes so much effort, I suggest that our entire relational attitude toward others can be summed up by our willingness to listen deeply with them.

> Our entire relational attitude can be summed up by our willingness to truly listen to others.

This definition of listening begins with *hearing* the other person. Hearing is the physical registering of someone's voice. Listening also entails *seeing* the other person so we might interpret their nonverbal cues. Offering "two-eye" attention improves reception.

Active listening requires us to *attune* to what is most relevant. We encounter millions of sounds and sights a day, but tune in to a mere fraction. As you read these words you are likely blocking out the whir of a laptop or music on your iPod. By choice you are attending to these words, and blocking out noises. We attune to friends by dropping what we are reading, giving them eye contact, turning our bodies toward them, and leaning forward. These behaviors tell them we are ready to listen. Do you do so?

Hearing and attuning are important, but, as already noted, we need to *understand* people's intended meaning. Is it possible to hear and attune but still not understand? I think so, especially when people speak vaguely or with poor syntax. Consider Megan, who says, "I'm feeling like ya' know, like I could do it if I had to, but so many things can, well . . . it's hard to say, ya' know . . . it's not easy." What does she mean? Abstract words such as "it" and "things" and her halting delivery make us strain to eke out understanding. Sometimes the context and topic do not even help. Here is where *responding* with questions and nonverbal affirmations plays in. Asking "What do you mean by 'it' Megan?" or "What kinds of 'things' make it difficult?" may keep you and Megan on the course to understanding. Furthermore, your quizzical look and thoughtful pause after you pose your questions will tell her that you await clarification. When we ask timely, thoughtful questions, or paraphrase our friend's ideas, we indicate that we are processing her message mindfully.

Hearing, attuning, understanding and responding are key, but the litmus test of true listening is *remembering* what was said.[34] One study indicated that men have a harder time remembering conversations they have had in the last six months compared to women. When asked if they had discussed household chores with their wives, only 19 percent of men responded affirmatively, while 71 percent of the wives did so. When asked if they had talked about having more children, men answered yes 15 percent of the time compared to 91 percent for women. I admit that I fit this pattern. Once a month or so I will ask Shelaine about an issue or event, and she will graciously comment that we have already discussed it.

. . . .

We are our own worst enemies when it comes to listening. The following examples crystallize how we should *not* listen if we want to engage in redemptive dialogue. Suppose a friend sat down with you and remarked, "I can't believe it! My sister is getting married and she isn't including me in the wedding party! Maybe I should just volunteer to park cars!" Consider how six poor listeners might respond.

> *The Pseudo (Fake) Listener*: "Uh huh. Yeh, marriage . . . it can be quite a party or a lot like parking cars." (The pseudo-listener is clueless to the intended meaning but has obviously heard something.)

The Selective Listener: "I didn't know your sister was getting married! Who's the lucky guy?" (The selective listener picks out only a portion of the meaning rather than the larger picture.)

The Monopolizer: "Ah, sister behavior!! Sisters can be so wrapped up in their own worlds sometimes. My own sister, Louise, once said that . . ." (The monopolizer takes over the conversation rather than allow the speaker to finish or expand on ideas or feelings.)

The Fixer: "You know what you should do? You *should* volunteer to park cars and she will feel so ashamed I'm sure she'll ask you to be in her wedding party. She'll figure out what's right, and you'll get what you want!" (The fixer seems to understand the speaker, but intends to fix the problem, not simply hear out the issue and emotions.)

The Ambusher: "I was just waiting for you to criticize your sister's wedding plans, and there, you've done it! Well I'll have you know that your life plans have not always pleased your friends and relatives either!" (The ambusher looks for opportunity to criticize the speaker, rather than support the speaker.)

The Defensive Listener: "So are you implying that I had something to do with it? I may know your sister, but please don't blame me!" (The defensive listener interprets descriptions as personal evaluations, rather than taking them at face value.)

These examples might make us chuckle, but, sadly, they represent how we often respond to others. James, the brother of Jesus, encouraged believers to be "quick to listen, slow to speak, and slow to become angry" (James 1:19). If we live out that second challenge—to be slow to speak—we will probably have time, and heart, to listen actively.

Summary

In this chapter we likened interpersonal communication to bowling, Ping-Pong, and charades. "Bowlers" picture communication as a one-way process largely dependent on hurling messages at passive recipients. "Ping-Pong players" acknowledge that receivers provide feedback, but still assume a predictable process of give and take until meanings are scored. "Charade players" view communication as a transaction whereby responsible symbolic exchange enacts relationships and changes participants through inter-human dialogue.

Redeeming our dialogue means guarding against nasty perceptual biases. We should guard against letting early, recent, novel, and negative information overshadow other things we know about them. We also need to guard against rationalizing that our behavior is driven by our environment, but others are driven by their choice; both are likely at work.

Redemptive dialogue also means that we engage words that edify or confirm, not tear down or disconfirm. It means seeking understanding, not winning, as we experience conflict, and dealing with issues sooner, not later. Finally, I suggested that our entire relational stance with friends is measured by our willingness to listen to them with an empathetic heart. Listening takes mental effort and requires an appropriate response. Active listening requires that we reflect back to the speaker what we hear him or her saying rather than charge off on our own agenda.

Many of our closest and most trying relationships occur with relatives. We turn to the family context in the next chapter to see how redemptive communication often does *not* happen.

 **WORTH THE TALK**

1. Do you agree or disagree with the four aspects of being human that Stewart and Buber suggest we should heighten in interpersonal communication? Those aspects include that we are unique, unmeasurable, choice-makers, and addressable. What features would you remove? Add? Why?

2. With whom do you enjoy a deep, soul-to-soul relationship where your interaction is typified by the transactional model? With whom do you interact more mechanically (Ping-Pong) or one-way (bowling)?

3. The underlying world view of the transactional model is communitarianism, or the basic belief that we define ourselves through our interaction with others. What is the truth value of this perspective? What cautions would you have about this perspective?

4. Which of the perceptual biases noted in this chapter plague college students most? What strategies would you suggest to guard against them?

5. Where on your campus do confirming messages occur? Disconfirming? Do you think bullying is an issue on your campus?

6. This chapter suggests that virtues such as humility and compassion help us manage conflict. Other people say we need to learn conflict-resolution skills and theories. What do you think?

7. What do you think are the top three barriers to active listening? How can we minimize them?

CONSIDER THE WALK

1. Keep a journal of your interpersonal communication with another person (e.g., roommate, friend, or parent). Choose someone you see regularly or someone with whom you think you have poor communication. Use ideas in this chapter for your reflections.

Ask: to what degree do you affirm each others' humanness? To what degree do you treat others like objects?
b. how do you perceive this person? Are any biases at work?
c. what kind of language typifies your talk?
d. how do you manage conflict? Do you fight fairly?
e. what is the quality of listening in your relationship?

2. Write a paper that reports and analyzes your findings from the journal noted in number one. Or, if you have not written a journal, use the same questions listed there to analyze your communication with one person or with people generally. The paper could accomplish two goals. One is to describe your communication habits with others (both the good and the bad). The second is to prescribe goals for your self for more redemptive relating.

3. Watch your favorite soap opera or prime-time drama and analyze the interpersonal communication between characters. Use the criteria noted in number 1. You will have to speculate about some of the dynamics.

4. Interview a person whose work is largely interpersonal communication (e. g., a student affairs staff, a counselor, a salesperson, a pastor), and ask what role interpersonal communication plays in that person's work. Write up your findings and share them in class with your classmates.

ONLINE CHALK

This chapter covers a wide spectrum of the interpersonal communication field. The following Internet search phrases attract academic and practical web sites concerning the themes addressed.

- Transactional model of communication
- Interpersonal perception and communication
- Language and social interaction
- How to deal with interpersonal conflict
- Good listening skills
- How to be a good listener
- Barriers to interpersonal communication

ENDNOTES

1 Larry Crabb, *Connecting: Healing for Ourselves and Our Relationships, A Radical New Vision* (Nashville: Word, 1997), 53.

2 These metaphors for interpersonal communication come from E. Griffin, *Making Friends (and Making Them Count)* (Downers Grove, IL: InterVarsity Press, 1987), chapter 1.

3 Works that typify the linear view include Harold Lasswell, "The Structure and Function of Communication in Society," in *The Communication of Ideas*, ed. Lyman Bryson (New York: Institute for Religious and Social Studies, 1948), 37-51, and Claude Shannon and Warren Weaver, *The Mathematical Theory of Communication* (Urbana: University of Illinois, 1949).

4 For a good overview of the interactive model, see David Berlo, *The Process of Communication* (New York: Holt, Rinehart, and Winston, 1960).

5 See Dean Barnlund, "A Transactional Model of Communication," in *Foundations of Communication Theory*, ed. Kenneth Sereno and David Mortensen (New York: Harper & Row, 1970).

6 E. Griffin, *Making Friends*, 16.

7 B. Aubrey Fisher and Katherine L. Adams, *Interpersonal Communication: Pragmatics of Human Relationships*, 2nd ed. (New York: McGraw-Hill, 1994), 18.

8 John Stewart, "Interpersonal Communication: Contact Between Persons" in *Bridges, Not Walls*, 5th ed. (New York: McGraw-Hill, 1990), 13.

9 See Martin Buber, *The Knowledge of Man*, ed. Maurice Friedman, trans. Maurice Friedman and Ronald Gregor Smith (n.p.: Balkin Agency, 1965). The excerpt titled, "Elements of the Interhuman" may be found in John Stewart, *Bridges*, 450-460.

10 Ibid., 18.

11 Ibid., (italics added).

12 Fisher and Adams, *Interpersonal Communication,* 30.

13 For a full treatment of this idea see Erving Goffman, *The Presentation of Self in Everyday Life* (Garden City, NY: Doubleday, 1959).

14 Stewart L. Tubbs and Sylvia Moss, *Human Communication,* 7th ed. (New York: McGraw-Hill, 1994), 57.

15 In addition to these factors, research indicates that people with higher intelligence are more accurate people perceivers. See ibid., 57.

16 D. E. Hamachek, *Encounters With Others: Interpersonal Relationships and You* (Fort Worth: Holt, Rinehart and Winston, 1982), 23-40, as cited in Ronald B. Adler and Neil Towne, *Looking Out/Looking In,* 6th ed. (Fort Worth: Holt, Rinehart and Winston, 1990), 98.

17 See Adler and Towne, ibid., 98.

18 See ibid., 99.

19 Cited in Fisher and Adams, *Interpersonal Communication,* 78, from E. Jones and R. Nisbett, *The Actor and the Observer* (Morristown, NJ: General Learning, 1971).

20 T. Pettigrew, "Three Issues in Ethnicity," in *Major Social Issues,* ed. J. Yinger and S. Cutler (New York: Free Press, 1978), as cited by William B. Gudykunst and Young Yun Kim, *Communicating With Strangers* (New York: Random House, 1984), 91.

21 For a description of this study and others like it see John Gottman and Nan Silver, *Why Marriages Succeed or Fail—and How You Can Make Yours Last* (New York: Simon & Schuster, 1995).

22 These criteria are from Evelyn Sieburg, "Interpersonal Confirmation: A Paradigm for Conceptualization and Measurement" (paper presented at the International Communication Association, Montreal, Quebec, 1973), as quoted in Kathleen Galvin and Bernard Brommel, *Family Communication: Cohesion and Change* (Glenview, IL: Scott, Foresman, 1982), 88.

23 Blaine Fowers, *Beyond the Myth of Marital Happiness: How Embracing the Virtues of Loyalty, Generosity, Justice, and Courage Can Strengthen Your Relationship* (San Francisco: Jossey-Bass, 2000), 83.

24 Ibid.

25 Specifically, the Pearson rho correlation coefficient for wives was .53, and for husbands .47 on a 0 – 1 scale. For full details see Bill Strom, "Communicator Virtue and Its Relationship to Marriage Quality," *Journal of Family Communication,* 3 (2003): 21-39.

26 Some of these ideas are based on Jack Mayhall and Carole Mayhall, *Marriage Takes More Than Love* (Colorado Springs, CO: NavPress, 1978), 83-85.

27 A. Lange, C. van der Wall and P. Emmelkamp "Time-out and Writing in Distressed Couples: An Experimental Trial into the Effects of a Short Treatment," *Journal of Family Therapy* 22 (2000): 294-407.

28 Two helpful sources on problem-solving in marriage include G. Margolin and B. Wampold, "Sequential Analysis of Conflict and Accord in Distressed and Nondistressed Marital Partners," *Journal of Consulting and Clinical Psychology* 49 (1981): 554-567, and S. Ting-Toomey, "An Analysis of Verbal Communication

Patterns in High and Low Marital Adjustment Groups," *Human Communication Research* 9 (1983): 306-319.

29 A good source on more than just problem solving is J. Wallerstein and S. Blakeslee, *The Good Marriage* (Boston: Houghton Mifflin, 1995).

30 See Deborah Tannen, *You Just Don't Understand Me!* (New York: William Morrow, 1990), especially the section "Put That Paper Down and Talk to Me!" 74-95.

31 David Augsburger, *The Love Fight* (Scottdale, PA: Herald Press, 1973), 3.

32 Alice Morgan's story is told in Neil T. Anderson, *Living Free in Christ* (Ventura, CA: Regal Books, 1993), 294.

33 See Steven Beebe, Susan Beebe, Mark Redmond and Carol Milstone, *Interpersonal Communication: Relating to Others* (Scarborough, Ontario: Allyn and Bacon, 1997), 103.

34 Ibid.

All families [peoples, nations] on earth will
be blessed through you.

Genesis 12:3
God's words to Abraham

Family Communication
Potential for the Best (& Worst)
Covenantal Relating

THE JOKE IS told of a forty-year-old man who wondered all his life why he didn't look like his younger brother or sister. He finally got the courage to ask his mother if he was adopted. "Yes, you were, son," his mother replied as she started to cry softly. "But it didn't work out, and they brought you back."

We might shrug this off as improbable in real life. However, recently two independent cases of parents posting ads on the web to sell their infant children shocked the world. A couple in Vancouver, British Columbia posted the following ad on Craiglist, an online classified advertising service:

> "Must have!!!! $10,000, a new baby girl, healthy and very cute. Can't afford and unexpected, Looking for a good home, Please call ASAP." [A cell phone number was included.]

The same month a German couple posted notice for their eight-month-old son on eBay for reason that he cried too much. The opening bid was for one Euro, or about $1.50 USD. In both cases the parents of the children were in their early twenties, and, when approached by police, declared their ads were hoaxes.[1]

Whether or not the parents were "just joking" may never be determined. If these ads actually were a hoax, they leave us wondering

"Why"? Why show a cavalier attitude toward one's child? And, if we were to learn that these couples genuinely intended to sell their children, we might well react with feelings of anger. We expect parents to welcome their children into the world and nurture them to adulthood. We assume covenantal commitment. These two stories, conceivably, signal symbolic abandonment.

While your family may be the image of love and functionality, the fact is, for many people, family spells struggle. With this in mind, the current chapter considers the dark side of family communication, in addition to its joys. I trust that this consideration will enable you to see that family interaction is pregnant with potential for redemption and damage, hope and hell. A political leader once said that if he could mold a child from infancy to age five, he would have that child for life. He was right. Family communication shapes our identity, our communicative skills, and our outlook on life.[2] It holds promise for the best, and worst, of close relating.

Defining Family Communication in Theoretical Perspective

Defining *family* has become increasingly complex. Simple definitions tend to cast families as two parents with 2.4 children living in the suburbs. This is the *nuclear family*, the combination of parents and their birth offspring. Some cultures, however, affirm *extended families* with uncles, aunts, grandparents, and cousins as much of a "family" as mom, dad, and siblings. Jewish people embrace this definition even today. Moreover, today we find *single-parent families* and *blended families* increasing in number. In *Understanding Family Communication*, three communication scholars define family broadly enough to capture its sociological diversity.

> A family is a *multigenerational* social *system* consisting of at
> least two *interdependent* people bound together by a com-
> mon living *space* (at one time or another) and a common
> *history*, and who share some degree of emotional *attach-
> ment to or involvement with* one another.[3] (their italics)

What do these features mean? Families are multigenerational in that they consist of older and younger people, usually parents and children, with the elder taking responsibility for developing the younger to adulthood. Together they form an integrated system with its own rules for interaction that yield emotional and communicative stability, and the means to change when challenges arise from outside, or inside, the group. They are interdependent in that each person—from grandma to infant—influences each other, and colors family culture. Family members usually share the same living area, a home, as well as psychological space, in mind and spirit, in order to meet personal and practical needs. Families interact over days, months, years, even centuries as they create, and recreate a family history through events, storytelling, and a life together. Through it all, families meet our deep need to connect, find purpose, and experience love. Even siblings who fight constantly share an emotional attachment that friends may never achieve.

Defining family *communication* is challenging as well. Scholars appreciate its complexity through three theoretical perspectives.[4] First, *social construction* theorists affirm the theme that we generate meaning and our social reality through symbolic interaction. In families we create, and then take for granted, many of our beliefs, values, and moral vision. Social constructionists parallel our covenantal approach which assumes that through communication we come together, and change—through family pacts, traditions, and history. The social constructionist approach accounts for the communication of the abusive husband referred to in Chapter 5. He genuinely believed that abusive behavior was normal—a practice modeled to him by his father and uncles.

Dialectical theorists emphasize a different theme. They see family communication as an expression of the polarities, paradoxes, and contradictions that families encounter. For example, a child's whining may indicate a need for more attention from dad, but dad's avoidance may indicate his need for space. This is an example of the connectedness—separateness tension we all negotiate. Some days we're happy with bumping elbows with family, but other times we crave isolation. Dialectical theorists view these tensions as neither good nor bad, but as the primary drivers of family interaction.

Finally, *systems* theorists believe that family interaction is best understood as a complex social organization consisting of people, rules for interaction, and the resulting relational mix. Any one member's communication is best understood in its relation to the whole family network. No one behaves individually; everyone contributes to a whole that is greater than its parts. In *A First Look at Communication Theory*, Em Griffin provides a vivid analogy of the family-as-system:

Picture a family as a mobile suspended from the ceiling. Each figure is connected to the rest of the structure by a strong thread tied at exactly the right place to keep the system in balance. Tug on any string, and the force sends shock throughout the whole network. Sever a thread, and the entire design tilts in disequilibrium. The threads in the mobile analogy represent communication rules that hold the family together.[5]

If family members play by the same rules, the system is said to be *homeostatic*, that is, in balance. Even if those rules do not encourage personal growth or moral discipleship, the system is still said to rotate in harmony. However, unless ugly rules are acknowledged, and recast anew, a system hums along in *deadly balance* as its structure slowly destroys the people in it. Some call this pattern *dysfunctional*, for it does not allow members to meet each others' need for love, acceptance, and control. Dysfunctional communication is cancer for true covenantal relating.

Covenantal Family Communication

Family interaction, more than any other communication context, reflects the way we come together to agree on how to do life in order to change for the better. This, in western culture, may be due to Judeo-Christian roots. As family researcher Annette Mahoney writes...

Within Judaism, for example, the relationships among family members are likened to the covenant between God and the people of Israel. Individuals are expected to show each other the commitment, trust, forgiveness, and love that they show to God and that God has shown to them. Within Christianity, relationship among family members are similarly covenantal, with bonds among family members compared to those between Christ and the Church.[6]

Family law expert Margaret Brinig, expands on these insights by noting that covenant "refers to the solemn vows that create and characterize the family," and covenants "derive most of their power from the family members' mutual commitment to one another to the preservation and protection of the family itself."[7]

Brinig also refers to the "parental covenant," with its lopsided nature, that mothers and fathers enter into when they have children. It is one-sided because parents do not seek a "fair" relationship with their kids. Rather than balancing costs and rewards, they give far beyond what is equal. She observes that a *parental covenant* is similar to God's love for us. "The biblical parallel to family covenants is God's generosity even when what we are given—or what we accomplish in return—may not be equal."[8] She continues: "Covenant… describes a relationship characterized by a special kind of love: one that is boundless and unearned. The person in a covenant relationship expects, with justification, that it will go on forever. The emphasis is on giving, not receiving; on enjoying the gifts given to others rather than reveling in the gifts one receives from them. Covenant, then, describes altruism in the framework of relationship."[9]

This may be your experience. Perhaps your parents have given tons. They have invested sleepless nights, emergency hospital visits, orthodontics, summer camp fees, thirty-year mortgages, beater cars, long walks, strained talks, and university tuition with few expectations from you except returned love. When we come from functional homes, it is easy to take these investments for granted.

However, this is not everyone's experience. Some families suffer from mild to chronic dysfunction where parents don't give and give, but take and take. Needy parents can foster needy children. Broken parents—people who experience woundedness from their own birth family—may limp along for years nursing their own hurts while attempting to cope by interacting with their kids in less than healthy ways. Our hearts should go out to them, for whether they intend to or not, they tear others down.[10]

Dysfunctional Communication: Tearing Others Down

Broadly speaking, dysfunctional communication is the use of words or actions that fail to edify others physically, socially, intellectually, and spiritually. Dysfunctional talk and behavior hammers people's spirits, constrains their options, subverts their intelligence, and rattles their emotions. To use the mobile analogy again, dysfunctional communication is a sign of less-than-redemptive "threads" or rules at work. Those rules, while rarely articulated, govern the twirl and twist of the entire family structure.

Scholars call these threads *regulative rules* because they guide what the family considers appropriate behavior. Unhealthy families often have a long list of rules for keeping their system in balance—rules that may seem odd to other families but which make sense to unhealthy families in light of their history. Consider the following rules, and how they are expressed in dysfunctional families.

Sometimes parents lay down these types of regulative rules explicitly, for example, "I don't want to catch you two talking about sex again!"

DYSFUNCTIONAL COMMUNICATION RULE	RESULTING COMMUNICATION
1. Yelling is acceptable. It shows you care.	A lot of yelling, in earnest.
2. Withdrawal is acceptable. It shows you know how to submit and admit that you are wrong	Concessions (e.g., "You're right, I'm wrong), and subsequent silence.
3. Critical joking is acceptable. It shows that you do not take yourself or others too seriously	Jabs, ridicule, sexist jokes, ethnic jokes, statements that the perpetrator is "just joking."
4. Children should be seen, not heard. To speak only when one is asked is a mark of good training	Silent children who may use disruptive behavior to gain attention.
5. Do not air personal problems nor expect an empathic ear. Strong people work out emotional issues on their own.	Talk that denies emotions ("You don't really feel that way"); children who turn to peers for support; a sense of not being loved.
6. Avoid talk about sex. Sex is a natural thing that happens wonderfully when you get married, and until then needs no discussion.	Confused children, especially during the hormonal years; children who meet their curiosity about sex by talking with friends or turning to media sources.

Other times, rules emerge through patterns, and family members pick up these patterns by osmosis. I recall how little my birth family talked about the matter when a girl at our church got pregnant. Her parents shuffled her away to have the baby in another town, and all we heard was that she was having a baby and giving it up for adoption. My parents did not discuss how Tina's boyfriend was equally responsible, nor what we might learn from this situation. Therefore, despite my belief that God made me a sexual creature and gave me the gift of sex, the lesson I learned from Tina's case was that sex was best left not discussed at home.

Disconfirming Messages: Signs of a Jilted Family Mobile

The silence rule my parents applied to sex is one example of disconfirming communication, not confirming communication. "Social scientists use the term *confirming communication* to describe messages that convey valuing, and *disconfirming messages* to define those that show a lack of regard."[12] A gag order on sex ignores a person's sexuality, and indirectly shows a lack of regard for this part of one's being. Any message that conveys a lack of regard is antithetical to covenantal communication. Disconfirming communication comes in several ugly shades.[13]

Verbal Abuse: communication that is meant to cause psychological pain. The verbal abuser may attack another person's competence ("You are an idiot"), role ("So all you do is run a cash register?"), perceptions ("You're wrong to feel that way"), sex ("Stupid blonde!"), body type ("Come here, fatso"), or race ("He's a honky [nigger, dago]"). The messages sent are "You are worthless" and "I am more powerful than you."

Complaining: communication that persistently finds fault with someone's behavior. We can so easily find fault with dad's cooking, sis' hogging the computer, or mom's gift to us. Even when a complainer justifies his or her complaining with a righteous motive ("I nag about your dirty room because I want you to be responsible"), the receiver can interpret the tone of the complaint as meaning "you can do little right."

Impervious Responses: communication that ignores the other person. The impervious responder gives the "silent treatment" or turns a "cold shoulder," whether in brief conversations or over a span of weeks or months. The dominant message received is "you don't exist."

Interrupting: communication that breaks into someone else's floor space. Verbal interruption is equivalent to stepping in front of someone on a sidewalk. Interrupters may be forgiven on first occasion, but repeated interrupting sends the message that the interrupter's agenda is more important than the listener's.

Irrelevant Responses: communication that is oblivious to what the other person just said. It may indicate that the speaker is simply daydreaming. But when used intentionally, irrelevant messages tell the listener "Your message wasn't worth attending to" or, again, "my agenda is more important."

Tangential Responses: communication that takes the speaker's comments in part, but shifts the topic down the responder's bunny trail. Suppose Glenda says, "We need to talk about whether we'll ski or not this weekend." If Brent answers "Yeh, speaking of skiing, you should see the snowboard I just bought," he has in effect disconfirmed Glenda's suggestion.

Impersonal Responses: communication that responds in the abstract or with clichés. Suppose a daughter, Susan, says, "Dad, I really need to talk about how I feel about your divorcing mom." If dad responds, "Glad to hear it. We all need to talk things out. Psychologists say talk purges the soul," he has, in effect, turned Susan's comment into a statistic about everyone. If he followed up with a statement such as, "So what do you think? I'm ready to listen," he is back on track.

Ambiguous Responses: communication that can be taken more than one way, leaving the receiver unsure of what is meant. In Chapter 3 we called this *equivocal language*. Suppose you say to your professor "Could I come by tomorrow to talk about my grade?" Your prof might respond with an ambiguous (but oddly welcoming) statement such as, "Uh, maybe so. Grades are important, and you have a right to ask about yours. Tomorrow's not too full." Does this mean "yes" or only "we'll see"? If it means "we'll see," you still do not know if the professor plans to contact you later about a time to meet.

Incongruous Responses: communication that contains two contradictory messages, one usually verbal, the other nonverbal. Suppose someone like Glenda asks her husband "Honey, do you love me?" only to receive an angry "Of course I do!" We know she will only pay attention to the tone of voice..

Disconfirming messages are insidious because they inflict personal pain. Researcher Anita Vangelisti examined *hurtful messages* from

"He's my new boyfriend. I know he's cold and unemotional, but on the other hand, he never criticizes me, he doesn't complain about my friends, and if things don't work out, he'll be gone in the Spring!"

family members and outsiders and their effect on our psyche. She found that attacks from family members registered just as hurtful as criticisms from non-family members.[14] Just because we are family does not lessen the pain. Vangelisti also found that hurtful messages create a distancing effect between recipient and attacker. Interestingly though, she found that we lose less social intimacy when family members hurt us than when outsiders do. Maybe this finding indicates that "blood is thicker than water" (i.e., family bonds are stronger than friendship ones), but the results are still disturbing. Like a dance with a beloved porcupine, we keep closely in step with parents and siblings, even when being bloodied by prickly barbs. Some family members, especially women and children, know no other family life but an intimately abusive one.

Verbal Abuse: A Closer Look

We have said that verbal abuse is communication intended to cause psychological pain. A synonym for verbal abuse is *verbal aggression*—talk that damages someone else's self-worth and self-concept.[15] Have you ever heard statements such as these?

> "Will you PLEASE explain WHY you can't do ANYthing RIGHT?"

"I suppose you think you're SMART, DON'T you? YOU think you did pretty WELL! RIGHT? Well, let me tell YOU..."

"GOODness! THAT outfit almost makes you look THIN!"[16]

Victims of such statements often receive them from other family members. If you read them aloud and emphasize the ALL CAPS words, you can tell that they drip with sarcasm. How widespread is verbal abuse, and what does it look like?

In a study of 6,000 families, about 75 percent of husbands and wives indicated that they were the targets of verbal abuse in the previous year.[17] While seventy-five percent seems high, keep in mind that it represents an entire year of a couple's interaction. What must be understood as well is that verbal abuse is not just tongue lashings and yelling profanities. It also includes subtle diminishing, cool indifference, one-upmanship, witty sarcasm, silent withholding, manipulative coercion, and unreasonable demands.[18] Patricia Evans, author of *The Verbally Abusive Relationship*, compares the values of verbal attackers with those who wish to nurture. These values may help you determine if you or someone you know lives with a verbally abusive family member.[19]

ABUSIVE RELATIONSHIPS EXHIBIT	HEALTHY RELATIONSHIPS EXHIBIT
Inequality	Equality
Competition	Partnership
Manipulation	Mutuality
Hostility	Goodwill
Control	Intimacy
Negation	Validation

For whatever reason, abusers have a strong need for being "one-up." They need to feel that they are the superior partner (inequality), the winner (competition), and the relational oarsman (control). To acquire these positions, the abuser twists words and perceptions (manipulation), gets angry easily (hostility), and refuses to acknowledge their victim's feelings, perceptions, values, and accomplishments (negation). A victim is especially thrown off center when the abuser's words are accompanied by seemingly loving and sensitive tones of voice. The result is what some authors call crazy-making—the sense of being confused, lost, off balance, and generally bugged by double messages.[20]

Power Is Key. Patricia Evans uses the concept of power to explain these dynamics. She writes, "There are two kinds of power. One kills the spirit. The other nourishes the spirit. The first is Power Over. The other is Personal Power. Power Over shows up as control and dominance. Personal Power shows up as mutuality and co-creation."[21] Verbal abusers relish Power Over. They feel that the family exists to meet their needs and they demand respect by virtue of their status. In contrast, family members who exhibit Personal Power thrive on mutual trust and assume good will. They value legitimate authority, but do not abandon their need to earn respect. A fair renaming of personal power could be *covenantal power*, because the intention of each is to mutually edify for the common good.

Dividing power into two types may be a bit simplistic. But what Evans is onto, and what others confirm, is that power is a telling feature of the family relational matrix. However power does not belong to a person; power is *a property of relationship* among group members. To use Griffin's mobile analogy again, a member who yanks rank on his or her relational string shocks the entire system.

Scholars who write in the area of interpersonal persuasion typically distinguish between more than two types of power. Family communication authors Galvin and Brommel summarize six bases for power. As you read them, consider what types are at work in your family.[22]

Punishment or Coercive Power: Punishment power is at work when family members promise or threaten physical or psychological pain. Parents may resort to name-calling or threaten not to pay tuition "unless you straighten up." Children may use punishment power when they threaten to run away from home or stonewall in silence until the parent apologizes. Coercive power is the *modus operandi* of the verbal abuser. It communicates, "Do as I wish, or else…."

Positive Reinforcement Power: Positive reinforcement is at work when family members promise or deliver something desired. A father's attempt to motivate a son toward the dean's list with the promise of a Disneyland trip is a good example. In dysfunctional relationships, however, such an offer may be taken as bribery or pure manipulation. I know of a case where a not-at-home dad made grand promises to his son to buy him an expensive birthday gift, but never followed through. Consider the head games that represents.

Expertise Power. Expertise influence is at work when we believe another family member knows more than we do. Young children are particularly suspect to expertise power because they in fact know less than their parents, but also because they believe that their parents know everything. Humility on part of the parents is crucial if the child is to learn that everyone is finite and fallible. Abusers typically lack this humility, even over-claiming what they know. Abusers often see themselves as experts on almost everything.

Legitimate or Position Power. This power comes when we acknowledge that some roles carry certain responsibilities and privileges. My wife is our family bookkeeper, and so her opinion about financial matters carries clout. If she says "Sorry, but we can't afford that this month," I listen. As noted above, abusers exercise legitimate power as an inherent right. If anyone ever said to you, "Why should you obey? Because I'm your father (or mother), that's why!" you've experienced legitimate power by mere role, not reason.

Identification or Referent Power. Identification power serves as a base when you see yourself as similar to someone else and desire to be like him or her. A daughter is more likely to identify with her mom than her dad. She is more apt to take her mom's advice on a wide range of issues because of their female connection. Identification can boomerang though, as in the tendency for children to take after their parents in a host of destructive habits.

Persuasion or Information Power. Persuasion power is at work when family members offer sound reasons and values for why others should agree with them. Abusers would likely abuse less if they imitated God's call to "Come now, let us reason together" (Isaiah 1:18). Offering good reasons is usually considered a highly ethical way to persuade others. However, this method can still be exploited. Consider someone who says, "You have two options: get a job or go to school. If you go to school, you'll cost me money, need to move, get homesick, and probably flunk out anyway." Their reasons may be true, but they limit choice and fail to acknowledge the advantages of college (e.g. character development, vocational training, or relational enrichments). Abusers in particular can be very bright, persuasive arguers, but their aim is not to reason together. Their goal is to win arguments with vise-grip logic.

This list makes power appear as an incarnation of evil. Not so. How we use power determines it moral force. Our choice is whether we regard power as a right (to lord over others) or as a responsibility (to meet family needs mutually). *Power-as-right* leads to domineering communication; *power-in-covenant* encourages mutuality where everyone pulls their weight within their role.

In traditionally conservative Christian homes the role of leader has fallen to the husband. Advocates see this model as biblical and healthy as a father provides resources, protection and care for his wife and children. Critics of the *Father Knows Best* model point out that in some cases it tends toward theological rigidity and power-as-right.

Without getting into strong prescriptions of do's and don'ts, I think it is worth suggesting some tips for functional family communication. We begin with a look at the role men play in the family mix.

Men as Relational Key

Research indicates that men benefit more from marriage than women. Marriage more often frees men to pursue career goals while simultaneously raising a family, getting involved in local community, and enjoying the status prestige. Women, traditionally, have supported men in these endeavors, carrying the load of child rearing and home management at the expense of career development. Even when women work outside the home, they wind up doing most of the housework. We are not surprised, therefore, that men report a higher quality of life after they wed than do women.[23]

Add to this, another interesting fact. In the long run, men control the quality of marriage more than women. Kenneth Ferraro and Thomas Wan examined this issue with couples who were about sixty years old. They summarize that "husbands are more able to control the social psychological evaluation of life in the marital context.... The well-being of husbands and wives is relatively stable... though husbands are more frequently the ones who affect changes in well-being."[24]

An explanation for this finding may go like this. Whether because of nature, nurture, or our sinfulness, men are inclined toward tasks and hierarchy, assertiveness and competition—things you need to build an army, not a family. Women have a tendency toward relationships and context, nurturing and intimacy—qualities that make a family mobile turn in positive balance. Left to their customary leanings, many men are less relationally savvy than their wives. Therefore, the soundness of a man's marriage and family life is dependent on his commitment to relationships and mutuality—two qualities he is perhaps not naturally inclined to do, but which are essential for covenantal relating.

I believe that Richard Halverson, past Chaplain of the United States Senate, understood this when he made this contentious claim:

> It is my deep, settled conviction that *one hundred percent* of the responsibility for the sustenance of the marriage relationship belongs to the husband. The scriptures tell us that as husbands we need to model ourselves after Jesus Christ, who gave Himself up in every way in order to present His bride to Himself without blemish or stain or spot or wrinkle![25]

Halverson may be no family communication expert, but his wisdom from forty-some years of marriage and family life give reason to pause. We often hear that marriage is a 50-50 arrangement, or a 100-100 one, each person giving it their all. But men may need to consider that they can't split this responsibility down the middle.

The call for men to take their family covenant seriously is underscored by sobering facts about homes without dads.[26]

1. Children raised with no father in the home have been shown to exhibit more antisocial behavior than their raised-with-dad counterparts.

2. Children from broken homes suffer from illness twenty to forty times more often than children raised in intact families.

3. Fatherless children are more likely to do poorly at school and are doubly at risk of dropping out of school than kids with dad at home.

4. Even among children with fathers at home, the average time spent in conversation with their father each day is eight minutes, and only four minutes if their mother also holds a job outside the home.

5. Many men involved in the current men's movement attribute their sense of lost identity and confused views about masculinity to their father's absence during childhood.

This evidence suggests that when men split the home scene, they contribute to the disintegration of families. And since more men leave the home than women, it seems justified to suggest that a family's relational health depends on dad's commitment and effort.

Men are also key because they tend toward verbal abuse, and women and children are their most common victims.[27] What Halverson intimates, therefore, I call straight up—men should not be less like men, but men should attempt to be more like women in terms of relational sensitivity.

Accepting this idea as a biblical truth has become easier for me after reading Jack Balswick's book *Men at the Crossroads: Beyond Traditional Roles and Modern Options.*[28] Balswick suggests that some believers have bought into a flawed theology that fuels men's beliefs that women and families are to be dominated, not nurtured. First he clarifies what "helper" means in Genesis 2:18: "The LORD God said, 'It is not good that man should be alone. I will make him a helper as his partner.'" The root for the term "helper" here is used fifteen times in the Old Testament, *always in reference to God.* Balswick concludes,

"Because I said so!"

"Needless to say, it would be a gross misinterpretation of Scripture to think of God as subordinate to humankind because the Bible says he is our helper."[29] The operative word in Genesis 2:18 is not "helper" but "partner." Just as God is our helper but not subordinate to us, so it is possible for a woman to be a helper but not subordinate to her husband in the negative sense. She is his partner.

Second, he explains that Eve's sin was the sin of going beyond the *dominion* given to her. She had already been given the whole of Eden except the tree of good and evil. For overstepping her God-given *dominion*, God's punishment to Eve was that she would be *dominated* by Adam. God said, "Your desire will be for your husband and he will rule over you" (Genesis 3:16). Balswick observes that "many have interpreted this sentence to mean that God *intends* (desires) for Adam to lord it over his wife—and that, therefore, Christian men today should dominate their wives as well. Within the context, however, God's statement is better understood as a consequence that will come from the curse placed upon Adam as well as Eve."[30] Adam's curse was that he would *want* to dominate Eve, but this was not God's original design.

Finally, Balswick turns to Jesus Christ as a role model for men today. To make his point he asks the reader to do an activity. I repeat it here because it is a real eye-opener. I hope you will take time to do it as I did.

First, locate a pencil and a piece of paper. Now take five minutes to list one-word descriptors of Jesus' characteristics. Base your list on what you know of his life on earth. Responses might include terms such as "loving" and "just." Make your list of Jesus descriptors now.

. . . .

Once you have made this list, reflect on how our society today typically defines "masculine" and "feminine" qualities. Now go back to your list and consider each descriptor one at a time. If a term seems to fit the "masculine" ideal, mark it with an "M." If it fits the "feminine" ideal, mark it with an "F." If it fails to fit either stereotype well, skip it, and go to the next word. Do this now.

What I found, and what Balswick finds time and time again, is that the "male" traits and the "female" traits come out about even. Jesus showed power, might, determination, and skill, but he also showed love, compassion, emotion, and concern. Balswick concludes, "A masculinized or feminized image of Jesus is not supported by the scriptural narratives. Taken alone, each view is incomplete. But taken together, they suggest the rich depth that characterized Jesus' human life. So we men need to turn to Jesus to find liberation from sterile, restricted definitions of manhood that are prevalent in modern culture."[31]

Balswick's call to men to avoid extreme stereotypes may be taking effect more readily these days as researchers have found that fathers are showing affection more today than they did three decades ago, albeit in masculine ways. Mark Morman and Kory Floyd studied fifty-year-old dads and their college-aged sons to find that dads and sons use supportive activities, such as helping, to show their affection, more than making out-right statements such as "I love you" or big bear hugs. While some scholars have lamented that men and boys don't use words to express their emotions as commonly as do women, others have suggested that sharing activities can be as rewarding as deep conversation. Morman and Floyd's study affirmed this view when they found that the more dads and sons engaged in supportive activities, the more they felt close, open, and satisfied in their relationship.[32]

The Sanctified Family: A Worthy Goal

What then should be our goal in family communication? We could aim for functionality. In Christian perspective, however, I believe the goal should be about faith, and "faithing" each other unto Christlikeness. In theological terms, this is sanctification.

The book of *Hebrews* indicates that Jesus' life enables us to be family with him and sanctified by him when the writer says, "In bringing many sons to glory, it was fitting that God ... should make the author of their salvation [Jesus] perfect through suffering. Both the one who makes men holy [Jesus] and those who are made holy [people] are of the same family" (Hebrews 2:10-11). I hope you can get past the gendered language to appreciate two key points. The first is that Jesus' suffering guarantees that he understands our family struggles as limited and tempted humans. We have reason to believe Jesus lived with his parents and siblings until his public ministry, and might assume that they experienced the normal trials and frustrations of family life. The second is that God, through Christ and his Spirit, works to make us holy or sanctified. The Revised Standard Version translates the above passage this way: "For he who sanctifies and those who are sanctified have all one origin. That is why he is not ashamed to call them brethren." God in us binds us as family with the larger goal of personal holiness.

Much more recently family researchers have asked how religious sanctification shapes family life.[33] Annette Mahoney and colleagues define sanctification as "a psychological process through which aspects of life are perceived by people as having spiritual character and significance."[34] While their language is not biblical in terminology, their theorizing is. They review how Christians see family life through God's eyes when we view marriage as sacred and dependent on God's blessings. Godly eyes also understand sex as God's gift, personal sacrifice as good, and commitment as a choice we make to get through financial and medical hardships. Finally, God's ways provide wisdom when we encounter conflict with each other.[35]

Additional research points out that parenting and general family functioning can be understood in sacred terms. Christian parents consider pregnancy and child birthing as "miraculous" and "divine," and consider child rearing to require godly virtues such as patience and love, as they "train up a child in the way he should go" (Proverbs 22:6). Parents encourage children to respect elders, act well toward others, and avoid destructive habits.[36]

If we buy into this idea that family communication's purpose is to redeem us, to sanctify us, then it is worth considering what redemptive family interaction looks like. In broad relief, covenantal families aim to avoid hurtful games based on dysfunctional rules, disconfirming messages, and power-over mentality. Rather, they strive for validation, intimacy, goodwill, mutuality, partnership, and equality. Let's look at its positive features.[37]

Healthy Relationships. Sanctified families develop relationships that are characterized as "affiliative, trusting, positive and optimistic, warm, unconditionally accepting, and relaxed."[38] Obviously, communication is key to establishing these relational traits. When our talk is self-centered, critical, and caustic, we poison relationships.

In healthy families, strong friendships form between pairs of people, but not at the exclusion of others. Nor do these dyadic bonds form coalitions against others.[39] Maybe you have a favorite brother, or find more time to spend with mom than dad. This seems to be fine as long as it does not create resentment among the rest of the family.

Covenant Power. Sanctified families consider how they can meet each other's needs rather than get what they want. Families who exhibit servant power acknowledge that someone needs to lead, but not the same person day in and day out. Servant power allows every member to have a say in how the family is run, but still acknowledges that dad and mom are most responsible, and that dad is accountable before God for the whole package. A father's accountability to God by grace is no basis for power-lording but rather humble steward-ship. Research bears out that *egalitarian leadership*—another term for servant power—is more functional than dominating authoritarianism, or having no leader at all.[40] Somewhere in between is the balance wherein everyone's view is heard.

Parents who think they have to control every family decision may be hiding behind stereotypes of leadership, or may be shoring up a low esteem.

Clear Role Differentiation. Healthy families talk about who does what, when, where, and why. In our home, I manage the lawn, the garbage, the repairs, the vacuuming and the dusting.

> A father's accountability to God by grace is no basis for power-lording but humble service to his family.

Shelaine manages the finances, the social calendar, the laundry, and the medical needs of our children. Together we garden and plan vacations. As our children mature we want to extend their responsibilities beyond cleaning their rooms. These roles are not set in stone though, and we negotiate new ideals in family councils and spousal chats.

Furthermore, healthy families communicate responsibility for member roles, and, when individuals mess up, they admit it. Since we have agreed that my job is collecting the garbage and taking it out once a week, I am willing to bear the consequences for its piling up. I cannot blame others ("Taylor's school project made for a whole bag of paper!"), complain ("This job is the pits"), or belittle the issue ("Come on! What's wrong with a little bad smell?"). Taking responsibility for our roles helps avoid blaming and complaining.

Good Problem Solving Skills. Healthy families talk through their problems, solve them, learn from them, and move on. Less functional families do not. Healthy families focus on the problem, not the person. They are more likely to use a win-win framework for discussing issues rather than a win-loss one. That is, they try to meet both party's needs fully rather than one person's needs at the expense of the other. Sometimes they compromise and meet half way. Other times they graciously agree to disagree on matters that do not matter.[41] They look out for each other.

In unhealthy families, communication itself is often the problem.[42] For about a year a distressed family lived adjacent to our home and our exposure to their talk gave us the sense that it played strange head games. From behind the hedge that separated us we heard a lot of yelling, in earnest, and many ultimatums. "Get OUT of the pool, now!" "If you don't get out NOW, you will go to your room!" "Don't you EVER do that again!" The saddest one, however, was "EVERYone, STOP SHOUTING!" We doubted that the mom was aware of the contradiction.

Above Board Discussion about Discipline. Perhaps the ultimatums shouted by our neighbor mom would be unnecessary if she and her husband could manage a family council with the kids where everyone signed off on family rules and consequences for breaking them. When everyone has a say in forming such rules, no one should need to shout to enforce them.

During the busy years of raising three sons, my wife and I have logged thousands of miles in car and van to soccer practices, job locations, and friends' homes. One day our youngest son, Eric, forgot an important form at home. He called his mom to ask if she could bring it to school. Shelaine explained that she would, but that the natural consequence of his forgetting was her lost time and gas consumption, so she was going to start charging him two dollars for such incidences. He agreed. A few weeks later Eric returned the idea when Shelaine arrived late to him up. "I've wasted ten minutes, Mom, and I think you owe me $2." Shelaine agreed, and the two continue to honor these rules in respect for each others' time and energy.

Congruent Communication. Sanctified families practice congruent communication. As noted in Chapter 4, congruency is expressing on the outside what one is thinking and feeling on the inside. It means being genuine, not phony. In some respects, it is the crux of covenantal communication—knowing what you agree on, and showing it in your family life. Sanctified families are not fakes; they do not deny what they stand for, nor shy away from the hardships that plague them. As noted earlier, my birth family *believed* that sex was God's gift to us for our pleasure to use responsibly, but our *talk* was not congruent with that value as we skirted sexual topics and only criticized sex in the media.

Functional families exhibit open, frank, and respectful talk about issues and needs. And as Miller writes, "Healthy families speak the truth in love, and parents and other older family members are willing to listen to the words spoken by 'mere children.'"[43]

Freedom to Express Emotions. Those who feel free to express emotion and how they do so are strongly influenced by our birth family and cultural heritage. Part of men's history has been the rule to suppress their emotions and play poker face. However, healthy families acknowledge that life has its joys and stresses with resulting elation, sadness, peace and depression. Healthy families realize that emotions are not right or wrong, but that they are foundational to being human and an important outlet for understanding each other. Men who hug sons and women who cheer on athlete daughters show emotional aptitude.

Healthy families take life with a grain of salt, and know how to party. As Janet Yerby and her associates observe, "Optimally functioning families are more spontaneous, playful, and optimistic than introspective. They are more energized and emotionally connected. They have fun together; they are humorous and witty. They can laugh at their problems and be playful."[44]

Freedom to Talk about Problems. One potential risk in families which strive to live by godly standards is an unwillingness to share openly about personal problems. The mentality is that if God is on our side, then personal problems are a sign of moral weakness and nobody wants to hear that someone is a failure. Rather than look struggles or sin in the face, the temptation is to tip toe around it and talk as if everything is fine. As one student reported in a study on family communication, "My friend's family never talks about what's wrong—they just pretend everything is OK when it's not."[45]

Henri Nouwen observes that our brokenness is a part of life, and we are better off admitting it, and giving it to God, than trying to ignore it. In one of his radio sermons he said,

> We are broken people. You and I know that we are broken. A lot of our brokenness has to do with relationships.

If you ask me what it is that makes us suffer, it is always because someone couldn't hold onto us or someone hurt us. I know each of us can point to a brokenness in our relationships with our husband, with our wife, with our father, our mother, with our children, with our friends, with our lovers. Wherever there is love, there is also pain. Wherever there are people who really care for us, there is also the pain of sometimes not being cared for enough. That is enormous.

What do we do with our brokenness? As the beloved of God we have to dare to embrace it, to befriend our own brokenness, not to say, "That should not be in my life. Let's just get away from it. Let's get back on track."

No. We should dare to embrace our brokenness, to befriend it and to really look at it. "Yes, I am hurting. Yes, I am wounded. Yes, it's painful."

I don't have to be afraid. I can look at my pain because in a very mysterious way our wounds are often a window on the reality of our lives. If we dare to embrace them, then we can put them under the blessing. That is the great challenge.[46]

Summary

Families promise the best and worst in relational communication. Hopefully yours is a harbor from the gales of life. Families manage meanings over generations as members influence each other in a common living space and create their own histories. For good or ill, families share an emotional attachment, unlike non-family bonds. In families, we have the opportunity to nurture children and affirm developing adults. Families begin with parents who normally engage in a lop-sided covenant of investment in their children which imitates God's investment of grace toward us.

Exceptions to this standard include families where rigid, critical, and domineering webs of entrapment snag children, teens, and parents. The presence of dysfunctional rules, disconfirming messages, and verbal abuse usually means that at least some family members are hung up on powering over others rather than serving others. Abusive environments are characterized by inequality, competition, manipulation, hostility, control, and negation. Men are more likely to verbally abuse others and leave home. For these reasons this chapter encourages men to seriously consider their talk and how they may conform it more to the richly balanced manner of Christ. Men, and families, who want to nurture healthy homes, will communicate equality, partnership, mutuality, goodwill, intimacy, and validation. By God's grace the outcome will be the sanctified family where members serve one another within clearly defined roles and problems are discussed openly with emotional freedom. How we talk with each other contributes to the successful construction of this covenantal reality.

Some people have left their birth families so long ago that the lack of communication effectively frees them from its bounds, but this doesn't mean they live as hermits. Rather they surround themselves with friends and find new identities by joining other groups. College students are prime examples. Examining the dynamics of non-family groups is the topic to which we now turn.

 **WORTH THE TALK**

1. Can you give personal examples to show that you family communication works like a "system"? Discuss how the words or behaviors of one person have a rippling effect throughout your family and on future communication.

2. What types of power do others exercise *over* you? *With* you? (The difference indicates whether they engage a Power Over approach or Servant Power approach.) Closer to home, what types of power do you exercise *over* others? *With* others? (Do you more commonly engage in Power Over or Servant Power?) You may want to refer to the six types of power reviewed in this chapter to aid your discussion.

3. Do you agree with the statement made by Richard Halverson, that 100 percent of the responsibility for marriage sustenance [and family functionality] belongs to the husband? Why or why not? Is it fair to expect so much of men?

4. How has your family attempted to make sanctification your aim? What examples indicate success or failure in striving to encourage each other toward Christ-like godliness?

 **CONSIDER THE WALK**

1. Dysfunctional communication begins with dysfunctional rules. Analyze your own family for dysfunctional communication by making two lists, one for rules, the other for resulting messages. Consider the rules that you might be most responsible for establishing and maintaining. Some time after you have written your analysis, sit down with your family (or one-on-one if necessary), and discuss what you have discovered. In a spirit of grace and reconciliation, admit where you are not serving the system well. Invite others to contribute their ideas, but don't force or demand change from them. Work cooperatively toward establishing a new set of rules and how your family talks.

2. Verbal abuse can be a slippery term unless we can recognize its various forms, both in our own communication and in others. In *The Verbally Abusive Relationship*, Patricia Evans lists eighteen verbal abuses. They include withholding, countering, discounting, abuse disguised as jokes, blocking and diverting, accusing and blaming, judging, criticizing, trivializing, undermining, threatening, name calling, forgetting, ordering, denial, and abusive anger. Write a paper about verbal abuse that defines these terms, and gives examples of them in family relationships. As part of your work, address whether or not power misuse is the underlying problem. As a case study, you may want to analyze your own communication with others or interview friends (with guaranteed confidentiality) to provide some original research for your writing.

3. Use ideas from this chapter to analyze how the characters of your favorite soap opera, situation comedy, prime-time drama, or feature film relate to each other. You might consider what rules are being followed, what disconfirming messages are typically sent, what types of power are being abused, and what hope there is for sanctified

communication. Try to give representative dialogue as proof of your analysis.

 **ENDNOTES**

1 These stories reported on in the National Post, a national Canadian newspaper, in May, 2008. See: http://www.nationalpost.com/news/canada/story.html?id=544227.

2 For a scholarly look at how parents pass on communication competence to their children see Brant Burleson, Jesse Delia and James Applegate, "The Socialization of Person-Centered Communication: Parents' Contributions to their Children's Social-Cognitive and Communication Skills," in *Explaining Family Interactions*, ed. Mary Anne Fitzpatrick and Anita L. Vangelisti (Thousand Oaks, CA: Sage, 1995).

3 Janet Yerby, Nancy Buerkel-Rothfuss and Arthur P. Bochner, *Understanding Family Communication*, 2nd ed. (Scottsdale, AZ: Gorsuch Scarisbrick, 1995), 13.

4 Ibid., 7-13.

5 Em Griffin, *A First Look at Communication Theory*, 6th ed. (New York: McGraw-Hill, 2006), 176.

6 Annett Mahoney et al., "Religion and the Sanctification of Family Relationships," *Review of Religious Research* 44 (2003): 224.

7 Margaret F. Brinig, *From Contract to Covenant: Beyond the Law and Economics of the Family* (Cambridge, MA: Harvard University Press, 2000), 1.

8 Ibid., 130.

9 Ibid., 131.

10 See Martin Rovers, *Healing the Wounds in Couple Relationships* (Toronto, ON: Novalis, 2005) for a study on wounded and communication in close relationships. Rovers describes wounds as emotions, behaviors, and thoughts that are reactions to past hurtful attacks on one's core self image, values, beliefs, or esteem that results in an identifiable or unidentifiable unresolved issue. This wound is triggered in the present by some action or words of a partner which then guides expectations for current relationships.

11 I constructed these rules, in part, based on features of the *functional* family as described in Kathleen Galvin and Bernard Brommel, *Family Communication: Cohesion and Change*, 2nd ed. (Glenview, IL: Scott, Foresman, 1982), 283-289.

12 Ronald Adler and Neil Towne, *Looking Out, Looking In*, 8th ed. (New York: Harcourt Brace College, 1996), 367.

13 This list and descriptions are based on Adler and Towne, ibid., 369-370.

14 Anita Vangelisti, "Messages That Hurt," in *The Dark Side of Interpersonal Communication*, ed. W. R. Cupach and B. H. Spitzberg (Hillsdale, NJ: Lawrence Erlbaum, 1994), 53-82.

15 For a full treatment of verbal aggression and its relationship to physical violence, see Dudley D. Cahn and Sally A. Lloyd, eds., *Family Violence From a Communication Perspective* (Thousand Oaks, CA: Sage, 1996).

16 These examples come from Suzettte Haden Elgin's book *You Can't Say That to Me! Stopping the Pain of Verbal Abuse* (New York: John Wiley & Sons, 1995), 1.

17 I am indebted to Adler and Towne, *Looking Out, Looking In,* 369, who cite this study by M. Straus, S. Sweet and Y. M. Vissing, "Verbal Aggression Against Spouses and Children in a Nationally Representative Sample of American Families" (paper presented at the annual meeting of the Speech Communication Association, San Francisco, CA, 1989).

18 This list is provided by Patricia Evans, *The Verbally Abusive Relationship* (Holbrook, MA: Adams Media Corporation, 1996), 17.

19 Ibid.

20 See George R. Bach and Ronald M. Deutsch, *Stop! You're Driving Me Crazy* (New York: G. P. Putnam's Sons, 1980).

21 Ibid., 29.

22 Galvin and Brommel, *Family Communication,* 126-127.

23 S. Sharlin, F. Kaslow and H. Hammershmidt, *Through Thick and Thin: A Multinational Picture of Long-term Marriages* (New York: Hawthorne Clinical Press, 2000), 80-81.

24 See Kenneth Ferraro and Thomas T. H. Wan, "Marital Contributions to Well-Being in Later Life: An Examination of Bernard's Thesis," *American Behavioral Scientist* 29 (1986): 434.

25 Richard Halverson, *No Greater Power* (Portland, OR: Multnomah Press, 1986), 118. I am indebted to Stu Weber's *Tender Warrior* (Sisters, OR: Multnomah Books, 1993), 118 for his citation of Halverson's book.

26 Items 1-3 reported in Charles Colson, *A Dance with Deception: Revealing the Truth Behind the Headlines* (Milton Keynes, England: Word, 1993), 187-188. Items 4 and 5 are reported in Colson, ibid., 185-186.

27 See M. Bogard, "Why We Need Gender to Understand Human Violence," *Journal of Interpersonal Violence* 5 (1990): 132-135, and L. L. Marshall, "Physical and Psychological Abuse," in *The Dark Side of Interpersonal Communication,* ed. W. R. Cupach and B. H. Spitzberg (Hillsdale, NJ: Lawrence Erlbaum, 1994), 281-311.

28 Jack Balswick, *Men at the Crossroads* (Downers Grove, IL: InterVarsity Press, 1992), 30.

29 Ibid., 54.

30 Ibid., 56.

31 Ibid., 59.

32 M. T. Morman and K. Floyd "A 'Changing Culture of Fatherhood': Effects of Affectionate Communication, Closeness, and Satisfaction in Men's Relationship with their Fathers and Sons," *Western Journal of Communication* 66 (2002): 395-411.

33 See Annett Mahoney et al., "Religion and the Sanctification of Family Relationships," 220-236.

34 Ibid., 221.

35 Ibid., 222-223.

36 Ibid., 223.

37 These insights derived from: David R. Miller, *Counselling Families After Divorce: Wholeness for the Broken Family* (Dallas: Word, 1994), 268-272; Yerby, Buerkel-Rothfuss and Bochner, *Understanding Family Communication*, 308-315; and John Caughlin, "Family Communication Standards: What Counts as Excellent Family Communication and How are Such Standards Associated with Family Satisfaction?" *Human Communication Research* 29 (2003): 5-40.

38 Miller, *Counselling Families After Divorce*, 269.

39 Yerby, Buerkel-Rothfuss and Bochner, *Understanding Family Communication*, 311.

40 Yerby, Buerkel-Rothfuss and Bochner cite W. R. Beavers and R.B. Hampson, *Successful Families: Assessment and Intervention* (New York: Norton, 1990).

41 I was reminded of this important rule recently while reading Romans 14. The issue Paul addresses is how to deal with differing opinions over types of food. Paul concludes, "Let us therefore make every effort to do what leads to peace and to mutual edification. Do not destroy the work of God for the sake of food. All food is clean, but it is wrong for a man to eat anything that causes someone else to stumble. It is better not to eat meat or drink wine or to do anything else that will cause your brother to fall" (verses 19–21).

42 See P. Watzlawick, J. H. Beavin and D. D. Jackson, *Pragmatics of Human Communication* (New York: Norton, 1967) for their discussion of meta-communication and its role in dysfunctional family systems.

43 Miller, *Counseling Families After Divorce*, 269.

44 Yerby, Buerkel-Rothfuss and Bochner, *Understanding Family Communication*, 313.

45 Caughlin, "Family Communication Standards," 12.

46 See Henri Nouwen's full sermon at: www.csec.org/csec/sermon/nouwen_3502. htm#anchor610088, or search for it using its title, "The Life of the Beloved."

Let us consider how we may spur one another on to love and good deeds. Let us not give up meeting together, as some are in the habit of doing, but let us encourage one another—

Hebrews 10: 24–25a

The Good Group

Community in the Making

IT WAS LATE November and our church council members were huddled around our conference table in an attempt to hammer out an overdue vision statement for our local assembly. The previous evening a guest speaker had spoken to us about vision-setting and planning. Now it was the next afternoon and we felt the time crunch to put ideas to pen and get on with our task.

We had just returned from lunch when Jack—a successful middle-aged real estate developer—proposed an unexpected turn. "I don't know about you folks, but I'm wondering if it's premature for us to discuss God's vision for our church before we examine how we stand before him and each other. Are we right with him? Are we right with each other? I think we need to settle these issues before we can discuss vision."

Several members glanced at the chairman for his response. He commented that we had sloughed off the vision task long enough and that our two-day retreat was intended to help us nail it down. But Jack's point was hard to ignore. If we harbored bitterness or unconfessed sin, how could we lead?

Then Lynn spoke up. "Maybe God would still honor our task even without a long confession-and-tears time. Maybe God can work through our good intentions and thoughtful discussion if we give it a try." From the nod of heads I could see a fence line go up mid-table.

On Jack's side were members who wanted to get relational, confess to each other, and bond in spirit. On Lynn's side were those wanting to pursue the task, trust in God's grace, and let cohesion take care of itself. We were at a standoff.

My council experience and the research of group communication scholars confirm a hunch you may have as well: groups can make you or break you—and they are practically unavoidable. We took a candid look at the family group in the preceding chapter. Now it is time to examine groups we choose to join, namely, task groups, relationship groups, and influence groups.[1] What we will find is that groups form a powerful matrix for covenantal change personally and corporately. Let's begin with features that define small groups generally.

> In the U.S. alone, 80 million people meet at least once per week in a small group.

Defining Groups

Take a minute to consider the groups you have chosen to join. These might include the student newspaper staff, a sports team, or a college-and-career class at church. By conservative estimates, about 33 million U.S. citizens have a meeting on any given day at their workplace, and about 80 million people attend groups each week for personal support and care. In fact the majority of groups which meet for support and care stem from churches and synagogues.[2] What distinguishes these kinds of small groups from the people who mingle around a Coke machine?

The answer, in part, is in how we define them. One definition is that a small group is "a limited number of people who communicate face-to-face, share a common understanding of an interdependent goal, influence one another, and express a sense of belongingness to the group."[3] These features are broad enough to include your college student newspaper staff and care group, but narrow enough to exclude the Coke crowd and those cheering on a football team. Let's examine each feature.

A Limited Number of People

How limited? Scholars do not always agree, but most see small groups as consisting of three to twenty members. What is true of a dyad (twosome) may be true of some groups, but what is true of a triad (threesome) better captures the group dynamic. Some add that an odd number is better than an even number if your group votes a lot and where one vote either way will swing it. Depending on a group's purpose, too few members (three or four) may mean too few resources. Your newspaper staff would be stretched with only three writers and one editor. But too many members (twelve to twenty) may create other concerns such as *coalitions* and *deadwood*. Coalitions are clusters of individuals who form cliques and nettle the nest with their own agendas. Deadwood members are usually isolates who fail to contribute for reason of boredom, personal insecurity, or simply lack of time. There is no perfect number for how large a group should be, but conventional wisdom and research indicate that somewhere between five to eleven members there resides much potential for a good group.

Who Communicate Face-to-Face

We take this for granted, for without symbolic interaction among its members, a group could not function. However, trying to measure or describe group communication has proven to be a complex task. The sheer number of messages that can be sent, even one-way, appears daunting in a small group.

Suppose only two writers, Allen and Betsy, show up for a newspaper staff meeting one week. The number of possible actions (messages sent one way) is two: A to B and B to A. If Carla, the editor, shows up the next week, the possible number of communicative actions shoots up to nine: 1) A to B, 2) A to C, 3) B to A , 4) B to C, 5) C to B, 6) C to A, 7) A to B & C, 8) B to A & C, and 9) C to A & B. And if that is not enough, groups of four yield twenty-eight possible actions, groups of five 75, groups of six 186, groups of seven 441, and groups of eight 1,056.[4] No wonder we say eight is enough! Numbers like these may look onerous until we recognize that each utterance comes to us one at a time and probably makes a lot of sense in context. But how can we categorize what gets said?

One answer is to observe the way comments and behavior function to fulfill group goals. We look at goals in the next section, but here it is enough to say that most groups exist to solve problems, whether task, relational, or personal. Two group communication scholars, Randy Hirokawa and Dennis Gouran, suggest that members are more apt to solve problems with quality decisions when their interactions perform four important functions: 1) they show a thorough and accurate analysis of the *problem*, 2) they express criteria that frame their ideal *goal*, 3) they identify as many alternative *solutions* as possible, and 4) they *evaluate* the pluses and minuses of each alternative in light of the criteria frame.[5]

My church's council members had long expressed the problem: we had no statement of mission, vision, or core values. We felt rudderless. Our goal was also clear: we wanted to write a mission statement, vision statement, and set of core values to guide our programs and initiatives. The night of our major impasse, we eventually split into four sub-groups to discuss alternative statements. Four groups of three members each toiled over their own versions of these statements. Finally, in future meetings, we returned to debate the two most likely proposals.

Although Hirokawa and Gouran's functions capture the rational decision-making process more than relational dynamics, one might use their model to figure out why a group flounders relationally. For example, group members who offer up irrelevant comments, false information, biased opinions, and mere silence may frustrate others and create conflict. Moreover, if group members fail to be mindful and vigilant, they might enjoy much fun en route to a poor decision.

Who Share a Commonly Understood Interdependent Goal

All groups do not pursue the same goal, yet their varying goals often determine the kind of talk members consider appropriate. Some, like a newspaper staff or church council, gather to get work done. We call them *task* or *decision-making* groups, and their meetings smack of all business. Others gather for friendship and fellowship—*relationship groups*—and their meetings appear mainly social. Still others come together for personal healing and growth through *influence groups*—their times can be emotionally charged.[6] In each case though, members realize that none of them can accomplish these tasks alone; they need each other to accomplish an interdependent goal, whether that be to plan a new building, to feel good through friendship, or to personally mature.

The Task or Decision-Making Group. Classic examples are school or work committees who manage programs and budgets. My church council is a task group with a relational overlay. Here is its purpose:

> <u>Church Council</u>: to provide administrative and visionary oversight to the policies, personnel and programs of our local church so that we might extend the work of God's kingdom in spiritual depth and numerical breadth.

You can bet that this calling influences our communication significantly. We hear a lot of reports, debate what our church members want and need, and vote on recommendations to take before the entire church body. All the while we manage courteous civility and a little fun too. As you see, task groups are mainly work and occasionally play.

The Relationship Group. Relationship groups consist of people whose main goal is to enjoy each other's company, but not by accident. Their interaction is planned and purposeful, as in dinner clubs, book clubs, and church care groups.

For several years my wife and I participated in a gourmet club with three other couples. We met four times a year to cook master-piece meals and consume them together. Life carried on after gourmet club disbanded a few years back, but during those years it was richer because of the Lundbergs, Camerons and Sawatzkys. Here was the purpose of our club:

> <u>The Gourmet Club</u>: to prepare and consume delectable international delights in the company of long-time friends and to encourage each other in our marriages, family life, and Christian walk.

We didn't have this goal written down in a manual, but we acted as if we shared it. For example, one night we got onto the topic of how we met our spouses. Ned told us of his initial attraction to Kim and his fear that she might be too good-looking for him. We didn't psychoanalyze Ned after his disclosure (despite four licensed psychologists in the group!) We simply chuckled and smiled our approval of Ned's willingness to be honest, and then we affirmed that Ned and Kim were highly suitable for each other.

The gourmet goers represented what some describe as a good relationship group. Members of relationship groups attend voluntarily, affirm each other, self-disclose openly and honestly, honor confidentiality, empathize with each other, hold each other accountable, and pray together.[7] Relationship groups socialize with a purpose, and their connecting is three-quarters the fun.

The Influence Group. Robert Wuthnow, small-group expert and author of *I Come Away Stronger*, asked a U.S. sample of over 2,000 people the following question: "Are you currently involved in any small group that meets regularly and provides support or caring for those who participate in it?"[8] Exactly 40 percent said "yes." The faithful and irreligious alike join influence groups because they recognize the need for changed attitudes and habits. And that is what the influence group's purpose is, to help people change their views of themselves and their relationships so they can move up the ladder of personal development. In covenantal perspective, the influence group best represents how people come together to agree on how they will live and regenerate through group interaction.

For some people their ladder is already in a very deep hole, and change means struggling back to ground level where life is "normal." For example, consider the purpose of groups such as Alcoholics Anonymous and Weight Watchers.

> The Self-Help Counseling Group: to help people who are caught in addictive and abusive behavior accept their dependence, and to assist them in moving toward a new identity with new expectations and behaviors towards others and the addictive substance.

Counseling groups like AA and WW require skilled leaders who understand the plight of group members and what they need for physical and emotional healing.

Other people's ladders are on firm ground, but they desire to go beyond the third rung spiritually or developmentally. Faith-discovery programs, such as *Alpha*, fall into this category. Members are not drug dependent; they seek God-dependence. What is their purpose?

<u>The Faith-Discovery Group</u>: to create a safe place where people may find out about Christianity and the person of Christ through theological education, personal testimony, and biblical insight.

It is key that members choose to be involved, desire to change, and are willing to do the homework and activities required to encourage spiritual growth. Influence groups express best the spirit of covenantal communication in that members realize that personal growth evolves through therapeutic talk engaged in over time through mutual commitment to change.

Who Influence Each Other

Robert Wuthnow's book title, *I Come Away Stronger*, indicates another truth of small groups—they empower us to handle life. But that empowerment requires change, and change requires openness to being influenced by others. My sense is that people who enter a group experience in humility will reap the most rewards, for in humility we listen better, reflect more, and consider how we might change. Rubbing elbows with others sharpens us, and we have opportunity to sharpen others. Two ways we become persuaded are through a group's leadership, and through the click and clash of conflict.

Leadership.[9] Without someone at the helm, most groups veer off course and float adrift. One researcher found that ninety percent of group members say their current group has a leader, more than those who say they have a stated purpose (84 percent), name (76 percent) or agenda (75 percent).[10] The questions are, who will lead or who should lead?

We used to think that leaders were born, not made. You either had leadership *qualities* or you did not. Of little surprise, we found that leaders were more intelligent, knowledgeable, and self-confident than followers as well as more attractive, taller, and verbally adept. The problem was that as the list of traits got longer and longer, the likelihood of finding anyone with each trait became slimmer and slimmer. In addition, many a short guy and average-looks gal who led groups admirably blew the whole formula.

What followed was an attempt to describe leadership *styles*. *Autocratic* leaders who cracked the whip and announced self-made decisions usually engendered aggression or apathy, depending on the followers. *Laissez-faire* leaders who took a "hands-off" approach did little to motivate, cohere, or even upset group members. *Democratic* leaders who encouraged group discussion and group decision-making were most likely to instill group satisfaction, cohesiveness, and quality decisions. But we have since discovered that the democratic leadership style doesn't work in some situations. If the college newspaper is two days overdue and the printer says she is about to go on vacation, what is needed is not a so-what-do-you-think democratic leader. The situation calls for a strong autocratic voice that can move sluggish writers to their laptops!

Thus came a shift to our search for *situational* factors that allowed for leadership. Later this approach was modified in *contingency* theory. This view combined the styles view with the situational view to suggest that effective leadership depends on both variables. Contingency researchers showed that leaders who are most motivated to meet interpersonal needs are best qualified to lead less-than-enthusiastic followers who face a complex, unstructured task. Leaders who enjoy pushing for task accomplishment perform best with admiring followers who undertake less complex, more routine jobs.

Today two valued views of leadership are the *functional perspective* and *transformative perspective*. Functional school advocates suggest that *leadership* is different than being a *leader*. Leadership is any behavior that helps the group accomplish its goals, whereas a leader is

© 2000 Randy Glasbergen.

"Memo: next week's Leadership Seminar has been postponed until we can find someone who's willing to take charge of the program."

the person designated as in charge. Some leaders perform poorly at leadership, while some "followers" perform it admirably because they influence the group toward task completion. If you read between the lines of the functional approach, you can see a biblical theme, namely, that she or he who serves the needs of the group, leads. Functional leaders aim to meet basic needs of group members, such as physical, safety, and belonging needs. The functional perspective endorses servant leadership.

Transformative leadership is said to build on functional leadership as it seeks to meet higher human needs such as building esteem and achieving group member's personal potential. To do so leaders set the bar high and convert people to a new way of thinking. Michael Hackman and Craig Johnson, in *Leadership: A Communication Perspective*, observe that transformative leaders are creative, interactive, visionary, empowering, and passionate.[11] Such leaders look beyond a group's successes and envision creative opportunities, and are masterful at capturing this vision "through images, metaphors, and models that organize meanings for followers."[12] Along the way, transformative leaders show passion for projects *and* people, and empower others with ideas, freedom, and resources to jump on board and accomplish the group's mission. Some transformative leaders might be considered *charismatic* in that they seem to embody superhuman, even super-

natural gifts uncommon to most earthlings. Charismatic leadership works ethically as long as leaders serve others humbly and welcome feedback and criticism from followers.[13]

Conflict. Small group members also change through encountering and working through conflict. Conflict can be defined as "an expressed struggle between at least two interdependent parties who perceive incompatible goals, scarce rewards, and interference from the other party in achieving their goals."[14] Council members Jack and Lynn expressed competing goals. Jack wanted to come clean with God and each other before we discussed church vision. Lynn wanted to discuss vision straightway. Most group members sensed that we had scarce rewards, such as time, and wanted to avoid costs, such as an extra meeting. We were also interdependently linked because we were committed to arriving at a unanimous decision. Jack saw Lynn as interfering with spiritual renewal. Lynn saw Jack as blocking task accomplishment.

We have a tendency in evangelical Christianity to believe that conflict signals disunity of the Spirit, and possibly moral failure. We may also buy in to the myth that Jesus was harsh with evil doers, but forever nice with his intimate twelve. From this thinking we may conclude that good groups are always polite, but perpetual politeness may lead to hum-drum groups with little genuine sharing.[15] Let's consider three other beliefs which I suggest are equally mythical and unhealthy.

> Myth #1.   Conflict is a sign of unhealthy diversity; the scriptures call us to unity.
> Reality. Paul called us to unity (see Romans 5:5–6), but not unity in all thought and behavior. He called us to unity in spirit for the purpose of glorifying God. I know Lynn and Jack. They want to glorify God through their actions. Their clash probably led us to a more robust group experience than had either kept mum. Unity, like harmony, requires two different voices with the same musical score. Unity does not mean sameness just as harmony does not mean monotone.

> Myth #2. Conflict is sin. Or, where there is conflict, sin must be present.
> Reality. Conflict can be sin, but not all conflict is sin. Carla's call for more editorial writing in the newspaper differs from Allen's goal for straight news, but both are legitimate newspaper philosophies; neither is immoral. Carla's hurling insults at Allen to win the argument is sin.

> Myth #3. Nice people do not conflict. (To be read: Holy people always agree.)
> Reality: Many godly people conflict. Consider how Jesus scolded Peter when Peter said that Jesus would not die. Jesus said, "Get behind me Satan!" (see Matthew 16: 23).

Or consider Paul and Barnabas, who in Acts 15:39, it is reported, "They had such a sharp disagreement that they parted company." Even role models of Christian faith experience conflict.

So what do we do with conflict in small groups? In Chapter 6, we noted the strategies of keeping our cool, taking a break, acting wisely, and aiming to understand and reconcile with one another. Recently communication scholars John Burtis and Paul Turman determined a helpful list of additional pointers:

1. Pick your battles carefully; debate what really counts.
2. Determine the worst thing that could happen, and live with it if possible.
3. Hold the view that you can learn from conflict.
4. Show value and interest in other group members, and when possible, talk to them privately away from the group.
5. Let people vent in the group.
6. Listen, listen, listen.
7. Write down—or at least paraphrase—the other person's issues, and discuss them until you understand them.
8. Ask everyone if there are other things to discuss as well.
9. Don't rush to conclude, but understand that conflict ends eventually.
10. Focus on the problem, not on individual people.
11. Do not agree to some future action unless you are really committed to it, and do not agree just to bring peace.
12. Admit your own mistakes, and plan ways to do better in the future.[16]

So how did we solve the impasse at the church council? Our senior minister suggested that we first spend time in personal reflection and public confession, and then divide into work groups to draft separate vision statements. Jack's side of the table appreciated the pastor's sensitivity to relational and spiritual matters, and Lynn's side saw that small groups could accomplish more than our clunky group of twelve. We met the true needs of each group member in a civil manner.

And Who Express a Sense of Belongingness to the Group

Feeling a sense of ownership is the last key to defining a small group. When we feel like we belong, benefits abound. Several years ago the students on my school's student newspaper staff felt they didn't belong. The editor was a top-down, opinionated individual who did little to instill a sense of team identity. Attendance at staff meetings plummeted and morale sunk to an all-time low. The group resembled a collection of rag tag reporters, not a *staff*.

Most small group scholars would say this editorial staff lacked cohesion. One writer defines cohesion as "the bond that links group members to the group, the degree to which the members are attracted to one another and the group, and the unity a group has toward its members."[17] This definition accounts for how people in diverse groups such as hockey teams and weight watcher clubs can feel pulled to the center or repelled to outer orbit. What are some of those forces?

John Cragan and David Wright suggest four important factors: 1) the communication that occurs (or not) and its quality, 2) the roles people play, whether contributing to or detracting from the group's goals, 3) the norms or rules for behavior that the group establishes for itself, and 4) how members manage conflict.[18] Cohesion is also strongest when group members 5) share similar attitudes, and 6) set and achieve workable goals.[19] It may go without saying, but lousy talk, competing roles, uncertain norms, habitual conflict, divergent attitudes, and vague goals spoil any hope for cohesiveness. I think the first and fourth of these factors squelched belongingness for the newspaper staff. The top-down edicts from the editor-in-chief stymied group discussion, and because no one addressed this issue with the editor, everyone suffered.

Groups are more likely to experience cohesiveness when members know their roles, play by the rules, manage conflict well and keep their talk and walk consistent. Cragan and Wright report that a cohesive blend leads to three desirable outcomes: productivity, consensus, and member satisfaction.[20] The more cohesive your group, in general, the better. Cohesion sounds like the holy grail of good groups. Find it, and you succeed.

A few people. Face-to-face communication. A common goal. Influence. Belongingness. You will find these criteria in most standard textbooks that explain small group communication.

What believers might be asking is whether Christian groups experience any more bliss than other groups for reason of our shared faith and spirit. It would sure be easy to think so, but it's tough to make absolutist claims when comparative data are hard to find. Besides, what a small group of believers considers bliss may differ from what newspaper staffers consider a good group.

What we do know is that small groups thrive when group members feel that their needs are being met. In one recent study researchers found that Christians who joined a weekly care group were largely motivated by the desire "to become more disciplined in [their] spiritual life."[21] And their small group experience largely met that need. After participating in the group, 56 percent said spiritual matters were more important to them now, 53 percent said church or synagogue were more important, 63 percent said prayer was more a priority, and 48 percent valued Bible study more. A considerable majority of 84 percent confirm that their faith and spiritual walk have been influenced positively by participating in a small group.[22]

What might be better than data on the devoted is a conceptual and biblical understanding of groups. There is nothing wrong with describing groups with criteria such as number of people, type of interaction, common goals, influence and belongingness; but there is the itch to ask, what may be missing? Does our faith contribute a theme that explains why Jesus molded his ministry around twelve disciples or why church growth pundits praise the small group movement?[23] Several authors who write about small groups in the church believe they are on to a theme. What's missing is *community*.

The word "community," like "communication," derives from the Latin word *communis*, which means *to share in common*. We speak of urban communities (where we live together), but we can also speak of spiritual community (how we commune with each other). First century witnesses of new Christians said, "Look how they love one another." Love for one another is the basis for *koinonia*, or believer fellowship. It is an ancient theme.

Before the Beginning There Was Community

Religious thinkers make some intriguing observations about God, people, and how we connect in community.[24] Their ideas apply not only to the small group context, but to our very definition of our person as self-in-community (see Chapter 5). Consider this theology of community.

God is Community. "From the beginning, God has existed as a community of Being. In human history God has revealed this community of Being as Father, Son and Spirit, an eternal small group, a Trinity of Being and relationship, around whom the greater community of beings is gathered, both angelic and resurrected."[25] The mystery of community in the Trinity has baffled theologians for centuries, but most recognize the Trinity as *one* community.

God desires community with us and among us. Despite the perfect community within the Godhead, God chose to create us—people—for fellowship with him. Everyone "is called to live in intimate, reciprocal, dialogical and growing relationship" with God.[26] Even if we have not found God, only through life with each other do we come to know who we are. Even if we reject God, our life with each other images the community of the Godhead.

God established a special community with his chosen people through a covenant. In the time before Christ, God entered a covenant relationship with the nation of Israel. As we have learned, a covenant is a promise, and God's promise to Abraham was that he would prosper and be blessed. God's requirement for Israel was that they be his people, his holy nation, his priesthood who realized that individual-in-community was God's design for human-human and human-divine relationships.

Jesus Christ came to re-establish community between God and us. The Jews struggled to maintain their integrity with God. We struggle to maintain our integrity with God. God knows that we fail again and again. Therefore, in his desire to re-establish divine-human community, God walked on earth in the form of Jesus Christ. In Christ we have a God model for how we ought to live with God (vertical community) and with each other (horizontal community). Jesus used the twelve disciples to epitomize the power of community and to establish his church.

The church locally and globally expresses human and divine community. Upon Christ's resurrection and ascension to God the Father, God sent his Holy Spirit to enable us to live out community in *ecclesia*—the church—and in the culture at large. We are called to love, honor, disciple, serve, wait for, care for, comfort, build up, maintain the peace with, be subject to, forgive, confess to, and extend hospitality to all people, especially those in the body. God's spirit binds all ecclesia together worldwide and some day Christ will return to unite with us.

Julie Gorman summarizes the spirit of community when she writes: "However much we may think of our relationship in individual terms, we are always seen by God as family, networked, honeycombed, related to one another as His children, His bride, His building."[27]

Features of Small Group Community

So what does community look like in a small group? Can we get beyond its theology to practical features? Scott Peck has attempted to answer that question in his book *The Different Drum: Community Making and Peace.*[28] Although his ideas may apply to lovebirds and large organizations, his main interest is small groups. As you read these features you might reflect on whether the groups to which you belong exhibit these qualities. If you can answer "yes" to a number of them, you will begin to see the centrality of community to group communication.

A place where everybody is welcome. Peck calls this "inclusivity," but it boils down to a welcoming spirit. Inclusivity is not an absolute though; it is something your group must negotiate, especially in fellowship and care groups. If

Early in life we learn how to communicate whether or not others are welcome in our group.

you let *anyone* in, you could kill the group. If you let *no one* new in, you could kill the group. The key is having a border that is neither a porous perimeter nor a brick wall.

I recall some acquaintances that struggled with inclusivity. Their growth group was in its third month and beginning to bond well through Bible study and mutual encouragement. Then a new couple arrived that had a different purpose in mind, namely, to question the faith. The original members thought their purpose was to edify believers, not attract dissenters. The group limped along for a few weeks and then breathed relief when the couple failed to show one night. The group's leader reported that the newcomers left because they felt coldly unwelcome. Your group members may need to discuss what your purpose is and how obviously they want to hang the sign "newcomers welcome."

A Place Where People are Committed to Each Other. In Chapter 2, we observed that communication flourishes when people commit to each other long term. In small groups, commitment means attending regularly, and listening openly. This is especially important when we clash with others over style or beliefs. The former chair of our church council was a detail-man, whereas I tend to be a global thinker who waxes philosophic. Don and I had to guard against judging each other unduly, because both functions enable a group to succeed. We expressed our commitment by faithfully attending council meetings and listening to each other's views. Don could recall obscure budget lines and important nuances of ancient conversations that I had long forgotten. Meanwhile, I sensed that he appreciated my futuristic look at church ministry as I asked how we might do ministry creatively.

A place where people make decisions by mutual agreement. Consensus creates community, and is a hallmark of covenantal relating. When we disagree, we have work to do. I like the cartoon that shows the juror standing outside the jury room giving the bailiff the carry-out order. "Eleven hamburgers, one frank. Eleven coffees, one tea. Eleven apple pies, one chocolate cake." Juries *must* come to unanimous agreement. It is part of due process. Most groups we belong to do not have to agree unanimously, but it's wise to shoot for it. As already implied, consensual agreement leads to a more cohesive bunch than when leaders bark orders to passive members or when voting results in a six to four split.[29] Arriving at consensus takes more time and patience than a vote or leader fiat because members need to listen to everyone's view.

Making decisions by mutual agreement can be a rule-of-thumb agreed upon by everybody in a group. In fact, healthy groups who are serious about commitment, decision-making, and cohesion often express their expectations in a group covenant. Figure 8.1 represents a group covenant established by students in a spirituality and discipleship course at a Christian university, but this pact would work just as well for a care group or newspaper staff. A small group covenant is group-negotiated list of expectations. From the example you can see that those expectations cover everything from attendance to confidentiality, and honesty to respect. You can find more such examples by searching the internet using the key phrase "small grou covenants."

A place where people are realistic about the world and themselves. In other words, community encourages looking outwardly as much as looking inwardly, and members are not duped about either reality.

Some time ago the Parents Council of the elementary school where my children attend held a meeting to determine whether uniforms should be required. One hundred and seventy five parents showed up to speak their minds about uniforms, money, identity, choice, and convenience. The arguments stacked up about even. Just before they voted, one mother felt that this issue pit parents against parents. She

---

Small Group Covenant

Attendance: I agree to be at the session each week unless a genuine emergency arises.

Participation: I will enter enthusiastically into group discussion and sharing.

Confidentiality: I will not share with anyone outside the group the stories of those in the group.

Honesty: I will be forthright and truthful in what is said: if I do not feel I can share something, I will say "I pass" for that question.

Openness: I will be candid with others in appropriate ways and allow others to share for themselves.

Respect: I will not judge others, give advice, or criticize.

Care: I will be open to the needs of others in appropriate ways.

Figure 8.1 This covenant indicates how members agree on communication rules in their small group. Used by permission from Dr. Gary Waller, Professor of Theology at Northwest Nazarene University in Nampa, Idaho.

stood and commented that this issue could be explosive and divisive—that it could destroy school unity and morale. Then she added that she didn't sense antagonism, but heart-felt passion for the welfare of the children. The vote eventually went 110 against to 65 for.

Community affords this luxury. It is a place where you can be true to yourself and speak your mind without the fear of attack. At the same time, however, community requires us to listen to each other. To use a political phrase, community encourages checks and balances to keep us on course with the felt needs of our members and the world at large.

> **Community affords the luxury to be yourself, and speak your mind, without the fear of group attack.**

A place of safety where one can contemplate, heal, convert, and grow. What Peck means by contemplation is not quiet meditation, but a heightened awareness of yourself and your group's purpose. Contemplation in this sense is asking, "How are we doing?" "Are we on target?" "Are we healthy?" "Where are we headed?" A good group protects your right to ask these questions. John Fischer laments that in some Christian circles people are not encouraged to ask certain questions. He writes,

> Have you ever been in a group of believers when some-one asked a question that didn't have an easy answer? Disapproving glances were probably thrown at the questioner as if to say, "Don't you know we don't ask such questions here?" There is a tacit understanding within many churches and fellowship groups that this gospel ship navigates best if you don't rock the boat.[30]

If your group discusses the same topics in the same patterns with the same outcomes meeting after meeting, then there is a good chance you would benefit from asking why you began the group in the first place. Community provides the freedom to ask tough questions.

In addition to contemplation, Scott Peck also suggests that community occurs when converting and healing take place. That might mean spiritual conversion (as in finding redemption in God through

Christ for the first time) or physical healing (as in release from alcoholism). But it can also mean personal discipleship in the iron-sharpens-iron manner of Proverbs 27:17. Church groups function this way. Robert Wuthnow found that most members of cell groups say they feel closer to God (90 percent), have a deeper love for others (87 percent), are better able to forgive others (84 percent), and are better able to forgive themselves (82 percent).[31] Indeed, most of them joined church groups because they wanted to learn more about God and develop their trek with him.

A word of caution though. Peck suggests that a leader's attempt to *program* healing and converting can backfire. Whether due to our western sense of rugged individualism or simple fear of change, most of us do not want to be considered someone else's project. We want to change on our own accord. Research by Wuthnow supports this idea. He writes,

> I have shown that many of the formal structures that have been discussed in the literature on small groups—such as contracts, terms, able leadership, and fixed agendas—contribute *less* to the successful functioning of groups than do informal norms and activities, such as encouraging all members to share, respecting their views, and making them feel appreciated.[32]

This does not mean that leaders should come unprepared or have a vague purpose. It means the goal should be to establish a safe place—a place where it is okay to not be okay. Communicating love and acceptance provides this kind of safe place where members can be vulnerable and accountable.

A place where people can fight graciously, influence others equally, and enjoy a spirit of unity. I relish these qualities in my breakfast group with Rick and Dan—two friends I have met with for sixteen years. Every other week meet at *Ricky's Family Restaurant* at 6:30 A.M. to discuss empty nesting, Vancouver Canucks hockey, worship wars, liberal-conservative politics, and more. We debate, cajole, and laugh over our diverse positions, and we solve the world's problems in an hour. Along the way we differ sharply, argue strongly, and come away friends. I think we reflect Peck's criteria that community fosters gracious conflict, mutual influence, and the Musketeer spirit of one for all, and all for one.

Those are Peck's features of community in small groups. If their contours remain a little fuzzy, that is probably a good thing. What we should garner from them is that community is more process (how things are done) than product (what gets done), more motive than behavior, more heart than head. Authentic Christian community is about sharing life with others under Christ's lordship. "This is what *koinonia* is all about. *Koinonia*, the …New Testament word for 'fellowship,' actually means *sharing something with someone*. This kind of relationship is deeper than that of acquaintances or even friends. It is marked by the quality of sharing that *good* friends with a *close personal relationship* enjoy—love for one another. This is a relationship characterized by openness, acceptance, warmth, and growth."[33]

Summary

Millions of Americans and Canadians belong to small groups where they work, fellowship, and heal. We defined a small group as a limited number of people who interact face-to-face over time toward a common goal. Group members typically enjoy equal opportunity to persuade each other and find identity with each other. Groups may have purposes that regard tasks, relationships, personal improvement or a mix thereof. Leaders in groups would be wise to ask how they may inspire creative solutions and meet group needs, rather than manipulate people to change. Being organized is important, but keeping the flow of discussion open, and affirming members, appears to be more important for success.

The notion of community goes beyond the realm of explaining group dynamics. Community explains, in part, the mystery of the Trinity, God's desire for fellowship with his creation, and his choosing of Israel as a special people. Community helps us understand Emmanual—God with us—in his incarnation through Christ, and it deepens our appreciation of what it means to be reconciled among fellow believers, whether in our local fellowship or worldwide.

Attempting to define community is a slippery venture, but Scott Peck's description gave us a start. Community exists when people feel welcomed, not shunned; are committed to each other, not dogged under gun point. Community is about making decisions together and being in tune to our purpose on earth. In community we are safe to reflect on the tough questions of life for the larger purpose of healing, changing and growing. Finally, community is where we can conflict graciously, influence one another mutually, and enjoy a spirit of unity. It's about getting along despite our differences.

Whether we can expect full-blown community in task groups might be wishful thinking, but task groups with no community are painful. How to nurture community without chasing it away may be our primary challenge.

 **WORTH THE TALK**

1. Is there any feature of small groups that you think is missing from the definition above? What feature would you add? Subtract? Why?

2. Do you think that the idea of community explains best the dynamic of God's relationship with us, and our relationship with other believers? If so, why? If not, why not? What idea would you use?

3. The idea of community may apply more easily to relational and influence groups where people intend to get up close and personal. But what about task groups? For example, what is the likelihood that a group such as your school's newspaper or yearbook staff will experience community? Is this realistic or pie in the sky?

 **CONSIDER THE WALK**

1. Consider a group to which you belong. Analyze its dynamics using the criteria for defining a small group (noted under the "Defining Groups" section of this chapter). Try to explain why your group members interact as they do. Use the criteria as a basis for suggesting ways your group might improve its experience.

2. Analyze a group to which you belong for its degree of community using the criteria described above. Suggest why you think your group suffers from a lack of community or relishes in ripe community. (Or perhaps your group falls somewhere in between.) Use these criteria for recommending attitudes or actions the group could use to increase community.

ONLINE CHALK

Consider the following search terms to learn more about small group communication, leadership, conflict, dynamics, problem solving, and covenants.

- Small group communication
- Small group leadership
- Small group conflict
- Small group covenants
- Understanding group dynamics
- Problem solving in groups

ENDNOTES

1 I take this typology from Em Griffin's *Getting Together: A Guide for Good Groups* (Downers Grove, IL: InterVarsity Press, 1983), 27-41, but need to acknowledge that various authors categorize groups differently. For example, Michael Argyle distinguishes between family and adolescent groups, work and committee groups, and therapy groups in his article "Five Kinds of Small Social Groups," in *Small Group Communication: A Reader*, ed. Robert S. Cathcart and Larry A. Samovar, 6th ed. (Dubuque, IA: Wm. C. Brown, 1992), 18-25. Griffin's categories are preferred because they appear to be more encompassing: family and adolescent groups are examples of relationship groups; work and committee groups are examples of task groups; therapy groups are one example of influence groups.

2 The 33 million figure is cited by Stewart Tubbs and Sylvia Moss, *Human Communication*, 7th ed. (New York: McGraw-Hill, 1994), 266; the 80 million figure is estimated by Robert Wuthnow, *Sharing the Journey: Support Groups and America's New Quest for Community* (New York: Free Press, 1994) where he shows that 40 percent of a national survey indicated they belonged to a support group. If, by conservative estimate, there are 200 million adults in the United States, the total number of people in support groups alone is about 80 million.

3 Beatrice G. Schultz, *Communicating in the Small Group: Theory and Practice*, 2nd ed. (New York: HarperCollins, 1996), 5. See Tubbs and Moss, *Human Communication*, for this second definition: a small group is a "collection of individuals who influence one another, derive some satisfaction from maintaining membership in the group, interact for some purpose, assume specialized roles, are dependent on one another, and communicate face to face" (267).

4 Robert Bostrom, "Patterns of Communicative Interaction in Small Groups," *Speech Monographs* 37 (1970): 257-263, as cited in Tubbs and Moss, *Human Communication*, 286.

5 This discussion of Hirokawa and Gouran's work is based on Em Griffin's description in *A First Look at Communication Theory*, 3rd ed. (New York: McGraw-Hill, 1997), 247-258. See also Dennis Gouran, Randy Hirokawa, Kelly Julian and Geoff Leatham, "The Evolution and Current Status of the Functional Perspective on Communication in Decision-Making and Problem-Solving Groups," in *Communication Yearbook 16*, ed. Stanley Deetz (Newbury Park, CA: Sage, 1993), 573-600.

6 Griffin, *Getting Together*, 27-41.

7 Ibid., 35-36.

8 Robert Wuthnow, ed., *"I Come Away Stronger:" How Small Groups are Shaping American Religion* (Grand Rapids, MI: Eerdmans, 1994), 369.

9 This concise review of leadership theory is based on Beatrice G. Schultz, *Communicating in the Small Group: Theory and Practice*, 2nd ed. (New York: HarperCollins, 1996), 94-102.

10 Wuthnow, *Sharing the Journey*, 135.

11 Michael Z. Hackman and Craig E. Johnson, *Leadership: A Communication Perspective* (Prospect Heights, IL: Waveland, 2000), 91-112.

12 Ibid., 103.

13 Ibid., 119.

14 Joyce Hocker and William W. Wilmont, *Interpersonal Conflict*, 3rd ed. (Dubuque, IA: Wm. C. Brown, 1991), 12, as cited in Tubbs and Moss, *Human Communication*, 195.

15 For a look at the myth that "good groups are polite" see Dan Williams, *Seven Myths about Small Groups* (Downers Grove, IL: InterVarsity Press, 1991), 82-97.

16 This list built from John O. Burtis and Paul D. Turman, *Group Communication Pitfalls: Overcoming Barriers to an Effective Group Experience* (Thousand Oaks, CA: Sage, 2006), 131.

17 Gerald L. Wilson, *Groups in Context: Leadership and Participation in Small Groups* (New York: McGraw-Hill, 2005), 254.

18 John F. Cragan and David W. Wright, *Communication in Small Group Discussions: An Integrated Approach*, 3rd ed. (St. Paul, MN: West Publishing, 1991), chapter 1.

19 Gerald Wilson, *Groups in Context*, 255-256.

20 Ibid., chapter 1.

21 Wuthnow, *Sharing the Journey*, 381.

22 Ibid., 382 and following.

23 Along with that praise comes a legitimate call for concern. For a balanced view of the small group movement in religious America, see Warren Bird, "The Great Small-Group Takeover," *Christianity Today*, February 7, 1994, 25-29.

24 Most of these ideas come from Gareth Weldon Icenogle's *Biblical Foundations for Small Group Ministry: An Integrational Approach* (Downers Grove, IL: InterVarsity Press, 1994), and Julie A. Gorman's *Community that is Christian: A Handbook on Small Groups* (Wheaton: Victor Books, 1993).

25 Icenogle, *Biblical Foundations,* 371.

26 Ibid.

27 Gorman, *Community that is Christian,* 23.

28 M. Scott Peck, *The Different Drum: Community-Making and Peace* (New York: Simon and Schuster, 1987).

29 See for example Cragan and Wright, *Communication in Small Group Discussions,* 20-21 and 269-270.

30 John Fischer, *What on Earth are we Doing?* (Ann Arbor, MI: Servant, 1996), 35.

31 Wuthnow, ed., *I Come Away Stronger,"* 382.

32 Wuthnow, *Sharing the Journey,* 133. See chapter 5 especially.

33 Thomas G. Kirpatrick, *Small Groups in the Church: A Handbook for Creating Community* (New York: Alban Institute, 1995), 5. For this definition of *koinonia* Kirpatrick quotes Gerhard Kittel, ed., *Theological Dictionary of the New Testament* (Grand Rapids, MI: Eerdmans, 1965), 797.

Now Stephen, a man full of God's grace and power, did great wonders and miraculous signs among the people. Opposition arose, however from members of the Synagogue. . . . These men began to argue with Stephen, but they could not stand up against his wisdom or the Spirit by which he spoke.

Acts 6:8–10

Principles for the Podium
Getting Started in Public Speaking

ONE YEAR AFTER 9/11, President George W. Bush delivered a speech in New York City flanked by the Statue of Liberty and an American flag. Bush began his speech with these words:

> Good evening. A long year has passed since enemies attacked our country. We have seen images so many times they are seared on our souls, and remembering the horror, reliving the anguish, re-imagining the terror, is hard—and painful. For those who lost loved ones, it has been a year of sorrow, of empty places, of newborn children who will never know their fathers on earth. For members of our military, it has been a year of sacrifice, and service far from home. For all Americans, it has been a year of adjustment—of coming to terms with the difficult knowledge that our nation has determined enemies, and that we are not invulnerable to their attacks.

The president went on to describe how these events challenged Americans and brought out virtuous character. He also noted that 9/11 spurred us on to think of important things—"love for our families, for our neighbors, and for our country; gratitude for life and to the giver of life." The terrorists, he asserted, attacked not only Americans, but also American ideals—ideals such as liberty, equality, human life, freedom, and opportunity. Following a description of America's successes in its war against terrorism, the president said he believed God has placed Americans together for a purpose. He then concluded:

> We are prepared for this journey. And our prayer tonight is that God will see us through, and keep us worthy. Tomorrow is September 12th. A milestone is passed, and a mission goes on. Be confident. Our country is strong. And our cause is even larger than our country. Ours is the cause of human dignity: freedom guided by conscience and guided by peace. This ideal of America is the hope of all mankind. That hope drew millions to this harbor. That hope still lights our way. And the light shines in the darkness. And the darkness will not overcome it.[1]

The Challenges and Responsibilities of Public Speaking

Few of us will encounter speaking assignments as difficult as those presented to presidents and prime ministers. However, the speaking assignments we do receive can loom large and seem impossible, and this can scare us. In fact, one out of five students in elementary school, secondary school, and university suffer from extreme fear of speaking in public. Another one in five experience "butterflies" before speaking.[2] And more people fear speech giving than fear heights, financial problems, dogs, or death.[3] Why does public speaking instill so much fear? I believe the answer is that, consciously or not, people recognize the sobering challenges and responsibilities that define public address. People also fear failure.

What if you gave a commemorative speech on September 11, 2011—ten years after the 9/11 bombings? What would you say? Would you inform your audience, console them, persuade them, or provoke them? What types of logical and emotional appeals would you use? What types of appeals do you think would be ethical? What research would you do? Do you think you would be the right person for such a task? These questions indicate challenges and imply responsibilities. As we consider each one, we will observe practical tips to guide our speechmaking.

Public Speaking Is a Purposive Activity

Perhaps no other communication activity is as intentional as giving a speech. We usually know the date, time, place, topic, prep requirements, and purpose before we stand behind the podium. The purpose of President Bush's speech was *to commemorate* the attacks, victims, and heroics of September 11. To commemorate means to remember, or to signal the memory of a person, place, or thing.

Your university speech instructor likely required you to give several types of speeches, each with its own purpose. At my school we require students to give a *personal narrative* speech to start the semester. Its purpose is to share two or three defining features of one's personal life (one's personal story), so others may get to know the speaker better. Later students prepare an *informative speech* with the purpose to introduce listeners to new ideas or information. Informative speeches sometimes take the form of *demonstrations* or *process explanations*, such as "How to wax a snowboard," or "How to apply for student aid."

Once students have gained experience with informative speaking, the course moves on to *persuasive speeches* that intend to alter an audience's beliefs, attitudes, or behavior on a controversial issue. For example, one of President Bush's goals, we presume, was to convince listeners to believe that Americans have risen from the rubble of terrorism, and remain undaunted in their battle against it. Additionally, he no doubt hoped that our attitudes toward America and American ideals were favorable. Finally, while he does not call his listeners to action, he justifies current military activity by saying "We fight, not to impose our will, but to defend ourselves and extend the blessings of freedom."

The point here is that we should know what we want our speech to accomplish. When we mix conflicting purposes, we are apt to confuse our listeners. I recall a student who wanted very badly for us to change our attitudes toward Native Americans, but her jokes and flamboyant delivery made some students think she was kidding. Better had she been mindful of her purpose to persuade, not entertain, and speak accordingly. What is the purpose of your next speech? Is it to inform? Persuade? Celebrate? Honor? Commemorate? Determine its purpose, and stick with it.

Related to your purpose is your *thesis*. A thesis is the main point you want to make about your topic. It is a sentence, not a phrase, and it makes a clear assertion. Examples of *poor* thesis sentences include:

America and terrorism. (These are two topics.)

Should 1st world countries forgive 3rd world debt? (This is a question.)

Land mines and leg-hold traps should not be allowed for use by military and hunters to kill people and animals because they are inhumane. (This one mixes two issues and includes a reason for the assertion.)

A good example of a thesis is as follows:
Attempting to eradicate terrorism is a lost cause.

This thesis is a sentence, it makes one assertion, and it pertains to one topic. It is wise to determine your thesis before you begin your research, or, to formulate it soon after you have discovered what your research supports.

Public Speaking Is a Research Activity

Research is one of those "ugh" topics. Few of us enjoy long days in the library or clicking through endless websites. We may even think that good speakers don't do research because they have the gift of gab and rich personal experiences. While these benefits help, the general rule is that good public speaking is still 90 percent perspiration and 10 percent inspiration. A friend of mine, Paul Chamberlain, serves as a case in point. Paul logged sixty hours of research on physician-assisted suicide so he could debate a local politician for thirty minutes. That is a 120-to-1 ratio for research-to-speaking time.

You probably do not have that kind of time, but you do have some decisions to make as you research your talks. How much do you know about your topic? How can you invest your time best to garner opinions and data? How might you weave in your own experience? Unless you tap in to the breadth and depth your topic represents, you might forfeit your right to be heard. The goal of research is to discover *evidence*. Stephen E. Lucas and colleagues define evidence as "supporting materials—examples, statistics, testimony—used to prove or disprove something."[4] Types of evidence that you might unearth include:[5]

Facts: things that have occurred and are verifiable as true. Bush cites several facts: that 2001–2002 was a year of adjustment, of children born who would not know their fathers, of great sorrow. Few would debate these assertions, for many people experienced them, and the media reported them.

Statistics: numerical facts that represent significant information. Statistics can be divided into *raw numbers* (e.g., 4,000 students attend the school), *descriptive statistics* such as mean, median, mode, and percentages, (e.g., 68 percent of students are female), and *inferential statistics* such as correlations (e.g., high school grade point average predicts university grade point average). Inferential statistics differ from descriptive ones in that they infer a relationship between two or more variables.

Opinions from experts: professional, informed judgments made by an expert about information in his or her field. These are not to be confused with the endorsements popular athletes or Hollywood stars make for consumer products. However, when the surgeon general maintains that Wheaties are nutritious, audiences listen.

Personal knowledge: your knowledge built on experience with the topic. Do not underrate what you know from first-hand experience, for many of your audience members may be relatively inexperienced with your topic. For example, your summer as a tree planter in northern Canada provides rich material about environmental issues, renewable resources, and logging companies.

Examples and illustrations: an incident or item which represents a more general state of affairs. From your summer up north you might use the example of clear-cutting 150-foot trees as proof that our generation will never renew a similar forest in our lifetime, thus the need for long-term planning. Or, a photograph of a forest before and after clear-cutting might illustrate the destruction of green space generally..

Anecdotes and stories: short or long narratives that make a point. Suppose you wanted to underscore our own mortality without being macabre. You could tell a humorous anecdote like this one: "A teacher was admiring a new photo of her students, and commenting that in twenty years they would look back and say 'Look, that's Jennifer—she's now a doctor; and that's Tim—he's now a professor.' There was a pause, and from the back of the room came a small voice, 'And there's Mrs. Burton, and now she's dead.'"

Quotations: cited material that captures a truth in a pithy or beautiful way. It is wise to use quotations when someone else has said something better than you can express it, but guard against making your speech a collection of other people's words. A quotation from Dr. Martin Luther King, Jr. is reminiscent of President Bush's closing lines about light and darkness. King said, "Darkness cannot drive out darkness; only light can do that. Hate cannot drive out hate; only love can do that."[6]

Definitions and descriptions: definitions outline the meaning of special words, and descriptions paint pictures of places, people, and objects. Both depend on well-chosen words for their effectiveness. A scholar who critiques the Bush Ellis Island speech notes, "I use the word 'myth' several times in this analysis. It is important to understand that I *do not* intend the connotation of 'untrue.' Rather, I use myth to indicate culturally-important stories a nation tells itself in order to understand its relationship to the world, i.e., who we are as a people."[7] This is an important definition if one wants to understand the scholar's analysis!

You can locate material from a variety of sources. Your goal should be to use the appropriate source, not the easiest or fastest one. Consider doing your research from:
- Magazines
- Books
- Scriptural texts

- Encyclopedias
- Statistical sources
- Interviews with experts
- Biographical sources
- Newspapers
- Government publications
- Computer databases
- Internet Websites
- Microfilm databases
- Special reference books[8]

Today the trend is away from print sources and toward electronic ones. Whether you use sources off-line or online, it is important to know how to assess their worth. Bill Badke, an expert on research strategies, suggests that the guidelines for assessing online documents run parallel to those for off-line ones.

1. Look for the name of the author and/or organization responsible for the information. Established authors and credible organizations are usually well known, or can prove their credentials on their site.

2. Look for signs of scholarship—good language level, analytical thinking, bibliography and/or footnotes, logical organization.

3. Look for signs of a *lack* of scholarship—lots of opinions without the support of evidence, indications of paranoia (as in *somebody's out to get us*, or *we're victims of a conspiracy*), poor spelling and grammar, lack of references to other sources, poor organization.

4. Ask yourself—does this person have a vested interest in promoting a viewpoint or is he/she simply sharing information? Vested interested may be okay as long as you are well aware of what they are. A site selling Toyotas is going to be different in its very nature from a site offering independent reviews of Toyotas.[9]

If you are accustomed to doing all your research by using major search engines such as Google, Yahoo, Window Live, or Ask.com, consider searching with academic search engines such as Google Scholar, CiteSeer, Scirus, Windows Live Academic, and getCITED. You may need to pay a user fee and enter a password to access full-text articles, but the results may be worth it. The URLs for these sites are provided at the end of the chapter along with some other database sites. Also, you should visit your university and master its in-house search engines. Our school subscribes to Academic Search Premier by EBSCOhost as well as several other academic databases. Use your library privileges liberally to access resources that Google cannot find or cannot access.

Public Speaking Is a Logical and Emotional Activity

The ancient Greek philosopher and rhetorician Aristotle used the term *logos* to refer to appeals we make to logic, and the term *pathos* to mean appeals we make to emotions. We typically use both when presenting speeches to inform, and more so in speeches to persuade. While the two look distinct, keep in mind that they overlap depending on the points we make in a speech. For example, if your thesis is "Regular exercise improves academic grades," you might use the following syllogism to prove it:

> Major Premise: Regular exercise reduces stress.
> Minor Premise: Low-stress students learn better than high-stress ones.
>
> _____
>
> Conclusion: Regular exercise can lead to better academic performance.

While this argument flows logically, it also makes subtle appeals to emotional states such as peace, calmness, and personal confidence. Or put another way, it would be hard for your audience to hear your argument and not feel the persuasive sway of these unspoken emotions.

While syllogistic reasoning is effective, it is not the only way to picture how we think logically. Stephen Toulmin, a British logician, offers another model for how we reason, and many public speaking students find his ideas helpful for analyzing their topic and building their speech.[10] His model consists of six main concepts, the first three serving as a must-have trio for a standard argument.

Claim: the assertion you want to prove. This could be your thesis, or a main sub-point in your speech.

Grounds: evidence that supports the acceptability of your claim. Examples, as already noted, include facts, statistics, illustrations, and expert opinion.

Warrant: the assumption or premise that allows the grounds to be taken as proof for your claim. Warrants work like the major premise in a syllogism.

If we apply these three concepts to the exercise-and-grades issue, a Toulmin depiction of the argument looks like Figure 9.1.

In this example, a study that shows how stress inhibits learning is only meaningful to the claim if one assumes that regular exercise reduces

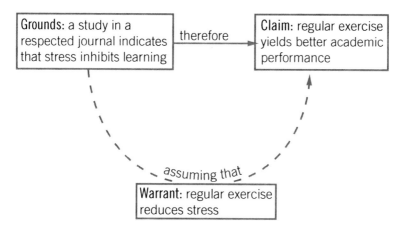

Figure 9.1 An application of Toulmin's three key concepts: claim, grounds, and warrant. We make claims based on grounds that seem reasonable given an assumed warrant.

stress. Toulmin's model goes on to add three additional concepts:

Backing: this is support or evidence that proves your warrant as true.

Reservations or rebuttals: these statements indicate, by your own admission, instances when your claim may not hold true

> **Qualifier**: a word or phrase that indicates your degree of certainty; terms such as "maybe," "usually," and "undoubtedly."

Someone might argue that finding time to exercise, or the fear of injury, makes regular exercise stressful. That person may demand proof that your warrant is true—that exercise lowers stress. You might back-up your warrant with a study or expert opinion that supports your assumption that exercise lowers stress.

Upon thinking through the issue, you might see that in some cases exercise causes more stress than peace. Toulmin would suggest that these are admitted reservations, or rebuttals, and they typically start with the word "unless." For example, "Exercise reduces stress *unless* one suffers from a chronic heart condition," or "Exercise reduces stress *unless* potential injury outweighs benefits." In this case, you might want to add a *qualifier* to your claim: "Regular exercise *usually* yields better academic performance." Your provisional language indicates that you are not boorish about the generalizability of your claim, but that you still believe in its essential truth value. A full Toulmin schematic is represented in Figure 9.2.

You might chart out your speech by placing your thesis in the "claim" box, and then inserting different pieces of evidence in the "support" box, and from there working out how the warrant, backing, rebuttals, and qualifiers play out for each piece of evidence.

Public Speaking Is a Symbolic Activity

Do you think Franklin Roosevelt's speech after Japan's attack on Pearl Harbor would have been memorable if he had begun it with, "December 7, 1941: A date which will live in world history"? That's how his assistant first wrote it. Roosevelt made one slight change, and now most college students can repeat, "December 7, 1941: A date which will live in infamy." Or consider if John F. Kennedy had said, "Stop looking for a government handout, and find some way to chip in your own two bits." Instead he penned, "Ask not what your country can do for you—ask what you can do for your country."

In Chapter 3 we discussed the power of words to refer to and create reality. That is perhaps no truer than in public speaking. Behind

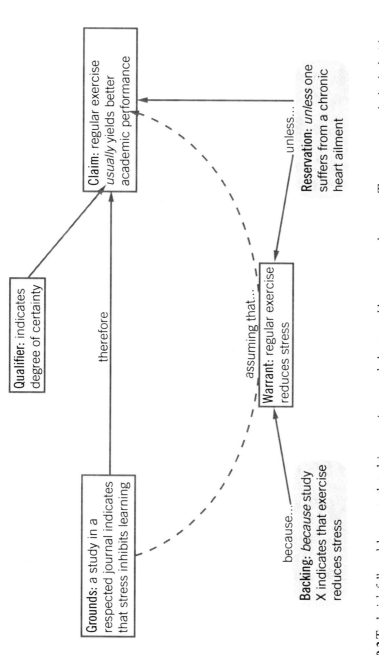

Figure 9.2 Toulmin's full model suggests that claims require grounds, buttressed by an assumed warrant. The warrant may be backed with support, and reservations might be articulated to anticipate listener rebuttals. Qualifiers indicate our degree of certainty.

the podium we *cite* incriminating evidence, *describe* war and heaven, *plead* the case of the innocent, *defend* our values, *proclaim* God's word, and the like. This is not to ignore the importance of vocal variety and appropriate gestures, but to highlight that without words we would have pantomime, not public *speaking*. In Chapter 3 we considered how words might be used intelligibly, culturally, worthily, as stories, and in speech acts. Here are some additional guidelines.

Define Terms Early. When we define key terms early in our speech, we provide our listeners with semantic pegs on which to hang the rest of our speech. For example, the scholar who defined "myth" as "culturally important stories" gave his readers a guiding definition to interpret his analysis. Therefore, when he said that Bush's speech "harkens back to our cherished myth [culturally important story] of a land blessed by God for the use of a great, free people" we know he is analyzing American culture, not calling the belief untrue or make-believe necessarily.[11] Therefore, a student who argues that regular exercise improves academic performance may want to define "regular exercise," "improves," and "academic performance."

Find the right word. Not the *morally* right word, though this may apply at times, but the *meaningfully* right word. Meanings are in people, but the right words vibrate them. "World history" might be correct, but Roosevelt's choice of "infamy" captures the evil and anger associated with the bombing of Pearl Harbor. Likewise, President Bush's speech tugs our hearts with phrases such as "seared on our souls," "horror," "painful," and "empty places" to mourn the loss of 9/11 victims.

Find the appropriate word. By *appropriate* I mean words that will not offend people inadvertently. Sexist expressions such as *dame* and *stud*, as well as stereotypical expressions such as *dumb blond* and *red neck* place people in boxes. Our language should show respect for people, even if we do not identify with them.

Avoid jargon. Jargon is technical language that creeps into our language when we become experts in a field or area. What would you think if your well-educated pastor began a sermon like this: "Lest our sanctification be hindered by iniquity, let us renounce our abominations and embrace Christ's propitiation." The statement is rotten with jargon. Better if your pastor simply said, "Let's admit that we've messed up and accept Christ's payment for our sins so we can grow spiritually." Both church-goers and non-church-goers can tap into this line's meaning.

You might be tempted to write out your entire speech before you give it, and that's not a bad idea. Doing so will probably guarantee precise word choice. However be careful not to get hung up on specific diction on first writing. I suggest you outline the speech in point form, and then tool the wording later on.

Public Speaking Is about Organizing Your Message

An old wag once said, "It's okay to have butterflies before you speak, just make sure they're flying in formation!" One way to control our nervousness is to be organized. In my public speaking course I require speakers to prepare a speech outline and hand it in the day of their speech. Once they know where they are headed, they are a step closer to a more controlled delivery.

Classic patterns for organizing speech material abound. The big picture usually follows this pattern: tell your audience what you will tell them, tell them, and then tell them what you told them. In other words, use an introduction, body, and conclusion.

Introduction. Your first words set the tone, scope, and purpose of your speech. Plan them well! A thoughtful introduction will 1) orient your audience to your topic, 2) build rapport between you and your listeners, 3) possibly give an internal preview of points you will cover, and 4) state your thesis. Beginning with a pithy quotation, a vivid story, an appropriate joke, or reference to the occasion may achieve each of these goals. Practice your introduction aloud several times so you can nail it.

Body. The body of your speech develops your thesis—that is, it proves what you think is true. Informative and persuasive speeches may follow a number of stock patterns for organizing material. You will need to decide which pattern works best for your topic:

> **Narration**: a lengthy story around which your entire speech is built. This is also called a *chronological pattern* because

your points retell events in time sequence. A personal testimony of faith fits this category.

Spatial: when your points reflect physical or geographic locations. A speech describing six places to vacation in your home state will refer to six locales, their features, and whereabouts. Or, your description of Florida's Epcot Center may be organized by exhibition.

Categorical or topical: when you organize your topic by natural divisions. For example, a categorical approach was used earlier in this chapter to describe types of speeches: speeches to inform, persuade, commemorate, entertain, and the like. Also, the material you are currently reading describes patterns of organizing speeches along five different categories.

Problem-Solution: to argue that a problem exists, and then offer a solution to solve it. Of course you may have two or three sub-points within each of these broad areas. President Bush's recollection of the terrorist attacks painted a bleak problem; his solution: "a sacred promise…we will not relent until justice is done and our nation is secure."[12] When your audience is unaware of the problem, you will need to prove that it exists before you offer a solution; in other cases, the problem is obvious, and you would be wise to focus on the solution.

Statement of Reasons and Refutations: to order your points as reasons for your thesis, and address anticipated refutations as well. A speech encouraging people to consider motorcycling would likely list reasons why such as: 1) motorcycles are economical on gas, 2) motorcycles are convenient, and 3) motorcycles cost less than cars. But motorcycles are also dangerous, so you might refute this idea with 4) motorcyclists who wear helmets and protective clothing suffer fewer injuries than those who do not.

Conclusion. Plan to wrap up your speech with some kind of summary, challenge, or unique final point. President Bush ended with a challenge for Americans to be confident, and claimed that their cause was "freedom guided by conscience and guided by peace." His biblical allusion to light shining in darkness, and the darkness not overcoming it, served as a vivid symbol of hope as he stood on Ellis Island. Keep your conclusion brief yet sufficient to provide closure for your audience. Tie up loose ends, and finish strong.

Public Speaking Is about Who You Are

Our plans to research, organize, word, and argue our speech will be for naught if our audience thinks we are foolish, insincere, or incompetent. So it is worthwhile to look inwardly to ask, are we worthy of this speech? This topic? This occasion?

In Chapter 3 we noted that our language spills from the condition of our heart (Matthew 12:33–34). That principle is a time-honored one. Plato bemoaned show-off speakers who devalued the truth.[13] These speakers, called sophists (pronounced *sah-fists*) were professional speakers who traveled the Greek islands impressing common folks with their ability to argue both sides of an issue, but avoided taking a personal stand. Plato likened them to "false lovers"—connivers who used public speaking to deceive and manipulate people in order to make an easy buck. Plato urged would-be rhetoricians to be "noble lovers"—people who spoke the truth and allowed the audience to respond in a way that benefited themselves, not the speaker.

Similarly Aristotle made a lot of being a person of character as a prerequisite for the public speaker. He argued that a speaker's *ethos*— that is, character, good will, and moral rightness—completed the trilogy of *logos* and *pathos*. To be sure, we make appeals to logic and emotions, but these appeals depend on our moral character to gain full effect.[14]

Furthermore, around the time of Christ, Roman teacher Fabius Quintilian defined the entire public speaking enterprise as "A good man speaking well." For Quintilian, a person was good if he or she was "free from all vice, a lover of wisdom, a sincere believer in the cause which he advocates, and a servant of the state and the people."[15] That is quite a high calling.

The contemporary term for ethos is "credibility." Credibility is the degree to which audience members perceive us as knowledgeable,

**"What software would you recommend to give
my presentation so much flash and sizzle that
nobody notices that I have nothing to say?"**

trustworthy, dynamic, attractive, and similar to themselves.[16] Choosing
a topic you genuinely enjoy or are passionate about will likely build on
your knowledge and trustworthiness. Dressing one notch better than
your audience and using an engaging delivery will boost dynamism
and attractiveness. Finally, if you can show how your values, beliefs,
or experiences ring true with your audience, they will regard you as
similar to themselves, and therefore more credible. Most importantly,
speak on topics that reflect your true self. Don't be a sophist. People
can see right through a phony.

Public Speaking Is an Ethical Activity

Being a person of integrity makes ethical speaking seem natural. As
the previous section implies, when our heart is right, our speech will
be right. But of course it is not always that simple. Saying what is right
also depends on the situation and on our audience. Quickly the issue
of what is the best, moral, right thing to say gets complex.

The field of ethics concerns rules for right behavior, for right
choices. And in public speaking, we make many choices in order to
speak. What topic should I choose? What language reflects it accurately? Is my research sufficient to make a strong case? What style of
delivery will impress but not deceive? What organizational pattern
will convince, but not manipulate?

Fortunately, philosophers and theologians have wrestled with this issue and provide moral maxims to guide our speechmaking. Moral maxims are like steel girders to which we might rivet our speech and behavior. A maxim such as "Integrity is more valued than image" might render the ethic (behavioral rule) "Don't make up proof in order to sound impressive." Let's briefly consider several classic maxims and their application to public speaking.[17]

Aristotle's Golden Mean: Communication is ethical if it reflects moral virtue. Moral virtue is that which is situated between excess and deficiency. For example, arguing for complete government control of media content is excessive; arguing for no government control is deficiency. Arguing for moderate involvement would be considered virtuous, hence ethical. As you prepare your speech, ask if you are arguing the virtuous center.

Situation Ethics: Communication is ethical if it is the most loving thing to do and if it adheres to the ethical maxims of a given place or culture. Therefore, there are no universal rules for ethical behavior, only cultural or situational ones.[18] Conservative critiques of situation ethics cast them as too relative, but the main maxim rings true with biblical truth. Consider how Paul said he became all things to all people so he might win some. He was willing to adjust his rhetoric to local cultural expectations so he might lovingly win them to his view. Will your audience consider your speech as loving?

The End Justifies the Means: Any communication strategy (the means) is ethical if the speaker believes his or her goal (the end) is noble and just. Quintilian, for example, believed it would be okay to lie to an audience if this strategy diverted an assassin from a victim, deceived an enemy to save one's country, or comforted a child who was sick. What concerns many believers, and non-believers alike, is that individuals such as Adolph Hitler and Ganges Kahn used what they believed to be moral ends to perform heinous acts of brutality as well as manipulative rhetoric. Better that our means are as noble as our ends.

John Stuart Mill's Principle of Utility: Communication is ethical if it brings the greatest good for the greatest number of people. Typically "greatest good" has been defined as the presence of pleasure and the absence of pain. Other scholars say that what is "good" includes the entire package of beauty, economic gain, honor, and the like. Do you think George W. Bush's commemorative speech brought the most good to his world of listeners? What benefits were gained by Americans? Allies? Enemies? What else could Bush say that would benefit more people?

Immanuel Kant's Categorical Imperative: This German philosopher suggested that you "Act only on that maxim which you can will to become a universal law."[19] Or, in other words, do only that which you are willing to allow everyone else to do. For example, if you or I fudge statistics to pad a weak section in our speech, Kant would ask us if we are willing to allow anyone, anywhere, to fabricate statistics too. If we answer no, then we have broken his maxim. On the other hand, we should be able to answer yes categorically (without reservation) to a host of other questions: Should all speakers research their topics thoroughly? Should speakers avoid manipulating audience emotions? Should speakers argue with sound logic? It is not difficult to uphold Kant's maxim if we follow standard textbook wisdom.

Democratic Rationalist Perspectives: Communication is ethical if it mirrors "equality of opportunity, free and open discussion, equality of individuals, belief in the inherent dignity of all human beings, [and] the right of freedom of information."[20] This perspective assumes that if you give rational people sufficient information, they can make the right decision. As public speakers this translates into the right for everyone to speak their mind and receive our respectful attention. It means speaking in a manner that invites discussion rather than squelches it, and acknowledges that we as speakers do not wield ultimate expert authority. A valid question is whether or not the media allow for a democratic, rational discussion of issues. Does CNN's coverage of Bush's 9/11 commemorative speech and the ensuing analysis of that speech by Larry King and other analysts, constitute a fair, open, level-headed discourse?

Dialogical Perspectives: Communication is ethical if it adheres to the rules of dialogue, not monologue. Dialogue resembles the charades model of interpersonal communication we discussed in Chapter 6. People who dialogue are genuine, empathetic, show unconditional positive regard for the other, and promote a spirit of equality and emotional support. Jewish philosopher Martin Buber popularized this perspective with his distinction between I-it and I-Thou communication. I-it rhetoric treats listeners as objects, while I-Thou considers them complex image bearers of God deserving of dialog, not monolog.[21] Theorists Karen Foss and Sonja Foss affirm a similar view when they suggest that rhetoric should be a process of wholeness, process, and cooperation, rather than the cool application of logic to dominate others.[22] Dialogical speakers strive to be audience-centered and audience-sensitive as they prepare and deliver speeches. They are eager to entertain questions following their speech, rather than flee to the comforts of off-stage.

Covenantal Ethics: Communication is ethical if it allows people-in-community the voice to participate in their understood common good.[23] Or, put in terms from Chapter 2, covenantal communication is ethical because it brings parties together to agree upon redemptive pacts to change together over time for their common good. Like those who call themselves communitarians, covenantal ethicists believe we can know the common good and aim to speak it into existence. A covenantal approach values the raising of questions for discussion as much as the declaration of one's own beliefs. It is talk that invites participation, and articulates the communal virtues of acceptance, patience, compassion, and generosity. Covenantal speakers speak *with* their audience, not *at* them.

> Covenantal ethics requires empowerment of people-in-community to voice their vision of the common good.

Speaking this way suggests that audiences have freedom to respond willfully to what speakers say. Em Griffin considers free will to be crucial to any ethic for presenting the gospel of Jesus to unbelievers. In *The Mind Changers: The Art of Christian Persuasion* he writes: "As ambassadors for Christ, we need to have an ethical standard which guides our appeal regardless of how people respond. I believe there is such a standard. Simply stated it is: Any persuasive effort which restricts another's freedom to choose for or against Jesus Christ is wrong."[24] Verbally abusive speeches that coerce listeners to "choose

Christ, or else" obviously fall outside Griffin's rule. Christ *calls* us to himself, and then allows us to choose.

Public Speaking Is a "Live" Activity

Have you ever experienced speakers who read their entire speech, or fixate on their PowerPoint slides, or drone on and on in monotone? Those delivery styles, I suggest, are dead, not alive. They ignore the fact that covenantal *public* speaking takes place with others, requires eyeball-to-eyeball connection, and engages the spirit. Coming together, in this covenantal fashion, requires thoughtful content and winsome delivery. Let's consider tips that deliver on delivery.

Delivery Styles. You can give your speech in one of three modes, or a combination thereof. In certain situations the *manuscript style* serves you well. A manuscript allows you to prepare all your material ahead of time, right down to precise word choice. Having a manuscript to read gives you peace of mind when your material is highly technical or when the situation requires carefully crafted pronouncements. Similarly, a *memorized style* puts the research and wording issues behind you, and allows you look right at your audience and kick in your best nonverbal skills. Short speeches and humorous talks adapt well to memorization. However, both styles have pitfalls: reading can sound monotone, and memorization can sound canned. You can lose your spot while reading, or misorder your twelve page manuscript. Memorized styles can lead to embarrassment should you pull a blank, or leave out critical points.

The delivery style I encourage my students to master is termed *extemporaneous*, or speaking from prepared notes. The extemporaneous speaker uses an outline as the basic skeleton, and then fleshes out the speech spontaneously, but not for the first time in front of an audience. If you practice your speech four or five times aloud using your outline, you will own your ideas deeply, and this will lead to wording that is fresh and precise when you "go live." Extemporaneous speaking provides an ideal balance between planned material and in-the-fray performance. It frees you to move about on the platform (if desired), give ample eye contact, and engage your voice to emphasize key points.

Your Voice and Dress. How you *sound* and how you *look* play key roles in your success as a speaker. What kind of voice do your listeners hear? Tinny? Airy? Soft? Recall from Chapter 4 that these qualities can make people jump to the conclusion that you are immature, inse-cure, indecisive, or weak.[25] You will promote a better impression with a full, rich voice if you follow these tips:

> 1) Project your voice with increased volume—about twice as loud as when you speak in regular conversation. Opening your mouth widely and taking full breaths will aid projection.

> 2) Vary your pitch to express your ideas. You might practice your speech in *monotone* as a negative example to compare with a bet-ter *variable tone.*

> 3) Change your rhythm and rate. That is, avoid a stylistic rut! Video capture your speech and listen for where variation is needed for effect.

> 4) Articulate and pronounce with care. Articulation is saying words *clearly*, and pronouncing is saying them *correctly*. Both will aid hearing and comprehension.

Your voice should carry well to your audience with conviction and vocal variety. Make sure everyone can hear you easily, and enjoy filling the room with the full, confident sound of your voice.

In Chapter 4 we discussed how the *artifacts* such as clothing, hair-style, and jewelry determine our appearance. Dressing casually tells others you are friendly, fair, enthusiastic, and flexible. Dressing for-mally conveys that you are prepared, knowledgeable, and organized.[26] Just how you should dress depends on the expectations of your audi-ence, and the situation. A chat with local school kids about car safety might call for casual clothes, whereas a year-end banquet speech at your workplace may require formal attire. A rule of thumb is that you consider what your audience will be wearing, and match it, or dress one notch up. You will want to avoid the extremes of under-dressing or overkill.

Eye Contact and Gestures. A final comment should be made about looking at people, and using your hands. In western society, eye con-tact communicates interpersonal warmth, respect, and attention. Don't leave home without it! You should know your speech well enough to freely connect with most audience members. Poor eye contact focuses on the podium, the back wall, or listeners' foreheads. Favorable contact engages in person-to-person contact for one to two seconds, spontaneously, and across the entire room. A helpful way to improve eye contact is to practice your speech with a mirror, and look at yourself. If you can endure your own glare, you can handle the eyes of your audience.

Chapter 4 described *illustrators* such as gestures that help visualize what we say. When I caught a thirty-four inch salmon one year, you can bet I was quick to stretch my arms wide to illustrate my prize. Illustrators come in handy when describing objects ("It was *this* long), or directions ("The new library will be past this green space and to the left"), or for emphasis (shrugging one's shoulders when asking, "Who could explain it?"). Illustrators come naturally as you become comfortable with your material, and show your enthusiasm and conviction.

This chapter has provided guidelines for preparing your first or fortieth speech. See Table 9.1 for a checklist for your personal preparation.

TABLE 9.1 - CHECKLIST FOR PUBLIC SPEAKING

- ✔ Know your purpose, and stick with it.
- ✔ Do the research your topic requires.
- ✔ Argue your position logically and emotionally.
- ✔ Word your speech for clarity and power.
- ✔ Organize your points sensibly.
- ✔ Be credible on your topic.
- ✔ Speak ethically.
- ✔ Deliver extemporaneously.

Summary

This chapter scopes out the skills and wisdom required to speak well. And the checklist just noted serves as a springboard for our summary. When you know your purpose, your speech will gain focus and clarity. Lack purpose, and you will confuse your audience.

Few of us enjoy research, but without it, we lack credibility. The same goes for our logic and emotional appeals. As God said to Israel, "come, let us reason together." We ought to reason together with our listeners, being sensitive to their assumptions and values so we can appeal to them ethically. In regard to emotion, our appeals to love or hope, disgust or fear should be appropriate and not cloud our listeners' capacity to reason. God made us complex creatures; our appeals should be similarly complex.

How we organize our material will determine how well our audience grasps it. Disorganized points fail to fall into the categories audiences expect. Similarly, a poor delivery distracts or bores our audience. Better to organize sensibly, and deliver with passion.

Perhaps most significant is speaking ethically. Have you considered the common good? Does your position, and your delivery, honor God? Have you avoided faulty logic, and appealed to valid emotions? If your conscience bugs you as you prepare, listen to it.

Finally, the wording, or diction, cloaks our speech in rags or fine linen. Sweating over appropriate, powerful word choice will pay off with your audience. May we be good people speaking well.

 **WORTH THE TALK**

1. What is your greatest fear about public speaking? Why do you fear it?

2. This chapter lays out numerous suggestions for preparing a speech. Which step do you find most challenging? Why?

3. Can you think of instances where a speaker used strong emotions to persuade you? Do you think the speaker acted ethically?

 **CONSIDER THE WALK**

1. Listen to a classmate's speech or another person's speech and analyze it from several ethical perspectives described in this chapter. Answer the question: Did the speaker use ethical means to accomplish an ethical end? The means of a speech deal with how it was organized, worded, researched, and argued. The end of speech is its goal. Did the speaker encourage the audience to adopt an ethical behavior?

2. Write a research paper that examines the ethics of a well-known speaker in world history. Some examples include Abraham Lincoln, Patrick Henry, Susan B. Anthony, Winston Churchill, Adolph Hitler, John F. Kennedy, Mother Teresa, Billy Graham, and Chairman Mao. Be sure you research more about ethics from other sources, and try to explain how this speaker's ethics enhanced or inhibited his or her success as a speaker.

3. Study the following cases. Write a one-paragraph response to each of the questions asked. Be prepared to discuss and expand on your answers in class.[27]

> a. A student in a speaking class has been assigned to give an informative speech in one week. He is very busy with required assignments in other courses and puts off the preparation of the speech until the night before it is due. He has great difficulty

finding a topic and finally resorts to using extensively an article from *Reader's Digest* as the basis for his speech. He makes no reference to the article in his speech. What are the ethical questions involved in this case, and how do you think they should be decided?

b. Is it ethical for a speech student to give a speech that was written by her roommate? Is it ethical for a politician to give a speech that was written by his or her speechwriter?

c. Is it ethical for a speaker to read her entire speech in a speech class? (Or, is a speaker acting ethically if she engages in no eye contact with the audience in this same class?). Would you make the same judgment for a preacher? Explain.

d. Are we ethically bound to listen to all persons who desire to speak to us? If not, why not, and when, if at all, should we refuse to listen to a speaker?

 **ONLINE CHALK**

The following key words generate a host of sites on speech preparation, delivery tips, famous speeches, and sermons. As always, use your own discretion as to the value of what you find at each site.

- How to give a speech
- How to speak confidently
- Great speeches
- Classical rhetoric
- How to preach
- Homiletics [an academic term for the art of preaching]
- See also AmericanRhetoric.com for audio and video recordings of speeches by well known American politicians and Christians

Following are some sites that may prove useful for conducting academic research on the Internet for your speeches or any other assignment.[28]

- Google Scholar: http://scholar.google.com
- CiteSeer: http://citeseer.ist.psu.edu/
- Scirus: http://www.scirus.com/srsapp/
- Windows Live Academic: http://academic.live.com
- getCITED: http://www.getcited.org/

 **ENDNOTES**

1 See Bush's Ellis Island commemorative speech at: http://election.rhetorica.net/bush/9-11_ellisisland.htm (accessed September, 2002).

2 For an excellent chapter on oral communication apprehension and how to deal with it see Donald W. Klopf and Ronald E. Cambra, "Anxious Communicators," in *Personal and Public Speaking*, 5th ed. (Englewood, CO: Morton Publishing, 1996), 77-88.

3 Reported in *The Sunday Times* of London, October 7, 1973.

4 Stephen E. Lucas, Juanita Wattam and Lazaros Simeon, *The Art of Public Speaking*, Canadian ed., (Toronto, ON: McGraw-Hill Ryerson, 2008), 371.

5 Most public speaking texts provide a full description of types of evidence. These lists were created with the help of Steven R. Brydon and Michael D. Scott, *Between One and Many: The Art and Science of Public Speaking*, 5th ed. (Boston: McGraw-Hill, 2006), 185-191.

6 See this and other quotations by Dr. Martin Luther King at: http://www.mlkonline.net/quotes.html.

7 On-line at http://election.rhetorica.net/bush/9-11_ellisisland.htm (accessed September, 2002).

8 For a fuller discussion of research sources see David Zarefsky, *Public Speaking: Strategies for Success*, 4th ed. (Boston: Pearson, Allyn & Bacon, 2005), 123-147.

9 See William B. Badke, *Research Strategies: Finding Your Way Through the Information Fog*, 3rd ed. (New York: iUniverse, Inc., 2008), 115-116. Note: the second sentence under point one is from the 2nd ed. of Badke's *Research Strategies*.

10 Stephen Toulmin, Richard Rieke and Allan Janik, *An Introduction to Reasoning*, 2nd ed. (New York: Macmillan, 1984).

11 See brief analysis following speech text at http://election.rhetorica.net/bush/9-11_ellisisland.htm (accessed September, 2002).

12 Ibid.

13 For a good overview of Plato, Aristotle and Quintilian's teachings on rhetoric see J. Golden, G. Berquist and W. Coleman, *The Rhetoric of Western Thought* (Dubuque, IA: Kendall/Hunt, 1983), chapters 2-4.

14 Ibid., chapter 2.

15 Ibid., 50.

16 Bert E. Bradley, *Fundamentals of Speech Communication: The Credibility of Ideas*, 6th ed. (Dubuque, IA: Wm. C. Brown, 1991), 69.

17 This list was compiled from several sources. For a fuller overview, I recommend that you consult a standard communication ethics text such as Richard Johannesen, *Ethics in Human Communication*, 3rd ed., (Prospect Heights, IL: Waveland Press, 1990).

18 This description of situation ethics is based on Joseph Fletcher's ideas as described by Bradley, *Fundamentals of Speech Communication*, 57. The work by Fletcher to which Bradley refers is J. Fletcher, *Situation Ethics* (Philadelphia: Westminster Press, 1966), 26.

19 Immanuel Kant, *Groundwork of the Metaphysics of Morals*, trans. H. J. Paton (New York: Harper Torchbooks, 1964), 88.

20 Vander Kooi and Veenstra, *Responsible Public Address*, 2nd ed. (unpublished manuscript, 1988), 17.

21 See Martin Buber, *I and Thou*, trans. R. G. Smith, 2nd ed. (New York: Scribner's, 1958), and Martin Buber, *Between Man and Man* (New York: Macmillan, 1965).

22 Karen Foss and Sonja Foss, "The Status of Research on Women and Communication," *Communication Quarter* 31 (1983): 195-204.

23 This definition based on Eric Mount, Jr., *Covenant, Community, and the Common Good* (Cleveland: Pilgrim Press, 1999).

24 Em Griffin, *The Mind Changers: The Art of Christian Persuasion* (Wheaton, IL: Tyndale House, 1976), 28.

25 See J. D. Burgoon, D. B. Buller and W. G. Woodall, *Nonverbal Communication: The Unspoken Dialogue* (New York: Harper & Row, 1989), 70.

26 These results were found for instructors dressed informally and formally and impressions students had of each. See L. A. Malandro, L. Barker and D. A. Barker, *Nonverbal Communication*, 2nd ed. (New York: Random House, 1989).

27 These examples are taken from Vander Kooi and Veenstra's *Responsible Public Address*, 19-20.

28 Badke, *Research Strategies*, 101-105.

Though I am free and belong to no man, I make myself a slave to everyone, to win as many as possible. To the Jews I became like a Jew, to win Jews. To those under the law I became like one under the law . . . so as to win those not having the law. To the weak I became weak, to win the weak. I have become all things to all men so that by all possible means I might save some. I do this for the sake of the gospel, that I may share in its blessings.

1 Corinthians 9:19–20, 22–23

Connecting with Strangers

An Incarnational Approach to
Intercultural Communication

MY CULTURAL UPBRINGING was rich yet narrow. From age four to eighteen, my roots were Jackson, Minnesota, population 3,400—a town nestled in the west fork of the Des Moines River valley. Surrounding that valley laid green-gold fields of corn and soybeans, and the outcropping of farmstead windbreaks. Half the students in my school were farm kids, the other half, town kids. The Worthington Trojans were our archrival in football, the Windom Eagles in basketball. The first African American I ever saw lived thirty miles away. In my early teens, a big trip meant visiting the Twin Cities three hours northeast. During high school, a band trip to Disney World brought the same sense of new and different.

I spent my university years nine hours from Jackson in the Chicago suburb of Wheaton, Illinois, and while the miles were great, the feeling was the same. Eighty-five percent of my classmates were white like me, and most were from middle- or upper-middle class homes. During those years I toured with a male choir that sang in Europe for six weeks. But even England, France, Switzerland, Germany, and the Netherlands looked safe from the elevated angle of a monster tour bus. After twenty years living in the U.S. Midwest, I needed a change and a challenge.

Therefore, after graduation, I decided to work overseas, and within three months I was on a plane for India as a short-term worker. There I got change and challenge.

Surrounding the orphanage where I worked were okra fields and orange orchards, and the occasional mango tree. Rather than football, I played *kubadi*, a form of chain-gang tag-and-tackle. I needed no big trip to get a buzz for the different. In nearby Chandur Bazaar, merchants sold freshly butchered goat and chicken, though a live chicken was preferred. Hindu shrines and naked Jain priests offered religious comment on beggars in shredded clothes and lepers with finger-less hands.

One warm summer night I was reminded of how India's ways extend through their modes of communication. I had just played a board game with Joey Meshramkar, the son of the orphanage director. Joey began walking me back to my bungalow, and as he did, he reached his hand for mine. I had seen Indian schoolboys holding hands in town, but this was different, I thought. We joined hands palm-to-palm and proceeded down the road. A few seconds later Joey adjusted his grip, and placed his fingers every other between my own. To a Minnesota boy, this type of hand-holding meant, "going steady." As a college graduate I knew it also meant "a cultural expression of friendship." You might imagine my ambivalence. A hundred steps later we arrived at the guesthouse and Joey let go. I was free at last. Thirty years later I can still recall my relief.

You might smile with me over such a little thing, but it was huge to me then. Showing friendship is a little thing, a godly thing. But *the manner* in which we show friendship is a cultural thing, and sometimes the differences count. Connecting with someone from a different background can bring variety and learning to a sheltered life. It can also establish a relational bridge for us to be God's ambassador to the world on our doorstep. Covenantal relating requires extra preparation and pure motives when we interact with culturally different others. How we might do that is the focus of this chapter.

Gazing at Our Cultural Navels? Today you do not have to go to India to find people of different races, cultures, and religions. The urban centers of the United States and Canada have become cross-sections of the global village. Within three houses of where I live reside a German couple from Paraguay, a couple from Brazil, and a couple from Greece.

Around the corner live two Indo-Canadian families. Your own neighborhood or school may be even more culturally diverse.

However, despite our increased opportunity to interact with people unlike ourselves, research indicates that we are far more likely to befriend people who are similar to us in age, sex, and race. We may enjoy work relationships and "activity friendships" on sport teams or in a choir with ethnic acquaintances, but we reserve relationships of trust and influence with those largely like ourselves.[1]

This pattern of whites befriending whites, blacks linking with blacks, and the like is important communicationally. We are more likely to develop a coherent personal and group identity, and experience harmonious use of language and nonverbal cues, within a single ethnic tradition. No one should blame anyone else for desiring these benefits. The problems arise when we begin to believe that how one group thinks and lives culturally is the only acceptable way. If I judge okra thumbs-down because it doesn't rate with Iowa corn, it is only a step away to judge Joey Meshramkar as "forward" because he failed to befriend me the Iowan way. Doing so suggests that I have gazed too long at my own cultural navel.

For believers, the urge to judge may be doubly strong, because we are tempted to equate what is culturally acceptable with what is morally (or even biblically) permissible. The two may overlap at times, but not always. For example, in central India it was common for Christian women to sit on the left side of the church sanctuary and the men on the right. Is this biblically required? I don't think so. Is it culturally expected? Yes—the same pattern was repeated in Bollywood movie theaters. Should I judge this split arrangement as evil? No. What I might do is ask a local Indian where this behavioral pattern came from, and then learn to live within its parameters. Doing so helps me, like Paul, to become all things to all people that I may influence some for God. Observing others and asking questions make us a student of their culture.

Understanding Culture

When we think of "culture" it is easy to conjure up images of burial site artifacts, painted masks, and dugout canoes (or for that matter, cemetery headstones, Avon cosmetics, and Ford Windstars). These are physical features of culture, but they are only a slice of its meaning.

Culture is the total life way of a people: how they think, how they behave, and what they create.

This definition is a composite of three aspects: the cognitive, the behavioral, and the artifactual. *Cognitive culture* is in our heads. It consists of our worldview, values, beliefs, and typical ways of thinking. An Indian student's value for family enmeshment compared to a Canadian student's value for personal independence is a good example of cognitive culture because they carry such values in their thinking patterns, and use them to make judgments about life. *Behavioral culture* is what we do, whether individually or as a group. It includes our micro use of space (proxemics), body movement (kinesics), and time (chronemics) as well as macro behaviors such as sports, driving styles, and celebrating holidays. Sunita's choice to visit her parents over spring break, but Susan's desire to spend time with friends on a road trip, reflect behaviorally Sunita's value for family and Susan's preference for independence. *Artifactual culture* is what we build, sculpt, design, plant, and create, and once created, these material objects affirm and continue to shape our worldview. In Sunita's hometown, the local Hindu temple and priestly garments of its monks re-affirm the role Hindu beliefs in Sunita's world and almost a billion others like her. In Susan's city glass and steel buildings preach the gospel of efficiency and progress while towering above diminutive church structures.

From a covenantal perspective, culture is a mammoth pact—a vast set of elements we agree upon to guide our cognitive, behavioral, and artifactual life. Of course not everyone will agree on every element, but a large majority will hold to a critical center, and will communicate it to succeeding generations. In cultural context we agree to love or hate God, play football or *kubadi*, and build homes from brick or bamboo. The process of learning our original culture is called *enculturation*, and the longer we spend time in that culture, the harder it is to adjust within another one.

Is Culture Good or Bad, of God or of Humans?

In Minneapolis, Minnesota the Mall of America boasts over 400 stores for one's shopping pleasure. In all of Chandur Bazaar the local merchants number about sixty. Both shopping areas are cultural efforts to meet material needs. Are 400 stores better than sixty? Do the eighty women's shops at the Mall represent a better system than the eight in Chandur Baazar? Or, regarding a different issue, if one were to start a church in either place, where would be its best cultural location—right in the Mall or business district, on the edge of town, or out in the country? Does location even matter?

Marvin Mayers, past Dean of the School of Intercultural Studies and World Missions at Biola University, wrestles with the question of whether culture is evil, neutral, holy, or what. To answer, he first grapples with the question of biblical truth and cultural reality. We know that the scriptures call us to holy living, but we also know that we live an okra-and-football world. Where is the truth for how we should live? In *Christianity Confronts Culture*, Mayers suggests a matrix for picturing how Christians may look at biblical truth and cultural reality.[2] We can look at both through the eyes of *absolutism* or through the tinted glasses of *relativism*. Together these two responses form four categories of thought (see Figure 10.1)

Bible and Culture as Absolute. Position 1 is taken by many conservative believers. They hold that the Bible and culture are both absolute, that is, complete and unchanging. In their thinking, biblical mandates are interpreted as having one cultural expression, so to change that expression is to question the authority of the scripture as containing the principles for guiding life and behavior. For example, some believers interpret the command to "not make for yourself an idol" in Exodus 20 a call for barren worship halls. Even a simple wooden cross or embroidered banner is forbidden. Such a view produces what Mayers

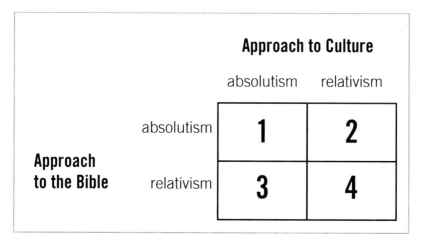

Figure 10.1 Four Ways of Thinking About Biblical Truth and Cultural Reality. (See Mayers, 1987, pp. 247-249)

terms cultural exclusivism, where "all other cultures and their life-ways are approached from the point of view of the person looking in."[3] Growing up in one culture within one religious denomination tends to create position 1 thinking. Such individuals use scripture and their own culture to evaluate what is good and bad in other people's cultures. The academic word for making such judgments is *ethnocentrism*.

Position 1 assumptions in the late 1800s to late 1900s in Canada and Australia led to the practice of removing aboriginal children from their families and placing them in residential schools in order to "kill the Indian in the child." In the classrooms and dormitories government teachers and church clergy forbade aboriginal kids to practice their native culture, punished them for speaking their original language, and required them to dress in western clothes and speak English.

Bible as Relative, Culture as Absolute. Position 3 is held largely by humanitarians who regard culture as the sole determiner of what to regard as truth and responsible behavior. In earlier chapters I have referred to these people as postmodernists. Postmodernists regard cultures as complete, whole systems that define and guide each cultural group toward their construction of truth and moral behavior. They believe that no outsider has the right to alter a culture's principles or lifestyle. The Bible is considered one of many sacred and secular texts that contribute to cultural life. The Bible is not considered the rule of life and behavior for all cultures, because it is the product of one culture—the Jewish, Greek, Roman mix of first century Palestine.

In 2008, position 3 thinking led the prime ministers of Canada and Australia to make public apologies to aboriginal people for the painful legacy of residential schools in the 1900s. In his speech, PM Stephen Harper said, "Today, we recognize that this policy of assimilation was wrong, has caused great harm, and has no place in our country," indicating that he no longer presumed superiority of dominant European culture over First Nations ones, or at least lamented how his white forefathers imposed their culture on others.[4] Similarly, PM Kevin Rudd, looked to "A future where all Australians, whatever their origins, are truly equal partners, with equal opportunities and with an equal stake in shaping the next chapter in the history of this great country, Australia."[5] Position 3 thinking places each culture on equal footing because it assumes each culture determines local truth rather than there existing an objective knowledge of truth handed down through any one culture.

Bible as Relative, Culture as Relative. Position 4 is held by many professors in the social sciences. Mayers cites Clyde Kluckhohn, Margaret Mead, and Ruth Benedict as examples, as well as Christian anthropologists Bronislaw Malinowski, A. R. Radcliffe Brown, and Robert Redfield. In this view, "culture is a dynamic [not absolute] process that is internally self-correcting and can be relied on to produce decisions that aid the society as well as the individual within society."[6] The Bible is regarded as one of many texts for moral guidance that helps people communicate and act responsibly. Position 4 is similar to position 3 in spirit but not degree. Position 4 Christians believe that we can rise above our cultural entrapping to understand the universal good, and the communicationally wise, in light of God's general revelation to everyone on earth.

Position 4 thinking is represented in the residential school apologies in that both prime ministers referred to standards for human betterment, and that each cultural group should have a say about those standards. To quote Mr. Rudd, "[We envision] a future where we harness the determination of all Australians, Indigenous and non-Indigenous, to close the gap that lies between us in life expectancy, educational achievement and economic opportunity."[7] Comments such as these imply that living a long life, being educated (not ignorant), and finding meaningful work are worthy goals for all people. Of note, however, is that Mr. Rudd ignores the role of spiritual awareness or religious practice in culture.

Bible as Absolute, Culture as Relative. Position 2 is the one Mayers suggests is significant for the church worldwide. It is the view that I favor in this book. He writes:

> The approach of biblical absolutism and cultural relativism affirms that there is a supernatural intrusion. Truth is from God. Truth does not change. [However,] the way truth is communicated in a given culture and language will change. Even as Christ through the Incarnation became flesh and dwelt among us [that is, became human and lived among us], so truth becomes expressed in culture. However, the

Word made flesh lost none of his divineness, and truth is not corrupted or changed necessarily by its expression via human sociological forms. It is always full and complete as truth. The moment truth is wed to [only] one cultural expression, there is a high potential for falsehood.

Mayers' would say that joining God's truth to only one cultural expression is position 1 thinking, and will lead to the kinds of hurt and confusion witnessed in residential schools. However position 2 assumes that God has crashed into history and life to reveal himself and his gospel of love and forgiveness through Jesus Christ. Position 2 also takes seriously the God has commissioned us to be his helpers in passing on this good news to every people group. Therefore our goal should be to discover appropriate sociological (or communicational) means for making Christ relevant to people. If appropriate, those means will be as redemptive as the goal to make disciples of Jesus.[8]

Culture as Good. Therefore, what Mayers means, by a position 4 stance, is that culture is at least neutral, or perhaps even a good tool for the expression of biblical (and other) principles for responsible living. If any thing or any one is evil, people are, not culture, so it is quite possible to convey God's unchanging message through cultural forms. Women sitting on one side of the sanctuary and men on the other may reflect cultural gender roles, but it does not undermine God's call that we treat each other as sisters and brothers in the Lord. Likewise, a church that holds its services at the Mall of America is simply playing Minnesotan. Even residential schools may be appropriate as long as parents and kids buy into them freely, and school teachers uphold God-honoring standards for nurturing young people. If Jesus lived a cultural life as a Jewish carpenter-gone-rabbi, we too can convey God's message to others through local forms. In short, Mayers is saying that most cultural forms are neutral or even good because they are created by made-in-God's-image people, and capable of communicating his truth.

Culture as Bad. Sherwood Lingenfelter, a colleague of Marvin Mayers, would underline "most cultural forms." He may even say that only a few cultural forms are so blessed. He reasons that if culture is the cognitive outpouring of sinful people into behavioral and physical forms, then some cultural patterns (if not a good many) are fallen too. For example, if we are "locked" into a Mall-of-America way of thinking, we are apt to worship money, not God eternal. Our cultural habits, though commonplace to us, are essentially keeping us from communion with God. He refers to Paul's writings to make his point that culture might be a "pen [or cage] of disobedience."

> Paul suggests that human beings are in a prison, a cell of disobedience: "God has imprisoned all human beings in their own disobedience only to show mercy to them all" (Romans 11:30–32 NJB). He repeats the same theme in Galatians 3:22, paraphrasing Psalm 14:1–3. He observes that "the whole world is a prisoner to sin." God has penned up all people in their self-created cells of culture, including Jew and Gentile, pagan and missionary.[9]

Taking Mayers' analogy of culture as a tool, Lingenfelter uses the same analogy with a different result. "Using the tool analogy, culture is more like a "slot machine" found in Las Vegas' gambling casinos than a wrench or screwdriver. Culture, like a slot machine, is programmed to be sure that those who hold power "win" and the common players "lose"; when or if the organized agenda is violated, people frequently resort to violence to reestablish their "programmed" advantage."[10]

To the degree that worship services in materialistic malls mock the simple lifestyle Jesus chose, they are pens of disobedience. To the extent that dividing women and men in worship leads to stereotyping of the other, it is a fallen cultural form. Insofar that a residential school system causes a child to feel abandoned by her parents, it is a cultural form best avoided.

So Who's Right? That is a tough question. Frankly, I do not think we should ask this question, because both perspectives deserve merit. Jesus didn't ignore the cultural means available to him, but neither did he involve himself in every cultural practice. Professor Mayers' optimism is based on Christ's use of first century cultural forms to convey his life-changing message. Professor Lingenfelter's pessimism stems from observing sinners who get side tracked by attractive, sinful forms. Some forms, like slot machines and inhumane housing complexes and nuclear bombs, are bent toward evil: the first two are designed to hook others for an easy profit and the third to wipe out an enemy rather than turn the other cheek. Determining what forms may pen us in and which ones bring new life may not be easy. What we do have is the life of Christ as a model for being spiritual and cultural beings. His method was to bridge the culture of heaven with the culture of earth through the mystery of the incarnation. That's a model worth considering.

What Is Incarnational Communication?

Put simply, to communicate incarnationally is to imitate the strategy of God in Jesus Christ. While it is similar to redemptive interpersonal communication (see Chapter 5), its scope is intercultural. As Rene Padilla writes, "All authentic communication of the Word is patterned on the incarnation and therefore, seeks to find a point of contact with [people] within [their] own situation."[11]

> **Some cultural forms are biased towards the abuse of power.**

More recently, Charles Kraft has written, "We believe that God wants His Church incarnated in the cultural way of life of every society (people group). Just as Jesus totally participated in first century Palestinian life, not as a foreigner but as a native son, so contemporary Christian communities should not be living like foreigners in their own lands, speaking their language with a foreign (usually Western) accent, performing foreign-looking rituals at strange times and in strange-looking places."[12] While these authors' comments refer to biblical translation of the Word and growing churches, their ideas apply to any intercultural situation where a person from culture A hopes to communicate with fidelity and integrity to a person of culture B. Such communication is receptor-oriented, respecting of the receiver's frame of reference, and motivated by love.

Love "Them" at the Expense of "Us." In a sense, Jesus' obedience to God led to an intense cross-cultural mission assignment. Jesus could have remained with God where his status and comfort were secure. However, he chose to love us at his own expense. While we were still broken, pathetic individuals, Christ became Emmanuel—God with us—so he could minister, teach, and die among us. Heaven would have been a safer place.

Similarly, we are safe and comfortable when we stay home and surround ourselves with same-culture friends. Such friends yield us benefits, but remember that identification with our in-group is often at the expense of out groups. We favor our own buddies when dividing up resources like money and affection, and we usually rate our own group more positively, even when the lines of distinction between "them" and "us" are minimal and arbitrary.[13] As one author concludes, "Because we evaluate ourselves partly in terms of our group memberships, seeing our own group as superior helps us feel good about ourselves."[14] Professor Lingenfelter might suggest that this kind of thinking is a pen of selfish disobedience.

Christ's example is so different. While he surrounded himself with close disciples, he did not shy from those unlike himself. Jesus was not a tourist to earth, content with an impersonal speaking circuit agenda. Nor was he on a three-week summer mission project. Jesus was into Jewish culture and world change for the long haul. His posture toward people, whether they were poor or rich, Jew or Samaritan, was to humbly love them. Granted, my first inclination toward my Paraguayan, Brazilian, and Greek neighbors might not be to become their best friends, but at least my orientation toward them should reflect humility and service, not judgment and avoidance.

Loving people who think and live differently than we do is not a natural thing, and the edict to love may sound difficult and concocted. How can liking them become as normal as phoning a friend? Here are some guidelines based on research and biblical insight.

Befriend people of similar socioeconomic status. Making contact with those of similar economic background may strike some as snobbish and unchristian. Jesus did not seem to hold to this pattern as he seemed equally comfortable with lawyers and doctors as with tax collectors and prostitutes. However, research in ethnic relations shows that strangers get along best when they hail from similar strata in society.[15] Jesus' blue-collar roots as the son of a carpenter made him a shoe-in with the likes of fishermen Peter, James, and John. His knowledge of the law made him attractive to Nicodemus (the Pharisee, see John 3) and Luke the medical doctor. Our own social status may be more uniform, but it is no sin to stack the deck in the direction of social status as we seek to influence others for God.[16]

A debate that continues in some Christian circles concerns the role of ethnic churches. Some suggest that dividing churches along ethnic lines sends the wrong message to outsiders. It makes us look like we preach love but practice racism. Murray Moerman disagrees. As coordinator of church planting for Outreach Canada, Murray has seen a lot of good in ethnic churches. He writes, "Anglo churches are best at reaching Anglos. Spanish churches are best at reaching Spanish people. Chinese churches are best at reaching Chinese people. Not only that, but professional athletes are best at reaching professional athletes, media people at reaching media people, yuppies at reaching yuppies, men at reaching men, women at reaching women and so on."[17] His examples highlight the wisdom of befriending people from similar backgrounds when possible. Their culture may differ, but their lifestyle and values likely align with our own.

> Through incarnation, Jesus set aside heavenly modes and took on earthly ones to accomplish his mission.

Pursue a common goal. Research indicates that intercultural relating is more harmonious when two groups join hands to defeat a common enemy or accomplish a common goal.[18] The opposing approach pits groups against group, each blaming the other for the problem. Suppose the problem is drought in Mali, Africa. Imagine the tension if North American relief workers criticize Mali nationals of being lazy or not innovative. Better to ask nationals for their own solutions to drought issues, and together focus on withered fields and parched lakes.

Or consider the problem of learning English. On most university campuses, ESL students struggle to master this language, not for lack of trying, but because English has inconsistent grammar and illogical pronunciation rules. A native English speaker who asks, "How can we tackle subject-verb agreement?" is water to a thirsty spirit. I have heard more than one report of good friendships developing between English tutors and their students when this attitude is taken. Working together directs us away from thinking "me" against "them." It helps us think "we" against "the problem."

Spend time together. This point may seem like common sense and moot, but consider Jesus' manner. After growing up thoroughly Jewish, he began his formal ministry by choosing twelve men with whom he spent the next three years. He walked, ate, joked, fished, preached, worshipped, philosophized and in every other way hung out with them. As Donald Smith suggests in *Make Haste Slowly*, communication boils down to involvement in other people's lives.[19] It requires shared experiences over coffee and *kubadi* so two can share meaning more easily. Involvement means bonding over mundane things, rather than squirming through a slick gospel presentation presented door to door. Other things equal, spending time together decreases stereotyping and prejudice, and increases attraction.

Be Teachable as to Their Culture and Language

It is hard to love others when you do not understand them. Worse yet, we tend to fear people whom we cannot figure out. So it is not surprising that the second element of incarnational communication is to know our audience thoroughly. It means becoming observers of their culture.

Over twenty years ago I moved to Canada where I began a crash course on Canadian life and culture I began by watching

> In Canada, a football can rest on the 53 yard line.

nothing but Canadian Broadcasting Corporation (CBC) news, read the local paper religiously, and quizzed my colleagues about their native land.. A year later I married a Canadian woman, joined a Canadian church, and became a fan of hockey. In 2005 I became a Canadian citizen, and today I am more apt to think like a Canadian than an American. I have been told by Americans that I "sound" Canadian. My acculturation took time and an open spirit. How do we show our willingness to learn a new culture's ways? I can think of at least four.

Develop the sense of "different and good." When we encounter strangers and enter new cultures, we are prone to focus on how they differ from our roots, and evaluate those differences negatively. Consider the last time you visited another country. What did you take pictures of? Many short-term missionaries return home to show slides of crowded sidewalks, open-air meat markets, shantytown poverty, and religious icons.

Audience members ooh, ha, and ugh their way through these pictures, and resolve that life is better in North America. These differences no doubt reflect worldview themes, but if we focus on the differences, and judge them negatively, we will tend to see others as "other," and rarely as people like ourselves. The fact is that the butcher in Chandur Bazaar shares much in common with me as a fellow human being. If I want to understand him, I will have to get past the blood-drained goat hanging on the butcher pole.

Become a student of their culture. We study other cultures in anthropology textbooks, but when we arrive on location the true learning begins. In my Canadian experience, I now understand that five-party politics symbolizes a strip of Canadian cultural diversity. It reflects Pierre Trudeau's push to make multiculturalism Canada's state policy, not the exception to the rule. (Quick. Who was Pierre Trudeau?) I am not sure what Canadian football rules suggest, but I have interpreted the three-down rule as one way Canadians gently say, "We are not Americans."

> The more similar we assume two cultures to be, the greater our shock when we discover their differences.

We can make sense of another culture's habits and forms of communicating once we understand what guides them. This is the logic behind the concept of *cultural relativism*: behavior makes sense in light of the underlying structure of society; what is meaningful depends on societal context. Behavior is like the tip of an iceberg with its own peculiar shape and look. If we understand the sub-aquatic factors, we will understand why the tip leans and dips like it does. Figure 10.2 pictures this relationship.

Studies in acculturation inform us that plugging in to local media is a safe way to acculturate to local culture, especially if we watch news shows rather than entertainment shows.[20] In the long run though, you will need to make friendships and "do culture" interpersonally. When in India for six months, I did not have a television or a radio. Instead, day after day, night after night, I got to know Indian culture by interacting with my carpentry students, the boys' home staff, and local mer-

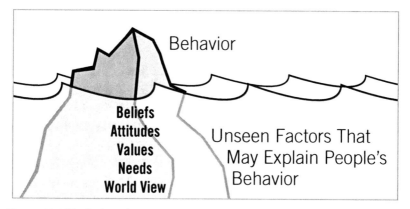

Behavior

Beliefs
Attitudes
Values
Needs
World View

Unseen Factors That
May Explain People's
Behavior

Figure 10.2 The Iceberg Analogy: People's behavior makes sense when we understand what lies beneath the surface.

chants. Personal contact is more draining than watching television, but you gain more than information; you begin to establish trust.

Become a student of their religious views. Recall how Paul argued his case on Mars' Hill, that place in Athens where all the latest teaches were taught? After strolling through the streets of Athens and seeing it filled with idols, he began his speech by noting "I see that in every way you are very religious. For as I walked around and looked carefully at your objects of worship, I even found an altar with this inscription: TO AN UNKNOWN GOD. Now what you worship as something unknown I am going to proclaim to you" (see Acts 17:22–34). First he observed their religious practices; then he spoke to their spiritual need.

If we do not understand someone's religious beliefs in even a religion 101 way, we will fail miserably at sorting out the specifics of his or her particular convictions. A comparative religion course that covers the tenets of Islam, Buddhism, Hinduism and New Age thought could prove invaluable in the future. Getting a hold of a comparative religions text, such as *Relating to People of Other Religions: What Every Christian Should Know* (Abingdon Press, 1997), is a close second option.[21] Knowing religious thought shows respect for someone else's convictions. It also helps us establish points of contact for communicating the Christian story.[22]

Learn the language of those you want to befriend and influence. In covenantal perspective, our first sign of wanting to come together to change for the good is to agree on a linguistic code. In humility it means learning—and loving—the language of those with whom we hope to serve. Too many cross-cultural efforts have failed because English-speakers have bought in to two myths. The first is that non-English speakers want to learn English anyway, so using English does them a favor. The second myth is that the demand for English education must indicate that English is superior. While it is true that English education is in demand world wide, the motive behind it is largely economic, not cultural. The international business elite require a single language, and English became the expedient choice after it was imposed by the British during their imperial conquests. In terms of being a "better" language, English gets a "D" for lack of consistency. (Did you know that *ghoti* is pronounced "fish."? It is possible with phonemes such as enough, women, and lotion.) Linguists are now convinced that there are no " primitive languages." Many languages spoken by "less developed" people—such as Spanish and Indonesian—are more consistent than English.[23]

Far beyond the transmission capacity of a language is its potential for identification. When we speak someone else's language, something clicks. Three years after returning from India, I taught communication courses at the University of Iowa. One semester an East Indian woman took my class, and I learned that her home was Mumbai, Maharashtra—the same state as Chandur Bazaar. I assumed she spoke Marathi, so asked, "Kussa kai, teek ahay?" She beamed, "Teek ahay." She had not heard Marathi in months, and her shock that I spoke a bit of her language soon turned to solace. All from asking, "how are you, fine?" Through Marathi we identified with each other.

Use Their Cultural Forms

In addition to loving dissimilar others at our own expense, and humbly learning about their culture, we know we communicate incarnationally when we succeed in discovering the cultural forms that convey God's truth and establish responsible relationships least obtrusively. As Wycliffe translator and scholar Eugene Nida puts it, "Our fundamental task is to 'relay' this communication [or truth] in still different forms, but with essentially an equivalent content, so that men in other times and places may be put in touch with the infinite God."[24] Those forms vary from culture to culture, but somehow, some way, God is able to use these forms—whether neutral or fallen—to show himself to others. Non-westerners do not have to give up their cultural heritage to live redemptively with each other and know God's grace. Cultural forms are means to impute God's message, and God's message is able to redeem fallen cultural forms. Let's consider what this implies for us as his ambassadors.

Recognize that you are the message. It has been said that Christians are the only Bible some people will ever read. That is, what many unbelievers know about God is what they see in us. That is a little scary.

A true-life example strikes this home. E. Stanley Jones, author and veteran missionary to India, said that the attack against Christianity in India came in three waves. First Hindus claimed, "It isn't *true* (i.e., these are the wrong truths), then, it isn't *new* (i.e., Hinduism has the same truths), and finally, it isn't *you* (i.e., you are not living the truth). The last of these was the most damaging, for it suggested that some Christians in India conveyed un-Christian messages.[25]

Are you fit for intercultural ministry? When I was finishing my college work, some guys in my dorm asked me what I was planning to do after graduation. I told them that my uncertainties about graduate school and the workforce were influential in making me consider short-term missions. It was true, but I wish I hadn't phrased it that way. Later one of them joked to another friend, "After finishing school you can either go to grad school or get a real job. But if all else fails, you can do what Strom did and become a missionary." I laughed it off, but the attitude there is a common one. Some believers feel that intercultural work is for those who cannot hack it at home. Thirty years later I know better. Missionaries, relief workers, and civil diplomats are among the best educated and morally alert people I know. One reason why they may look "culturally off" in Des Moines is because their heart is in Dhaka.

One of the mysteries of our faith is how God not only lived with us as Christ, but that he lives in us by his Holy Spirit. Despite our fallenness, we have God's Spirit to help us witness a life for him. That is our hope as messengers for him.

Tap in to the "flow of truth." In addition to living the truth, we need to figure out how a culture pursues truth, for every cultural group has its ways of determining what is true and what should be done about it.

Western cultures use democratic politics, university systems, the mass media, and the church to meet this need. We are more likely to agree with the results of a scientific study about cancer covered on the six o'clock news than embrace the ranting declarations of a scruffy psychopath atop a soapbox in Central Park. To put it another way, we need to discover the structure of decision-making and work within it. As Mayers notes, "The truth of God must come to each man completely and effectively in keeping with what he is socioculturally."[26] If we impose electronic media on people who value a shaman (holy person) atop a stump in the village center, there is a good chance they will miss our message for all the noise of the medium. Will they respect a message that comes by way of television when they are accustomed to receiving truth from a respected elder?

In certain agricultural cultures, information travels quickly along the path en route to the rice fields. If you want to be in the know, *get on the path*. If you want your message known, *get on the path*. Donald Smith notes that once we know the structures by which truth and decisions are determined, our strategy for reaching people in that culture should vary accordingly.[27] We should do it their way.

"I understand, Bobby, but this isn't Rome."

Find the right words and nonverbal cues. This was the wisdom of Chapters 3 and 4, and yet interculturally it takes on monumental significance. Our language and body cues carry the bulk of our message. And, conversely, what we think, and how we think, are intimately linked to our words and actions. Both views remind us that managing symbols requires responsibility, especially when working within someone else's code.

How would you express that you feel tired and worn out? In English we might say "I'm bushed" but a Korean might say, "I want to die." How do you indicate your name to someone? You probably say, "My name is _____," but a French-speaker would say, "I name myself _____." How do you express "yes" with your head? In the United States and Canada we nod our heads up and down, but East Indians wag their heads back and forth. How might you beckon someone to you? Probably by holding your hand out, palm up, and "hooking" her towards you with your pointer finger. In India, the palm faces down and you "scoop" her toward you with all your fingers.

The challenge is to find the *functional equivalent.* That is, you want to find the word or action in the receptor's culture that creates the meaning you hope to import from your home culture. If a "scoop" functions to create the equivalent meaning of a "hook," then use a "scoop."

Bible translators know the principle of functional equivalence well. For example, in some cultures, the part of the body used to refer to the soul is not their word for "heart," (as in North America). Some language groups use the word "abdomen," "throat," or "liver" to mean soul. "Hence, certain familiar passages must be rendered in quite different ways, e.g., 'Let not your liver be troubled' (John 14:1), 'So you have sorrow now, but I will see you again and your livers will rejoice' (John 16:22), and 'These people honor me with their mouths, but their livers are far from me (Matthew 15:8)."[28] For position 1 Christians who may dispute such "tinkering" with scriptural texts, the position 2 believer asks, "What has changed?" The words, yes. God's Word, no.

Meet human needs, find points of contact and use redemptive analogies. These are three strategies for making the gospel message intelligible. The first is to recognize that people everywhere have basic life needs, and a message that meets a need will be more readily considered.[29] International relief ministries such as Samaritan's Purse and the Mennonite Central Committee (MCC) understand this principle.

When drought hits Sudan and bombs drop on Afghanistan, relief workers meet physical needs first, and other needs later. They take Jesus' words to heart when he said, "I tell you the truth, whatever you did for one of the least of these brothers of mine, you did for me" (Matthew 25:40). Meeting physical needs develops trust, and tills the ground for meeting other needs.

Second, our message will be more likely considered if it engages our listener with a slice of shared experience or a conceptual container. These *points of contact* serve as the basis for meaningful dialogue. In these years after September 11, commentators and teachers have made public statements comparing Islam and Christianity. Here and there they observe points of contact for mutual dialogue. For example, Muslims believe that God reveals himself to us, but that he would not become human to do so. Christians believe that God reveals himself to us, and in his omnipotence is able to visit earth as a human. The concept of "revelation" is therefore a point of contact with a Muslim, even though the full-fledged doctrines behind this term share no common ground.[30] But we can enter meaningful dialogue about revelation generally.

Third, we can further link with culturally different others by employing *redemptive analogies*. Redemptive analogies compare aspects of the gospel message to some ritual, practice, word, or behavior in the receptor's culture that opens the floodgate of understanding to what God has done for us through Jesus Christ. Don Richardson's book, *Eternity in their Hearts*, provides example after example of how God has prepared many cultures with such a comparative vehicle.[31] For the Sawi of New Guinea, the floodgate opened when they saw Christ as their "peace child." Sawi chiefs from warring tribes exchange one of their children as a sign of trusted truce. As long as each child is alive and well, the two chiefs' tribes live in peace. If either child dies or is mistreated, there are grounds for war. Richardson developed the analogy that God and the Sawi were once at war, but God has now given them his peace child. As long as Jesus is alive and well among them, peace reigns. This comparison brought such understanding that Richardson witnessed hundreds of Sawi people trusting Jesus. Today two-thirds of the Sawi profess Christ as their Lord.

What If We Do It the Old Way?

Valuing other cultures and their modes of communication typifies the incarnational model. This culturally sensitive approach has been encouraged by Christian missionary scholars such as Donald McGavran, Alan Tippet, and Eugene Nida since the 1960s, and echoed by a second generation, such as Paul Hiebert, Charles Kraft, and Marvin Mayers. Their books are worth considering.[32]

However, for many years—even centuries—many Christians took a strong position 1 approach, the old approach, to intercultural missions. Viewing the Bible as their guide for holy living (a good thing) but adding the view that western culture was superior to others (a bad thing), yesteryear attempts to reproduce believers interculturally led to ugly methods such as resident schools for aboriginal children. In an attempt to right these wrongs, advocates of interfaith dialogue and one-world religion have swung the pendulum to the opposite side of the arc, and argued for melding all faiths. Both approaches fail to be appropriate to the teachings of scripture, and appropriate to the people who seek after God. Let's look at each briefly.[33]

How Not to Share God's Message Interculturally. The first ineffective model is the head-on approach. "This is the method of aggressive refutation and condemnation of other faiths. This attitude assumes that all other religions are the work of the devil, are false, and devoid of value. There are, therefore, no points of contact or bridge-points for preaching the gospel."[34] This method entails the condemning of idol worship, the condemning of false gods, the tearing down of pagan temples, and force-feeding the gospel. Without choice, many people in Africa, South America, and Southern Asia have become Christians not by choice but by default. They were never given the opportunity to understand the gospel message well enough to make their own decision to choose God and destroy idols. They are mere cultural Christians—people who display the outward signs of western Christianity, but have no personal relationship with Jesus Christ.

In response to the inadequacy of the head-on approach, some believers have swung the pendulum to the other extreme and used the shake-hands approach.[35] This is the method of accommodation, that is, the watering down of the gospel so that it is easier for others to accept. David Wilkerson believes that the seeker-sensitive movement among mega-churches has accommodated the gospel. He writes,

Accommodate means to adapt, to make suitable and acceptable, to make convenient. A gospel of accommodation is creeping into the United States. It's an American cultural invention to appease the lifestyle of luxury and pleasure. Primarily a Caucasian, suburban gospel, it's also in our major cities and is sweeping the nation, influencing ministers of every denomination, and giving birth to megachurches with thousands who come to hear a nonconfronting message. It's an adaptable gospel that is spoonfed through humorous skits, drama, and short, nonabrasive sermonettes on how to cope—called a seeker-friendly or sinner-friendly gospel.[36]

At a more symbolic level, accommodation may occur through the words we use to convey spiritual truth. One year the student committee in charge of our school's Missions Week decided on the motto: La Mission: To Go Where No One Has Gone Before. The phrase "La Mission" was a take-off from a then popular LaBatts beer commercial, and the "To Go Where…" phrase was borrowed from *Star Trek*. While attempting to be culturally cool, the phrase fumbled its meaning amidst images of Captain Kirk and other Enterprise crew members tilting back cold ones. It also conjured up the idea that some gospel crew, rather than God, draws people to himself.

The result of a coercive head-on approach and an anything-goes shake-hands approach is often the same: syncretism. Syncretism is the mixing of two religions to form a mutant offspring. As Eugene Nida writes, "Syncretism . . . involves an accommodation of content, a synthesis of beliefs, and an amalgamation of world views, in such a way as to provide some common basis for constructing a "new system" or a "new approach."[37] We want to avoid syncretism, but we take this risk when we use cultural forms from a receptor culture to communicate the gospel. Jesus took this risk when he conveyed God's will for us through first-century Palestinian culture. Our goal, like his, is appropriate contextualiation—to live and proclaim the redeeming message

> God's communication model is characterized by incarnation and covenant.

of God with local forms of communication so that others can hear God's still small voice and colossal love.

Incarnation and Covenant as Intercultural Strategy

God's grand plan to enter the world through Jesus, the Christ, shows us his covenantal love. In his omnipotence, he may have chosen other means to draw us to himself, but he chose to get down and dirty with his creation. In fact, God's communication model represents these two great themes: incarnation, and covenant. By putting on flesh God took on human cultural form in order to communicate his message of committed love. Charles Kraft, author of *Communication Theory for Christian Witness*, provides a tightly written summary of godly communication. What he discovered in his analysis parallels incarnational, covenantal communication.

> The Scriptures provide us with communicational models to imitate. We see there a God who refuses to stay on the other side of an enormous communication gap. He seeks a relationship with us that will elicit from us a commitment to himself and his cause. To bring this about he develops a strategy to assure that he will be understood on our side of the gap. In this strategy he is receptor-oriented, entering our frame of reference in a trusting, dependent, even vulnerable manner to show his love, acceptance, and respect toward us in a way that we cannot misunderstand. God is personal and identifies with us by incarnating himself and himself becoming the message he sends. Furthermore, God assures that his messages come with impact. He develops high credibility, deals specifically with his receptors and the issues that concern them, leads his receptors to discovery, and trusts them to carry on the cause.[38]

If we can imitate God's method of getting a hold of us, we might better understand how he would have us help others get a hold of him. Consider these implications of Kraft's ideas as applied to covenantal, intercultural ministry:

> 1. We need to close the culture gap by getting outside our comfort zone and into the culture we seek to learn from and influence.

2. We should be receptor-oriented by entering the host culture's frame of reference, and agreeing to express ourselves as they would express themselves.

3. Our relationships should not be safe and professional, but vulnerable and personal as we seek to build trusting, interdependent relationships with host members.

4. If we want to see genuine change, we must be willing to change as well, as we present our ideas credibly with the goal to meet felt needs.

5. Like Jesus, we need to commit to the long term, not short term. Time and experience together improves communication and better guarantees change.

Summary

If you think about it, the principles for covenantal relating with people from different cultures are identical to those at home. Know your audience, form your message, use words your audience will understand, and engage nonverbal cues that lend credibility to what you say; spend time with them and develop shared experiences so you can play charades, not Ping-Pong or bowling; choose to listen and choose to love; agree together how you may meet physical and spiritual needs. Intercultural communication requires the same principles.

To know your audience means studying their culture and religious views. It may mean missing the service at First Baptist so you can attend First Buddhist. It definitely means that God's call for us to be in the world, but not of it, does not put us on the sideline, but in the thick of our world, always seeing culture through God's eyes and seeking to redeem it and people. Culture is his vehicle through which we create our lives and come to know God's life.

This was the manner of Jesus. He left heaven to don human garb to walk dusty roads with Jews, Greeks, Samaritans, and Romans. His teaching reflected his knowledge of their history and occupations, their rituals and language. In this chapter, we considered the wisdom of imitating his manner. Spending time with relatively similar others toward some common goal builds trust. Taking a stab at their language, or immersing ourselves in it, builds bridges. Discovering how locals make and communicate important decisions puts us on the right path. Finding points of contact and redemptive analogies will help meet spiritual need.

 **WORTH THE TALK**

1. What do you think of the students' choice to use "La Mission: To Go Where No One has Gone Before" as a missions week motto?

2. One author has these tips about how to interact with people of different faiths.[39] Do you agree with them or not? Why?

> a. Be assured that Christ is the Truth, but show humility in that this is entirely God's doing, not our own.

> b. Show the attitude of tolerance (open-minded, fair-minded, sympathetic, and empathetic), but do not compromise the gospel's truth.

> c. Make love your primary manner, and respect the person's freedom to choose for or against Christ.

3. Consider Figure 10.1 again. Where do your thoughts lie on the issue of biblical truth and cultural reality? Can you figure out why you think this way?

4. It is easy for us to think that Christian faith has been communicated in North American culture by way of indigenization (the use of our local forms), with little if any syncretism (the mixing of Christian beliefs with non-Christian ones). Can you think of examples of beliefs or behaviors that we take for granted as biblically Christian that are really culturally Christian?

CONSIDER THE WALK

1. Attend a worship service where your language is not spoken. Do a little ethnography (see Chapter 14). In particular, observe communication forms and identify what function they appear to perform. Typical functions of worship include 1) to praise God, 2) to speak with God, 3) to hear from God, and 4) to fellowship with other believers. How does the church you normally attend accomplish the same purposes with different forms?

2. Interview an international student. Focus your questions on how the Christian faith has been communicated within his or her home culture. Explain the idea of "indigenization" to the student, and try to determine if knowledge of the gospel came by way of "home-grown" communication vehicles or "imported" ones. You may need to do some book research about his or her culture to gain fuller understanding.

3. Play cross-cultural simulations in class. This suggestion is aimed mainly at your instructor, but you might help get the ball rolling. Look for organizations such as Simulation Training Systems, P.O. Box 910, Del Mar, CA, 92014 and request their list of simulation games for cross-cultural experiences. STS sells the games "Where Do You Draw the Line?" (about cross-cultural ethics), "Star Power" (about power, its use, abuse, and how it is communicated in culture), and Bafa Bafa (about intercultural communication, culture shock, and cultural norms). I have also developed an intercultural communication simulation called *Waffles*, and it is available by contacting me personally at strom@twu.ca. After playing a game, analyze your experience by using ideas in this chapter as well as intercultural communication textbooks. This analysis may take the form of a thorough debriefing after the simulation (led by your instructor) or a paper written by you.

ONLINE CHALK

The Internet abounds with links to mission organizations and missionary causes. However the following search terms are intended to help you link with sites about intercultural communication generally.

- Intercultural communication theory
- Intercultural effectiveness
- Functional equivalent translating
- Nonverbal emblems in other cultures
- Preparing for intercultural work

ENDNOTES

1 See Carol Werner and Pat Parmalee, "Similarity of Activity Preferences Among Friends: Those Who Play Together Stay Together," *Social Psychology Quarterly* 42 (1979): 62-66, and Denise B. Kandel, "Similarity in Real-Life Adolescent Friendship Pairs," *Journal of Personality and Social Psychology* 36 (1978): 302-312.

2 Marvin K. Mayers, *Christianity Confronts Culture* (Grand Rapids, MI: Zondervan, 1987), 247-249.

3 Ibid., 241.

4 See http://news.sbs.com.au/worldnewsaustralia/text_of_harper39s_apology_549118 for Prime Minister Stephen Harper's apology speech (accessed June 13, 2008).

5 See http://www.pm.gov.au/media/Speech/2008/speech_0073.cfm for Prime Minister Kevin Rudd's apology speech (accessed June 13, 2008).

6 Mayers, *Christianity Confronts Culture*, 248-249.

7 Rudd's opening comments, http://www.pm.gov.au/media/Speech/2008/speech_0073.cfm.

8 Charles H. Kraft, ed., *Appropriate Christianity* (Pasadena, CA: William Carey Library, 2005).

9 Sherwood Lingenfelter, *Transforming Culture: A Challenge for Christian Mission* (Grand Rapids, MI: Baker, 1992), 17-18.

10 Ibid., 23.

11 Quoted in John Stott and Robert Coote, *Gospel and Culture* (Pasadena, CA: William Carey Library, 1979), 97.

12 Charles H. Kraft, *Appropriate Christianity*, 12.

13 See, for example, the work of Henri Tajfel and Michael Billig, "Familiarity and Categorization in Intergroup Behavior," *Journal of Experimental Social Psychology* 10 (1974): 159-170, and Henri Tajfel, "Social Psychology of Intergroup Relations," *Annual Review of Psychology* 33 (1982): 1-39.

14 David G. Myers, *Social Psychology*, 3rd ed. (New York: McGraw-Hill, 1990), 345.

15 See Y. Amir, "Contact Hypothesis in Ethnic Relations," *Psychological Bulletin* 71 (1969): 319-342.

16 Of note, the work of Christian missions in India has had the strongest impact on two groups: the high caste Brahmans and the untouchable Harijans. Christian missionaries, largely from wealthy countries of the United States and Britain, have related well to the socially elite Brahmans. What explains outcast conversion to Christianity is the Christian doctrine of "no caste in Christ." Harijans have, therefore, identified with the "spiritual status" of missionaries who do not claim to be superior on a spiritual ladder of caste.

17 Murray Moerman, "Ethnic Communities are 'Bridges of God' to Spread the Gospel," *Christian Info News*, May 1996, 6.

18 Amir, "Contact Hypothesis in Ethnic Relations," 319-342.

19 Donald K. Smith, *Make Haste Slowly: Developing Effective Cross-Cultural Communication* (Portland, OR: Institute for International Christian Communication, 1984), chapter 6. See also his textbook, Donald K. Smith, *Creating Understanding: A Handbook for Christian Communication Across Cultural Landscapes* (Grand Rapids, MI: Zondervan, 1992), 23-40.

20 See for example Young Y. Kim, "Communication Patterns of Foreign Immigrants in the Process of Acculturation," *Human Communication Research* 4 (1977): 66-77.

21 M. Thomas Thangaraj, *Relating to People of Other Religions: What Every Christian Should Know* (Nashville: Abingdon, 1997).

22 See John T. Seamands' *Tell It Well: Communicating the Gospel Across Cultures* (Kansas City: Beacon Hill, 1981) for excellent chapters that address how to share the gospel with Hindus, Buddhists, Animists, and Muslims.

23 A missionary friend of mine to Indonesia described Indonesian as a "perfect language" because it holds consistently to its rules for spelling, pronunciation, and grammar.

24 Eugene A. Nida, *Message and Mission: The Communication of the Christian Faith*, rev. ed. (Pasadena, CA: William Carey Library, 1990), 28.

25 Reference to Jones made by Seamands, *Tell It Well*, 109.

26 Mayers, *Christianity Confronts Culture*, 116.

27 Smith, *Make Haste Slowly*, chapter 14, "Structure Determines Strategy."

28 Nida, *Message and Mission*, 139.

29 This is the observation on which the work of Abraham Maslow's theory of hierarchical needs is based. He suggests that all people experience the need for physical well-being, safety, a sense of belonging, self-esteem or self-respect, and self-actualization. See A. H. Maslow, *Motivation and Personality*, 2nd ed. (New York: Harper & Row, 1970).

30 Nida, *Message and Mission*, 18, is critical of Christians who promote a "common ground" approach to communicating the gospel. He writes "We insist upon a "point of contact" approach rather than a "common ground" orientation because it is impossible to take any element of belief out of its context and still have the same belief. Religions are systems, and the individual beliefs have meaning only in terms of the system to which they belong."

31 Don Richardson, *Eternity in Their Hearts* (Ventura, CA: Regal Books, 1981).

32 Key works by the three authors not referred to yet in this chapter include: Donald McGavran, *The Clash Between Christianity and Cultures* (Washington, D.C.: Canon Press, 1974); Alan R. Tippet, *Verdict Theology in Missionary Theory*, 2nd ed. (Pasadena, CA: William Carey Library, 1973); and Paul Hiebert, *Anthropological Insights for Missionaries* (Grand Rapids, MI: Baker, 1985).

33 These two criteria—appropriate interpretation of the Scriptures and appropriate contextualization in a people group's culture—are the defining features of the most recent thinking by Charles Kraft and others. See Charles H. Kraft, *Appropriate Christianity*.

34 Seamands, *Tell It Well*, 75.

35 Ibid., 78.

36 See David Wilkerson, *The Dangers of Accommodation*, sermon text, http://www.ag.org/EnrichmentJournal/199901/078_accommodation.cfm (accessed June 16, 2008).

37 Nida, *Message and Mission*, 131.

38 Charles Kraft, *Communication Theory for Christian Witness* (Nashville: Abingdon, 1983), 34.

39 Seamands, *Tell It Well*, 54-56.

Do not love the world or anything in the world. If anyone loves the world, the love of the Father is not in him. For everything in the world—the cravings of sinful man, the lust of his eyes, and the boasting of what he has and does—comes not from the Father but from the world. The world and its desires pass away but the man who does the will of God lives forever.

I John 2:15–17

Electronically (Dis-) Connected
Arguments Against the Media

IT WAS LIKE most days in speech class. Five students were prepared to give persuasive speeches. Four topics that day elude me just now. Ben Ridley's will stick with me for a long time.[1] What I knew of Ben was that he enjoyed sports and hoped to be a sports journalist someday. I got the sense he valued watching ESPN and Canada's equivalent, TSN. For classmates who knew Ben, I suppose they were expecting a topic such as "You should consider sports journalism as a career," or "How to curb steroid use in professional sport." Our expectations were off.

Ben stood behind the lectern and declared, "For years we've been hearing about all the bad stuff television does to us. We hear that it attacks our values and makes us do things we normally wouldn't. Well I'm an avid TV watcher, and I'm here today to convince you that TV isn't harmful."

Ben proceeded to defend his case with personal examples. He said that while he loved to watch murder mysteries, he never felt the urge to murder anyone. Despite TV's brash commercialism, he claimed he had his buying behavior in check. Even though he watched fights break out during hockey games, he said he never punched a friend

Ben's experience with television is a starting point for the next two chapters as we examine today's media. Without doubt, today's youth are growing up in a media-saturated environment, and it is possible that many share Ben's cavalier attitudes. On average, students who are eight to eighteen years-old engage media for six and a half hours per day, including two-and-a half hours of multitasking with more than one medium. Among young people, the national U.S. average for television watching and DVDs is about four hours per day, while the average for listening to CDs, MP3s, and the radio is just under two hours per day. Add to this about fifty minutes of video games and forty-five minutes of reading magazines, and one can understand why only five and half hours remain to parse out for time with parents (2.25 hours), physical activity (1.5 hours), homework (50 minutes), and chores (thirty minutes).[2]

> Believers respond to media based on their understanding of what it means to be in the world but not of it.

When the second edition of this book came out in 2003, MySpace was a year old and Facebook had yet to launch. Today over 200 million people manage personal profiles between these two social networking sites with another half million patrons joining everyday.[3] You likely belong to one or the other, and begin and end your day checking your wall or inbox email. In one day alone it is possible that you will wake up to music on a clock stereo, check email two or three times, view an instructional DVD, Google sources for a research paper, listen to music on your iPod, smile over a YouTube video, watch a TV drama or two, and play a video game.

This litany of media consumption requires us to ask to what degree it matters. Does it matter that time with media per week approximates the hours spent at a full-time job? Are we comfortable with media personalities and values presented on TV, in movies, and on the web? Might believers bring particular criteria to their media consumption to make sense of their choices?

Since many other books can help you understand the media industry complex, it is my desire to address how Christians have responded to media content and technology. Observing their responses—and reasons for their responses—will help us understand people like Ben as well as believers quite unlike him as well. To that end, I build Chapter 11 and 12 around a model of Christian responses to the media (see Figure 11.1). This chapter introduces all five responses, and then addresses the first one at length. Chapter 12 will address two other responses that I believe are relevant to most Christians today. Let's begin with the model.

Christian Responses to Media: Reject, Accept, Critique

Through the centuries, believers have engaged popular culture in varied ways based on their understanding of what it means to be in the world but not of it. In John 17:14–16, Jesus prays to God the Father to protect his disciples as they enter the world. He says,

> I have given them your word and the world has hated them, for they are not of the world any more than I am of the world. My prayer is not that you take them out of the world, but that you protect them from the evil one. They are not of the world, even as I am not of it. Sanctify them by the truth; your word is truth. As you sent me into the world, I have sent them into the world. For them I sanctify myself, that they too may be truly sanctified.

Christians have taken Jesus' words differently depending on their understanding of worldliness and sanctified living, but generally their responses have fallen into three camps: 1) reject the world as evil and attempt to live apart from it in a counter-cultural manner, 2) engage culture with the mind of Christ in an attempt to critique and transform it unto his image, and 3) embrace the good that God has bestowed, through common grace, in all people and culture.[4]

To explain these responses with respect to engaging the media, Christian writers have wrestled with two issues. The first is to determine a posture regarding technology generally. Doing so requires them to assess the benefits and drawbacks a technology brings to humankind, and to discern godly engagement with it. The second issue is to determine criteria to judge media content such as news, stories, heroes, and entire worldviews. Doing so requires believers to discern godly criteria for the rejecting, accepting, and/or engaging of media content while maintaining the broader goal of being sanctified, or holy, as Jesus prayed.

The model depicted in Figure 11.1 attempts to grid these responses along two axes. The horizontal axis represents believers' responses to media technologies, with the three possible responses being reject, accept, and/or critically engage. Likewise, the vertical axis represents the continuum on which we respond to media content through avoidance, acceptance, and/or critical engagement. The combining of these two issues, and our potential responses to them, creates four quadrants, or four primary postures of responding to media. In addition, the center of the model represents a fifth "quadrant" of thoughtful engagement, if one assumes that between "acceptance" and "rejection" is not mind-numbing neutrality, but critical consideration. While any one person's posture might straddle two or three quadrants, let us consider each quadrant as a pure type.

The Separator, Position 1: Reject Media Technologies and Media Content

If you saw the movie *The Witness*, you will have observed this view at work in the life of the Amish. Some Christians, including the Amish, certain Mennonite groups, and Hutterites outrightly refuse to bring communication technologies into their homes. They believe that being in the world but not of it means to live a simple lifestyle, and to work and worship communally. "To the Amish, worldliness denotes specific behaviors and lifestyles. High school, cars, cameras, tape recorders, television, films, showy houses, certain farm machinery and bicycles, all tagged *worldly*, are censured."[5] The Amish do not use telephones, for example, because telephones undermine the separatist call to find one's place in Amish community and not relate to outsiders. In addition, the Amish value for contextual family interaction, as opposed to telephone's decontextualized form, help us understand why they reject phones.[6]

We do not have to be Amish to respect their response or admit that we have responded similarly. Any time we refuse to clutter our lives with one more media toy and rightly judge media content as dishonoring to God, we are holding a position 1 stance. In order to understand why some Christians ban or censor the ugliest of media content from their own consumption, we will look at their arguments in the second half of this chapter.

The counter-cultural life of position 1 Christians may avoid the negative effects of media, such as impersonalization and questionable values. In their media-less environment they enjoy the intensity of community in which they find identity and accountability. What they lack, however, is any basis for changing the media industry or enjoying God's general revelation these media may offer.

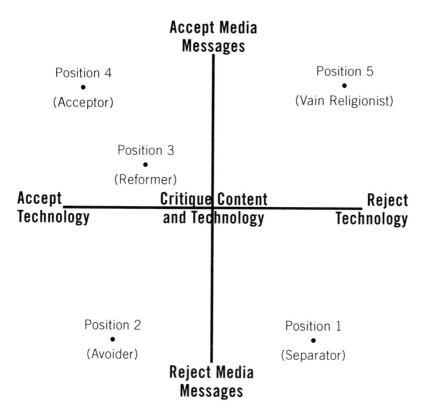

Figure 11.1 A grid for understanding people's responses to media technology and media content.

The Avoider, Position 2: Accept Technology, and Avoid Questionable Content

If you experience your walk with God in an evangelical tradition, there is a good possibility you hold an avoider response to the media. Most evangelicals consider media technologies as gifts from God sprung from human innovation. Avoiders believe technologies are benign, but content is morally charged. The evangelical community is particularly concerned with mediated depictions of sex, violence, profanity, and the occult. Avoiding such programming, and choosing wholesome or family values material, is a strategy used to cope in today's media environment. Evangelicals are likely to praise the media for their educational and informational role in alerting us to the material and spiritual needs of others (e.g., *World Vision* television specials). They also consider media channels as gifts from God so we might assist him in drawing others to himself. Christ's great commission to make disciples of all nations (see Matthew 28) compels these believers to embrace radio, television, and the Internet as means by which Christians can proclaim the Good News of Christ.

You are likely in position 2 if you approve of Chuck Swindoll's radio program *Insight for Living,* or Billy and Franklin Graham's televised crusades. If you own a raft of CDs by Christian artists, subscribe to *CCM* (Contemporary Christian Music) Magazine or enjoy clicking on ministry Internet cites for resources, then it is evident you accept these media but selectively choose your content.

Position 2 Christians might condemn the media's most obvious ills, but overlook less overt woes such as crass materialism or blind nationalism. Moreover, some position 2 Christians are indifferent to mediocre professionalism, claiming that Christian content trumps all. Even still, these Christians usually avoid the ugliest and most demeaning of media fare because they choose to avoid it. We will look more deeply at their arguments for accepting media technology in Chapter 12.

The Reformer, Position 3: Critique Technology and Messages from a Christian Perspective

While evangelical theology emphasizes worldly detachment and personal holiness, reform theology highlights the Lordship of Jesus over all his creation—even our media-soaked planet. Reformers emphasize that God not only gave us a great commission, but also a cultural mandate to redeem cultural institutions, including the media. By redemption they mean the process of finding the moral good that already exists in culture, and attempting to transform cultural institutions to the glory of God, whether those institutions are school systems, governments, or the media industry. Reformers take Philippians 4:8 seriously when it encourages us to think upon whatever is true, noble, right, pure, lovely, admirable, excellent or praiseworthy, whether it originates from scripture or not. Reformers reject the split between "sacred things" and "secular things" that some Christians believe demarcate God's world. Rather, reformers believe that if all truth is God's truth, and if the media can be used as a vehicle for conveying truth, then we should search and use the media to know him through culture, and advance his kingdom. Therefore, reformers represent the center position in the model, for they encourage believers to be continually engaged and critically evaluative of media technology and content.

We exercise a position 3 stance when we genuinely search for faith-affirming interpretations of family life among the Barones on *Everyone Loves Raymond*, or grasp someone else's pain and despondency from a segment of *ER*. Reformers define holiness as not the avoidance of sin or its depiction, but our response to sin when we encounter it.[7] We also exercise a transformer response when we consider how the structure of a medium, such as television, sends its own message apart from the programming. For example, realizing that watching television promotes a sedentary lifestyle is one such insight.

> While evangelical theology emphasizes worldly detatchment, reform theology highlights the Lordship of Jesus over all his creation - even our media-soaked planet.

Christians who hold a position 3 response to media sometimes walk a fine line between being in, understanding, and attempting to change the world, yet not succumbing to its mold. Some may fool themselves when they think they are able to rise above hurtful or deceptive media content and walk away better people. Sometimes, they gain a fuller understanding of sin in the world at the price of their own moral sensitivity and spiritual walk. We will look more fully at position 3 in the following chapter.

The Acceptor, Position 4: Accept Media Technology and Content

Ben Ridley represents believers who have a carefree attitude about media. They freely purchase cutting-edge media gadgetry and daily consume full doses of television and other electronic media. Their response is justified by at least three ways of reasoning. One is to believe, like the reformers, that God's message is available to us through cultural expressions, including the media. His grace might hide in the shadows of a *CSI* episode, but it is there if we look for it. The second is the belief that we are able to defend ourselves against messages that are antithetical to the faith. They believe that we are not sponges, but Spirit-filled critics. And third, they think that God is more concerned with behavior than attitudes or intentions. As long as Ben does not punch his brother as they watch *World Wrestling Entertainment's Smackdown*, then God has few qualms with his media choices. These assumptions free acceptors to engage film, music, and television with the calm assurance that tucked away therein is an expression of God's goodness to us. If they fail to find it, and cross the line, they believe God's grace abounds.

"Am I mindful when I watch TV? Sure I am. Touch my TV and you'll see how much I mind."

While some believers may manage to please God plopped in front of the tube with a highly discerning spirit, there is an equal or greater likelihood that they experience self-deception, or at least illogical thinking. Consider the results of a study by Karen Foss and Alison Alexander who interviewed twenty people who watch at least six hours of television per day. The researchers discovered that heavy viewers tend to see their TV watching as motivated by outside forces rather than personal choice, believe that TV watching has negative effects on people generally but not them specifically, and say that TV viewing is *not* important to them.[8] I suggest that people who blame their environment for their habits, consider themselves immune to media, and label a six hours-a-day activity unimportant, are not the mindful critics noted in position 3.

The Vain Religionist, Position 5: Reject Media Technologies but Accept Media Values

I am not sure I have ever met a position 5 believer, but it is possible to imagine someone who rejects media hardware on ideological grounds, but embraces media values to cope with life. I believe Ted Kaczynski was such a person.[9]

Theodore John Kaczynski was the infamous Unabomber who fled to the Montana wilderness to write a 35,000-word anti-technology manifesto, and mail package bombs to high-tech industry CEOs from the mid 1970s to the mid 1990s. The hit list FBI agents found tacked to his shack wall targeted the airline industry, the computer industry, and geneticists. From his wooded seclusion, he mailed death packages to Thomas Mosser, a New Jersey advertising executive, and Gilbert Murray, a timber-industry lobbyist. Both died. In all, Kaczynski killed three people and injured twenty-nine others.

The sad consistency of Kaczynski's behavior was that he rejected human community along with technology. Unlike the Amish whose community is the defining feature of their worldview, Kaczynski defined himself an independent Marlboro man. Although he denounced technology, he used technology to murder those he believed were ruining society. Hollywood promotes similar solutions when "good guy" characters injure, punish, and kill "bad guy" characters in order to make things right. The point here is that rejecting technology generally, or media specifically, is no guarantee toward godliness.

The label "vain religionist" comes from my reading of James 1, where the apostle says that people who consider themselves religious, but who cannot control their tongues, practice a worthless faith (1:26). By parallel, believers who claim godly values in their decision to not own a television or attend the cinema, but who still embrace negative media values, may only be fooling themselves.

If we exclude the acceptor and vain religionist positions as serious contenders for our attention, we might regard the avoider and reformer positions as the only realistic options for Christians today. However, for some believers, the best option is still avoidance. For some that means not owning a television set, and being highly selective in their media use. Two adult friends of mine fit in this category. Behind their position is the belief that despite our best efforts otherwise, we may still succumb to banal and base media content if not careful. Just as Paul said that eating meat was not for all Christians, so too consuming media may be a decision each of us must make. If there is anything to this belief, then it is worth considering why some believers separate themselves from media.

A Case Against the Media

A good number of separatist (position 1) and avoider (position 2) Christians believe that media deliver as many drawbacks as advantages, present ungodly values, waste our time, and rely on sex and violence too easily to maintain our attention. Both value enmeshment in human community and dependence on God more than entanglement in digital reality. Let's consider five arguments they marshal against the media.

The Medium-as-Amputator Argument. In 1967, media futurist Marshall McLuhan said, "The medium, or process, of our time—electric technology—is reshaping and restructuring patterns of social interdependence and every aspect of our personal life. It is forcing us to

Copyright © 1997 Randy Glasbergen.
www.glasbergen.com

GLASBERGEN

**"Thank you for calling. Please leave a message.
In case I forget to check my messages, please
send your message as an audio file to my e-mail,
then send me a fax to remind me to check my
e-mail, then call back to remind me to
check my fax."**

reconsider and re-evaluate practically every thought, every action, and every institution formerly taken for granted."[10] McLuhan's point was that every technology introduces change to a culture, and in the case of media technology, that change occurs apart from—or in addition to—the changes brought by its content. The medium alone changes us.

McLuhan argued that technology serves as *extensions* of our bodies—the car as an extension of our feet, the radio as an extension of our ears, the television as an extension of our eyes, and the like. When a new technology emerges, we often praise it for its beneficial qualities. However, McLuhan also pointed out that technology *amputates* previous benefits. The car increases speed of travel, but removes the need to walk and the health benefits of walking. When families rely on television for continuous entertainment, family members lose their ability to create their own fun, or think each other funny. BlackBerrys connect us to our work, but can lead to addiction and the inability to leave work alone. During the April 2007 crash of BlackBerry's email server, David Hyman awoke to his addiction. "I push that button like a nervous habit, all day, all night. When you don't get your email, you're like a drug user cut from your source."[11]

You can determine what a medium gives, and takes away, by asking four questions McLuhan asked. 1) What function of the human body does the medium or technology extend? 2) What has been retrieved—or gained, positively—from the new medium? 3) What does the medium or technology make obsolete? And 4) what does the technology reverse into if it is overextended?[12] Overextension occurs when new problems and amputated benefits associated with a new medium outweigh, and therefore, reverse its benefits.

Position 1 and 2 believers point out the ills of media amputation and overextension. They cite facts such as the difficulty for family members to hold meaningful, personal conversations when the television glows in the family room an average of eight hours per day. Or that the obesity rate among high television viewers is greater than for people who watch little television. Or that our enmeshment with palm-pilot organizing, 180-cable channel availability, and billions of searchable Internet sites distracts us from finding a quiet place with God.[13] Their argument, therefore, is that for all the good media do to build global community and world awareness, the media also cut off previous joys, and muddle a once simpler life.

The Values Argument. A second argument against the media is that they promote values that believers find objectionable or misplaced. Values are concepts of the desirable.[14] We value what we think is important. Separatist and evangelical believers argue that we are better off avoiding media programming that runs contrary to kingdom values. If you have clicked through twenty channels only to determine "there's nothing good on," this probably indicates that your values do not square with the media's. Christian values such as selfless love, service to others, deferred gratification, and devotion to God find little space in popular media. Let us consider three media values that conflict with the call of Christ.

Media Value #1: You Deserve A Comfortable Life. In an average year, American advertisers churn out 12 billion display ads, 2.5 million radio commercials, and 300,000 television commercials. If you watch television for three hours straight, including the ads, you will see about thirty-six minutes of advertisements, or forty-five to sixty ads depending on how many are thirty seconds or sixty seconds. If you surf the World Wide Web for two hours per day, you may encounter fifty to a hundred ads. Within this flood of advertisements, a uniform message emerges, namely, that we are what we buy, and only when we have bought enough will we accomplish the American dream and be content. Madison Avenue advertising executives would like us to believe that she who dies with the most toys wins. In contrast, Jesus modeled a simpler life free from material entrapments. Upon his death, the soldiers fought over his cloak, the only personal item referred to at the crucifixion scene in the biblical story.

> Adolescents who watch a lot of TV tend to want easy, high-paying jobs, with long vacation time.

Author Ben Stein analyzed television programming and determined that it looks a lot like happy brightness of Sunset Boulevard because it reflects the comfortable lifestyles of producers and actors in Los Angeles, California.[15] While Stein made his observations over twenty-five years ago, they still hold true today as television glorifies the rich and famous. Programs such as *Entertainment Tonight* or dramas such as *Desperate Housewives* and *The OC* focus on upscale living among celebrities and characters alike. Moreover, game shows such as *Wheel of Fortune* and *Deal or No Deal* make it tough to shake the notion that what counts is our material comfort.

Does this message really affect us? Can we rise above it? One television study on adolescents' perceptions of work suggests not. The researcher found that "heavy viewing adolescents were more likely [than low viewers] to want high-status jobs that would give them a chance to earn a lot of money but also wanted jobs to be relatively easy with long vacations and time to do other things."[16] This evidence suggests that increased exposure to the posh and privileged makes us devalue a simpler life, and perhaps disparage our own.

Media Value #2: You Deserve an Exciting Life. The media depict fast moving dramas that grab our attention, and stimulate our minds and emotions. The subtle message is that we should emulate celebrities, extreme sports heroes, and product-rich living as a matter of course. Advertising especially promotes the idea that products yield excitement. We can all recall ads that claim certain shampoos bring orgasmic ecstasy, a razor's shave attracts beautiful women, and beer guarantees a party.

Media critic Seth Stevenson points out the myth behind recent beer advertisements for Amstel Light, Heineken Premium Light, and Corona. The marketers attempt to associate their beers with historical Amsterdam (Amstel), the cosmopolitan life (Heineken), and Mexican beaches (Corona). He comments,

> There's no weight or integrity to these brand "stories." HPL [Heineken Premium Light] won't make you popular with people from all corners of society, just as Amstel won't make you a Dutch hipster and Corona won't transform you into a beach bum. We all know this. I'm not pretending it's a revelation. But once in a while, advertising's insistence that brands have meaningful personalities fills me with a sky-graying, soul-shrinking sense of ennui.[17]

These television examples pale in comparison to graphic horror films and video games intended to increase one's heart rate. Elizabeth Perse believes that some people are wired naturally for high stimulation. She calls such people "high sensation seekers," and she examined how they meet their need for a stimulating life. She found that high sensation seekers (HSS) attend more horror films, like horror films more, watch horror films for the gore and thrills, prefer rock music, consume more x-rated magazines, books, and movies, express more willingness to watch erotic films, and spend more time watching action movies in experimental conditions than low sensation seekers.[18] Although Perse treats HSS as a personality trait that influences media choices, you can see how the material chosen only confirms and strengthens the value for excitement. In the case of serial killer Ted Bundy, exposure to absorbing material increased his threshold for what produced a kick. Eventually he raped and murdered young women as a means to achieve the same stimulation provided earlier by pornography.[19]

Media Value #3: You Acquire Friends through Things. The media industry is committed to the belief that material gain equals social acceptance. Therefore we should not be surprised when advertisers imply that wearing cologne will seduce mates, or driving a roadster will gain friends' approval. Of particular concern is the myth propagated by the 100,000 alcohol ads we see by age eighteen. These ads show the party crowd relishing in fellowship, but experiencing no addiction, impaired driving, or morning-after hangovers. As implied earlier, their message is clear: drink booze and you will be a social magnet. Bacardi rum commands us to "Unleash the party."

Another concern is that the media depict a fallen view of friendship. Christian media critic Quentin Schultze casts relationships on soap operas in Darwinian terms. He says soaps reflect "an evolutionary naturalism in which human society is a collection of animalistic individuals battling for survival. There is no God and no place for transcendent values from a god."[20] Producers of television, rock videos, and R-rated movies are too willing to portray self-centered, back-stabbing, and sex-based friendships as the norm, and chalk it up to survival of the fittest.

When we remember that the media are businesses, we understand their values. Media producers are out to sell goods—whether programs or perfume. To gain our attention, they sell us an attractive bill of goods: comfort, excitement, and friends. They do not want relationship with us; they want revenue through advertising, and we guarantee them revenue when we tune in.

The Time Use Argument. A third argument separators and avoiders advance is that many hours with the leisure of media is a waste of time if our larger goal is to glorify God. In Paul's exhortation to the believers at Ephesus, he encourages them to "be careful then, how you live—not as unwise but as wise, making the most of every opportunity, because the days are evil" (Ephesians 5:15–16).

How much time does a typical person spend with media sources?[21] According to the U.S. Department of Labor's Bureau of Labor Statistics for 2006, people in America aged fifteen years and older have about 5.1 hours of free time on average each day (weekdays, weekends, and holidays included). Within this period, exactly half of it is spent watching television (2.6 hours), and 19 minutes is spent playing video games or surfing the web. Other activities include socializing with friends and family (46 minutes), reading (22 minutes), exercising and recreating (17 minutes), relaxing and thinking (19 minutes), or some other leisure activity (29 minutes). Young people aged fifteen to nineteen tend to watch less TV and play more video games, whereas the elderly over seventy-five watch almost double the TV (4.2 hours) and play hardly any games.[22] In Canada, individuals average 21.4 hours of television per week (or a little over three hours per day), according to Statistics Canada, a government service.[23]

The U.S. statistics are conservative, however, in that they are based on the "primary activity" survey participants noted in activity diaries, rather than recording primary *and* secondary activities. In other words, they do not account for multitasking. A.C. Nielsen, a private ratings company, account for multitasking by using a combination of self-report diaries and electronic meters. According to their 2006 results, individuals averaged four hours and thirty-five minutes of television viewing per day, while households total an average of eight hours and fourteen minutes per day.[24]

Although comparable statistics for protestant Christians is difficult to find, we can piece together that believers may engage media in ways similar to the broader population. According to The Barna Group, a Christian polling company, in 2005 two-thirds of Christian households (67 percent) had Internet access at home, equivalent to the general population, and slightly more born-again Christians used a cell phone (75 percent) compared to the general population (72 percent). With respect to social networking, Barna writes, "People within the Christian community are just as immersed in (and dependent upon) digital technologies as those outside of it. Both evangelical Christians and other born again Christians emerged as statistically on par with national norms...."[25] Regarding podcast use, Christians are more likely (38 percent) to download a sermon or church teaching than other adults (17 percent), which is not surprising.

In addition, most born again teens (64 percent) believe that copying CDs and unauthorized music from friends is not a moral issue, much like their non-Christian counterparts (66 percent), and active church attenders were almost as likely to engage in piracy as non-attenders (78 percent and 81 percent respectively).

> Youth spend about 8.5 hours with media each day, compressed into 6.5 hours due to the common practice of multitasking.

Moreover, the most widely purchased media by Christian adults for their children in 2007 were DVDs of movies and television programs (about 84 percent) followed by CDs (60 percent), and video games (51 percent). Across these categories, however, anywhere from a quarter to nearly a half of parents said they were concerned about the moral content of the media product, but bought them anyway.[26]

Finally, a 2006 study of 806 Protestant ministers and 1,184 adults who attend Protestant churches indicated that both groups consume, on average, twice as much secular media programming as religious programming. This was especially true for movies, where only 17 percent of films were Christian, and least true for music, where 42 percent was faith-based. The study also considered television, websites, radio, non-fiction books, fiction books, and magazines where percentages fell more mid-range.[27]

Again, these figures are not proof that the rates of media consumption by people who consider themselves Christians are equivalent to non-Christians, but the trend of other practices, such as ownership, purchase behavior, and use of social networking, would indicate so.

In light of all this consumption, let us admit that we use media to meet personal needs, and not just to wile away the day. Yesterday I spent nine hours on my computer (while writing this chapter), two hours watching the Celtics win over the Lakers for the NBA championship, and another hour of *America's Got Talent* with my son Eric. As McQuail, Blumler, and Brown observe, we use media to gratify felt needs. "People wanting *information* may tune in *The MacNeil/Lehrer News Hours* on public television; individuals seeking to clarify their personal identity may watch *Oprah*; viewers searching for clues about social interaction may turn on *All My Children*; and people looking for entertainment may select *Wheel of Fortune*."[28] Position 1 separators and position 2 avoiders suggest, however, that despite these genuine motives, time with media can steal important time with people in real time and space. In light of exponential addiction to MySpace and Facebook, David Kinnaman of the Barna Group observed,

> Church leaders have to strike the delicate balance between the spiritual and cultural potential of tech tools without surrendering to the false promise of these tools. Having the means of reaching the masses—for instance, through podcasting—is a good thing. Yet, nothing matches the potency of life-on-life discipleship. In this respect, social networking and blogs can be effective tools to intimately connect with a small, natural network of relationships. The key is using the technology in a way that is consistent with your calling and purpose, not just an addictive self-indulgence.[29]

Some believers question whether it is wise to spend as much time with media sources per week as one would on a full-time job. Does it glorify God? Position 1 and position 2 Christians doubt so, and attempt to redeem their time in community with others.

The Spoiled Sexuality Argument. The fourth argument against the media is one that separatist and evangelical Christians make often and make clear. It asserts that media producers are far too willing to depict spoiled versions of our sexuality in media content, and that these images pain the heart of God. The orthodox Christian view of sexuality is that God gave erotic love for pleasure and procreation within a loving, committed marriage relationship. Through our sexuality, we consummate the mystery of two becoming one and show each other agape love. Eros love, or sexual love, is of God, but people have abused eros for personal gain and perverted pleasure. For single individuals, sexuality is an area for practicing God's grace and self-control. People of faith are concerned with the pervasiveness of media sex, and the distorted messages these depictions convey.

The Pervasiveness of Sexual Material in the Media. Your own experience will likely affirm that sex is a common theme in the media. The amount you consume depends, in part, on your choices. Other times, it seems sexual material follows us, even when we think we have chosen programming that contains little or none at all. The sheer quantity of sexual content in media often makes it impossible to avoid.

Take television as a case in point. According to a Kaiser Family Foundation report, the incidences of sexual scenes on television in 2005 were *double* that of 1998. The study looked at over 1,000 hours of programming across all genres (dramas, sitcoms, etc.) except for news, sports, and children's programming, and found that 70 percent included some sexual content, and 45 percent included sexual behavior. By "sexual content" the researchers meant talk about sex or talk leading to sex, talk about one's sexual preferences or habits, as well as sexual behaviors such as physical flirting, kissing, oral sex, implied intercourse, and depicted intercourse. The study also counted references to possible risks and responsibilities regarding sex, such as experiencing emotional fall-out (when learning a partner is not a virgin), becoming HIV positive, using contraception, abstaining from sex, and being sexually active against parents' wishes.

The results indicated that 92 percent of TV movies talked about or depicted sex, sitcoms such as *Family Guy* and *That 70s Show* registered 87 percent, drama series such as *Desperate Housewives* and *24* measured 87 percent, soap operas were close behind with 85 percent, while reality shows, such as *Survivor* and *American Idol*, had the least sex (28 percent). The number of sexual scenes totaled 3,780 in 2005, compared to 1,930 in 1998, which translates into five scenes per hour in 2005 compared to 3.2 scenes in 1998.[30] In regard to depictions of intercourse, "About half of all scenes …(53 percent) involve characters who have an established relationship with one another [down from 61 percent in 2002]. One of every five scenes of intercourse (20 percent) involves characters who know one another but have not yet established a relationship, and another 15 percent of scenes present characters having sex when they have just met (compared to 7 percent in 2002)."[31]

While current data are not available regarding the depiction of unmarried versus married sex, research from the early 1990s indicated that in soap operas—watched most often by teens—the ratio of unmarried-to-married sex was 2-to-1.[32] In teen-favorite prime time shows the ratio was 6-to-1.[33] And, in a sample of thirty R-rated movies that teenagers said they preferred to watch, the ratio rocketed to 32-to-1.[34]

What cumulative effect this content has on people is hard to tell since we certainly learn a lot about sexuality from our parents and friends as well. Even so, some effects are measurable, and we turn to those now.

Impact of Sexual Material. If the impact of this material ended with increased heart rates and sweaty palms, perhaps fewer Christians would be in a huff about its prevalence. But the effects go beyond mere physical arousal. Sexual themes influence how we think, feel, and treat people around us. The Kaiser Family Foundation researchers summarize the current research on sexual depictions in the media and its impact on young viewers in particular.

> Important research evidence in recent years has confirmed and extended our understanding about the influence of media sex. Observing talk about sex has been shown to influence adolescent viewers' beliefs about normative sexual patterns and practices…, expectations about how sexual relationships evolve…, and attitudes toward casual sex….. New data have strengthened the previous finding that exposure to sexual content on television is significantly correlated with teenagers' sexual behavior, while extending the association to other media….. And in arguably the most compelling study to date, a longitudinal panel study with a nationally representative sample demonstrated a causal [not casual] relationship between adolescent exposure to sexual talk and behavior on television and the acceleration of sexual activity including intercourse….[35] (bracketed phrase inserted)

"Normative" means kids take media content as the norm in everyday life, "correlated" means that watching media sex tends to predict adolescents' sexual conduct, and "causal relationship" means that after controlling for everything else (i.e., socioeconomic status, parental oversight, and teen's mental health, self-esteem, and religiosity), exposure to sexual talk and behavior on TV pushes kids to initiate intercourse with friends.

What these general findings indicate is that teenagers watching scenes such as Julie and her ex-husband Jimmy make love on *The OC* are likely to extend this dramatic fiction to real life as a standard and ideal. What impressions might they gather? In one episode, Julie and Jimmie lay naked under bed covers kissing passionately. Julie mumbles that it has been a long time, and Jimmy remarks that it's like riding a bike. Julie questions if her behavior is adulterous (now that she is remarried), to which Jimmy responds, "Technically I think it does." Julie complains that her husband hasn't touched her for months, and is headed for jail. Jimmy asks if she wants to stop, and Julie firmly responds, "No." The two continue as the music volume increases and the camera shifts to an outside shot. Regular exposure to scenes like this might create the impression that cheating on a bad spouse makes sense, cheating at all is okay, and one can solve personal problems by pressing the flesh with someone new (or in this case, old).

Of course watching just one scene like this will not result in the viewer becoming an adulterous spouse or sexually active teen, but five scenes per hour, for four hours a day, or 140 scenes per week, just may. Add to Julie and Jimmy the likes of characters Dr. Jack Hodgins and Angela Montenegro on *Bones* who video capture their love-making and watch it at work, Cheyenne Hart-Montgomery and Van Montgomery on *Reba* leading each other up the stairwell with knowing eyes, or Dr. Gregory House's many references to making it with Dr. Cuddy, or with his ex, or with a guest-actress midget, and one cannot escape the sense that television cultivates beliefs and values with furrowed consistency. As the Kaiser report authors conclude, "Because media influence tends to be gradual and cumulative in nature, it is the overall pattern of messages across programs to which viewers are exposed that is of primary interest for explaining effects."[36]

For a smaller group of people, sexual depictions in the media means regular use of pornography. Research on pornography suggests that viewing sexually explicit materials even once can lower one's appreciation for his or her sexual partner. In three different studies, male subjects viewed videotapes of attractive nude models in various types of sexual activity. Soon after they rated their own partners as less physically endowed, reported loving their own partners less, and were more likely to proposition a female interviewer during the debriefing period than were guys who were shown a control (non-sexually explicit) video.[37]

Like prolonged engagement with televised sex, viewing pornography over an extended period influences one's perceptions of real-life lovers. Researchers Zillmann and Bryant had male and female subjects watch pornographic videos weekly for several weeks, and found that:

> respondents seeing the explicit films reported, relative to a control group, less satisfaction with the affection, physical appearance, sexual curiosity, and sexual performance of their real-life partners. They also saw sex without emotional involvement as being relatively more important than the control group did. They showed greater acceptance of premarital and extramarital sex and a lesser evaluation of marriage and monogamy. They also showed less desire to have children and greater acceptance of male dominance and female submission. Results generally did not differ for males versus females or college students versus non-students.[38]

The reason for this result is due to the nature of pornographic material in which gorgeous models entwine in nontraditional positions and experience nirvana-like ecstasy in a childless, relationship-free vacuum. Few real life friends and lovers measure down to this spoiled, but highly idealized view of sex.

Sexual messages in the media today have become seemingly schizophrenic. On one hand, entertainment programming preaches that sexual involvement is natural, necessary, common, and free from responsibility. Consenting partners meet and hop into bed at their earliest convenience. On the other hand, health and government authorities advocate responsible sexual involvement in safe sex campaigns, and women's groups lead the charge against sexual abuse. The first group preaches freedom, the latter responsibility and self-control. On a positive note, young people who watch TV stories that preach sexual responsibility, sex's negative consequences, and appropriate condom use, are less likely to initiate sexual intercourse the year following this viewing than kids who don't watch such programming.[39]

The statistics, however, suggest that the entertainment industry is winning, and the fall-out is not just increased promiscuity. As one author concludes, "At a time when half of all new HIV infections in this country are among young people, when one in four sexually active teens contracts an STD every year, and when one in three girls become pregnant before the end of their teen years, it is important to know that Hollywood has the potential to play a positive role. While many TV executive are already taking initiative, Hollywood's full potential has not been realized."[40]

The sexuality argument alone is sufficient for some people of faith to cancel their cable, restrict their movie choices, and filter their email. Others do the same because of media violence.

The Violence Argument

"Don't worry kids, that's not <u>real</u> blood."

The fifth argument against the media that separatists and evangelicals muster is that media producers are far too willing to depict violent behavior between people. They follow the lead of George Gerbner, noted media violence researcher, who comments, "We are awash in a tide of violent representations such as the world has never known, and the consequences are very troubling."[41] Just how deep is this tide, and should we care?

Prevalence and Nature of Violent Material. On a blog site dedicated to votes for the most violent video game, a contributor named "Aliasing" writes [typed as found]:

> God of War 2 should be right at the top of the list..... I'm about two hours into the game and to date I've
> Torn about 1000 wings out of screaming harpies
> Killed dozens of gryphon's by shearing both wings off in mid air.
> Torn off a soldiers arm and killed him with the his sword in his dismembered hand.
> Broken another solider in half and used one half to beat a man to death.
> Used a small dog as a soccerball.
> Watched in horror as a large bird eats the internal organs out of Prometheus in graphic detail
> The burned Prometheus alive in a pit of coals
> Killed a siren by tearing off the top and its head at the mouth.
> Literally liquidfied a mans head by repeatedly slamming a metal door against it, after impaling him against a wall with a giant spear.[42]

"Aliasing" fits a favored storyline in violent video games, which is "a human perpetrator engaging in repeated acts of justified violence involving weapons that result in some blood shed to the victim."[43] Recently in Australia, the Classification Board declined the distribution of the sci-fi shooting game *Dark Sector*, citing that it contains graphic violence including "decapitation, dismemberment of limbs accompanied by large blood spurts, neck breaking spurts, neck breaking twists and exploded bodies with post-action twitching body parts."[44]

By comparison, violence on television is not as numerous, graphic, or interactive. Nevertheless, its prevalence has increased compared to several years ago, which is not encouraging. In an examination of programming on ABC, CBS, NBC, Fox, UPN and WB, the Parents Television Council observed that violent depictions increased by 75 percent from 1998 to 2006, averaging 4.41 instances per hour up from 2.25. The researchers at PTC counted person-to-person violence (as in shooting, stabbing, fighting), self-inflicted violence (such as attempted and successful suicide), medical violence (as with gory autopsies), and general mayhem (earthquakes, explosions, car crashes, and the like).

The PTC study also reported that television violence is becoming increasingly sexual as rapists, sexual predators, and fetishists attack victims during prime time, particularly on shows such as *Law and Order: S.V.U., C.S.I* (all three series), *Medium, Crossing Jordan, Prison Break, E.R.,* and *House.* For example, in *Medium,* Allison encounters a brain-injured man who, prior to his accident, murdered several prostitutes and buried them in the desert. Alison has a vision of him suffocating his victims in bed with a pillow while their hands were tied to the bedposts.

Impact of Violent Content. John P. Murray summarizes the growing and definitive research on violent media's effect on people, and particularly young children. In 2008 he observed that

> Fifty years of research on the effect of TV violence on children leads to the inescapable conclusion that viewing media violence is related to increases in aggressive attitudes, and behaviors. The changes in aggression are both short term and long term, and these changes may be mediated by neurological changes in the young viewer. The effects of media violence are both real and strong and are confirmed by the careful reviews of research evidence by various scientific and professional organizations that are concerned with children's mental health and development.[45]

The short-term effects of exposure show up in priming violent tendencies, arousing aggressive emotions, and providing models to imitate. The long-term effects of exposure include watching and learning hurtful scripts from violent characters, becoming emotionally desensitized to graphic gore, and building a general sense of fear.[46] Among people with well-developed imaginations, media violence may also perform a cathartic or blowing-off-steam function, though this is rare.[47] Catharsis is the only positive effect of media violence that scholars propose. All other effects are negative or potentially so.

In particular, *arousal* is the stirring up of emotions such as anger, hatred, or revenge and *priming* means making people susceptible to similar situations in real life. For example, a man who returns home after watching one of the *Saw* flicks to find his partner doing something that upsets him, is likely to respond aggressively toward her. The smallest thing can cue people to violence. In one study, second- and third-grade boys watched a violent video in which perpetrators used walkie-talkies as part of their equipment. Later, these boys were much more aggressive while playing floor hockey in a room where adult supervisors were using walkie-talkies ostensibly to do "sports interviews." The kids who saw a non-violent video (showing no walkie-talkies) played hockey less aggressively.[48]

Disinhibition is the process by which exposure to mediated aggression lessens people's inhibitions to act anti-socially. For example, a ten year longitudinal study indicated that the amount of TV violence consumed by eight year-old boys was a strong predictor of their aggressiveness as eighteen year-old men. The more they watched as kids, the more aggressive they were as young adults.[49] More recent evidence indicates that this effect occurs when kids watch over one hour of television per day. Jeffery Johnson tracked

> Serial killer Ted Bundy admitted that a steady intake of pornography and alcohol desensitized him to the heinous nature of his crimes.

707 children's television habits and behavioral tendencies over a seventeen-year period and found that kids who watched two or more hours of television per day were four times more likely to act aggressively in everyday life.[50] Repeated images of violence appear to develop a set of values and response options that make real-life aggression acceptable to heavy television viewers.

Imitation is to copy violent behavior after viewing it in the media. Although children are most susceptible to this kind of immediate social learning, there are also cases of young adults doing something similar to what they have viewed. Years ago, after MTV's Beavis and Butthead lit aerosol can contents, some viewers tried the same with terrifying results. In Moraine, Ohio a two-year-old girl died in a fire when her five-year-old brother mimicked B&B. In Sydney, Australia, an entire apartment complex burned down when a group of teens followed suit.

Desensitization is the lessening of emotional angst to violent content and the increasing acceptance of violence in real life. As noted earlier, a poignant example is the testimony of serial killer Ted Bundy. In his final interview with family activist James Dobson, Bundy admitted that he required increasingly more violent material to get the same buzz. Violent pornography and alcohol dulled Bundy's emotional response to heinous acts. He eventually murdered twenty-six young girls and women.

Since many of the effects noted here are behavioral, some Christians might believe that they would never go so far as to act aggressively or destructively towards others. Like Ben Ridley, who argues for "no effect," they use this reasoning to explain recreational reading of *Playboy* or laughing their way through a slice-and-dice movie. Separatist and evangelical believers bemoan this libertarian philosophy that people have the right to do as they please as long as they do not hurt others. This philosophy also conveys an ill-conceived view of purity and godliness that assumes God is only interested in our behavior. Students like Ben may forget that the God whose eyes are so pure he refuses to look on evil (see Habakkuk 1:13) requires his children to exercise self-control and be holy like himself (see 1 Peter 1:13–16).

A typical comeback by position 3 and 4 believers to avoidance arguments is that the conservative arm of the church focuses largely on media woes. In response, they point out that the media also inform, educate, and provide acceptable entertainment for those who look for it. Transformers also point out that God said, "to the pure all things are pure" (Titus 1:15). What they mean is that God has not made us machines who always respond in hard-wired, cause-effect ways to ugly media content. Rather, our frame of reference, and Spirit-led interpretations of media, weaken their negative impact and, at times, brightly discover Gods truth. The media offer benefits for all, including Christians. We will look at these positions in Chapter 12. For now it is sufficient to acknowledge what separatists and evangelicals have in their favor to argue rejection of certain media.

Summary

1. Media technology gives and takes away. Its benefits include ease, speed, and efficiency to communicate, and unbridled access to information. However, media necessarily remove, or amputate other benefits, and when overextended, create their own problems.

2. Media sources largely ignore Christian values. They espouse a life of excitement brought on by material comfort, immediate gratification, and artificially induced community. Sorely lacking are strong messages of altruism, sacrificial love, long-term commitment in relationships, and peace in God.

3. Media use can be a waste of time. While we may learn about the world and realize that people are badly in need of support and salvation, the blunt facts are that we spend more free time sitting idly with entertainment media than with needy others.

4. Media sources shed more lust than light upon human sexuality. The treatment of women especially as objects for personal gratification thwarts God's sacred view of sex.

5. Media sources confirm that we are like Cain—sinners prone to violence—but at the expense of creating more Cains. Exposure to mediated violence results in negative arousal, disinhibition, imitation, and desensitization.

For all the clout these five arguments pack, this chapter has not mentioned other issues perhaps equally disturbing. These include the effect of depreciated reading skills among heavy TV viewers, and the biased flow of world information from the likes of CNN. Other scholars claim that the subtle messages of racism, ethnocentrism, and blind nationalism are more insidious than overt sex and violence. These concerns also weigh into the equation against the media.

 **WORTH THE TALK**

1. What position represents your place on the media grid? Think through your position and discuss it with a friend.

2. Is the separatist's call for media abstinence a viable one? Specifically, what actions would you need to take in order to live in a media-less or low-media environment? Is it possible or desirable with regard to print media? Is it possible or desirable with regard to electronic media?

3. How valid is the avoider, evangelical position? Can Christians tiptoe around objectionable content? *Should* Christians tiptoe around objectionable content?

4. Position 3, the reformed view, suggests that we can redeem (find the good in) media messages and redeem (change for the good) the media industry. Do you agree with these views? Why or why not?

5. Ben Ridley's position 4 is based, in part, on the belief that media provide harmless fun. Another assumption is that a life of entertainment, within reason, is okay in God's eyes. What do you think?

6. The research regarding sexual and violent material in the media paints a bleak picture of their redemptive value. What do you think of the evidence? To what degree do you think it applies to you?

 CONSIDER THE WALK

1. Survey or interview students at your school as to their views on what a Christian response to media ought to be. See if their responses fit the model presented in Figure 11.1 or if some other model works better.

2. Pick up copies of *Seventeen, Mademoiselle,* or other women's magazines and analyze their photographs and articles for sexual messages.

What myths do these materials depict? What truths?

3. Write a paper that compares violence in R-rated movies with violence in the Bible. See what scholars say on both issues and use ample examples. Try to grasp the similarities and differences between filmic and biblical violence. Determine the purpose of each.

ONLINE CHALK

This chapter catalogues arguments against the media. Its tone and perspective represents people who bemoan media's negative effects. You will find additional material to support these arguments using the following Internet search terms.

- Media effects model
- Media cultivation model
- Violence in the media
- The Kaiser Family Foundation
- Parents Television Council

ENDNOTES

1 The name "Ben Ridley" is fictional, but this illustration is not.

2 "Generation M: Media in the Lives of 8-18 Year-olds," Kaiser Family Foundation Study, executive summary posted March 2005, http://www.kff.org/entmedia/upload/Executive-Summary-Generation-M-Media-in-the-Lives-of-8-18-Year-olds.pdf (accessed June 17, 2008).

3 See Jeremiah Owyang's commentary and information about the Internet at http://www.web-strategist.com/blog/2008/01/09/social-network-stats-facebook-myspace-reunion-jan-2008 (accessed June 17, 2008).

4 The challenge of living in the world as members of God's kingdom has fascinated Christian writers through the centuries. A significant work, to which I am indebted, is Richard Niebuhr's *Christ and Culture* (New York: Harper & Row, 1951).

5 Donald Kraybill, *The Riddle of Amish Culture* (Baltimore: Johns Hopkins University Press, 1989), 38.

6 Ibid., 144-145.

7 For an insightful and readable reformed view on culture and how evangelicals might respond see John Fischer, *What on Earth are We Doing? Finding Our Place*

as Christians in the World (Ann Arbor: Servant Publications, 1996). Fischer gives examples of finding God's message in cultural expressions as diverse as rock music lyrics and baseball games.

8 Karen A. Foss and Alison F. Alexander, "Exploring the Margins of Television Viewing," *Communication Reports* 9 (1996): 61-68.

9 See the entry for Theodore Kaczynski at Encyclopedian, http://www.encyclopedian.com/te/Ted-Kaczynski.html (accessed June 18, 2008).

10 Marshall McLuhan and Quentin Fiore, *The Medium is the Massage* (New York: Random House, 1967), 8.

11 James Granelli and Alex Pham, "BlackBerry Outage Leaves Users Thumb-Founded," http://articles.latimes.com/2007/apr/19/business/fi-blackberry19 (accessed April 17, 2008).

12 For a summary of McLuhan's four questions see Todd A. Kappelman, *Marshall McLuhan: "The Medium is the Message,"* http://www.probe.org/docs/mcluhan.html (accessed May 17, 2003).

13 With regard to hearing God's voice amidst media din see Joseph Bentz, *Silent God: Finding Him When You Can't Hear His Voice* (Kansas City: Beacon Hill, 2007).

14 Richard D. Rieke and Malcolm O.Sillars, *Argumentation and Critical Decision Making*, 5th ed. (New York: Longman, 2001). See especially chapter 10, "Support:Values."

15 Ben Stein, *The View from Sunset Boulevard: America as Brought to You by the People Who Make Television* (New York: Basic Books, 1979).

16 N. Signorelli, "Television's Contribution to Adolescents' Perceptions About Work" (paper presented at the annual conference of the Speech Communication Association, Chicago, November, 1990).

17 See Seth Stevenson, "Less Filling: Beer Ads Just Aren't Doing it for Me Anymore," http://www.slate.com/id/2193692/?GT1=38001 (accessed June 19, 2008).

18 Elizabeth M. Perse, "Sensation Seeking and the Use of Television for Arousal," *Communication Reports* 9 (Winter 1996): 37-48.

19 Serial killer Ted Bundy acknowledged the role that pornography played in increasing his need for greater stimulation. See James Dobson, *Fatal Addiction: Ted Bundy's Interview with Dr. James Dobson*, VHS (Colorado Springs: Focus on the Family Films, 1989).

20 Quentin Schultze, *Television: Manna from Hollywood?* (Grand Rapids, MI: Zondervan, 1986), 47.

21 Peter C. Clemente, *The State of the Net: The New Frontier* (New York: McGraw-Hill, 1998).

22 See the U.S. Labor Department's Bureau of Labor Statistics' website, http://www.bls,gov/tus/charts/leisure.htm (accessed June 18, 2008).

23 See Statistics Canada's report, http://www40.statcan.ca/101/cst01/arts23.htm (accessed June 18, 2008).

24 See Gary Holmes, "Nielsen Media Research Reports Television's Popularity Is Still Growing," Nielsen Media Research, posted September 21, 2006, http://www.nielsenmedia.com/nc/portal/site/Public/menuitem.55dc65b4a7d5adff3f65936147a

062a0/?vgnextoid=4156527aacccd010VgnVCM100000ac0a260aRCRD (accessed June 18, 2008).

25 "Barna Technology Study: Social Networking, Online Entertainment and Church Podcasts," posted May 26, 2008 at http://www.barna.org/FlexPage.aspx?Page=BarnaUpdate&BarnaUpdateID=29 (accessed June 18, 2008).

26 All statistics were posted at The Barna Group, http://www.barna.org/FlexPage.aspx?Page=Home (accessed June 18, 2008).

27 "Survey: Christian Media Used Often, but there is Room to Grow," posted June 28, 2006 at http://www.bpnews.net/bpnews.asp?ID=23557 (accessed June 27, 2008).

28 This quotation is from Em Griffin, *A First Look at Communication Theory*, 2nd ed. (New York: McGraw-Hill, 1994), 330. For a full description of the "uses and gratification" model see D. McQuail, J. G. Blumler and J. R. Brown, "The Television Audience: A Revised Perspective," in *Sociology of Mass Communications*, ed. D. McQuail (Middlesex, England: Penguin, 1972), 135-165.

29 See "Barna Technology Study: Social Networking, Online Entertainment and Church Podcasts," posted May 26, 2008, http://www.barna.org/FlexPage.aspx?Page=BarnaUpdate&BarnaUpdateID=299 (accessed June 18, 2008).

30 "Number of Sex Scenes on TV Nearly Double Since 1998," Kaiser Family Foundation News Release, posted 2005, http://www.kff.org/entmedia/entmedia-110905nr.cfm (accessed June 19, 2008).

31 "Sex on TV 4," Kaiser Family Foundation Report, executive summary posted 2005, http://www.kff.org/entmedia/7399.cfm (accessed June 19, 2008).

32 Bradley S. Greenberg et al., "Sex Content on Soaps and Prime-time Television Series Most Viewed by Adolescents," in *Media, Sex and the Adolescent*, Bradley S. Greenberg, Jane D. Brown and Nancy L. Buerkel-Rothfuss (Cresskill, NJ: Hampton Press, 1993), 35.

33 Ibid., 39.

34 Bradley S. Greenberg et al., "Sex Content in R-Rated Films Viewed by Adolescents," in *Media, Sex and the Adolescent*, 49.

35 "Sex on TV 4," Kaiser Family Foundation Report, posted 2005 http://www.kff.org/entmedia/7399.cfm (accessed June 18, 2008), 57.

36 Ibid.

37 Richard Jackson Harris, "The Impact of Sexually Explicit Media," in *Media Effects: Advances in Theory and Research*, ed. Jennings Bryant and Dolf Zillmann (Hillsdale, NJ: Lawrence Erlbaum, 1994), 247-272.

38 Ibid.

39 "Sex on TV 4," Kaiser Family Foundation Report, executive summary, 2.

40 Ibid., 13.

41 George Gerbner as quoted in the *Video Resources for the 21st Century 1996 Catalogue* (Northampton, MA: Media Education Foundation, 1996), 8.

42 Posted November 12, 2007 by "Aliasing," at http://digg.com/gaming_news/Top_10_Most_Violent_Video_Games (accessed June 19, 2008).

43 S. L. Smith, "Perps, Pimps, & Provocative Clothing: Examing Negative Content Patterns in Video Games," in *Playing Video Games—Motives, Responses, and*

Consequences, ed. P. Vorderer and J. Brant (Mahwah, NJ: Lawrence Erlbaum, 2006), 57-75.

44 Asher Moses, "Violence and Sex May Get Thumbs Up," posted February 25, 2008, http://www.smh.com.au/news/technology/violence-and-sex-may-get-thumbs-up/2008/02/22/1203467345267.html (accessed June 19, 2008).

45 John P. Murray, "Media Violence: The Effects Are Both Real and Strong,' *American Behavioral Scientist* 51 (2008): 1212.

46 This summary of effects comes from René Weber, Ute Ritterfeld and Klaus Mathiak, "Does Playing Violent Video Games Induce Aggression? Empirical Evidence of a Functional Magnetic Resonance Imaging Study," *Media Psychology* 8 (2006): 39-60.

47 B. Gunter, "The Cathartic Potential of Television Drama," *Bulletin of the British Psychological Society* 33 (1980): 448-450.

48 W. Josephson, "Television Violence and Children's Aggression: Testing the Priming, Social Script, and Disinhibition Predictions," *Journal of Personality and Social Psychology* 53 (1987): 882-890, as cited in Jo Eunkyung and Leonard Berkowitz, "A Priming Effect Analysis of Media Influences: An Update," in *Media Effects: Advances in Theory and Research*, ed. J. Bryant and D. Zillmann (Hillsdale, NJ: Lawrence Erlbaum, 1994), 43-60.

49 L. D. Eron, L. R. Huesmann, M. M. Lefdowitz and L. O. Walder, "Does Television Violence Cause Aggression?" *American Psychologist*, 27 (1972): 253-263, and L. R. Huesmann and L. D. Eron, eds. *Television and the Aggressive Child: A Cross-national Comparison* (Hillsdale, NJ: Lawrence Erlbaum, 1993), 174, as cited in Gunter, "The Cathartic Potential".

50 Maggie Fox, "Guide, Limit TV Viewing, U.S. Experts Urge Parents," posted March 2002, http://www.thefreeradical.ca/March_2002_tv_violence_study.htm (accessed June 23, 2008)

He who seeks good finds good will, but evil comes to him who searches for it.

Proverbs 11:27

To the pure, all things are pure, but to those who are corrupted and do not believe, nothing is pure.

Titus 1:15

Electronically (Re-) Connected
Arguments for the Media

IF YOU ACCEPT the idea that reading a good book redeems you, then you understand the unshakable assumption that many believers hold about media, that whatever their form, Christian media can shape, nurture, test, and inspire us. So compelling this belief, some believers show faith in the medium akin to faith in God. For example, when God TV launched in the United States from its origins in the United Kingdom, founders Rory and Wendy Alec greeted new viewers thus:

> We are so excited about all the Lord is doing through GOD TV and thankful for everything He has done. ... The Father loves you so much that He sent his only Son and everything Jesus talked about pointed to Him. GOD TV is the Father's network, and everything points to the Father, and we pray He would use our programmes as a vessel to pour out more of His presence in your life.[1]

Executives at another Christian network play a similar theme in a statement titled "Renew Your Faith in Television with Sky Angel":

> Once again, we're at the technological forefront with Sky Angel IPTV – the next step that will help us advance our mission to build and operate a global communications

system to reach the world with the life-changing message of Jesus Christ. Powered by the Internet and delivered straight to your television, our new IPTV television service gives you more channels, more choices and more control. ... We believe Sky Angel IPTV will create a better viewing experience for you, while nurturing your spiritual growth and providing you with many more positive entertainment choices. This is TV for a better you.[2]

This chapter expands on the rationale behind evangelical uses of media, as well as reformer responses as described in Chapter 11. Why do evangelicals generate such excitement about media's potential? How is it that most Christians adopt media gadgets with hardly a blink of an eye? On what basis do many believers watch the same television shows and rent the same movies as unbelievers?

Position 2 Revisited: Glory in the Technology, but Guard Content

Even though few Christians may practice this position right down to the last video rental, its pattern and thinking is common to the Christian population. What reasons shape this position to accept technology yet guard content? I think there are at least five.

Technology is Neutral. Neutral? In what way? Most believers in this position mean technology is morally neutral; TVs and DVD players are soulless, therefore not sinful or redeemed. Lynn White claims that this idea took root when Christian views of nature replaced animistic ones during medieval times.[3] The Greeks and Romans believed that spirits existed in trees, rivers, and hills, and that messing with nature meant disturbing the gods. Christians believed otherwise, and read the scriptures to say that God created the earth, but did not emanate within the earth. With no fear that God would be distressed, Christians felt free to investigate the earth's resources and develop new technologies.

One and a half millennia later, you can still find scholars who affirm this way of thinking. As one writes, "Technology in itself is neutral and should not be labeled 'good' or 'bad.' It is the uses to which we put new scientific developments that enhance or degrade personal well-being and prosperity."[4] Another writes that technology is "essentially amoral, a thing apart from values, an instrument which can be used for good or ill."[5]   Clifford Christians captures the moral dynamic when one claims that technology is value-free:

> Technology is not at fault, but the uses to which we put it [are]. ... A knife in the surgeon's hand saves a life and destroys it when used by a murderer. ... The same video player shows pornography and National Geographic specials. Television technology can promote salvation rather than commerce.[6]

Evangelicals agree with this reasoning, and are therefore eager to use the media to transmit familyvalues and gospel-clear material to whomever is searching for it.

Technology Improves Life. Avoiders, or position 2 Christians, adopt media technology readily because they believe it improves life. Some would note that just as medical discoveries have staved off diseases from reaching epidemic proportions, so too media sources have curtailed widespread global ignorance through news and educational programming. Similarly, just as nutritional insights have lengthened our life span, so too media have enriched life through arts and entertainment. Quentin Schultze calls this "technological optimism," and makes comment on Americans and televangelists in particular.

> The national imagination [of Americans] has always linked technological development with human progress. As a result, Americans, including televangelists, have generally been technological optimists. In the case of television, cable channels, remote controls, satellite transmitters and receivers, VCRs, large screens, and enhanced audio all become symbols of what most people believe are better and more pleasant ways of life."[7]

Dennis Callaway captures this optimism in an article titled "Missions in Cyberspace." He describes the situation where a missionary senses that a seeker is close to making a decision to trust God for salvation. The missionary wants to mobilize believers to pray, so he emails a prayer request to one of his support churches in Long Beach, California. The pastors photocopy the request for the midweek group leaders, and within two days, 400 believers are praying for the seeker.[8] Position 2 Christians applaud speed, efficiency, choice, and convenience because these qualities appear to make the work of the church more effective.[9]

God Keeps On Giving Us Technology. A third reason why Christians use media technologies freely is because they consider them signs of God's progressive revelation.[10] This way of thinking also began in medieval times when the Christian linear view of history replaced pre-Christian Greek and Roman cyclical views. Augustine read the scriptures to mean that we are not spinning our wheels historically or culturally but that we are actors in God's drama—creation, fall, Christ's intervention, and kingdom consummation. All along the way, God speaks with us and reveals himself to us. Part of that revelation is the garden of scientific knowledge and the produce of technology.

In *Faith in Reading: Religious Publishing and the Birth of Mass Media in America*, author David Paul Nord argues persuasively that the rise of the publishing industry in the 1800s was driven by evangelical Christians within the American Bible Society and American Tract Society. While today's secular media operate largely for profit, Nord points out that yesteryear Christians were more often willing to give away the gospel message and church literature because of their faith in God, and recognizing their role in sharing it with others.[11]

Today many Christians continue to view technological advances as gifts from God and proof of his grace. In writing about the Internet,

one Christian media scholar wrote, "*There comes a time when the church of Jesus Christ has to be bold enough to lay claim to a new medium. As I like to put it, new technologies are part of the unfolding of God's Creation. We don't own these technologies; God does.*"[12] Many ministers, youth leaders, missionaries, and professors would agree.

Responsible Ambivalence. While many position 2 believers view technology as morally neutral, others feel uneasy about lumping TVs and VCRs in with non-media machines. Is there not a fundamental difference between a DVD player and the Salk vaccine for polio? Between a stereo system and a Volkswagen Jetta? The difference is that the vaccine and car were developed with narrowly defined beneficial ends: eradicate polio and to ease transportation. While it is true that the narrow goal of media technology is to communicate efficiently with millions, others point out that the message conveyed is the broader goal, and content, is morally charged.

This uncertainty towards media technology goes deep in Christian thought, and prevailed in the 1920s and 30s. In those days, many believers and bullet theorists cast the newly invented medium of radio as a powerful shaper of public opinion. Hitler's successful propaganda campaign fueled this model through the 1940s. In 1946, the founder of a large missionary radio station in Quito, Ecuador expressed concern about radio's potential.

> The phenomenal speed and size of the growth of radio .... indicate[s] vast potential for future good or evil. Whether mankind is to be blessed or blighted by this scientific marvel . . . is chiefly a moral and spiritual question for which individual Christians and the Church of Christ do well to assume a responsible attitude.[13]

More recently, the editors at *Christianity Today*—the flagship magazine for mainstream evangelical thought—describe a similar ambivalence toward the Internet.

> Technology's blessings have unexpected side effects. Technology accelerates change in ways that are difficult to handle. Even as the internet can bring the gospel into the privacy of seeker's homes, it can also create a "virtual

Christianity," unconnected to a living, breathing body of believers. Just as it can deliver information rapidly and efficiently, it can also fracture church and society into niche groups pursuing their special interests.[14]

So Much Christian Material to Choose From. The fourth reason why evangelicals find media consumption easy and beneficial is that fellow evangelicals produce ample media fare. Today believers and non-believers alike can avail themselves to Christian comic books, DVDs, TV talk shows, Internet chat lines, call-in radio programs and magazines galore. Consider this review of faith-filled media.

Magazines Galore. Magzines succeed because publishers carve out niche markets, and the same is true for Christian publishers. *Denominational magazines,* such as the Presbyterian Church of America's *byFaith* and the Evangelical Free Church's *Pulse* magazine, nurture group identity through reports and articles linked to the denomination's activities, personnel, and doctrine. *Scholarly journals,* such as the *Journal of Biblical Literature, Christianity and Literature,* and *Theology and Sexuality* offer venues for scholars to debate matters of biblical interpretation and life ethics. *Professional ministry magazines,* such as *Leadership* and *YouthWorker Journal,* resource ministry personnel with sermon outlines, counsel on tough body-life questions, and reflections by nationally recognized leaders. *Family improvement magazines* provide articles on parenting, marriage, budgeting, school concerns, and health. *Marriage Partnership, Today's Christian Woman,* and Promise Keepers' *New Man* are prime examples in a crowded field. Finally, *Christian trade magazines* appeal to a broad yet targeted readership as in the cases of *World Magazine* (a news magazine), *Christianity Today, Campus Life* and *Contemporary Christian Music Magazine,* Much like *Newsweek* or *Psychology Today,* these magazines appeal to a wide readership, and gain revenues by selling advertising space for everything from pews to a college education.

The pattern here reflects magazine publishing generally; publishers search out specific markets and develop magazines to meet the needs of readers. No matter what you are looking for, you are bound to find it eventually.

Radio: Sound Success. Few media historians would squabble over the claim that the invention of radio was simultaneously the birth of religious radio. It is reported that Samuel Morse's first telegraph message in 1837 was "What hath God wrought?"[15] and Reginald Aubrey Fessenden's first wireless voice transmission in 1906 was a Christmas eve service consisting of a reading of Luke's Gospel, a singing of Handel's *Largo*, and a violin solo of "O Holy Night."[16] Religious broadcasters haven't looked back since.

Pulpit and podium radio programs began in the 1920s and continue today with ministries such as Chuck Swindoll's "Insight for Living" and Woodrow Kroll's "Back to the Bible." *Talk shows* and *call-in talk shows* such as James Dobson's "Focus on the Family" and Hank Hanegraaff's "The Bible Answer Man" tackle questions head-on with no-nonsense answers, guest experts, and facts on cults and culture.

Christian music programming fills more air time than talk shows or preaching ministries, though you will find all three on Christian radio stations. This pattern is unlike secular commercial radio that tends to be all-talk or all-music (what the industry calls *format radio*). Christian stations have typically conformed to *program radio* (a mix of, talk, preaching, news, and music). Finally, *missionary radio* has been developed by evangelical groups who praise its ability to transcend geographic and political borders. Today Trans World Radio, Far East Broadcasting Company, and HCJB Global—the three major networks—broadcast biblical teaching and music in over 150 languages to within reach of most the earth's population via satellite, cable, Internet and local AM and FM radio. HCJB (which stands for Heralding Christ Jesus' Blessings) also engages in healthcare, medicine, education, and leadership consulting. Increasingly, mission radio groups have developed Internet ministries so listeners may connect in virtual community.[17]

Christians' use of radio will likely not die out soon. Its relatively low cost, personal feel, and omnipresence in kitchens, cars, and offices of the world's urban centers and remote jungles make it an appealing medium for people with a message.

Film: Mixed Reviews. If there were a medium that people of faith love to hate, yet feel guilty loving, it is film. Diatribes against the cinema from conservative Christians dot the historical landscape, including Stephen Paine's classic piece *The Christian and the Movies*. In 1957, he wrote pointedly, "We [Christians] don't attend movies. . . . Even if it were possible for you to attend the movies without personal detriment, . . . you would still be an accomplice to an industry that is causing untold crime and moral degradation among the young people of our country."[18]

However, this condemnation sounds foreign to most of us who nursed on television and DVD rentals during primary years, and relished our first trip to the cinema soon after. However, Paine's sentiment may explain why secular filmmakers have been slow to depict religion in movies, why Christians filmmakers entered the industry late in the game, and why Christian film critics see-saw in their praise for Hollywood's flashiest medium.

This love-hate relationship probably explains why you can find three types of religious movies today: the Biblical epic film, the universal thematic film, and the explicit evangelistic film. Biblical epic films date back to the oldie goldies when D. W. Griffiths and Cecil B. DeMille were new masters with a new medium. Griffith's *Intolerance* (1916) and DeMille's *The Ten Commandments* (1923, 1956) led the way for other Biblical drama such as *David and Bathsheba* (1951), *Ben Hur* (1959), *The Greatest Story Ever Told* (1965), *Jesus of Nazareth* (1977), and most recently, *The Passion of the Christ* (2004). As with many movies based on true life, these films have been criticized for falling short in authenticity, playing heavily on sentimentality, and brandishing the sensational. Even still, these films create a scriptural presence in film history.

More common to your viewing, perhaps, are thematic films that portray devout Christians in dramatic relief. For example, *A Man Called Peter* (1955) retells the life story of Methodist minister Peter Marshall in a most positive light. *Tender Mercies* (1983) depicts character Mac Sledge who finds religion among members of a Baptist church choir and experiences the first pains of new birth. More recently, in *Dead Man Walking* (1995), Susan Sarandon plays a Catholic sister who shows unreturned love to a convicted murderer played by Shawn Penn. The sister's strong testimony of God's love leads the convict to eleventh-hour repentance. Finally, *The Chronicles of Narnia: The Lion, the Witch, and the Wardrobe* (2005) and *Prince Caspian* (2008) serve as allegories of Christian faith and struggle based on the theology and novels of C. S. Lewis. Unlike many pictures put out by Christian studios, these feature films depict characters who struggle in their search for God, and who find him without the help of a sermon. They are more *show* and less *tell* about a life with God.

Gospel Communications and Billy Graham's World Wide Pictures account for a good percent of the *evangelistic films* produced. (WWP has produced over sixty films since the 1950s.) Films such as *The Hiding Place* (1975), *The Prodigal* (1983), *Power Play* (1994), and *The Climb* (2002) use biography and drama to show God at work in the lives of well known and everyday believers.[19]

The cumulative viewings or listenings to the *Jesus* film, produced by Campus Crusade for Christ, now totals over 6.5 billion times, making this movie the most watched or heard in world history. It is now available in over 1000 languages.[20] The film is based entirely on Luke's telling of Jesus life, and holds to scripture for its script. Paul Eshleman, Director of the *Jesus* film project, comments that this has made it a draw among many mission agencies.

> The power of the film is not in the cinematography, the presentation or even in the actors, but the power is in the Word of God. Because it stays close to the Scripture, it can be used like the Bible and that is why mission organizations want to use it. It presents Christ in such a powerful way.[21]

The *Jesus* film project coordinators report that 221 million individuals have indicated their decision to trust Christ for salvation after a viewing of the film (38.5 million more since the 2003 edition of this book). A commitment by local believers to follow-up new believers is required before *Jesus* is shown.

Like any medium, film has potential to present Christian faith in positive or negative perspective. Ministry films, while short on aesthetics, attempt to make God's word and work front and center. Commerical films represent diversity of quality and themes, but tend to feed human stardom, entertain for escapism, and depict our brokenness with no gospel answer. This may explain why many evangelical believers give the cinema one thumb up and one thumb down as an avenue for redemptive art.

Television: Famine or Feast. As noted in the previous chapter, we tend to spend more time with television than with any other medium, and our likelihood of encountering religious themes in television is scant to plentiful, depending on our choice.

Can you recall the last time religion made network news headlines, and the story was positive? In a study of religion in network news, the staff at the conservative watchdog Media Research Center reported that, "TV news coverage of religion has doubled in ten years, but [the] tone [is] still negative." From the mid-1990s to the mid-2000s, total network news coverage of religion increased from two stories per week to six stories in newscasts by ABC, CBS, and NBC. However, these figures represent only 3 percent of all news stories covered during that time, up from 1 percent in 1994.

The reason for more recent upswing was likely due to the twenty-fifth anniversary of Pope John Paul II, the release of Mel Gibson's *The Passion*, and religious freedom stories from Iraq. However, the president of the Media Research Center noted, "Religious stories are more prevelant, but the prevailing attitude at the networks seems to be it's only a good story if it casts faith in negative light, or if it evokes a political controversy."[22] For example, ABC's George Stephanopoulos on *This Week* referred to the Pope's positions on sexuality and women as "somewhat authoritarian and antiquated" and NBC's Dawna Friesen on *Nightly News* described the Pope's anniversary as "bittersweet" for his alienating Catholics over his conservative views on homosexuality, divorce, abortion, and contraception.[23]

In the world of prime-time dramatic programming, religious themes have also increased in number due to PAX Network (now ION Television) and the WB (Warner Brothers) network (now merged with UPN-United Paramount Network to form The CW Television Network), which target the conservative religious market. However, the overall presence of religious characters, and programming, remains small compared to general programming available through ABC, CBS, NBC, and FOX. In particular, communications professor Scott Clarke found that only 32 of 549 characters in prime time television (or 5.8 percent) could be identified as religious in 2003, a figure that virtually mirrored findings from 1994 (5.6 percent). Generally characters are nominally religious (3.8 percent) rather than devoutly so (2.0 percent). This world of religion-slim television compares sharply with the U.S. population where 77.7 percent consider themselves religious.[24] However, in a trend away from research in the 1970s, 1980s, and 1990s, religious characters in the 2000s were more likely to play central characters rather than supporting roles.[25]

Some believers take these positive signs as reason to target the major networks for Christian programming. While this strategy appeals in theory, the financial and artistic hurdles are great in an industry where only one in 3000 new shows pitched per year make it to the air.[26]

One response to these odds has been the creation of entire Christian networks for the sole purpose to broadcast faith-friendly programming. William F. Fore notes in *Television and Religion*, that the Christian network represents the fifth generation of Christian leaders using television. In the 1950s, Billy Graham used television to *cover* his rallies. Later Oral Roberts typified a *participative* style in that he offered to heal viewers if they would place their hands on their TV sets and provided viewers with telephone numbers for calling in to his ministry headquarters. Rex Humbard and Robert Schuller represent the *production* generation in that they built churches expressly for producing television-ready services. The fourth strategy, the *host-show program*, is embodied in Pat Robertson's "The 700 Club" (running continuously since 1966), which combines talk show and news show formats as Robertson and other anchors banter with co-hosts, cut to ministry commercials, and dialogue with studio audiences. Finally, the *genuine TV network* has emerged as a Christian presence in the cable network system. Most notably is Robertson's *Christian Broadcasting Network*, Paul and Jan Crouch's Trinity Broadcasting Network, Robert Johnson's Sky Angel, and Rory and Wendy Alec's God TV.

The continued development of the internet as a means for online television has made accessible a growing list of Christian broadcasting networks. The web service *Christian Tuner* (christiantuner.com/live/tv.asp) allows users to scroll through no fewer than fifty options worldwide, including the big three just noted.

Critics of Christian programming point out that even Robert Schuller's *The Hour of Power* (the most widely viewed of all TV ministers) attract at best 2 million households per week, and those largely Christian viewers.[27] In effect, any salt these programs attempt to spread falls back into the shaker. A positive interpretation is that faith-based television meets a spiritual need for millions worldwide.

The Internet: Cyberspace Sanctuary? A rough estimate of the World Wide Web's popularity for talking about Christianity is to run a simple test—to search for references to "Jesus Christ," "God," and, for comparison, "Bill Gates," using a standard search engine. Previously in 1996, using Alta Vista, results were 25,000 references to Gates, 146,000 to Christ, and 410,000 to God. In the spring of 2003, "Bill Gates" drew 580,343 sites, "Jesus Christ" 3.1 million, and "God" 16.6 million. In summer of 2008, the week following Mr. Gates' retirement from the Microsoft Corporation (a major news story), the results still favored the divine duo: Bill Gates (90.5 million) Jesus Christ (134 million), and God (1.4 billion). Using Google, the results were analogous: Gates (34 million) Jesus Christ (46 million) and God (673 million).

Behind this exponential growth in Christian sites is a strong position 2 mentality. As Jason Baker, author of *Christian Cyberspace Companion* writes, ". . . the machine is neither inherently good nor evil; it is simply a tool to further the ideology of the person using it. [T]he Internet can be employed to build God's kingdom or assault it."[28] So how are Christians using it for God's glory?

One way to find out is to visit Gospel Communication's gospel.com website. This site serves as a hyperlink nexus for institutions and individuals involved in Christian ministry, education, media development, missions, relief work, and more. In addition, you have no doubt watched YouTube videos, but you may have yet to discover GodTube.com, a Christian clone where content is monitored to present faith-affirming speakers, short films, and ministry videos.

Research suggests that the more religious you think you are, the more likely you will use the internet, even after accounting for other variables such as age, gender, education, and ethnicity. However, this finding is less true for religious people involved in local ministries such as small group study, talking with your pastor, or volunteering time to serve others. This finding, generated by data gathered in 2001, may be less true today if online activity involves increased social networking rather than merely surfing.[29] Whether or not we can connect with Christ's body, the church, as easily online as face-to-face is an important issue. A simple response is to recognize that human community still delivers a richness of exchange unmatched by e-interaction of individuals with noses to monitors. We would be wise to recall the encouragement in Hebrews 10:23 that reads, "Let us hold unswervingly to the hope we profess, for he who promised is faithful. And let us consider how we may spur one another on toward love and good deeds. Let us not give up meeting together, as some are in the habit of doing, but let us encourage one another—and all the more as you see the Day approaching."

We Can Assess Content According to our Values. A final reason why evangelicals engage media with ease is their conviction that one can rely on conservative values to sort through media fare. While values may be defined narrowly as objects, practices, or ideas we consider important, they may also be defined more broadly as "belief systems, ideologies, and cultures" which represent our general orientation in life.[30]

Communication professor Thomas Christie defines values this way and proposes that we filter media content against this backdrop. He cites research that suggests filtering is necessary on a regular basis because of the "values divide" between journalists (who tend toward liberal values) and mainstream Americans (who, by comparison, tend toward conservative ones), a fact which both groups recognize and accept.[31] In particular, people who are conservative, vote Republican, over sixty, and live in the south are more likely to think the news media less credible and criticize it more than people in the Northeast.[32] With respect to fundamentalist Christians, this posture of criticizing the media may be founded in the fact that network television news tends to cast them as intolerant, racist, violent, and eager to impose their beliefs on others.[33]

Christie also proposes a model, which his research supports, indicating that our values guide our media choices, especially with regard to traditional versus non-traditional news sources. Using language much like the accept-reject-critique model of Chapter 11, he shows how most people begin their search for news with traditional sources such as *ABC News* or *CNN*, and if the perspective there resonates with their values, they accept it. However, if consumers encounter values quite unlike their own, they will reject the material or seek values-consistent coverage in alternative media such as talk-show radio. If they continue with listening to or watching the traditional news show, they will do so with a more critical eye in order to "negotiate" the good found therein. In his study of 3,000 adults chosen randomly from across the United States, he found that people's values were very likely to predict whether or not they tuned in to *The Rush Limbaugh Show* and *Focus on the Family* as a source for cultural commentary.[34]

The idea that we "negotiate" media fare with discernment serves as an appropriate transition to a fuller explanation of the position 3, or reformer response to media. We consider it now as the last reasonable response Christians might engage with the media.

Position 3 Revisited: Critique Technology and Content within a Christian Worldview

Christians who hold a position 3 response to media (I called them transformers) differ in significant ways from those holding position 2. First off, they are not convinced that technology is value-free; they say it is *value-laden*. Second, they have more faith in the human spirit; they believe that critical thinking and a pure heart help us understand and benefit from media material. And third, while they affirm the production of overtly Christian content, they suggest that believers diversify their strategies in order to redeem media and their audiences. Let's take each in turn.

Technology is Not Value-Free. Like their Amish brothers and sisters, transformers are skeptical that technology is neutral or value-free; rather, they suggest that technology is inherently *value-laden*, that is, it represents and nurtures the inventor's values. Take computers for example; they didn't just happen, they were developed by sensing, valuing, religious (in some way) people, such as Bill Gates, who had a goal in mind: to crunch numbers efficiently, send messages quickly, and connect the world in community. The values of efficiency, speed, and connection embody your PC. Marshall McLuhan would say they are the "message" of the computer medium.[35] However, as we noted in the previous chapter, technology may *amputate* current benefits, or it may overextend and create new problems.

Clifford Christians argues that technology is value-laden from initial conception to everyday use:

> Technology, in my view, is the distinct cultural activity in which human beings form and transform natural reality for practical ends. From this perspective, I would argue that valuing penetrates all technological activity, from the analytical framework used to understand technological issues, through the processes of design and fabrication, to the resulting tools and products. Although valuing is surely

involved in the uses to which people put these technological objects, valuing saturates every phase prior to usage as
well.[36]

Perhaps we align our values with our technology, or, rather, our
technology shapes our values. The relationship is likely symbiotic.
For example, at least one study has shown that computer compulsives
(that is, heavy-weight programmers) think and act differently toward
people than most of us. "In their interaction with spouses, family, and
acquaintances, they are often terse, preferring yes-no responses. They
are impatient with open-ended conversations and are uncomfortable
with individuals who are reflective or meditative. Computer compulsives demand brevity and view social discourse in instrumental terms,
interacting with others as a means of collecting and exchanging useful information."[37] Again, it is difficult to discern which came first,
programmers' compulsive personalities, or the effects of working with
efficiency-oriented technology. However, other things being equal,
the technology likely feeds the personality.

Computer technology may consist of inert, soulless microchips
and fiber optic cables, but the impact of computers on human life
and consciousness belies their bias. Quentin Schultze comments that
computers technology encourages "informationism"—an almost religious faith "in the collection and dissemination of information as a
route to social progress and personal happiness."[38] Informationism is
one sign of a culture in love with electronic gadgetry. These gadgets
may have been created for practical ends, yet they shape our values
and experience.

What this means is that we need to critique each medium by
asking at least two key questions: What values are inherent in this
medium (my TV, iPod, and DVD)? What change does this medium
introduce in my relationship with others and with God?

Let's look at the inherent biases of television as another example.
For good or for bad, television values images over words, and encourages us to think that *seeing is believing* more than *reading or hearing
is believing*. Also, television values the seven second dramatic cut and
the two-second advertising cut compared to a long-term event, like a
date or worship service. Television values interruption (or what Neil
Postman has called the "now this…" phenomenon[39]) rather than the
continuity found in a Bach symphony or Tolkien novel. Television

biases you toward physical inactivity as you watch the Olympics, and discourages your immediate effort to exercise. Finally, television images attract attention to its screen, at the cost of attention to people beside us. Hence, the values inherent in television viewing include image-over-word, visual interruption, physical passivity, and social distraction.

Transformer believers suggest that analyzing media technology for their inherent values is a godly craft, and allows us to rise above technology's built-in biases. Once aware of biases, the critically minded person is more likely to balance image-oriented media with oral and written sources, fight the urge to interrupt others, seek physical exercise, and turn off the tube when a friend needs to talk. Acknowledging the structural biases of a medium empowers us to choose our own course.

People Are Mindful Agents, Not Passive Sponges. This chapter began with two verses that embody this point. The writer of Proverbs says, "He who seeks good finds good will, but evil comes to him who searches for it" (Proverbs 11:27), and Paul writes, "To the pure, all things are pure, but to those who are corrupted and do not believe, nothing is pure" (Titus 1:15). Transformers take these teachings seriously and

suggest that what we bring to media will determine what we get from them. If we expect evil, we will find it; if we look for the good, it will light on our shoulder.

So while position 1 and 2 believers feel that an evil ace is an evil ace and will corrupt one's soul, (a position akin to the objectivists described in Chapter 1), transformers are interpretivists, and more optimistic. With regard to movie going, Lloyd Billingsley notes, "To assume that everyone will imitate [in belief and behavior] what they see [in a movie theater] is practically to deny free will, spiritual discernment, or moral courage."[40] He believes, rather, that we can engage in beneficial meaning-making from most media sources so long as we are armed with a godly heart and a critical mind. The same holds for evaluating a medium. If we approach it mindfully, we should be able to discern its beneficial features. In short, we need to be *media literate* by the Spirit's empowering.

Media literacy "refers to evaluative commentary on media use at the cognitive, emotional, aesthetic, and moral levels of individual experience."[41] Or as some media educators define it: "Media literacy is the ability to choose, to understand, to question, to evaluate, to create and/or produce and to respond thoughtfully to the media we consume. It is mindful viewing, reflective judgment . . . an ongoing process. . . ."[42] This means that we are committed to being television viewers, not mere watchers, and music appreciators, not mere consumers.

Media literacy is largely about asking questions that lead to understanding, and a balanced evaluation, of a media product. Questions such as:

- Who produced this product, and what is his or her worldview?
- How are people defined? How is the human condition depicted?
- Is the natural world depicted in its glory, or is it ignored and marginalized?
- Is this material artistically well done or is it imitative and plastic?
- What is predictable about this message? what is unique and refreshing?
- Does this material mirror world history or is it history-less?
- Is the church present? affirmed? absent? attacked?
- What value for people and God does this message depict?
- Are dramatic characters believable or are they simplistic and static?

- Are people depicted as accountable, moral agents or do they get away with murder?
- How does this message relate to my world today? What responsible action does it inspire?

Keep in mind that position 3 believers do not use critical thinking as a license for consuming garbage. Few would suggest that you rent *I Spit on Your Grave* or cruise Internet porn sites to eke out puny moral revelation, such as sin happens. They understand that God calls us to be transformed by a renewed *mind* (Romans 12:2), and that some material is not redeemable.

We are Called to Redeem Culture As Well As People. Transformers want to do more than redeem people with the gospel message. Many feel called to the cultural mandate. They see all of God's creation under his lordship—every person, animal, city, vocation, technology, and cultural product. They believe that our role is to be co-regents with God in managing, nurturing and stewarding earth and culture so both experience God's goodness and grace.

When transformers speak of "redeeming" the media, they mean activity such as improving laws that regulate media, lessening the profit-motive of commercial media, advancing programs with moral themes, and creating material that shows respect for human life. As one position 3 writer comments, "Together we have to support cultural advances that are life affirming—promoting growth, justice, freedom, and human dignity—and work to reform those that are dehumanizing or oppressive."[43] Here are some practical ways you can redeem the media.

Work in the media industry. Just as the heart of the king is in the hand of the Lord (Proverbs 21:1), so too the media industry is ultimately claimed by God. As God seeks Christ's lordship over our careers, we can offer media careers to God as a sweet smelling sacrifices. This does not mean media industries brim with godly virtue. What it does mean is that you can be a Christian in the thick of the media complex. Some media might stand for ideals opposed to Christian ones, but they will likely not change their ideals without a moral option.

When Eduardo Verástegui (lead actor in the film *Bella*) committed to living for God and making redemptive art, he joined up with like-minded screenwriter Alejandro Gomez Monteverde and former *Twentieth Century Fox* business director, Leo Severino. Together they founded *Metanoia Films* with the goal to "entertain, engage, and inspire." Monteverde explained his motivation behind *Bella*:

> I wanted to write a love story that isn't just about the romance between a man and a woman, but about self-sacrificial love—and a story about how each other's pain become each other's redemption. And I wanted to make a film that shows there's always a choice that doesn't have to lead to moral pain.[44]

Create Pre-evangelistic Cultural Products. Another strategy position 3 believers encourage is the creation of pre-evangelistic material. If you have ever walked out of a movie theater deep in thought about the big questions of life (for example, Why are we here? What is our dilemma? Where are we headed?), you may have viewed a pre-evangelistic film. Such material does not present Christ; they prepare the way for Christ. Like John the Baptist, it goes before, nurturing, prodding, hinting, and prophesying that life without God is hollow and eternity without God is hell. In short, pre-evangelistic content encourages people to ask questions *that lead up to* their search for a Savior.

For example, the documentary *Ridding the World of Landmines* may raise questions about war, civilian casualties, and the meaning of life. Similarly, an episode from the BBC's *Planet Earth* may cue people to the possibility that God was the mastermind behind nature's intricacy and balance.

Or consider your role as a restorative journalist. For example, some time ago a local news story featured the plight of a woman confined to a wheel chair at the brusque handling by taxi cab drivers. The woman commented that she felt more like cargo than a person as she was bumped in and out of city taxis by insolent operators. Stories like these may lead us to fight for justice and human dignity in our communication careers as we serve God.

Promote Media Literacy in Your School, Church, and Home. Transformers also encourage Christians to stop complaining about media content and start promoting new ways of encountering it. For example, you might host a "DVD club" where friends gather to view and analyze films. One would not want to get bogged down with too much theory and criticism, but at least be as committed to discussion as to the popcorn. Adding a media professor would also spice things up.

Along the same lines, a transformer might teach a class at church titled "The Christian and the Media." Even if you are not an expert, you can get parents talking with their kids, invite special guests, and evaluate movie clips for their redemptive value. Or you may look into attaining the Center for Media Literacy's media literacy kit to guide your discussion.[45] Parents of young children are especially eager to learn criteria and strategies for evaluating and managing the media at home.

Encouraging others to be media literate is challenging yet rewarding. The role I play with my sons is akin to a sports commentator who frames the action on the field. My goal is to help my boys rise above the medium, and its message, to bracket them with a dose of reality. Recently on an episode of *Bones*, we witnessed Dr. Temperance Brennan barge into the home of her colleague, Special Agent Seeley Booth, to confront him about a personal issue. The scriptwriters required her to enter his bathroom, without knocking, as he bathed in the tub. Of course, he stands up to make a point, all the while maintaining eye contact with Bones. It didn't take much thought to ask, "How realistic is that, guys? Would most work colleagues act similarly?" We answered "no" and figured that it was a case of TV's formulaic use of sex to garner attention.

Keep Your Pencil Sharp and Your Invention Skills Active. A fourth and final suggestion position 3 advocates often make is that we provide feedback to media producers and take a stab at being producers too. When you see a program you like, or read an article that inspires you, you might email the people responsible, and affirm their redemptive work. People respond well to strokes rather than swift backhands.

You can keep your creative juices flowing by finding ways to create your own redeeming material. Investing in film school, or attending the Los Angeles Film Studies Center (associated with the Council for Christian Colleges and Universities), is a start. Creating top-notch film shorts and entering them in contests such as the Damah Film Festival (see www.damah.com) will network you with filmmakers. Or sign up for an intensive seminars such as Act One: Writing for Hollywood (see actoneprogram.com/) to boost your skills.

Summary

While Chapter 10 presented arguments against the media, this one has presented arguments for the media. Those arguments are divided along two camps: the position 2 view contends that media technologies are neutral conduits through which morally charged messages are sent. The position 3 view suggests that technologies are value-laden, and critiquing them and their content requires a pure heart and Christian worldview.

Position 2 Christians see technology as gifts from God and are keenly optimistic that they improve life and help save the lost. This has motivated many to use magazines, radio, film, television, and the Internet to convey the clear message of Jesus Christ's gospel to people world wide, though sometimes with mixed results. While confident that media channels are amoral, position 2 Christians are often ambivalent toward new media because they know, that like any tool, they may be used to affirm or undermine God's kingdom. In order to tip the moral balance to God's end, these believers value the production of material deemed unquestionably Christian for the purpose of ministry and missions.

Position 3 believers also regard media technology as blessings from God, but they contend that such technologies are not morally neutral. They hold that technology embodies the values and goals of people who often pursue a profit. Transformers believe that we can rise above media content, and interpret it redemptively. Doing so requires a pure and faithful heart lest material become a stumbling block (see Romans 14:23). Finally, they suggest numerous strategies for how believers can redeem the media, including a career dedicated to creating morally uplifting and pre-evangelistic programs, education in critical thinking about the media, and active feedback-giving to media producers.

WORTH THE TALK

1. Where do you tend to side? Do you identify with the evangelical position 2, or the transformer position 3? Why do you see yourself this way?

2. Research indicates that most Christians consume media in patterns which are much like the unchurched. Does this give support for position 1 or position 3? Does is support either?

3. Which do think is better—a television program that makes explicit reference to God's work among people (e.g., *Seventh Heaven,* Robert Schuller's *The Hour of Power*), or a program that depicts people struggling people yet moral reflection (e.g., *Reba*) What criteria might we use to judge one "better"?

 CONSIDER THE WALK

1. Evaluate the best in Christian broadcasting, publishing, or computing and try to determine what makes their messages successful. For example, you might use *Christianity Today* magazine as a case example and describe its format, features, departments, editorial policy, and audience.

2. Try your hand at television or film criticism in the manner of a transformer approach. Select a show or movie and then draw the good it contains from a godly perspective. Criteria you might use include the ones noted under the section titled "People are mindful agents."

3. Write a proposal for a radio program, television show, film, or Internet website that you think would be pre-evangelistic. Write as if you were pitching your idea to a producer who wants to produce moral content but is cautious about overtly religious material. Your proposal should address:

Format: Will it be a drama, talk-show, information resource, comedy? Moral questions: What tough questions will be characteristic of your product? Will it consider the after-life? Ethics in the work place? Origins of the world?

How will you convince an audience that your product is worth watching/hearing/ buying? That is, why do you think today's culture is ready for your program?

ONLINE CHALK

Christian ministry websites abound on the Internet, as this chapter notes. However, sites that analyze media in Christian perspective are less easy to find. Here are some key sites for both, but favoring the latter.

- Gospel Communications
- Center for Media Literacy
- Hollywood Jesus
- The Center for Parent/Youth Understanding
- Media Education Foundation

ENDNOTES

1 Rory Alec and Wendy Alec, "A Huge Thank You to all Our Viewers, Founder Families and Partners, We Greet and Bless you in Jesus Name," posted at http:// us.god.tv/Group/Group.aspx?id=1000009051 (accessed June 30, 2008).

2 "Renew Your Faith in Television with Sky Angel" posted at http://skyangel. com/About/Index.asp?Reference=Welcome&~ (accessed June 30, 2008).

3 Lynn White, Jr., "The Historical Roots of Our Ecological Crisis," *Science, 155* (1967): 1203-1207 as quoted in Stephen V. Monsma, (Ed.), *Responsible Technology: A Christian Perspective.* (Grand Rapids, MI: William B. Eerdmans Publishing Company, 1986), 41.

4 Richard R. Landers, *Man's Place in the Dybosphere*, (Englewood Cliffs, NJ: Prentice-Hall,1966) 207 as quoted in Monsma, (Ed.) p. 24.

5 R. A. Buchanan, *Technology and Social Progress.* (Oxford: Pergamon Press, 1965) 163 as quoted in Monsma, (Ed.), 24

6 Clifford G. Christians, "Religious Perspectives on Communication Technology," *Journal of Media and Religion 1*, (2002): 38.

7 Quentin Schultze, *Televangelism and American Culture*. (Grand Rapids, MI: Baker Book House, 1991) 49.

8 Dennis E. Callaway, "Missions in Cyberspace," *CBInternational Impact*, Fall 1995, 8-9

9 This view imitates the apostle Paul's report that he used all possible means to save people (1 Cor. 9:22). See, for example, Marvin Mardock, (Ed.), *By all means: Trends in World Evangelism Today*.(Minneapolis, MN: Bethany Fellowship, Inc.,1969). Murdock includes the 1 Corinthians 9:22 passage opposite the book's title page. Chapters cover twelve means: aviation, television, laity involvement, international students, athletics, translation, mass rallies, relief work, literature, anthropology, medicine, and radio.

10 Lynn White, Jr. as quoted in Monsma, (Ed.), p. 41.

11 David Paul Nord, *Faith in Reading: Religious Publishing and the Birth of Mass Media in America* (New York: Oxford University Press, 2004). See also the review *Faith in Reading: Religious Publishing and the Birth of Mass Media in America*. by: Quentin J. Schultze, *Journalism & Mass Communication Quarterly 82*, (2005): 458-460,

12 Quentin J. Schultze, *Internet for Christians,* (Muskegon, MI: Gospel Films Publications, 1996), 11.

13 Clarence W. Jones, *Radio: The New Missionary*, (Chicago, IL: Moody Press, 1946) 7.

14 "Media in Motion: Evangelicalism's Mission and Message Outlast Evolving Technologies," *Christianity Today*, October 2006, pp. 38-39.

15 Hal Erickson, *Religious Radio and Television in the United States, 1921-1991*. (Jefferson, NC: McFarland & Company, Inc., Publishers,1992)1.

16 J. Harold Ellens, *Models of Religious Broadcasting*, (Grand Rapids, MI: William B. Eerdmans Publishing Company,1974)14.

17 For example, you will find Trans World Radio at http://www.twr.org, Far Eastern Broadcasting Company at http://www.febc.org and HCJB at http://hcjb.org.

18 Stephen Paine, *The Christian and the Movies*, Grand Rapids, MI: Eerdmans, 1957) 5 & 70 as quoted in Lloyd Billingsley, *The Seductive Image: A Christian Critique of the World of Film*, (Winchester, IL: Crossway Books, 1989)17. William Orr represents this position as well when he writes, "I have absolutely nothing to say against the invention of moving pictures. . . . . But what I want to mention particularly is the [Hollywood] *amusement* industry. For this industry I have only the severest condemnation. . . . These companies have become monsters, rich, unprincipled, and corrupt. And the commercial pictures of today are dramatized and produced by sinful, wicked people, and their influence is a vile curse upon our land," in William Orr, *The Christian and Amusements* (Chicago, IL: Moody Press, 1960) 93.

19 You can check out films by both groups online at http://www.gospelcom.net/gf/ and http://www.wwp.org.

20 For statistic on the *Jesus* Film Project, see jesusfilm.org/progress/statistics.html (accessed July 1, 2008).

21 "The *Jesus* Film Project Takes on the World," *Mission Frontiers: Bulletin of the U.S. Center for World Mission 19*, (1997): 7-12.

22 "New Media Research Center Study Finds TV New Coverage of Religion has Doubled in Ten Years, But Tone Still Negative," News Release posted at http://mediaresearch.org/press/2004/press20040406.asp (accessed June 30, 2008).

23 Quoted by Tim Graham in "Religion on TV News: More Content, Less Context," page 4, posted at the Media Research Center, http://mediaresearch.org/SpecialReports/2004/report040604_p1.asp (accessed June 30, 2008).

24 Scott H. Clarke, "Created in Whose Image? Religious Characters on Network Television," *Journal of Media and Religion 4*, (2005): 137-153.

25 Scott H. Clarke, "Created in Whose Image?" 147-148.

26 The 1-in-3,000 figure comes from Todd Gitlin, *Inside Prime Time* (New York: Pantheon Books, 1985) 21.

27 In the mid-1980s, Robert Schuller's program attracted 1.27 million households. See William F. Fore, *Television and Religion: The Shaping of Faith, Values, and Culture*. (Minneapolis, MN: Augsburg Publishing House, 1987) 84.

28 Jason Baker, *Christian Cyberspace Companion*, 2nd Edition. (Grand Rapids, MI: Baker Book House, 1997) 23-24.

29 Christopher Paine, "Exploring the Relationships Between Religion and Internet Usage," Paper presented at the International Communication Association Annual Meeting, November 1, 2004, New York, NY.

30 Thomas Bryan Christie, "The Role of Values in Predicting Talk Radio Listening: A Model of Value Equivalence," *Journal of Radio Studies, 14* (2007): 26.

31 Thomas Bryan Christie, 22.

32 Ibid, 22-23.

33 Peter A. Kerr, "The Framing of Fundamentalist Christians: Network Television News, 1980-2000," *Journal of Media & Religion, 2* (2003): 203-235.

34 Thomas Christie, "The Role of Values…" 30-32

35 McLuhan captured this idea in his now famous adage, "The medium is the message." See Marshall McLuhan, *Understanding Media*, (New York: McGraw-Hill,1964).

36 Clifford G. Christians, "Religious Perspectives on Communication Technology," *Journal of Media and Religion, 1* (2002): 38.

37 Jeremy Rifkin, *Time Wars: The Primary Conflict in Human History*. (New York: Henry Holt and Company,1987) 17.

38 Quentin Schultz, *Habits of the High-tech Heart: Living Virtuously in the Information Age*. (Grand Rapids, MI: Baker Academic, 2002) 21.

39 Neil Postman, *Amusing Ourselves to Death: Public Discourse in an Age of Show Business*. (New York: Viking, 1985) see Chapter 7, 99-113.

40 Lloyd Billingsley, *The Seductive Image*, 21.

41 Daniel A. Stout, "Religious Media Literacy: Toward a Research Agenda" *Journal of Media and Religion, 1* (2002) 50.

42 *Curriculum Report, 26*, No. 4, (Reston, VA: National Association of Secondary School Principles, March 1997).

43 William D. Romanowski, *Eyes Wide Open: Looking for God in Popular Culture*, Revised and Expanded Edition (Grand Rapids, MI: Brazos Press, 2007) 53.

44 As quoted in Amanda Shaw, "Something Beautiful in Hollywood," *Comment Magazine*, posted at the Work Research Foundation http://wrf.ca/comment/article.cfm?ID=296, p. 3 (accessed January 4, 2008).

45 You may find how to order a media kit at the Center for Media Literacy, http://medialit.org/ (accessed July 1, 2008).

Yet for us there is but one God, the Father, from whom things came and for whom we live; and there is but one Lord, Jesus Christ, through whom all things came and through whom we live.

1 Corinthians 8:6

Looking at the Social Sciences

A Christian Perspective

A couple years ago, our campus hosted Donald Miller, author of *Blue Like Jazz*, and itinerant speaker. Donald connects well with university students, so it was not surprising that our auditorium brimmed with students and faculty eager to hear his ideas. If you have never heard him speak, you might check out his resource site at donaldmillerwords.com, and see one of his online videos.

Donald's speeches serve as a basis for examining how scholars study communication. One might assume that his speaking ability represents above average accomplishment, but explaining *why* he succeeds will differ depending on one's school of thought within the field of communication. Social scientists—or people we called objectivists in Chapter 1—might suggest that Donald excels because he is credible in the eyes of his audience, uses two-sided arguments with skeptical crowds, and uses plenty of easy-to-grasp, relevant material. All three features increase speaker persuasiveness according to research in persuasion studies.[1]

Humanities scholars—or people we called interpretivists in Chapter 1—might suggest that we judge Donald a fine speaker because he handles scripture well, appeals to our logic and emotions, practices what he preaches, and articulates his ideas clearly. These factors, they would argue, may be observed from watching him and reflecting on his performance. One would not need science to prove so.[2]

Finally, communication practitioners, while not ignoring these other interpretations, would likely add, "And his delivery works." Donald Miller not only speakes articulately, but breathes life into his message with a genuine voice, personal eye contact, and illustrative hand gestures.[3] Practitioners would point out that even great ideas fall flat if not delivered engagingly.

This chapter and the two that follow examine the social science, humanities, and performance approaches to our field from a Christian perspective. They will help you understand how scholars arrive at defendable truth claims. To do so, we will look at their methods for marshaling proof, and their assumptions about reality and truth. My hope is that you will develop a discerning eye for research as you sift through books, articles, and websites during university and beyond. To

"So let me get this straight, ump. You're tellin' me that because the strike zone is a human creation, you can make it as big as you like?"

begin, let us take a bird's eye view of how scholars view truth, and then we will consider social scientists in particular.

The Three Umpires: Three Views of Truth

If you know baseball, then the "strike zone" is familiar. This zone is an imaginary rectangle in front of the batter that reaches from the knees to the top of the numbers on the jersey, and is as wide as home plate. The umpire's job is to determine when a pitched ball touches any part of this area. If it does, then in theory, it is a strike. When not, it is called a ball.

The story is told of three umpires enjoying cold drinks after a baseball game discussing their philosophy on calling balls and strikes. Their ideas parallel scholarly views of "calling" truth. The first umpire says, "There's balls and there's strikes, and I call 'em the *way they are*." The second responds, "There's balls and there's strikes, and I call 'em *how I see* 'em." The third umpire chimes, "There's balls and there's strikes, but they *ain't nothin' until I call 'em*."[4] The first ump appears to be an *objectivist*, the second a *subjectivist*, and the third a *constructivist*.

Umpire #1: The Objectivist. Ump #1 believes he can call balls and strikes exactly as they are with no slippage. He puts faith in his eyes to read the ball's position precisely, whether in the strike zone or not. Some communication scholars—objectivists—have a similar view of seeing and calling reality. They assume that our five senses objectively tap into our external reality, and that we can use language to describe this reality in truthful terms. Thus claims to truth, such as "Donald Miller is a good speaker," can be judged true or not in light of objective evidence. When evidence proves the claim true, we can say we *know* Don speaks well. Therefore, objectivist scholars are *foundationalists* in that they assume we can know something for sure because it is based on a stable foundation such as science, history, reason, or God.[5]

Some people of faith are objectivists. Surrounded with Scripture and blessed with common sense, they believe we are able to discern God's truth regarding our physical, spiritual, and social reality. Objectivists tend to interpret God's scriptures more literally than others. If God said it is so, they assert, it must be true.

Umpire #1 represents what philosophers call a modernist approach to truth—the idea that a stable singular reality is knowable through reason or science. One can be a natural scientist, social scientist, or

English professor and embrace modernism. The natural scientist assumes that God's creation presents itself objectively for our study and labeling. Social scientists believe one can study human behavior free from personal bias through experimentation and surveys. English professors assume they can understand the true meaning of an author's story by knowing the author's intentions, audience, and context.

Umpire #2: The Subjectivist. In contrast to ump #1, ump #2 believes that his limited senses, flawed reasoning, and personal biases keep him from seeing balls and strikes as they are every single time. Sometimes dust blows into his eyes and his vision is blurred. Other times he draws a mental blank as to what he just saw. Still other times he calls strikes on players he dislikes, even though the pitches were clearly balls. He would like to be a realist, but calls himself a *critical realist*, because to him the pursuit of truth is a subjective affair. What he *perceives* (rather than *receives*) is influenced by sensory limitations, brainpower glitches, and sin.

Communication subjectivists support this view of truth with studies from social perception—the study of perceiving other people. For example, in one classic study researchers showed a group of people a picture of an incident on a New York subway, for just a few seconds. The picture showed two men: one white and one black; one wearing a business suit and one in blue-collar clothes; one holding an open razor in a threatening manner, the other showing fear in response. Many of the white subjects reported later, from memory, that a black laborer was robbing a white executive. In fact, the picture showed a white man in denims holding a razor to a black man in a business suit.[6] Although everyone saw the same picture, some people's recollections were thwarted by expectations or stereotypes. Somewhere along the way, the truth was edited.

Some Christians consider themselves subjectivists. In faith they believe that the entire creation is a certain way (and is known by God as a certain way), but in humility they acknowledge that humans still see through a glass darkly while attempting to understand and describe God's created, social, and spiritual order (1 Corinthians 13:12). In other words, truth is defined best as "an honest and full accounting of what you perceived."[7] Even with regard to the scriptures, believing subjectivists think Christians can know its mysteries only in a limited sense. They recognize the role of the Holy Spirit to lead them into all truth, yet what that looks like in everyday life is sometimes difficult to grasp.

Umpire #3: The Constructivist. The last umpire claimed that balls and strikes do not even exist until he declares them so. Technically, he is right. We have all been at ball games where the pitcher missed the strike zone, but the umpire still calls it a strike. Even when the batter, manager, and fans protest, the strike still goes in the record book. In a very real sense an umpire is able to "call a game" (i.e., determine its outcome) by virtue of his status and how he labels reality. These two features—the power position we hold in our society, and how we wield language—are two central principles of constructivists.

Constructivists point out that it is powerful people that label reality and "call it" for less powerful others. For example, professors, politicians, and pastors resemble umpires as they label the world with academic, political, and theological language. Students like yourself are required to master what others hand down as "truth" if you want to succeed, whether you agree with it or not.

Constructivists represent the postmodern spirit that tends toward relativism—the idea that what is true for you may or may not be true for me. Postmodernist writer Walter Truett Anderson, author of *Reality Isn't What It Used To Be*, summarizes the constructivist view.

> The constructivists . . . say that we do not have a "God's eye" view of nonhuman reality, never had, never will. They say we live in a symbolic world, a social reality that many people construct together and yet experience as the objective "real world." And they also tell us the earth is not a *single* symbolic world, but rather a vast universe of "multiple realities," because different groups of people construct different stories, and because different languages embody different ways of experiencing life.[8]

Believers who have wrestled with the propositions of postmodernism give it mixed reviews. Of most concern are its claims that there exists no metanarrative—no overarching story of God's redemptive role in the world from beginning to end—to explain human experience, and that we have no hope to know anything objectively. However, Christians may appreciate postmodernism's critique of modernism.

Christians agree with postmodernists when they lament the modernist view that individualism, yields scientific answer that will cure all human ills. Despite the benefits of science, medicine, and technology, modernism has often come at the price of wisdom, and a search for God.[9]

Even if you do not believe in ultimate truth, your role as a student will require you to ponder three big questions: What is true?, What is good?, and What is beautiful? Interestingly, each year millions of students sign up for university courses in pursuit of *truth that is true enough*. Every semester thousands of students debate policies and values they consider *good that is good enough*. And every day classmates evaluate television programs, theater productions and website designs for *beauty that is beautiful enough*. These kinds of activities hint at standards for truth, goodness, and beauty that existence outside of those studying it and arguing for it. Many Christians point to the person of Christ as the *logos* of the universe who existed before all things and in whom all things hold together.[10] In him, they suggest, we understand why knowledge, morality and elegance are worth pursuing in our communication.

> Christians point to Christ, the logos of the universe, to fathom why knowledge, morality, and elegance are worth pursuing in our communication.

Social Science: Agreeing to Stick with a Method

Even though a good number of communication scholars think like Umpire #3, another group identifies most with Umpires 1 and 2. Social scientists, in particular, fall into this group, because they assume we can measure, describe, and predict communication objectively. Social science reflects the covenantal theme of this text because scientists agree on appropriate ways to gather and interpret data. Scientists rarely work alone, but, instead, rely on the scientific community to assist and guide their research.

By now you have heard or read of investigations reported in this manner: "According to a study at State University, researchers discovered facts XYZ that seem to support theory Q about human communication." Communication scientists believe we interact in patterned, generalizable ways, and their goal is to discover and measure variables that predict communication outcomes. To do so, they ask questions, observe communication activity, and answer their questions the best they can. In more expanded form, they follow the following five steps.

Step 1. Look Into It. Researchers review books, articles, and communication activity to determine a question that scientists have not yet answered. This is a *literature review*.

Step 2. Form A Hunch. From their reading and casual observations, researchers form a hypothesis or hunch about communication. A scientific article will usually label this section *hypotheses*.

Step 3. Observe Others Systematically. Scientists set up a study that employs a standard method to gather data/information (for example, a questionnaire, experiment, or interview process). Scientists take great pains to explain carefully this *methodology*.

Step 4. Report the Data. Scientists explain what they found and whether or not their hypotheses were supported. This reporting is called the *results* section of a scientific article.

Step 5. Discuss Importance of Results. Researchers suggest implications of their findings for future research and theorizing. These *implications* often point to *future research*.

Assumptions Social Scientists Hold

This five-fold scientific method indicates how social scientists see the world. Like umpire #1, they assume that reality is a certain way and that our senses and method can discover it. They sit squarely in the *objectivism* camp. At the same time, some scientists assume, like umpire #2, that the scientific method suffers from human flaws that render knowledge partial. Thus some social scientists sit in the *subjectivism* camp. Regardless of these differences, most hold the following assumptions about reality, and how we come to know it.

Social Scientists Assume Some Form of Objectivism. That is, they assume that a method for collecting information can be free from human bias, and that the data they collect with that method is pure information about the world. *Objective realism* is the idea that the social, physical and spiritual worlds are a certain way regardless of how we try to express them. Our truth claims about reality might be cloudy, but reality remains rock solid. *Objective methodism* is the idea that we can use scientific methods to examine reality without bias—that we can remove ourselves from reality and study it dispassionately at arms length.

Social Scientists Assume a Stable and Discoverable Reality. That is, they assume that a phenomena, such as credibility, is always at work in human interaction and that one can tap into that dynamic pattern. They are not saying that someone's credibility never changes, rather, they assume that credibility won't go away, and always contributes to the outcome. What we need, they suggest, are tools, such as credibility scales and attitude scales, to discover how a speaker's high or low credibility impacts attitude change.

Social Scientists Assume A Generalizable and Replicable Reality. If what's true for Donald Miller generalizes to other public speakers, then other scientists should be able to replicate (that is, repeat) this finding in their own studies. If what holds for Miller's rhetorical success does not generalize to other public speakers, we have a poor base for writing public speaking textbooks or requiring students to take a course in it. Scientists who desire to replicate earlier findings are required to use the same method as the original researcher. This would include using the same type of subjects, the same scales for credibility and attitude change, and the same statistical analysis for examining the data. If the results are consistent, we consider them replicable.

Social Scientists Assume Distinct Criteria to Develop Communication Theories. A theory is a scholarly attempt to describe reality, just as a map attempts to picture land, water, and roads. The goal of scientists is to describe reality, with the skill of a cartographer, while still acknowledging that social reality is not as easily drawn as hills and dales. Em Griffin, at Wheaton College, explains in *A First Look at Communication Theory* the criteria scientists use to guide their theorizing.[11]

1. Explanation of the Data. A good scientific theory explains an event or behavior. For example, the idea of credibility explains why different audiences experience little or much attitude change, when the speaker's credibility is low or high respectively.

2. Prediction of Future Events. A good scientific theory predicts what will happen. For example, based on research, we can predict that the opinion of an expert will be more widely accepted than a high school student's, even if the opinions are identical.

3. Hypotheses That Can Be Tested. A good scientific theory is testable. The hypothesis that "high credibility leads to attitude change" can be measured with surveys, and analyzed with statistics.

4. Relative Simplicity. A good scientific theory is as simple as possible. A theory that suggests that credibility influences attitude change is simpler than one that says variables D, E, F, and G influence attitudes. Both may be true, but the first takes fewer ideas to explain.

5. Practical Utility. A good scientific theory is useful. The credibility theory implies that public speakers should establish their credibility early in a speech if they hope to persuade their audience.

Gathering Data in the Social Sciences

Common methods scientists use to gather data include experiments, surveys, interviews, and observation. Understanding each may help you understand better articles in *Communication Monographs* or *Human Communication Research* (two of several scientific journals in our field).

The Experimental Method. Experiments are considered the "tightest" form of scientific research because they give scientists control over what interests them. For example, if you wanted to measure the effect of high and low speaker credibility on audience beliefs, you could show a DVD of a speech to 100 subjects, but alter how your subjects viewed the speaker's credibility. You could tell fifty subjects that the speaker was Dr. Judee Burgoon, a highly respected researcher in non-verbal communication, and tell the other fifty that the speaker was Ms. Nicole Burton, a local organizational consultant. If the topic concerned "nonverbal cues related to interpersonal deception," we could assume subjects would regard Burgoon more credible than Burton. Any differences the two groups showed in their attitudes toward nonverbal interpersonal deception would be attributed to differences in speaker credibility, because all other variables were tightly controlled.

Despite their scientific rigor, experiments are sometimes criticized for being artificial and not generalizable to the real world. Experiments also require ample planning, organizing, training, and follow-up data analysis. Even still, many insights about human communication have been gained through experiments.

"According to my research, laughter is the best medicine, giggling is good for mild infections, chuckling works for minor cuts and bruises, and snickering only makes things worse."

The Survey Method. Whereas experimenters manipulate variables in a laboratory setting, survey researchers use questionnaires to measure variables as they exist already in communicators. For example, you could study speaker credibility by asking subjects to indicate their "credibility rating" of the president or prime minister, and then ask several questions regarding public life. Surveys, such as the national census, typically use *demographic* information about age, sex, education level, job, residence, and religious affiliation to paint a picture of the country's population. A survey researcher could measure a thousand individuals' impressions of a leader's credibility a day or two before the speech, and then measure the same opinions after the speech. Later the researcher can determine if people's impressions of the speaker's credibility changed from time one to time two, and also learn if young people or women or urban folks changed their credibility ratings or opinions more than the elderly, male, and rural subjects.

Although constructing valid questionnaires is a time-consuming chore, the resulting data is often ripe for understanding communication. You can use existing questionnaires or develop your own surveys for customized research.

The Interview Method. The interview method is a cousin to the survey method except that you, as researcher, ask questions orally, and record answers on a form. Interviews are conducted door-to-door, by telephone, and by appointment. The *standardized interview* "consists of a set of prepared questions from which the interviewer is not allowed to deviate,"[12] whereas the *unstandardized interview* "allows the interviewer as well as the respondent considerable latitude."[13] Standardized interviews are commonly used by market researchers who want to determine people's purchase habits and intentions (e.g., "Which of the following brands of television have you heard of? ___ Panasonic ___ Zenith ___ Sanyo ___ JVC ___ other: please specify.").

Interviewers use *closed questions* to retrieve brief responses such as "yes-no," or "Panasonic—Sanyo." *Open questions* allow the respondent to answer in a lengthy, unspecified way, as in, "What is your opinion about the violence chip for television monitoring?"

Interviewing requires a capable researcher who listens actively, records accurately, and avoids biasing the questions or the answers. Journalists often interview one or two individuals to write a story, and social scientists may interview 30 to 300 individuals to grasp broad patterns of communication.[14]

The Observation Method. If you have ever counted the number of times a speaker says "um," you have engaged in observational research. Observation is a "direct" approach to measuring behavior. Some think it is superior to interview research because it does not depend on a person's memory or honesty. Rather, observation research "gathers data through systematic watching, studying, or interpreting the source

You may have already done some sort of observational research.

of the data."[15] For example, you could video tape the 100 subjects in your Burgoon-Burton study, and then go back and code their facial expressions. Head nods and smiles would score as "agreeing with the speaker" and head shakes and frowns would score as "disagreeing with the speaker." You could then see if high-credibility Burgoon received more "agreeing behavior" than low-credibility Burton. Observation research is at work under a variety of different labels including case studies, content analysis, interaction analysis, relational analysis, network analysis, and naturalistic inquiry. What holds them together, however, is that each attempts to describe the status quo (that is, how communication is), and each uses observation.[16]

An important point is that a good scientist asks a research question first, and then determines the right method to answer that question. The researcher may enjoy, say, interviewing, but a topic may be too sensitive for face-to-face questioning. For sensitive issues, a survey would be more appropriate.

Christian Responses to Social Scientific Scholarship

By now you have evaluated the social science enterprise for yourself. You may be drawn to its value for objectivity and crunching of statistics to discover laws of communication. Or you may feel uneasy, noting that so much science smells of determinism. Where does our free will fit in to all this? Your response mirrors how other believers respond to this modernist project. What follows is an attempt to show that Christians have responded to the social scientific enterprise a bit similar to their response to media. Some pay little attention to it; some see it as harmless; others see it as a direct line to God's general revelation.

Rejection or Ignoring of Social Scientific Scholarship. Believers who place preeminent worth on the Bible as God's source of truth may regard human science as being at odds with faith. Such individuals first point to the adjective *social* in social science and note that its focus is on people, not God. They observe that the modernist agenda, with its promise to solve human problems through social research, has given us few answers and false hope. If people are made in God's image, they assert, then we should begin our study of humans by studying God and our relationship to him.

Others note that the social sciences gave us the notion of "cultural relativity" and they find this a cancerous concept for absolute truth.[17] Cultural relativity is the postmodern idea that what is true or right for one culture is best understood relative to its worldview and assumptions. Although social scientists intended cultural relativity to be an antidote to ethnocentrism, conservative Christians attack it for undermining any sense of universal truth. As one critic writes, "To make cultural relativism an absolute is precisely to destroy objective truth and normative values," and "either there is a 'transcultural' common truth which is intelligible to 'all the nations,' or the Great commission is impossible of implementation."[18]

> Some Christians believe that good science is one more means by which we discover truth about God's creation.

Another reason why some believers are wary of social science is because of its link with determinism. *Determinism* is the school of thought that suggests that we do not have free will, but only react to forces around us. For example, some Christians may suggest that if a communication problem, such as verbal abuse, can be explained by the abuser's environment, then it is too easy to excuse the abuser.[19] They feel that abdicating our responsibility for sinful habits may be worse than the habits themselves.

Other Christians are not antagonistic toward social science research; they simply pay little attention to it. Four communication books written from a scriptural and humanities perspective include Charles Kraft's *Communicating Jesus' Way* (1999), Emma Justes' *Hearing Beyond the Words* (2006), Jeff Rosenau's *Building Bridges Not Walls* (2003), and Graham Johnston's *Preaching to a Postmodern World* (2001). Donald Miller's *Blue Like Jazz* (2003) and *Searching for God Knows What* (2004) are similar in that all of these authors cite few, if any, scientific studies as they make great points on communication, listening, conflict management, preaching, and finding God. Rather than science, they rely on scripture references, personal examples, anecdotes, poems, and rhetorical concepts to enliven their message. It seems that these books probably reflect the authors' fondness for stories, words, and principles rather than outright disdain for the social sciences.

Subjugation of Social Scientific Scholarship to Christian Teaching. Other believers welcome insights from the social sciences but with one proviso: God's Word still trumps science. As some Christian sociologists have written, "The Christian's main concern with any model is whether or not the model squares realistically with Christian conceptions of human nature and needs."[20] And another writes

> Any approach to sociology [or we could just as well say communication] that ignores the biblical account of the origin of humans and its implications, as well as the effects of the fall and the potential of redemption, will always come short of the full truth. An understanding of the scriptural view of human nature is essential for a valid sociology [or, study in communication].[21]

With this said, we should note that conservative Christians seem to be more concerned with the worldview and resulting interpretations scholars bring to communication data, than the data alone. For example, a study on lying indicates that people deceive others for a variety of reasons, including: to gain personal needs (such as money), to increase desired relationships, to protect their self-esteem, and to gain some personal satisfaction.[22] These are facts that believers will admit describe why people lie. However, any attempt to interpret these facts to suggest that lying is justified or natural may be deemed a non-Christian perspective.

Acceptance of Social Scientific Scholarship as General Revelation. Another group of believers suggests that good science is one more means by which God reveals himself and his creation to us. They echo the scripture verse that begins this chapter. If "there is but one God, the Father, from whom things came" and "one Lord, Jesus Christ, through whom all things came," then discovering the structure of everything is entirely about finding God's revelation to us (see I Corinthians 8:6). As Richard Bube writes, "Christian science is good science. And good science is science that is faithful to the structure of reality."[23] David Myers resounds this view when he writes, "To do science means to remain open to reality and not to force upon it prior conclusions from any source."[24] These believers are optimistic that science can deliver God's truth. But they are not so boorish as to place science above scripture. They are not even willing to place scripture above science. Of one conviction they are sure: our sinfulness and our limited brain-power inhibit our ability to make definitive truth claims about God or humans. In reform theological manner, Myers and co-author Malcolm Jeeves write:

> If God has written the book of nature [including human communication nature], it becomes our calling to read it as clearly as we can, remembering that we are humble stewards of the creation, answerable to the giver of all data for the accuracy of our observations. Indeed, it is precisely because all our ideas are vulnerable to error and bias—including our biblical and theological interpretations as well as our scientific concepts—that we must be wary of absolutizing any of our theological or scientific ideas.[25]

These writers suggest that the scriptures may all be true, but all the truth God has for us is not restricted to the scriptures. This means that knowing God's truth is not an either (scripture), or (science) proposition. These faithful scientists are bent on pursuing both/and truth, yet humbly so.

These responses recognize that scientific scholarship is not a perfect method for inquiry. Moreover, we have to admit that it is a method based on a modernist view of the earth and its inhabitants. Finally, we have to acknowledge that even facts are subject to interpretation given one's worldview.

Summary

For some Christians, the idea of discovering God's truth about communication scientifically is very attractive. For them the belief that God knows things *as they really are* is sufficient motivation to study his creation. These people relish in being able to say, "Miller is a great speaker, and I have the facts to prove it!" Good-meaning professors of sound and humble faith work entire lifetimes examining human interaction scientifically. I think most of them would agree with these summary statements about science and faith.

1. Social scientists endeavor to describe law-like relationships between communication variables by using standard methods of data gathering, analysis, and interpretation.

2. Social scientists assume objectivity of reality and method. Even still, most admit that the interpretation of their data is a subjective, human affair. Christians recognize that our sin and limitedness undermine our ability to grasp reality absolutely.

3. Christian responses to science range from rejection to acceptance. The moderate view is that social science is one more means to discover general truth, but with the qualifier that scientific research is inherently linked to a modernist agenda, a worldview that complements and contests the faith.

WORTH THE TALK

1. Do you agree with the assumptions that social scientists hold about the world? To what degree do they align with what we know from Scripture?

2. If you and your friends were the last people on earth, and you could continue living with only one source of written information, given the choice, which would you choose: 1) a copy of the Bible, or 2) all the back issues of *Human Communication Research* and *Communication Monographs*? Why?

3. If scientists are able to measure ways that people generally communicate, and therefore our behavior is predictable, how can we also claim that we have free will? Is our behavior a result of sources outside us, or do we choose to act freely? Is it a mix?

CONSIDER THE WALK

1. Interview a social science professor in your department. Ask him or her how science and faith interplay in their research. Also ask how their view of human nature can (or should) influence the way social scientific research is performed.

2. Carry out your own scientific research project on a topic that interests you. Consult a research text, such as Frey, Botan, Friedman, and Kreps (2008). *Investigating Communication: An Introduction to Research Methods*, (2nd ed.) Englewood Cliffs, NJ: Prentice Hall. Ask your professor to help you.

ONLINE CHALK

Searching the web for practical, useful documents on scientific approaches to communication is a difficult task. Diverse topics, academic sites, and tons of sites make for heavy slogging. Even still, if you type in these search phrases into Google using quotation marks, you may find some helpful material.

- How to conduct surveys
- Observational research[26]
- Social science and faith
- Faith and social science[27]

ENDNOTES

1 See Robert Gass and John Seiter *Persuasion, Social Influence and Compliance Gaining*, (Toronto, ON: Allyn and Bacon, 2006) for these and other social scientific findings on persuasion.

2 The practice of interpreting scripture is known as hermeneutics, and the theory that we persuade others by appealing to logic, emotions, and our credibility via our style of language goes back to Aristotle, four centuries before Christ.

3 The study of speech delivery as a high art form reached its peak during the British rhetorical era (1700–1880AD), most notably among the elocutionists. Their efforts arose out of a frustration that Greek, Roman, French, and Italian scholars had written much on creating speech material, organization, and wording, but little on delivery. See "The Elocutionary Movement," in James Golden, Goodwin Berquist and William Coleman, *The Rhetoric of Western Thought*, 4th ed. (Dubuque, IA: Kendall / Hunt, 1989), chapter 8.

4 This example and a full discussion of these worldviews may be found in Walter Truett Anderson, *Reality Isn't What It Used to Be* (San Francisco: Harper & Row, 1990).

5 This point is made by Patricia Waugh, ed., *Postmodernism: A Reader* (London: Edward Arnold, 1992), 5, as quoted by Gene Veith, *Postmodern Times: A Christian Guide to Contemporary Thought and Culture*, (Wheaton, IL: Crossway Books, 1994), 50. She does not refer to God, but Christian objectivists would include God as a foundation for revelation in addition to science, history, and reason.

6 Gordon W. Allport and Leo F. Postman, "The Basic Psychology of Rumor," *Transactions of the New York Academy of Sciences*, 2nd ser., 8 (1945): 61-81, as cited in Em Griffin, *Making Friends (& Making Them Count)* (Downers Grove, IL: InterVarsity Press, 1987), 81.

7 Brian McLaren, "An Open Letter to Chuck Colson," 3

8 Walter Truett Anderson, *Reality Isn't What It Used to Be*, 6.

9 See Stanley J. Grenz, *A Primer on Postmodernism* (Grand Rapids, MI: William B. Eerdmans Publishing Co., 1996). See especially Chapter 7: "The Gospel and the Postmodern Context," 161-174.

10 See Colossians 1:15-20 for scripture that describes the supremacy of Christ in Christian faith.

11 Em Griffin, *A First Look at Communication Theory*, 5th ed. (New York: McGraw-Hill, 2003), 39-43.

12 Stewart L. Tubbs and Sylvia Moss, *Human Communication*, 7th ed. (New York: McGraw-Hill, 1994), 244.

13 Ibid., 244.

14 The small group research developed in Robert Wuthnow's *Sharing the Journey* (see Chapter 6) was based on interviews with approximately 2,000 people, half of whom were members of ongoing groups and half of whom were not. This kind of interviewing requires a well-trained team of interviewers to guarantee consistency. It also requires ample funding to pay the interviewers.

15 Raymond K. Tucker, Richard L. Weaver, II and Cynthia Berryman-Fink, *Research in Speech Communication* (Englewood Cliffs, NJ: Prentice-Hall, 1981), 109.

16 Ibid., 110.

17 See Charles E. Garrison, *Two Different Worlds: Christian Absolutes and the Relativism of Social Science* (Newark, DE: University of Delaware Press, 1988).

18 Joe Carson Smith, "Contextualization or Christ?" *Christian Standard* 114 (1979): 427, as quoted in Garrison, *Two Different Worlds*, 19.

19 In "Serial Batterers: What Turns Boys into Brutes?" *Homemakers Magazine*, April 1996, 54-61, John T. D. Keyes cites Don Dutton, professor of forensic psychology at the University of British Columbia. Dutton testified at the O.J. Simpson trial, and he suggests that Simpson's upbringing mirrored three traumatizing factors that often lead to abusive tendencies as an adult: "a shaming or disparaging father who regularly humiliates the boy, often in public; an insecure attachment to the mother figure, … and experiencing or witnessing an abusive home environment," 57.

20 Charles P. DeSanto et al., *A Reader in Sociology: Christian Perspectives* (Scottsdale, PA: Herald Press, 1980), 14, as quoted in Garrison, *Two Different Worlds*, 142-143.

21 Stephen A. Grunlan, "Sociology and the Christian," in *Christian Perspectives on Sociology*, ed. Stephen A. Grunlan and Milton Reimer (Grand Rapids, MI: Zondervan, 1982), 411-412 as quoted in Garrison, *Two Different Worlds*, 147-148.

22 Carl Camden, Michael T. Motley and Ann Wilson, "White Lies in Interpersonal Communication: A Taxonomy and Preliminary Investigation of Social Motivations," *Western Journal of Speech Communication* 48 (1984): 309-325.

23 Richard Bube, editorial, *Journal of the American Scientific Affiliation* 23 (1971): 1-4, as quoted by Myers in *The Human Puzzle*, 10.

24 Myers, *The Human Puzzle*, 25.

25 David G. Myers and Malcolm A. Jeeves, *Psychology Through the Eyes of Faith* (San Francisco: Harper, 1987), 15.

26 A helpful source is "Observational Field Research" located at socialresearch-methods.net/tutorial/Brown/lauratp.htm (accessed June 24, 2008).

27 See especially Mary Stewart van Leeuwen, "North American Evangelicalism and the Social Sciences: A Historical & Critical Appraisal," located at: http://www. asa3.org/ASA/PSCF/1988/PSCF12-88VanLeeuwen.html (accessed June 24, 2008).

When he was at the table with them, he took bread, gave thanks, broke it and began to give it to them. Then their eyes were opened and they recognized him, and he disappeared from their sight. They asked each other, "Were not our hearts burning within us while he talked with us on the road and opened the Scriptures to us? … Then the two told [the other disciples] what had happened on the way [to Emmaus], and how Jesus was recognized by them when he broke the bread.

Luke 24:30–32, 35

Looking at the Humanities
A Christian Perspective

JESUS' BREAKING OF bread with two disciples after his resurrection reminds us that meaning lags behind at times, and then bursts into our consciousness almost recklessly (see facing page for Luke 24:30–32, 35). Peter and Cleopas knew Jesus intimately, yet for hours did not recognize him as they strolled together toward Emmaus with Jesus explaining prophecies about himself. Not until Jesus ate, prayed, and broke bread with them were their eyes opened and they recognized him. How many times before had Jesus handed out bread? How many times had he given thanks? Did Peter and Cleopas recall Jesus' words, "this is my body, broken for you"? As one interpretive scholar observed, "Communication is a participatory ritual in and through which we create, maintain, and change culture."[1] Jesus' rituals, however, common, resurrected new meaning for his disciples.

For some of you, the calculated methods of social science, described in the previous chapter, strikes an inhuman chord. For you, something does not sit right when a scientist presents a survey to determine the meaning of a Donald Miller speech, or your web design in COMM 230. Making sense of Miller and site requires human involvement, not statistical significance. If that is your sentiment, then you can probably figure out the features that unify cultural creations—artifacts as diverse as Miller's speech, your web pages, roadside billboards, *The Lord of the Rings: The Two Towers*, and even the covenantal communication model in this text. The answer, I suggest, is they are all intentional, human, symbolic expressions. *Intentional* means a creator gave forethought, planning, and purpose to their creation. They were designed. By *human* I mean created by people, not nature. Humans create cultural artifacts as an extension of their God-given creativity. *Symbolic expression* means the crafting of words, images and sound to create messages that signify emotion, objects, or abstract ideas. Like the breaking of bread by Jesus that signaled to his dinner guests "I am the risen Christ," all symbolic expressions are interpretable. Broadly speaking, they are all art.

Welcome to the Humanities

When we define art as any intentional human symbolic expression, we go beyond notions of pencil drawings and baked pottery to broader fields such as novels, films, music, dance, architecture, and theater. Still others add television shows, radio programs, Internet sites, magazine articles, billboards, posters and music videos. In the humanities, scholars call these "texts," because they are open for our interpretation, enlightenment, and enjoyment.

Scholars who study symbolic texts dot your campus map, but most teach in the humanities—departments of literature, languages, philosophy, music, drama, art, and communications. Another word for a humanities scholar is "humanist." Since the rise of modernism in the 1600s, a primary type of humanism North Americans have experienced is *secular humanism*—the idea that people, not God, are the measure of all things, and that one should appeal to human reason, values and creativity alone to understand a billboard, or *The Lord of the Rings*. But humanism comes in various stripes. As Bruce Lockerbie notes,

> ...there are differences among the humanisms, of which secular humanism is only one; others to be reckoned include naturalistic humanism, biomedical humanism, ethical humanism, to name only a few. Then there's also Christian or biblical humanism.[2]

Despite its negative connotation in some Christian circles, *humanism* has noble roots and educational benefits. In fact, it was in Christian medieval universities that students were required to take *studia human-*

itis (humanities studies) before preparing for professions in theology, law, and medicine. What held these courses together was their focus on the creative, cultural accomplishments of humans, rather than the actions of God. But this focus was not deemed a fumbling of God's truth to us, but an exercise in discovering his general revelation.

For example, around 100 AD Justin Martyr wrote, "Whatever has been uttered aright by any man in any place belongs to us Christians." Around 400 AD Augustine wrote, "Every good and true Christian should understand that wherever he may find the truth, it is the Lord's." Eleven hundred and thirty years later, John Calvin urged his readers to "not forget those most excellent benefits of the divine Spirit [namely, human competence in art and science], which he distributes to whomever he wills, for the common good of mankind." Similar views were expressed by Martin Luther, John Knox and other reformers.[3]

> The passion of Christian humanists is to discern, through the eyes of faith, creative human accomplishments.

The passion of Christian humanists today, like their medieval parents, is to understand, through the eyes of faith, creative and cultural accomplishments. They begin with the assumption that our creativity is a gift from the Creator God, and though not every creative effort pleases him, creativity is in its own right good. They also subscribe to the doctrine of *common grace*—the belief that God mercifully holds back the full brunt of sin's consequences so that everyone, unbelievers included, may discover and express moral truth and beauty in the world. However, the idea of common grace does not replace the need for God's Spirit to understand spiritual wisdom (see 1 Corinthians 2:6–16).

The craft of Christian humanists differs across the field. A speech professor who analyzes a prime minister's speech exercises "rhetorical criticism," and a serious Roger Ebert type practices "film criticism." *Criticism* is the practice of applying interpretive principles to communicative artifacts in order to describe their content, and assess their aesthetic merits. Other scholars practice "historical analysis," "cultural analysis" and "textual analysis." Still others roll up their sleeves as writers, actors, playwrights, screenwriters, orators, and artists. In his book,

Eyes Wide Open: Looking for God in Popular Culture, Bill Romanowski, a communications professor at Calvin College, describes cultural engagement for thoughtful Christians:

> The relationship between faith and culture is creational, part of our humanness. To be God's image bearer is to be human, and to be human is to be a cultural agent carrying on God's creative work by fashioning ways of life that promote love, creativity, kindness, mercy, justice, truth, and stewardship. ... I believe Christians should be studying, discerning positive and negative aspects, and working to redeem culture.[4]

Assumptions Humanities People Hold

By now you have figured out that Umpires #2 and #3 would feel quite at home in the humanities. Umpire #2, the subjectivist, is convinced that our worldview, limited knowledge, and sinful condition influence how we interpret the world. He calls reality as he perceives it. Umpire #3, the constructivist, takes these ideas a step further, and suggest that we construct reality in our heads with plank-like ideas, and riveting beliefs. How do they figure? In brief, they come to these convictions based on their assumptions about reality, art, and people like you and me.

Humanities Scholars Assume a Subjective Reality. Whereas Umpire #1 and social scientists believe in an objective "out there" reality, humanists believe that reality is personally constructed and uniquely meaningful "in here" (in the person). *Subjective* means "of or resulting from the feelings of the person thinking; not objective; personal."[5] For example, the film *The Lord of the Rings: The Two Towers* may be an objective cultural artifact, but the mental reality we make of it is a personal affair. Extreme advocates of this view might go to the wall claiming that no one—absolutely no one—interprets the film identically. We may all identify with the heaviness of Frodo's journey, the wisdom of Gandalf, or the film's good-versus-evil mega-theme, but after that, a lot is up for grabs. The ugly Orcs might remind you of a hurtful uncle, or you may see yourself in Arwen the Elf, played by Liv Tyler. Despite our mental overlap, we will not share identical meanings or mental worlds.

The moderate view, however, is that symbolic texts are open to a limited number of interpretations. If you think of Uncle Pat because he is unattractive and mean, we will understand your connection with Orcs. However, if you argue that *Two Towers* is a parody of *Star Wars*, we will say you are wrong because J. R.R. Tolkien died before George Lucas created *Star Wars*, and could therefore not make social commentary on it in his novels.

So, whereas scientists study law-like patterns of communication, humanists study personal and cultural meanings they interpret from intentional symbolic expressions. While we may not agree with each other's interpretations, we agree on enough to avoid chaos.

Humanities Scholars Assume That Art Depicts a Worldview. Or put more specifically, humanists assume that artists express their worldview in their creative work. We assemble our worldview through interaction with parents, peers, and the media. As one scholar defined it, a worldview "consists of basic assumptions and images that provide a more or less sensible, though not necessarily accurate, way of thinking about the world."[6]

Some worldviews become wildly popular, while others remain unique and personal. But whether an artist holds a publicly creedal worldview, such as feminism or postmodernism, or a uniquely spun blend, they likely express their worldview in their art.

In the larger scheme, Christian faith is a worldview, and its themes, values, and history shape us and in turn shape how we interpret contemporary culture. The covenantal paradigm introduced in Chapter 2 is one such expression because it draws on biblical covenants to understand communication.

Interestingly, Tolkien, a devout Catholic, believed his mythical stories were not allegories of Christian faith, but he asserted that they might be shrapnel of the "true light." Tolkien writes, "Man is not ultimately a liar. He may pervert his thoughts into lies, but he comes from God, and it is from God that he draws his ultimate ideals... Not merely abstract thoughts of man but also his imaginative inventions must originate from God, and in consequence reflect something of the eternal truth."[7] And later, "In making a myth, in practicing 'mythopoeia,' and peopling the earth with elves and dragons and goblins, a story-teller... is actually fulfilling God's purpose, and reflecting a splintered fragment of the true light."[8] Thus Tolkien believed his work reflected God's truth in broad terms, a belief associated with Tolkien's Christian faith worldview.

Humanities Scholars Assume That We Are Active Interpreters. Humanists agree with the position 3 transformers described in Chapter 11 and 12. People are not sponges, but active interpreters. John Fiske, a communications professor, suggested that the sponge metaphor casts people as mere spectators, but "active interpreters" pictures people as *viewers.* In regards to television he writes, "A viewer is engaged with the screen more variously, actively, and selectively than is a spectator."[9] Obviously, our mindfulness is a matter of degree and effort.

However, mindfulness does not occur in a vacuum; critical thinking requires the application of principles taken from *some* worldview. As David Naugle writes on the role of worldview, "This vision is a channel for the ultimate beliefs which give direction and meaning to life. It is the integrative and interpretive framework by which order and disorder are judged; it is the standard by which reality is managed and pursued; it is the set of hinges on which all our everyday thinking and doing turns.[10]

Thus one cannot underestimate the role worldview assumptions play when interpreting life, especially when messages are vague. For example, Tolkien's middle-earth in *The Lord of the Rings* offers various readings, some Christian, others pagan. As one Christian author notes, "Gandalf eventually defeats [his enemy Balrog], but lies near death until he is supernaturally revived and healed.... The parallels to Jesus' defeat of Satan through his death, burial and resurrection can be recognized for those who look."[11] Quite contrary readings are also possible. On the back cover of a tarot-card gift box sold in London, England, one may read: "The realm of the Middle Earth lies within each of us, so cast the gold ring over the map, and foretell the future through the cards. The Lord of the Rings Oracle is a new and extraordinary divinatory system based on the bestselling *Lord of the Rings...* a story laden with mysterious magic."[12]

In Chapter 1 we observed that interpretivists make meaning through rules for interpretation based on their values and worldview. If we default to society's worldviews, we will fumble the opportunity to see things Christianly. Thus, Christian humanists underscore point to themes and theology of the faith as rules for interpretation. For example, in this book I have used the Christian ideas—and ideals—of

"I don't see depression or even a Big Mac. All I see is Mrs. Hugadorn hauling me off to the principal's office."

covenant, reconciliation, sanctification, and incarnation to understand communication.

Humanities Scholars Assume Distinct Criteria for Communication Theory. In the previous chapter, we observed five criteria Em Griffin proposed to judge scientific communication theories. Similarly, he offers five standards for evaluating interpretive theories.[13]

Before we discuss his ideas, however, let us review the guiding ideas of the covenantal perspective, and then we will assess the covenantal model using Griffin's criteria. The covenantal approach proposes that: 1) Covenantal communication recognizes us as persons-in-community, 2) covenantal communication is motivated by our steadfast love for the benefit of the other, 3) covenantal communication requires responsible symbolic expression, 4) covenantal communication results in redemptive pacts as to how we will live together, 5) covenantal communication changes us together, and 6) covenantal communication exercises long-term commitment for maximum benefit. We summarized these principles thus: Covenantal communication is the process by which people-in-community, who are motivated by unconditional love, use symbols responsibly to agree upon redemptive pacts in order to change together through committed loyalty over generations.

How does the covenantal model rate on Griffin's five criteria? Is it a valid picture of how communication is, or might be? This brief analysis shows the utility of Griffin's scheme to judge humanities theories.

1. New Understanding of People. Griffin suggests that a good humanistic theory helps us understand what it means to be human. It plumbs human experience, expresses human needs, and paints frescos of human ideals.

The covenantal perspective defines humans as symbol-using creatures, designed for relationships, and molded by interaction with others. It assumes our communication choices determine the quality of our community as people agree to a moral vision for getting along.

2. Clarification of Values. A good humanistic theory makes clear a theorist's values, and empowers cultural interpreters with a language for assessing cultural life.

Covenantal thinking reflects my value on the biblical story to enlighten our earthly pilgrimage, and it places commitment, community, and holiness in the spotlight. The covenantal approach downplays our rationality, individuality, and personal rights. It assumes a biblical God-view of our communication.

3. A Community of Agreement. A good humanistic theory gains the acceptance of a wide number of scholars because it has been scrutinized openly in the marketplace of ideas. Scholars promote their ideas at conferences, in academic journals, and in books, hoping to gain support for them. Rallied support usually earns a theory's position in standard textbooks as valid cultural knowledge.

The covenant theme draws from the biblical writers, and numerous contemporary scholars such as Pava, Mount,

Balswick, and Botman (see Chapter 2). It draws on previous theorizing in language, psychology, sociology, and communications. Drawing on other scholars' work signals that these ideas have precedent and recognition in the scholarly community.

4. Aesthetic Appeal. Griffin also suggests that a good humanistic theory not only makes claims about art, but is art. That is, a theorist's turn of phrase and vivid analysis appeals to readers' artistic standards.

My style is not literary, but informal and descriptive. However, the chapter titles attempt to capture covenantal truth artistically: "Changing Together through Committed Agreement," "Exercising Congruency and Grace," and "Community in the Making" are subtitles for Chapters 2, 4, and 8. Moreover, coining the term "redemptive pact" (to describe agreements we make together for the collective good), seeks to enlighten with new meaning.

5. Reform of Society. A good humanistic theory creates change in the culture when its advocates promote it. For example, the works of feminist writers, such as Chris Kramarae, have altered how we understand, and talk about, women.

Clearly the covenantal approach is prescriptive. It calls for application to redeem our use of language, self-talk, relationships, small group community, intercultural ministry, and media consumption. It does not call for change in government or the church, but has potential for this kind of application.

Humanities Methods for Interpreting Meaning. The meanings we interpret from symbolic texts, and the broader theories we construct about cultural art generally, require methods that differ from those used in the social sciences. Let us consider three.

The Historical-Critical Approach. This method requires the humanist scholar to examine historical events and then critically assess their meaning and significance. Some historical-critical scholars lean towards objectivism and believe that their method "involves reconstruction of the past in a systematic and objective manner by collecting evidence, evaluating it, verifying it, and synthesizing it to establish facts and to reach defensible conclusions."[14] The authors of introductory textbooks in the mass media employ this method when they describe the invention, proliferation, and impact of media technologies from the printing press to the Wii.

More recently, however, postmodern historians suggest that even this analysis is not completely objective, but a social construction based on the judgment, and choices, of the historian. E. H. Carr argues that, "The belief in a hard core of historical facts existing objectively and independently of the interpretation of the historian is a preposterous fallacy."[15] He would argue that historians must focus on some events, leave out others, and make sense of it all with their own worldview. Since historians have typically focused on the activities of powerful and well-to-do males, newer trends attempt to include the traditionally voiceless in society, including women and visible minorities. Thus, a media textbook might focus on the power struggle between inventors, government, and consumers, and present case studies of how minority groups respond to new technologies. As Tom Dixon writes, these "social historians [seek] to discover the history of the voiceless masses. . . . . They claim that although such peoples kept no official history, they left tracks that can be detected in their cultural practices and forms. The study of these forms and practices, *cultural history*, consists mostly of studying symbolic behavior ...."[16] This kind of historian is less apt to ask what happened, in preference for what people thought happened.

Since neither historian—objectivist or constructivist—can work in a vacuum, their starting point includes the events, facts, opinions and testimonies with regard to historical events. Somewhere they will sift through newspapers, books, newsreels, and eyewitness reports to discern a defensible truth.[17]

Cultural Interpretation or Ethnography. One practices cultural interpretation and ethnography by sitting in, and soaking up, the communication activity one wants to understand. This method attempts to get into the heads of the communicators. For example, when Ben Stein wanted to understand television from the inside out, he proceeded to spend time with television executives, directors, and actors in Hollywood. Like a short-term missionary, he observed carefully, asked questions appropriately, and took notes copiously. As James Spradley would say, Stein became a "participant observer" of, and with, Hollywood's elite, so he could see television their way.[18]

> Ethnography is the practice of sitting in and soaking up the communication activity or culture one seeks to understand.

Anthropologist Clifford Geertz calls this the "thick description" of a culture. It entails absorbing a people's cultural ways and then describing them.[19] One scholar describes Geertz's approach this way: "As a sensitive observer of the human scene, Geertz is loath to impose *his* way of thinking onto a society's construction of reality. He wants his theory of communication grounded in meanings that people within a culture share. Getting it right means seeing it from *their* point of view."[20]

Have you ever done cultural interpretation or ethnography? Our students take a stab at it when they write up their internship reports. Some students work in television stations, others in public relations firms, and still others for non-profit relief agencies. In each case they report on the communication dynamics of the workplace. Their assessment is based on thirteen weeks of rolling up their sleeves as camera operators, PR writers, and the like.

Hermeneutics. Hermeneutics is "the careful and deliberate interpretation of texts," and may be broken down into several branches, including the "interpretation of scripture (exegesis), interpretation of literary texts (philology), and interpretation of human personal and social actions (social hermeneutics)."[21] Broadly speaking, all humanities professors do hermeneutics (pronounced her-men-new-tics). That is, they attempt to interpret the primary and secondary meanings of a text, where "text" means any intentional symbolic expression. Literature professors wrestle with novels by Keats, film instructors critique films of Ingmar Bergman, and popular culture experts muse on lyrics by Ice

T. The goals of textual interpretation are to explain the text, understand deeper messages, and consider its influence on the reader.[22]

For example, while driving near Portland, Oregon our family saw a billboard that showed a woman's hand bedecked with a brilliant gold diamond ring. The wording read: "For the marriage with no planned exits." Cleary the primary message of the ad was "you should buy one of our rings." While those words did not appear on the sign, the context of the billboard led us to interpret it so. However, there was a deeper message too, namely, that we can choose lifelong marital commitment. How did the ad influence us? I made comment to my wife about being committed for life, but I resisted buying her another ring.

How Christians View Humanistic Scholarship

I have already described *Christian humanism* as a worthwhile activity. However, some believers would consider this phrase an oxymoron—a contradiction of terms. They consider the wisdom of people to be foolishness (see 1 Corinthians 3:19), and stick to the scriptures. On the other hand, some believers are open to new ideas, and rarely distinguish between Christian ones and others. They regard the best of culture Christian, whatever its source. A third set of believers find a balance between rejection of humanistic scholarship and acceptance of it.[23]

Reject Culture—The Separatist Response. As just noted, some Christians put a higher value on personal piety and knowledge of God's word than learning about culture through the writing of humanists, Christian or otherwise. Rather than engage culture, they would rather live within well-defined expressions of spirituality considered safe and holy.

One of the early church fathers, Jerome, came to this conviction after a nightmarish dream where he encountered God as judge. To that point in time, Jerome, a rhetorical scholar, felt free to read the best of Cicero and other Roman speech scholars. Then one night he dreamt that he stood before God, who thundered, "Thou art not a Christian, but a Ciceronian. Where thy treasure is, there is thy heart also."[24] Following this dream he wrote, "What communion hath light with darkness? What concord hath Christ with Belial? What has Horace to do with the Psalter, Vergil with the Gospels and Cicero with the Apostle [Paul]? . . . we ought not drink the cup of Christ and the cup of devils at the same time."[25] Scholars have shown that Jerome's writings did not refer to scholarly works for fifteen years following his vision.

In the media chapter, we saw how this thinking translates into modern-day separatism. The Amish in Pennsylvania and Iowa, and Hutterites in North Dakota and Manitoba, live and worship communally with little exposure to televised culture or worldly books. They take seriously, and narrowly, Paul's instructions to

> For many students, the separatist response to the humanities seems difficult if not totally untenable.

Roman believers to "not conform any longer to the pattern of this world, but be transformed by the renewing of your mind" (Romans 12:2). They contend that physical separation better guarantees a mind for Christ.

For most students at Christian universities or Bible schools, the separatist response is hardly an option. Sticking our heads in the sand ignores the incarnational strategy of God in Jesus Christ. He entered the world in time and space, as a Jew in Roman-ruled Israel, to use cultural forms of communication, and the heritage of Jewish law, to convey his radical message. The separatist response to humanistic studies ignores that we are spiritual *and cultural*, and that God can reveal himself through the still small voice of sinful believers and unbelievers alike.

Embrace Cultural Excellence as an Expression of God's Truth and Goodness. At the other end of the continuum stand believers who do not consider Christian thought as a type but as a quality. Christ is not *against* culture, rather Christ is *of* culture, in the sense of what is excellent and pure and good. These believers hold that "the Christian system is not different from culture in kind but only in quality; the best culture should be selected to conform to Christ."[26]

This perspective came alive to me as I contacted Christian scholars years ago about the idea for this book. I mailed a one-page survey to 200 scholars at Christian institutions to solicit their opinions about the need for a Christian communication textbook. In addition to completing the form, several made additional comments. One person wrote, "A 'Christian' approach begs the question that the pursuit of academic excellence by the practitioner in the field is somehow inadequate. Isn't good scholarship Christian? I don't believe in 'spoon feeding' people just because they have a christocentric philosophy of life!"[27] I suspect the person who wrote this would position himself in the Christ *of* culture camp. Like other believers, he believes that Christian activity and thought is consumed with the pursuit of "*whatever* is true, *whatever* is noble, *whatever* is right, whatever is pure, whatever is lovely, *whatever* is admirable" (Philippians 4:8, italics added). Anything that is excellent or praiseworthy is fair game for our thought.

Accept Cultural Forms and Moral Content—The Centered Evangelical Response. Between the rejection position and the excellence position stand believers who see merit in both poles. Remember their response to media? It was the view that technology is morally neutral, but its content is morally charged, therefore, use technology freely, but avoid questionable content. Some hold the same view with regard to humanistic scholarship. As long as the truth we discover there complements biblical truth, then believers should feel free to read widely and consume cultural art carefully. But beware. Falsehood loves to masquerade in eloquent, fine-sounding argument (see 2 Timothy 4:2–4 and Colossians 2:8).

> Augustine reasoned that if public speaking were a neutral tool, then Christians should use rhetorical theory to advance God's gospel.

St. Augustine was perhaps the most prominent rhetoric scholar in all of northern Africa when he was attracted to the preaching of Ambrose. When Augustine converted to the faith, he had a decision to make about studying non-biblical books. He came to a quite different resolve than Jerome, when he wrote, "Now, the art of rhetoric being available for the enforcing either of truth or falsehood, who will dare to say that truth in the person of its defenders is to take its stand unarmed against falsehood?"[28] In other words, Augustine reasoned that if public speaking was a neutral tool, Christians should use rhetorical theory from respected secular scholars in order to advance God's gospel through better speaking.

The same mentality applies today across the curriculum in communication departments. You are apt to read Dov Simens' *From Reel to Deal* (Warner Books, 2003) because Simens is an expert. You might read Judith Martin and Thomas Nakayama's *Intercultural Communication in Contexts* (Mayfield Publishing Company, 2006) because Martin and Nakayama are established scholars in this field. This is not to suggest that everything Simens, Martin, and Nakayama say about communication may square with our read of scripture, but there is an assumption that truth belongs to God wherever it is found.

However, some believers in this camp hasten to add an important proviso. While experts may know their field, the field may not entirely honor God. Because some humanistic theories may be sheep in wolves clothing, it is best to be shrewd as serpents but innocent as doves when engaging human cultural scholarship (see Matthew 10:16).

Critique Cultural Form and Content—The Centered Transformer and Paradox Response. Other believers in the church-of-the-center do not see things in such black-and-white terms. Transformers ask evangelicals if it is possible to distinguish between social and secular truth. Knowing the difference is not only difficult, but also makes us tiptoe through culture like soldiers fearful of landmines. Is not God-in-us bigger than that, they might ask. In fact, if we do not understand the landmines we seek to avoid, we are worse off than those who do. As James Sire writes, "We have more to fear from naiveté with regard to error than we do from clear knowledge of error that we recognize as error."[29] That is, we should be more afraid of being culturally ignorant, than worried about wrong ideas entering our heads from time to time.

Paradox believers express frustration with living with one foot in God's kingdom and another in Los Angeles. They want to follow the Saviour, but they live in the culture of Hollywood and jewelry store billboards. They conclude that a foot in each kingdom is no problem as long as we remember which kingdom is influencing the other, and that God is sovereign over all. Even if humanistic scholarship and popular media depict wrong-headed ideas or a fallen world, we are better off understanding these messages so we may speak to them in our relationships with people who embrace them. Like the medical student who studies disease so she can better understand health, our study of fallen culture may actually enhance our understanding of God's truth. As Leland Ryken writes in *Culture in Christian Perspective,*

> The question that has perennially engaged Christians is not whether culture requires their attention, but how does it. Christian thinking on the question has moved between the poles of total rejection and total affirmation of culture. . . . [but] neither extreme does justice to the biblical data. To think Christianly about culture and the arts means to look at them through the "lens" of biblical doctrine.[30]

Polishing Our Lens

Ryken's metaphor of a Christian "lens" to interpret communicative culture is akin to using a telescope to view the cosmos. The cleaner, larger, and better polished your telescopic lens, the more refined your vision of the Big Dipper. However, if a lens becomes cracked, smudged, or unfocused, one's picture turns to fuzz. Similarly, our ability to view communicative culture Christianly depends largely on the Christian lens through which we view it. A biblically robust lens deciphers truth amidst error, beauty in the beastly, and virtue in the vile. However, a biblically bankrupt one defaults to standards that may blur understanding. Some implications from this metaphor seem appropriate to end this chapter.

> Francis Schaeffer suggested that culture holds signs of fallenness and rays of hope—what he termed the minor and major themes of our faith.

A Christian humanist knows the faith. Lens crafting is a time-consuming job, but once polished to concave or convex perfection, a lens helps us see more clearly. So too with faith. Spiritual maturity and biblical knowledge do not form overnight, and grasping doctrine evolves over years of study. While quick-fix advocates would like us to believe that this CD, or that practice, will disciple us into Augustines or Teresas in seven steps, we know the journey is long. Do we have more than a Sunday-school knowledge of the scriptures? Have we ever considered the history of the faith from AD 33 until today? Can we cite the creeds that embody our teaching? Do we have the mind of Christ? If we shrug off the task of mastering the faith, we will be poorly equipped for encounters with the world.

Christian humanists understand other worldviews. For some that means attending graduate school to discover how romanticist, structuralist, feminist, Marxist, and postmodernist ideals apply to everything from classical literature to episodes of *CSI.* For others it means not just understanding these lenses, but borrowing features from them that appear to enlighten the Christian mind. For example, for all the difficulties that postmodern thought poses to the faith, Christians can appreciate its dethroning of individualism as the ideal, and its value on authentic community. We may not agree with its notion that truth is a construction of our language group, but appreciate its position that our naming reality gives purpose and meaning. Until we understand the worldviews that find their way into popular media and art, we will have a tough time placing them in God's larger puzzle. They may even dupe us.

Christian humanists look for Christian meaning in non-biblical texts. That is, a rose-colored lens should create rose-colored images of everything it examines. Christian thinker Francis Schaeffer suggested culture holds signs of fallenness, and rays of hope, or what he termed the *minor theme* and the *major theme* of our faith.[31] As we read human scholarship or consume popular culture, we are bound to observe the minor theme that people—believers and unbelievers alike—displease God with sinful choices, selfish motives, and hurtful communication. However, this negative theme sets the stage for the major theme, namely, that God offers meaning and purpose to life through salvation offered us in Jesus Christ. We might find particular truth in the *scriptural claims* by a radio minister, or the *symbolism* in *The Two Towers,* or in *value statements* that judge one thing more worthy than another. Looking only for the minor theme betrays the hope within us; focusing entirely on the major theme yields unrealistic romanticism.

Summary

The humanities represent a common approach to studying human communication. Humanism is the study of creative achievements in literature, philosophy, music, art, drama, and communication. Christian humanism is the commitment to understanding communicative art through biblical faith. Christian humanists delve into scholarly writings and popular culture to discover God's generally revealed truth, beauty, and moral presence.

The methods humanities scholars employ assume a less rigid model than ones used by social scientists. Their use of historical research, cultural interpretation, and hermeneutics provide the basis for a rich understanding of cultural life. These scholars typically see life through a grand paradigm to make sense of art, literature, and media. Christian scholars value the lens of biblical faith and doctrine to enhance their read on culture for signs of our sinfulness and rays of God's hope, in grace, through Jesus Christ.

 **WORTH THE TALK**

1. Do you agree with the assumption that we create meaning as a response to cultural reality rather than cultural reality presenting itself objectively? Why or why not?

2. Consider a television show or movie you have watched recently and discuss with a friend the Christian themes or values you discerned as present or not.

 **CONSIDER THE WALK**

1. Interview an art instructor or a media production instructor on your campus to determine his or her perspective of God in the arts. Discover the professor's pilgrimage with regard to responding to the humanities approach.

2. Write a position paper that describes and defends where you stand with regard to humanistic scholarship. Make an effort to include your religious convictions and biblical references to articulate your stance.

3. Expand on number two under "Worth the Talk." Write a paper

that describes the scriptural truths, inherent values, Christian symbolism, and other messages that a television show or movie depicts. Consider using the idea of a *minor theme* and *major theme* noted by Schaeffer to explain its messages and evaluate its moral worth.

4. Use the covenantal model as a lens for interpreting a story in cultural life. Discern if the creators depict characters as boldly independent, or enmeshed in community. Ask if people show steadfast love for others, and engage communication responsibly. Consider if characters create redemptive pacts that guide their lives toward a common good, and how people change or not. Finally, consider if characters show commitment to each other, themselves, and to God.

ONLINE CHALK

The humanities examine the artistic and cultural accomplishments of people. These key phrases put you in touch with sources to wrestle with the task of seeing those accomplishments Christianly.

- Christian humanism
- Through the eyes of faith
- Christ and culture
- Christianity and culture

ENDNOTES

1 Quentin J. Schultze, *Communicating for Life: Christian Stewardship in Community and Media* (Grand Rapids: Baker Academic, 2000), 55.

2 D. Bruce Lockerbie, *Thinking and Acting Like a Christian* (Portland: Multnomah, 1989), 84.

3 These quotations of Justin Martyr, St. Augustine and John Calvin are from ibid., 87 and 92.

4 William D. Romanowski, *Eyes Wide Open: Looking for God in Popular Culture*, Revised and Expanded Edition (Grand Rapids, MI: Brazos Press, 2007), 16.

5 *Webster's New World Dictionary of the American Language*, rev.ed. (New York: Warner Books, 1984),

s. v. "Subjective."

6 Michael Kearney, *Worldview* (Novato, CA: Chandler & Sharp, 1984), 41.

7 Quoted by Colin Gunton in *A Far-Off Gleam of the Gospel: Salvation in Tolkien's The Lord of the Rings*, in Jospeh Pearce (Ed.) *Tolkein, A Celebration*, (San Francisco, CA: Ignatius Press, 2001), page 130.

8 See this and other Tolkien quotations at Catholic Education Resource Center. Retrieved June 23, 2008 from: http://www.catholiceducation.org/articles/arts/al0012. html

9 John Fiske, *Introduction to Communication Studies* (London: Methuen, 1982), 17.

10 David Olthuis,. "On Worldviews," *Christian Scholars Review* 14 (1985): 153-64 as quoted in *Worldview: The History of a Concept*, David K. Naugle, (Grand Rapids, MI: W. B. Eerdmans Pub., 2002), 349

11 Ken James, movie review, *The Lord of the Rings: The Two Towers*, ChristianAnswers.net. Retrievable from: http://christiananswers.net/spotlight/movies/2002/thetwotowers.html

12 Terry Donaldson, *The Lord of the Rings Oracle* (New York: Sterling Publishing, 1998).

13 Em Griffin, *A First Look at Communication Theory*, 6th ed. (New York: McGraw-Hill, 2006), 44-48.

14 Raymond K. Tucker, Richard L. Weaver, II and Cynthia Berryman-Fink, *Research in Speech Communication* (Englewood Cliffs, NJ: Prentice-Hall, 1981), 68.

15 E. H. Carr, *What is History?* (New York: Random House, 1961), 10, as quoted in *The Death of Truth*, Dennis McCallum, ed. (Minneapolis: Bethany House, 1996), 131.

16 Tom Dixon, "Postmodern Method: History," in ibid., 133-134.

17 For two examples of the historical-critical approach, see Harold Innis, *Empire and Communication* (Toronto: Oxford University Press, 1950), and Harold Innis, *The Bias of Communication* (Toronto: University of Toronto Press, 1951).

18 For a full description of this research method see James P. Spradley, *Participant Observation* (New York: Holt, Rinehart & Winston, 1980).

19 Clifford Geertz, *The Interpretation of Cultures* (New York: Basic Books, 1973), see pp. 6-7, 9-10, 12 & 14.

20 Em Griffin, *A First Look*, 18.

21 Stephen W. Littlejohn and Karen A. Foss, *Theories of Human Communication*, 8th ed. (Belmont, CA: Wadsworth, 2005), 128.

22 See Stephen W. Littlejohn, *Theories of Human Communication*, 5th ed. (Belmont, CA: Wadsworth, 1996), 211-213.

23 These three responses to humanistic scholarship are based loosely on the analysis provided by H. Richard Niebuhr in *Christ and Culture* (New York: Harper & Row, 1951).

24 This translation is from Pierre DeLabriolle, *The History and Literature of Christianity from Tertullian to Boethius* (New York: Kegan Paul, 1924), 11-12.

25 Jerome, Epistle XXII (CSEL, LIV) in *The Attitude of the Early Christian Latin Writers toward Pagan Literature and Learning*, trans. Gerald L. Ellspermann

(Washington, D.C.: Catholic University of America Patristic Studies, 1949), 2:159-160.

26 David J. Hesselgrave, *Communicating Christ Cross-Culturally* (Grand Rapids, MI: Zondervan, 1978), 79-80. Hesselgrave is not advocating this view, but is discussing the book *Christ and Culture*, in which Niebuhr describes the "Christ of culture" position as one of five responses Christians have often taken.

27 For reason of confidentiality, I am unable to provide the author's name and educational institution. I received his note in 1994.

28 Augustine, *On Christian Doctrine*, bk. 4, section 3.

29 James Sire, *The Joy of Reading* (Portland: Multnomah, 1978), 146.

30 Leland Ryken, *Culture in Christian Perspective: A Door to Understanding & Enjoying the Arts* (Portland: Multnomah, 1986), 12.

31 Francis A. Schaeffer, *Art & the Bible* (Downers Grove, IL: InterVarsity Press, 1973), 56.

King Solomon sent to Tyre and brought
Huram. Huram was highly skilled and
experienced in all kinds of bronze work.
He came to King Solomon and did all the
work assigned him.

1 Kings 7: 13, 14b

Building Temples
Engaging Communication Gifts

IN THE FILM *Bella*, Latino star Eduardo Verástegui plays "José," the head chef at a Mexican restaurant in New York City. Along side him co-star Tammy Blanchard plays "Nina," an attractive waitress, who learns that she is pregnant and whose life begins to spiral out of control, including getting fired. "José" supports her so far as to quit his job, introduce Nina to his family, and encourages her to choose adoption. *Bella* went on to win the People's Choice Award at the Toronto Film Festival in 2006.

As a young actor, Eduardo Verástegui rose quickly in Latino culture as a heartthrob in *telenovas*, or Latin soap operas, and enjoyed magazine-cover popularity akin to Brad Pitt and Tom Cruise. Writer Amanda Shaw tells his story: "...Verástegui—named one of *People en Espagnol's* '50 Most Beautiful People'—found himself typecast as the Latino Don Juan, playing the part all too well. That is, until he met a wise woman—a woman who taught him to speak English, a woman who taught him to speak to God. 'How are you using your talent? Who is God in your life?' she challenged him. He had no answers and he knew it. Verástegui recounts:

> We [Latinos] have been stereotyped in movies as banditos, drunkards, prostitutes, criminals. And if you're good looking, then you're a Casanova, a womanizer, and a liar. And

that's the person I had become. But this woman opened my eyes to the grace of God… God changed my heart and I had to repent of my past. And from that day on, I promised that I would never do anything that would offend God or my Latino heritage. I would never do anything to compromise my faith. That's the moment I realized that the purpose of my life was to know and to love God."[1]

Eduardo's story is one of redemption, not only for his soul, but also for his career. Following his conversion, and years before *Bella*, Eduardo left the *telenovas* scene, declined many offers for sexualized lead roles, and lived on the verge of homelessness due to lack of work. His convictions cost him, and at one point, he considered missionary work or joining a monastery. Upon hearing Eduardo's thoughts, his pastor chuckled, "No, no, no, you're not going anywhere. We have plenty of missionaries over there in that jungle. But you know what, we have very few here in Hollywood. And this is a bigger jungle. Our Lord put you right there for a reason."[2]

Eduardo's convictions led him to excellence in creating an award-winning film—one that broke away from hurtful stereotypes of *machismo* men, and embraced God's call to love unconditionally beyond emotional romance. Have you considered your convictions? Your talents? This chapter challenges us to give both to God. Whether blessed with one, five, or ten talents, the principle remains the same: God gives gifts so we may offer them back as sweet-smelling sacrifices. Using our gifts for God's purposes builds up others, transforms culture, and molds our self-identity.

The Problem

Unfortunately, not everyone in the church has a similar value on excellence. One of our drama instructors joked with his students that "skit" was a four-letter word. He meant that a skits pale in comparison to superb *drama*. I do not think he was being elitist. Generally, in North American culture, we have become so accustomed to template websites, banal television, and hurtful relationships, that we lower our expectations and settle for less. The same mentality creeps into Christian circles as it pertains to ministry where some are apt to think that gospel trumps gifts, and theology beats technique. The conviction is that getting the word out is more important than quality control.

"I have a delivery for you: 1000 pens with the slogan 'Excellence is in the Detales' and 500 factory-second, slightly irregular coffee mugs that say 'Quality Matters'."

This issue arose in a church business meeting I attended when someone asked why the board asked a pastor to resign. The moderator answered that, among other things, people were not pleased with his preaching. In defense of the pastor, a man stood up and said, "That's atrocious. The only grounds on which we should ever ask a pastor to resign are heresy and sexual infidelity." The room fell silent, and people wondered if they had committed a grave harm against the pastor. Then a mature member stood up, a man who had been a pastor and knew the demands of the position. He said, "Brother, preaching is a lot like food preparation. We expect food placed before us to be *more* than simply not poisonous. We also expect it to look and taste good as well." Heads nodded and some offered similar commentary. The congregants felt it was not too much to expect sound theology *and* fine preaching.

Barbara Nicolosi might suggest that pastors who preach poorly owe their congregations, and God, an apology. As a Christian scriptwriter and script consultant, she has observed the church's struggle to excel in media arts. In a "Prayer of Forgiveness," she writes:

> Let us repent of sloth and fear, the dearth of professionalism and depth...Let us ask forgiveness of those whose lives have been scarred by our failure to find a compelling forum for the Church in the arts and media... Too often the world has rejected our art as being banal, and our writing

as being nothing but platitudes, and too often, the world has been right.... For the bad example we have given others by wallowing in mediocrity and that which is unworthy, we are sorry.[3]

Not all Christians feel as Nicolosi does, and some may even feel that media art done too well isn't spiritual. In his book, *The Christian, The Arts, and Truth*, Frank E. Gaebelien describes believers who settle for second best, but critically judge those who excel. He writes:

> They are the kind of people who look down upon good music as high-brow, who confuse worship with entertainment, who deplore serious drama yet are contentedly devoted to third-rate television shows, whose tastes in reading run to the piously sentimental, and who cannot distinguish a kind of religious calendar art from honest art. For them better aesthetic standards are "egghead" and spiritually suspect.[4]

Nicolosi and Gaebelien are believers who take our creativity seriously. To them, creativity is good in and of itself, and beautiful creativity honors God. Some creative work may not please God, but tacky creativity mocks his Creator character. These authors would likely agree with theologian Elton Trueblood who quipped, "Holy shoddiness is still shoddiness."

Down deep, however, there is another issue besides excellence. See if you can discern it from these recollections. In Chapter 3, we observed that our heart spills to our lips. In Chapter 4, we noted that our emotions leak out toward others. In Chapter 5, we saw self-talk shapes relational talk. In Chapter 14, we understood that an artist's worldview peaks through her art. Clearly, our character and spiritual identity is linked intimately with our communication. Our soul shows in honest art and genuine skills.

Put more broadly, the issue is how we live life. I like the way Francis Schaeffer summarized his essay on art and the Bible. He writes:

> No work of art is more important than the Christian's own life, and every Christian is called upon to be an artist in this sense. He may have no gift of writing, no gift of composing

or singing, but each man has the gift of creativity in terms of the way he lives his life. In this sense, the Christian's life is to be an art work. The Christian's life is to be a thing of truth and also a thing of beauty in the midst of a lost and despairing world.[5]

Schaeffer's comments to artists extend to communicators. We may think we are short on gifts such as speaking, writing, or creating. We may earn our degree and still long for talent like an Eduardo Verástegui, or a roommate filmmaker. Schaeffer's point is that life requires more than skills; it begs for dedication to God.

But let us return to the key point. Until we understand that God is as concerned about our craft as our content, we will continue to consider skills second class. We will settle for sub-par sitcoms, sloppy journalism, and Sunday-school drama. Professional communicators begin with different assumptions and strive for higher standards. Before we discuss these elements, however, allow me one more reference to my experience as a communicator.

> Our communication craft is intimately linked to our character and spiritual sensitivity.

The Sixteen- and Thirty-Six-Year-Old Ventriloquist

Every summer, while growing up, my family attended a ten-day Bible conference where children like me enjoyed a kids program each evening. That is where I met Wally Schoon, a ventriloquist. I could hardly wait to hear him and his dummy "Leroy" duke it out with verbal jabs and hilarious slapstick. I was hooked. I spoke with Wally, and eventually read Bob Hill's book *You Can be a Ventriloquist.*

From age fourteen to sixteen, I dabbled with this intriguing craft. In the summer, you could find me on my front steps with dummies "Arthur" or "Charlie" and six neighbor kids huddled around. Other times I performed for small audiences at my home church. Later I joined a Youth for Christ singing group for two years, and performed over sixty times during our concerts with my new professional dummy, "Archie."

I will never forget my first public performance with that group. I had written the dialogue myself, and had practiced it enough to get through it in private. The crowd numbered only fifty, but I was nervous that they were adults, not children. In addition, my peers were listening in the wings for my debut.

I delivered the first few lines well, with "Archie" getting the best of me. My voices rang clearly with the aid of the sound system. I set up the joke, and "Archie" polished it off. I asked a question, and he retorted with a nutty answer. It began like clockwork.

Then tragedy struck. I figured out later that my routine was not much more than a string of jokes held together by a thinly glossed theme. Remembering which joke came next was not easy. I forgot a line, and then another. Try as I may, I could not get back to the string of jokes I had planned. Sweating profusely, and feeling self-conscious, I ad-libbed a few corny jokes, wrapped it up, and ended my five-minute routine at the two-minute mark. My friends told me it went well, but I could see through their praise. I felt awful.

Twenty years later and over 100 performances under my belt, my dean asked me to perform for our chapel. I knew our auditorium would be overflowing with 600 students, and 100 faculty and staff. I did not want to let them down. Therefore, two weeks before the performance, I put pen to paper and wrote a three-minute dialogue. I considered the theme the dean requested, thought of audience members who could take a joke, and began memorizing the script. My family listened patiently as I practiced aloud, with "Archie" on my knee. By the tenth time, my three-year-old son was beating me to the punch lines! By show time, I had written and practiced the three-minute gig for five hours. What a difference compared to my high school experience! I was ready to face 700 expectant people.

The practice paid off, and the event became my best-ever ventriloquial performance. I did not forget a single joke, and managed to recall 90 percent of the wording I had practiced in my living room. I read my audience well, played to their laughter with timely pauses, and even ad-libbed two choice lines. My colleagues seemed pleased, despite the jabs poked their way.

Writing and practicing my gig was hard work, but they resulted in a professional performance. Let's consider the values and assumptions that professional communicators hold.

Assumptions Professional Communicators Hold

By "professional" I do not necessarily mean *paid for one's services*, but that is not a bad standard. When professional speakers charge $1,000 for a talk, or when video editors require $100 per hour to edit raw footage, you know they justify these fees based on their competence. To be sure, you usually get what you pay for. However, "professional" also means *the highest standard in the field*. We can aim for excellence without charging a dime, and we begin with some foundational assumptions.

You Can Improve Your Communication Gifts. When I was sixteen-year-old ventriloquist, I could write dialogue, speak without moving my lips, and develop a personality for my dummy. What I lacked were memory skills, and the ability to put it all together under the stress of public performance. After twenty years of practice, those skills have become refined.

College administrators understand that practice makes perfect, and that students like yourself can improve your skills if given opportunity. That is why they often require skill-based courses in English, art, and communications—so you can improve your writing, creativity, and expression. Some students dread these courses. I can think of at least two reasons why.

One is that some believe our God-given skills are locked in at a certain level, and that no amount of practice improves them. My

Improved public speaking skills are a key advantage you will take from your university education to your new career.

experience teaching public speaking to hundreds of students proves otherwise as green speakers enter my course and leave confidently mature. In addition, while it is true that God gives gifts variously according to the grace given us (see Romans 12:6), the apostle Paul also says, "Since you are eager to have spiritual gifts, try to excel in gifts that build up the church (1 Corinthians 14:12). His admonishment to *try to excel* in certain gifts indicates that we can improve on our talents and deficiencies.

The other reason people hope to dodge skills courses is they think communication is a natural, easy skill. They liken it to breathing and eating. This mentality shows up when students spend hours fiddling with new software programs with no serious attempt to understand editing theory, story boarding, design principles, and the like. It also shows up in the belief that relationships just happen, and that no training or counseling can improve interaction with others. Film editors and relational counselors would think differently. Skills may begin with natural gifting, but their development requires effort.

Improving Our Gifts Requires Effort. In our convenience culture, hard work sounds burdensome. We can put that burden in perspective, however, when we realize that professional athletes, musicians, actors and speakers achieved fame only after much effort. Remember my colleague who debated the politician? Paul invested 120 hours in research before approaching the podium for his thirty-minute speech and rebuttal. We may not have a lot of time during the blur of a semester, but somewhere individuals like Paul will rise to the occasion, and the rest of us will be watching from padded chairs.

In the book, *Publish, Don't Perish*, Joseph Moxley smashes a few myths about published authors. He dispels the idea that writing is easy and fun. His research showed that:

1. Published people work hard
2. Are not necessarily brilliant
3. Do not enjoy the rigors of writing
4. Write regularly (e.g., 30 minutes a day) to promote creativity
5. Are not overly self-critical, especially on first drafts
6. Get bright ideas away from their desks
7. Have their own style[6]

These facts convinced me, while writing this book, that I was not alone in my trudge up publish mountain. It seems other writers feel overworked and overwhelmed as well. At times, they wish they could toss their laptops out the window, but they stick with it.

Plato knew the challenge of becoming a great orator. He wrote, "Several years of silent inquiry are needful for a man to learn the truth, but fourteen in order to learn how to make it known to his fellowmen."[7] We might ace the material, but mastering the means to convey it requires equal, if not more attention.

Enhanced Skills Reform Our Personal World. Specifically, improving skills makes us think differently about ourselves, and our potential. Only a few masterful artists are geniuses. Most of us are plodders. I did not rival Wally the ventriloquist in those early years, much less Edgar Bergen and Charlie McCarthy. However, with time came opportunity to stretch my wings beyond the singing group's concert settings. I performed ventriloquism at mother-daughter banquets, church gatherings, and talent shows. Eventually, I believed I could perform anywhere.

I have observed that a cycle of learning-experience-confidence-learning evolves when we test our skills through acts of faith. For example, after writing articles in our program's *Writing for Publication* course, students have learned theory and technique, experienced writing articles, and gained confidence from classmates' and instructor's feedback, all in the relatively safe confines of COMM 212. For some,

"Actually, success is 2% inspiration, 97% perspiration, and 1% deodorant."

however, the next step is one of faith to submit articles to a magazine or website editor. It only takes one acceptance to add confidence, which motivates more writing, yields increased success, and expands learning. Students' identity, writing, and goals change with time as God opens gates to exercise their gifts.

As an academic, I experienced this cycle when writing my first serious web articles on humility, self-control, and faithfulness in marriage communication. Until a few years ago, I had only written academic articles, conference papers, and this textbook. After writing my first web piece, I sent it to a writing instructor colleague, and asked her to respond to it. Like a nervous student, I read her copious comments in the margins, and licked my wounds. After a few more revisions with her guidance, I finally submitted it to an online editor. My image as a writer broadened when the editor commented that the piece required little editing before posting.[8]

Serving Others with our Gifts Creates Covenantal Culture. This book began with the premise that covenantal communication requires us to invest in our community so we may change together. How bleak and boring our journey would be if teachers and parents, friends and family had not blessed us with their creative gifts. Along the way, it will be payback time, and your generation will re-invest gifts in your communities. Gifts are best shared.

In the opening chapter, we saw the struggles of Burkitt Financial whose toxic communication required organizational overhaul. That facelift took place only after a consultant discerned the problems, envisioned a new course, and rallied the employees to treat each other humanely. The consultant invested her wisdom in Burkitt Financial to foster covenantal culture. Her remarkable gifts in human relations and conflict management hewed redemptive potential from fallen trees.

In a more proactive manner, the administrators at my university invested their wisdom in our campus community with distinctly covenantal language. For several years, we prepared ourselves for the new school year by quoting, in unison, a campus covenant. This covenant reflects numerous principles discussed in this book. I thought it a fitting example of covenantal practice for nurturing redemptive change.

Trinity Western University Employee Covenant

As members of the larger Trinity Western community, we enter into covenant with the Lord and with one another.

On this 19th day of August in the year 201X, we reaffirm our acceptance of and our loyalty to the Bible as the Word of God, and strive to be obedient to its precepts. We bring our lives, our values, our opinions, our ministries, our relationships, and our vocational activities under its authority.

We reaffirm the Lordship of Jesus Christ. Our lives are His. The organization we serve is His. We reaffirm His centrality, pledge ourselves to seek His glory, and rededicate our lives to fulfilling the ministry we have received from Him.

We covenant with the Lord and with one another to pursue diligently the goal of personal holiness. Although we are far from perfect, we want to be more like our Lord and strive toward godliness.

We commit ourselves afresh to the goal of excellence. We resolve to do our work as unto the Lord Himself and to serve with personal integrity and an attitude that is Christlike.

We believe in the mission of our organization, and will uphold its standards as a disciple-making academic community. We recognize changes and challenges as God-given opportunities to refine and improve our work for God's glory.

We value community and seek to be a people who positively support and exhort one another. When conflict arises, we aspire toward forgiveness and reconciliation. We pledge our ministry to one another during this coming year. Those gifts and resources graciously given us by the Lord, we give back to Him to be used as instruments of blessing in our larger campus community.

Through the grace of God and the enabling of His Holy Spirit, we commit ourselves to do justly, to love mercy, and to walk humbly with the Lord our God. In the presence of Almighty God we enter into this covenant and trust in His grace and power to ensure its fulfillment.

To Him be glory and honor, forever and ever. Amen.

Joining with three hundred believers in this ritual created a corporate covenantal speech act. The mere uttering of the covenant, in unison, symbolized the community we call Trinity Western University (see Chapter 3). Affirming the lordship of Jesus Christ over us personally and corporately signaled a made-in-God image anchored within a symbolic community (Chapter 5). Recognizing that we fall short of perfection, and require humility in conflict, biases us toward reconciliation, not warfare (Chapter 6).

Breaking into the film industry represents one challenging avenue for you to be a culture shaper.

This campus covenant looks more like a family commitment than a professional contract (Chapter 7). The agreement committed us to each other, to excellence, and to God's place in our lives. Committing ourselves "to do justly, to love mercy, and to walk humbly with the Lord our God" resonated with dialogic values such as equality, partnership, goodwill, and servant power (Chapter 7). The covenant recognizes our university as a "disciple-making academic community." We favor teamwork and moral development over showy individualism. The Trinity Western covenant attempts to nurture a campus community where people sense belongingness, relish long-term relational commitment, and feel safe in asking tough questions (Chapter 8). Arriving there means getting along despite our cultural and denominational diversity as we view differences graciously, pursue common goals, and try to communicate empathetically within other people's frame of reference (Chapter 10).

Finally, this campus covenant indicates our dependence on God, first for enabling us with gifts, and then for "grace and empowerment" to enact them for transformational change (Chapters 12 and 15). We believe that his truth and grace—as revealed in his word, Spirit, and creation—frees us from ignorance, sin, and defeat (Chapters 13 and 14). Gifts and grace; grace and gifts. Together they build covenantal culture.

This campus covenant is, therefore, an exemplar of a redemptive pact—an agreement that symbolizes the moral vision for all parties involved. More broadly, its engagement embodies the definition of covenantal communication noted in Chapter 2: Covenantal communication is the process by which people-in-community, who are motivated by unconditional love, use symbols responsibly to agree upon redemptive pacts in order to change together through committed loyalty over generations. As T.S. Eliot wrote, "What life have you if you have not life together? There is not life that is not in community, and no community not lived in praise of God."[9]

Summary

This chapter calls us to invest our communication gifts for God's glory. After God entrusts us with gifts, talents and skills, it is our turn to re-invest them in others and culture.

Jesus tells the story of the master who entrusted his property to three men before taking a long trip. The employee who received five talents "went at once and put his money to work" and made five more talents. The servant who received two talents did the same and made another two talents. But the third man "dug a hole in the ground and hid his master's money" (see Matthew 25:14–28).

You probably know how the story ends. The master praised the first two for being faithful with their talents. However, the master called the third man a "lazy, wicked servant" because he failed even to bank the money to earn interest. The master entrusted the first two with more responsibility, but stripped the third of his one talent and threw him out of the house.

The last servant did not have evil intent. He did not squander or misplace his gift; he failed to use it to bear more fruit. The parallel to investing our communication knowledge and skills is a fitting end to this chapter and book. Will we speak worthy words, and enact congruent nonverbal cues? Will we find our identity anchored in Christ and seek to edify others? Will our dialogue with friends and family members be full of grace and nudge them closer to God? Will our public speeches and intercultural interaction reflect incarnational love and responsible ethics? Will we exercise critical and godly thinking as we consume and produce media messages? Will we make wise choices in what we view and read? Will we employ the humanities and the sciences to probe the human spirit so we may meet people's deepest longing? God enabling, it is our choice whether or not we enact covenantal communication to his glory.

 **WORTH THE TALK**

1. What communication gifts do you have? Share with a friend what you believe to be your strongest suit.

2. What do you think is the relationship between content and delivery? Is there some validity to the idea that what we say is more important than how it is said? Put another way, what validity is there in the view that truth is more important than style or performance?

 **CONSIDER THE WALK**

1. Compare the quality of two major motion pictures using standard criteria found in a film text. One should be by a Christian production firm, the other not. Make recommendations for improvement for plot, character development, script, and cinematography. Which film is better? Why?

2. Make a list of the communication skills you know God has given you. Be more generous than critical. Take this list to your campus career center and ask the staff to direct you to material about communication careers. Compare your skills with those listed for each field. Do some dreaming and praying about where God might want you after graduation.

ONLINE CHALK

Establishing your career where your gifts are best suited takes time. The best place to start, however, is becoming aware of careers in our field. These terms and titles put you in contact with career information, and assessing where you fit in.

- Careers in communications
- Communication careers
- What Color is Your Parachute? (a bestseller on determining your gifts)
- JobHuntersBible (website associated with What Color is Your Parachute)
- Intercristo (a Christian job search service)

ENDNOTES

1 Amanda Shaw, "Something Beautiful in Hollywood," posted January 4, 2008 at *Comment*, website of the Work Research Foundation, located at wrf.ca/comment/article.cfm?ID=296 (accessed January 4, 2008).

2 Ibid.

3 Barbara R. Nicolosi, "Christians and Media: A Prayer of Forgiveness" posted at churchofthemasses.blogspot.com/2008/04/Christians-and-media-prayer-for.html (accessed June 27, 2008).

4 Frank E. Gaebelein, *The Christian, the Arts, and Truth: Regaining the Vision of Greatness*, ed. D. Bruce Lockerbie (Portland: Multnomah, 1985), 50-51.

5 Francis A. Schaeffer, *Art & the Bible* (Downers Grove, IL: InterVarsity Press, 1973), 63.

6 Joseph Moxley, *Publish, Don't Perish: The Scholar's Guide to Academic Writing and Publishing* (Westport, CT: Greenword, 1992), 3-14.

7 Plato, "Phaedrus," in *Readings in Classical Rhetoric*, ed. Thomas W. Benson and Michael H. Prosser, trans. H. N. Fowler (Bloomington, IN: Indiana University Press, 1972), 22-42.

8 The article "Are You Humble? Six Ways Your Spouse Can Tell" was multi-posted at the following sites: womentodaymagazine.com, mentodayonline.com, christianwomentoday.com, and retirementwithapurpose.com

9 T. S. Eliot, Choruses from *The Rock* (1934).

Index of Subjects & Names

Index of Scriptures